WRITING FOR HIRE

Writing for Hire

Unions, Hollywood, and Madison Avenue

CATHERINE L. FISK

Harvard University Press

Cambridge, Massachusetts & London, England

2016

Second printing

Library of Congress Cataloging-in-Publication Data
Names: Fisk, Catherine L., 1961– author.
Title: Writing for hire : unions, Hollywood, and Madison Avenue / Catherine L. Fisk.
Description: Cambridge, Massachusetts : Harvard University Press, [2016] |
Includes bibliographical references and index.
Identifiers: LCCN 2016027993
Subjects: LCSH: Authorship. | Copyright—United States. | Television authorship—
United States. | Screenwriters—Labor unions—United States. | Motion picture
authorship—United States. | Screen Writers' Guild.
Classification: LCC K1440 .F57 2016 | DDC 346.7304/82—dc23
LC record available at https://lccn.loc.gov/2016027993

ISBN 978-0-674-97140-0 (hardcover)

For Erwin

Contents

Abbreviations Used in the Text

AAA   American Authors Authority

AAAA   American Association of Advertising Agencies

ABA   American Bar Association

ABC   American Broadcasting Corporation

AFL   American Federation of Labor

AFM   American Federation of Musicians

AFTRA   American Federation of Television and Radio Artists

AMPTP   Alliance of Motion Picture and Television Producers

ASCAP   American Society of Composers, Authors, and Publishers

BBD&O   Batten, Barton, Durstine & Osborn advertising agency

BMI   Broadcast Music, Inc.

CBS   Columbia Broadcasting System

DGA   Directors Guild of America

FCC   Federal Communications Commission

HUAC   House Un-American Activities Committee

IP   Intellectual property

JWT   J. Walter Thompson advertising agency

MBA   Minimum Basic Agreement

NABET   National Association of Broadcasting Employees and Technicians

NBC   National Broadcasting Company

NLRA   National Labor Relations Act

NLRB   National Labor Relations Board

RKO   Radio Keith Orpheum

RWG   Radio Writers Guild

SAG   Screen Actors Guild

SP   Screen Playwrights

SWG   Screen Writers Guild

WGA   Writers Guild of America

WGAW   Writers Guild of America—West

WRITING FOR HIRE

Introduction

[P]erhaps the ghost-writer is among the honest literary men; in him
alienation from work reaches the final point of complete lack of
public responsibility.

—C. Wright Mills, *White Collar*

To be a writer is not the same thing as to be an author. Writers are people
who write as a vocation, or at least as an avocation. (People around Hollywood today are prone to say that you can't say you're a writer until you sell
your screenplay or get hired to write on a TV show.) But to be an author
means something more—authors are writers who in either a legal or a collo-
quial sense own their work and are recognized as authors of their work. In
American law, and in popular understanding, when writers work for hire,
they are often not authors of what they write: they don't own the work, they
have no right to have it attributed to them, they can't prevent the owners from
changing what they write, and they have what C. Wright Mills called a "complete lack of public responsibility" for their work. This book is a history of the
thirty-year struggle of writers to become authors of film, television, and,
briefly, radio. Through their union, Hollywood writers won some (but not all)
of the rights of authors. And it is also the story of how and why advertising
writers, who never formed a union, largely failed to wage that struggle at all.

"Written by": The Law and Norms of Attribution

In 1973, three Hollywood screenwriters each received a phone call from their
union, the Writers Guild of America, which since 1938 has represented film
and television writers in collective negotiations with studios, production
companies, and TV networks. The Guild's screen-credits administrator wanted

to know if the three writers would be willing to serve as arbitrators of a dispute over screen credit for writing the screenplay of a movie that a major studio was to release shortly. Three writers and a producer-director had written various drafts of the screenplay, and one of the writers was upset that the studio proposed to eliminate him from the screen credits.

Under the collective bargaining agreements between the studios and the Writers Guild, the Directors Guild, and the Screen Actors Guild, credits appear at the beginning of the movie, superimposed over the opening scene or a title sequence. These credits appear in a defined order, usually beginning with the studio and the various production companies that financed the film, followed by the names of the actors in starring roles, individual producers, the cinematographer, and certain others (the editor, composer, and so forth). The credit for the director is always on the screen by itself (Directed by . . .) as the last credit before the action begins. The writing credit (Written by . . . or Screenplay by . . .) always appears on a screen by itself just before the director's credit and for the same amount of time, and it identifies no more than two or three people as writers of the film, even if many helped write it.

The request to arbitrate a dispute over screen credit was a perfectly ordinary one for established writers to receive, as the Writers Guild is required by the collective agreement to resolve disputes among the many writers hired to work on movies. As in every such arbitration, the Guild chose three experienced writers to read all the versions of the script to decide who made the most significant contributions to the script from which the movie was finally shot.

The arbiters did not think much of the movie. One thought it was unoriginal, jesting that credit should be given to the writer of a recent acclaimed film on a similar theme. Another noted that crediting four people as writers "wouldn't help any of them," except that each of them would get a small share of the profits "if it ever gets on TV" (which the arbiter seemed to doubt). The third arbiter wondered "why anyone would want a credit on this picture, let alone why anybody would want to film it." The arbiters unanimously decided to grant credit to the production executive and the two-writer team. Acknowledging the likely disappointment of the writer who wrote the first two scripts and who would not get screen credit, one arbiter said the writer should "not be anguished" because "to tell the absolute, honest-to-God truth in confidence, I think he might be better off not to have his name on this."

The studio released the movie with writing credits as the arbiters decided. Audiences who paid attention saw superimposed over the action in the opening scene, "Written by X and Y & Z." Hollywood insiders would have known that the ampersand meant that Y and Z wrote as a team; the "and" meant that X wrote separately and probably wrote the first draft. (As a condition of being allowed to read dozens of credit arbitration files from the 1950s to the early 2000s, I promised not to mention the names of any films or people involved in the arbitrations.) Although the uncredited writer must have been disappointed, he could make no appeal and no legal claim to challenge the arbiters' decision.[1]

The arbiters were wrong about the movie. It was a hit with critics and audiences alike. It was profitable. It became an icon of the genre. It remains on many critics' lists of the top movies of the 1970s. One of the credited writers went on to a hugely successful career in the industry. Two others found moderate success. The uncredited writer did not. He had one credit prior to that movie and none since, which means his career as a Hollywood writer ended with that movie, and it probably ended because he did not get credit for writing it.

The studio owned the copyright in the film, and the studio is the legal author of the film and of the scripts and story outline upon which it was based. None of the writers owned the copyright in their script because, under the work-for-hire provision of the United States Copyright Act, "the employer is the author of a work made for hire."[2] Film critics and the public often describe the director as the author (in French, *auteur*) of a film.[3] This practice greatly irks writers, all the more so because most writers work in obscurity but create the basis for celebrity for directors and actors. As explained by screenwriter Charles Brackett—who won four Academy Awards for writing classic films in the 1940s and '50s, including *The Lost Weekend* (1945) and *Sunset Boulevard* (1950)—even a successful film writer will "never be familiar to the general public. Nobody will fight for your autograph. When you drive to the premier, the crowd in the bleachers will peer into your car and say, 'Oh, that's nobody.'" In his 2006 manifesto *The Schreiber Theory: A Radical Rewrite of American Film History,* critic David Kipen, using the Yiddish word for author, argued that treating the director as the author of a film is like treating a book's editor as its author. But in law, neither the *auteur* nor the *schreiber* matters; neither is the author of the work.[4]

The literature on copyright has drawn a distinction between authors and owners, at least since Mark Rose published his seminal history of copyright.[5] Rose shows how copyright law evolved in eighteenth-century Britain from a regime of censorship and licensing of publication (in which authors were publicly responsible for their work but not owners of it) to a regime that defined authors as the owners of works. American copyright defines an author as the owner, even when the owner did not write the work. So the distinction I wish to emphasize is the one between authors and writers. When my daughter was young, she won as first prize at a horse show a plaque saying, "You are the author of your own life story." To be an author, the plaque suggests, is to have the power and responsibility to create history. Film and TV writing is unique in American letters in having a worker-controlled process for deciding when a writer is an author, for deciding the meaning of authorship (authorship in the ordinary sense, not in the copyright ownership sense), and for compensating workers based on the union's own credit determinations. In so doing—and this is the first main argument of this book—the Writers Guild reclaims for writers some of the rights and responsibilities of authors, rights and responsibilities they lost under the copyright work-for-hire rule.

The collectively bargained Minimum Basic Agreement (MBA) between the Writers Guild of America (WGA) and the Alliance of Motion Picture and Television Producers gives power to determine screen credit to the Guild. The credit rules are detailed in Schedule A, a thirty-page addendum to the MBA, and in the Screen Credits Manual, which the WGA drafts and WGA members vote to adopt. (A similar MBA with a similar Schedule A and credits manual apply to television writing, although credit arbitrations are rare because TV writers usually resolve credit disputes through informal negotiation.) These complex credit rules are the most detailed statement in American law of the meaning of authorship. They are drafted by a committee of WGA members appointed to represent film and TV writers who have differing viewpoints on the roles of the first writer, subsequent writers, and production executives; and, from time to time, the entire WGA membership votes on changes to the credit rules.[6]

Disgruntled writers who believe the Guild's credit arbitration violated their rights rarely sue. While the Guild, like all labor unions, has a legal duty of fair representation to administer its contracts, including the credit system, fairly and competently, that legal duty simply requires the Guild to avoid arbitrary, invidiously discriminatory, or bad faith conduct; ordinary mistakes in credit arbitration do not violate the duty. And writers cannot sue the studio directly, for there is no provision in any individual writer's contract of hire or for sale of a script governing the allocation of screen credit except a standard term stating that credit will be awarded per the WGA's minimum basic agreement with the studios. At the urging of the WGA's lawyers, courts have resisted every effort to add more searching judicial oversight to the union's administration of the credit system.[7] This situation requires everyone to take seriously the Guild's role in credit determinations, and it enables the Guild to make trade-offs among competing goals.

Credit and the intellectual property rights and compensation tied to it— especially residual payments (for reuse of the work, as when a theatrical movie is shown on TV, or for when a TV show is broadcast, streamed, or downloaded after the first exhibition) and separated rights (to write a novel, stage version, or sequel based on the story and to reacquire the screenplay if it is not made into a movie within a stated term)—are established in the MBA, and they may not be negotiated in a writer's individual contract.[8] Writers have these rights because the founding Guild leaders spearheaded an effort in 1933 to secure writer ownership and profit participation. They were the most vocal and visionary proponents of writers becoming owners of their work, and when in the 1950s their efforts finally came to fruition, the credit system that was originally designed solely for attribution became a system that affects writers' compensation in very direct ways. The system depends on the WGA's fairness and rigor in administering credits. It took writers three decades of hard work between 1933 and 1960 to achieve this state of dominance in determining writing credits. This book is, in part, a history of that effort.[9]

A second main argument of this book is that the efforts of film and TV writers to gain legal rights as authors (some measure of ownership, creative control, and the credit or blame that goes with having one's name associated with a work) is a usable past, especially in the post-industrial, fissured economy of today.[10] By unionizing, this group of highly educated freelance writers was able to negotiate for control over who was recognized as an author of works and for compensation that turned on that recognition. The survival and flourishing of unionization in this narrow sector of the American economy, especially in a sector that valorizes individual achievement, reminds us that collective representation of labor, even highly compensated labor, matters in post-industrial American capitalism. Writers unionized in Hollywood for good reasons, and they remained fairly militant unionists because they understood the power of collective action in the early version of the "gig economy" that was Hollywood. Although writers have always believed that talent is highly individual, and some have made millions while others barely scraped by, they united over their common issues and held their union together through tumultuous strikes, persecution of leftists, industry downsizing, and huge changes in the way that movies and TV are created and delivered.

A third argument of this book is that screen credit is a form of contractually created intellectual property. It is one of the very few forms of intellectual property in the modern economy that is designed by workers for workers and without the involvement of the corporations that control most intellectual property policy. Norms about attribution became rights once employees unionized. Critics of unions have lamented the tendency of unions to create and insist on adherence to rules, sometimes at the expense of worthy goals like customer service, efficiency, or productivity. But rules are essential if we are to have rights, and rights are essential to fairness, equality, and property. The substantive and procedural credit rules distinguish the WGA and Hollywood from any other area of cultural production, and they are unique in the law. They bring the rule of law—uniform rules, fairly applied, based on evidence and reasoned argument—to the question of what it means to be the writer of a story. Unlike other places in both law and culture where authorship is taken as a (relatively) easily discernible *fact*, credit arbitrations treat authorship as contestable and as something that can be determined only through a process designed and administered by and for Guild writers. Everyone in Hollywood knows that credited authorship is, in some sense, a fiction when multiple writers have worked on a film or TV show. As one screenwriter put it: "We regularly sign our names to work we have not written. . . . Behavior that would be a disgrace for a novelist and grounds for dismissal of an academic is business as usual for us. Our defense is that we do it openly, and everyone knows it's being done. It's part of the lore of the movie business." In short, a film's legal authorship, and sometimes even its credited authorship, is not factual authorship and is a legal fiction in every sense of the term. But it is important to writers that it be a *legal* fiction.[11]

The legalism of the credit system matters because compensation (residuals, separated rights, and bonuses) is tied to credit. In fact, credit affects the labor market for writers and the willingness of companies to invest in projects. The WGA does not formally decide who gets hired or what gets written. But in determining who is credited for writing, the WGA effectively determines who will be hired in the future.[12] Credit influences the judgments of film critics, agents, producers, and knowledgeable consumers. Credit affects how studios evaluate ideas and how they attract investment capital to finance production. The importance of Guild credit determinations for the labor and product markets in Hollywood explains, in part, why the Guild survives conditions that in other industries have led to de-unionization. In a high-velocity labor market in which people switch jobs frequently and demand for the product is unpredictable, the perceived reliability of screen-credit determinations helps production and finance companies match investment capital with human capital. Moreover, residuals compensate writers during periods of slack employment, thus keeping their human capital in the industry. The WGA plays a significant, albeit indirect, role as an intermediary in the market for ideas that lead to projects and to creating a market for the completed projects.[13]

Advertisements, of course, have no signed author. As in Hollywood, men and women working on Madison Avenue made a great deal of money writing in the middle decades of the twentieth century. They worked for executives who knew—as one 1950s ad executive put it—that the company's most valuable assets rode down the elevator every night.[14] Agencies worked hard to identify and nurture writing talent, and many noted writers started their working lives in advertising. Unlike film and TV writers, however, advertising copywriters are largely unknown to the public. There is no formal system of attribution. When advertising awards are given, they name the ad agency, its creative director, and its art director; they do not name the individual writer or artist. An ad is almost invariably unsigned, even when a celebrity writer, director, photographer, or illustrator has participated in creating it. This anonymity has existed even during periods when the community of ad writers and film and TV writers overlapped and even when valorizing the individual creator might have benefitted the product, the advertiser, and the ad agency who recruited a noteworthy writer or artist to work on an ad campaign. This book explores what ad agency employees have said about why Madison Avenue does not publicly attribute work, and also explores the work practices within one large ad agency that occasionally created forms of crypto-attribution.

In 1923, Helen Landsdowne Resor, an executive at J. Walter Thompson, which was then the largest advertising agency in the world, hired Edward Steichen to bring his modernist photographic eye to a campaign for Jergens lotion. Steichen was a well-known artist; Landsdowne Resor chose him for the campaign because she was an admirer of modern art. (She was not alone among ad executives in admiring all things modern and modernist. She also was not alone in recruiting fine artists to work on advertisements, although she was more serious about her interest in art than some; she became a trustee of the New York Museum of Modern Art.) Beginning in September 1923, Steichen took all the Jergens advertising photographs, and he continued to do so until the 1930s. They were beautiful and arresting modernist images of women's hands and arms in close-up. As one senior copywriter said of the Jergens campaign, Steichen's photos "succeeded in getting some very charming illustrations on what hands can do in building romance." Although Steichen occasionally included his Jergens and other advertising photographs in the art gallery shows of his work in the 1920s and 1930s, his photographs were never attributed to him in the advertisements.[15] Yet doing so might have helped Jergens by suggesting it was a high-class product. Hoping to attract new or better consumers and add cachet to a product by associating the product with great art, a number of ad agencies recruited eminent art painters (including Georgia O'Keeffe and Stuart Davis), photographers, and illustrators (Norman Rockwell is today the most famous; others included Maxfield Parrish and Rockwell Kent).[16] In radio and television in the 1930s and 1940s, noted screenwriters did freelance work on shows produced by ad agencies. Although occasionally artists signed artwork and actors were credited in radio, writers were never credited in ads.

While today we consider attribution of authorship to be normal in film and television and inconsistent with the very nature of advertising, there is no reason that this should be so. Screen credit could be given only to the studios that made and financed movies or shows; screen credit could be superimposed on TV commercials; and the artwork and copy of print ads could note authorship in small print just as photo credits and bylines are given in newspapers and magazines. To whatever extent it may be true today that the "entertainment" portion and the "advertising" portions of what appears on a screen are made by different people working for different companies under different conditions and subject to different attribution norms, there was a great deal more overlap at mid-century. The people who freelanced for ad agencies writing advertiser-sponsored radio and TV programs were many of the same people who wrote films. And even those who wrote only ads or only radio, films, or TV were demographically similar—they went to the same colleges and universities, they lived in the same cities (principally New York, Chicago, and Los Angeles), and they traveled in the same circles. This book uncovers the history of the mid-twentieth-century labor practices that created the very different norms of authorship in two closely allied and overlapping industries that employed similar (and sometimes the same) people to write.

Writers in Hollywood, unlike writers on Madison Avenue, had their names attached to their work because Hollywood writers formed a labor union. While today substantial nonunion sectors exist in nondrama cable and reality television, since 1938 all Hollywood motion pictures and scripted television shows—now including shows created by Netflix, Amazon, and Hulu for streaming on the internet—have been produced by workers where everyone from the director, actors, and writers to the gaffers, grips, and drivers belongs to a union. Writers wanted to claim the cultural status and some legal rights that they would (or did) enjoy as authors of novels, plays, and short stories, and they used the power of unionization to create binding, writer-controlled legal norms mediating creation, ownership, private attribution, and public recognition. It was in the interests of studios, too, for their products to be authored, just as were other high-status cultural products, even if the public did not recognize the names of film authors as easily as they recognized the names of novelists or actors. Movie moguls sought legitimacy as creators of art by attributing authorship to writers and directors just as plays, novels, and short stories were authored. Ad executives, in contrast, thought ads were more effective if they read as if they were a message directly from the advertiser to the consumer, without identifying the text and image as the product of a creator's imagination. Nevertheless, two different labor law regimes in two similar occupations resulted in very different work cultures, compensation systems, and approaches to attribution and intellectual property.

Although ad writers sometimes chafed at the anonymity of their work, their nonunion workplace provided no institutional framework to channel their frustration into organized demands for change. Instead, they embraced a self-conception as professionals devoted to the interest of their clients to justify their own invisibility from public notice in the field in which they worked. Even the so-called Creative Revolution in advertising of the 1960s did not change the attribution norms, notwithstanding that ads acknowledged their nature as ads and ad copy occasionally explicitly acknowledged the existence of a copywriter. A 1965 Avis ad, written as a first-person narrative of a copywriter whose Avis rental car did not live up to a promise Avis had made in a previous ad, said, "I write Avis ads for a living. But that doesn't make me a paid liar. . . . So if I'm going to continue writing these ads, Avis had better live up to them. Or they can get themselves a new boy."[17] The ad is arresting because it breaks the convention of ignoring the existence of a writer behind the ad, and it is effective because it suggests that the writer uses and cares about the product he sells. Still, neither the agency nor the writer was identified.

In the absence of law requiring credit to the actual author, economic sectors that value accurate attribution developed norms and some contractual rights to attribute work to individuals. Newspapers came to use bylines, and in the wake of scandals about fabricated stories, some papers expanded the credit to include every reporter who had worked on the story. Academic journals require accurate attribution of authorship, and some limit the number of authors to prevent diffusion of responsibility for false claims.[18] Courts require lawyers to sign pleadings. Hospitals require doctors to sign medical charts. Architects must sign blueprints. Other norms and laws require attribution, but without the involvement of an employee representative, most aspects of attribution have been treated as company assets or as systems to protect the public, not as a protection for the rights of employee creators or as a device to share profits of the enterprise.[19] Democratically adopted and regularly applied legal rules requiring credit to employees is a signal achievement of the WGA.

Thus, a fourth argument of this book is that the difference in attribution between Madison Avenue and Hollywood is due in significant part to the different labor practices and, specifically, the unionization of Hollywood writers and the embrace of norms of professional duty to clients by advertising writers.

Law, Norms, and the Industrialization of Authors

In the twentieth century, creative work in the production of texts, images, and sounds—that is, the work of authorship—often occurred as part of a commercial enterprise. Corporations became the creators, authors, and owners of many of the texts, technologies, images, and information that constitute popular culture because the law by 1930 was clear that employees are not "authors" of their works; their employers are. Authorship in the sense in which everyone other than copyright lawyers understands it became largely disconnected from ownership.

That disconnection bothered writers. It was, and remains today, a major impetus for writers' unionizing. Erik Barnouw, who in the 1940s was the second president of the Radio Writers Guild and became a professor at Columbia and an historian of the radio-and-television business, was a passionate critic of the legal fiction of corporate authorship. In *The Television Writer,* his book about "the world of the television writer" as it stood in 1962 after the first full decade of the business, Barnouw excoriated "the industrialization of the writer," which was his shorthand for the paucity of legal rights of writer employees of media companies. His particular target was copyright law. The Constitution, Barnouw maintained, singled out only two occupations for special protection: "authors and inventors," to whom Congress could give "the exclusive Right to their respective Writings and Discoveries." The copyright work-for-hire doctrine, Barnouw maintained, was anathema to this goal. The Founding Fathers, he said, "considered it important to strengthen the independence of writers and inventors by giving them control, at least for a time, over uses made of their work and revenue from it." But the work-for-hire doctrine became "the Magna Carta" of twentieth-century media corporations because it took away writers' independence. Barnouw used the example of his first script for the radio show *Cavalcade of America,* which he wrote as an employee of the advertising agency retained by

DuPont, the show's sponsor. Although Barnouw received on-air credit for his episode, "Dr. Franklin Goes to Court," the copyright registration in the Library of Congress read: "by Erik Barnouw. Author: E. I. Du Pont de Nemours & Company."[20]

Writers have generally accepted that corporate ownership of collectively created works facilitates management and renewal of copyright in them. But Barnouw—channeling the refrain of many twentieth-century writers— complained that the "industrialization of writers" had gone too far. The writer

> almost never received air credit, was not paid for rebroadcasts, and did not share in subsidiary rights. Revisions were made without his consent and even without his knowledge. Scripts could be made to mean the opposite of what the writer intended, and sometimes they were. The writer could be barred from rehearsal, and on many series he was, as a matter of policy. It was precisely as if the founding fathers had written: "Congress shall have Power to deprive Authors of all Right to their respective Writings."[21]

Noting that for every form of contemporary corporate entertainment "to be set in motion, a lonely man still has to think and work with pencil or type-writer," Barnouw insisted that industrialization's divorce of writers from their legal and cultural status as authors was enabled by the copyright law and was a terrible injustice.

The Writers Guild sought control over screen credits to fight against this injustice. Guild leaders wanted screen credit to reflect the historical fact of authorship. Authorship designations should be *authentic* so that writing credits retain meaning to writers, studios, and the public. Yet, and somewhat contradictorily, the Guild decided to concentrate credit on one or two people to create the impression that the screenplay (and thus the film) reflects the creative vision of those persons. This strategic use of the concept of author-ship enhances writers' status vis-à-vis directors by portraying movies as the *creative vision* of a distinct author as opposed to a committee. Writers since the beginning of film have debated whether to credit every writer who worked on a film. An "additional writing by" credit existed in various forms before 1948, and the Guild debated reviving it in 2000 for writers who contributed significantly to a script but less than the amount required to get "screenplay by" credit. Its defenders say it is inequitable that people get no credit for significant contributions. Others say that too many credits diminish the significance of all writing credits. The view that has prevailed is that writers will be regarded as authors of film, in the sense of being creators of its creative vision, only if and when one or two writers control, and are perceived as controlling, the script content and the story construction.[22]

The work relationships of writers in mid-twentieth-century film, television, and advertising are where authorship was constituted. That is, workplaces generated legal and social norms mediating creation, ownership, attribution, and public recognition as dominant features of twentieth-century authorship. Résumés, references, and portfolios make claims about creation of quotidian work in the recent past, and biographies and histories tell the story of biography-worthy people and their work. Gender played a surprising role in enabling attribution of work, especially in the anonymous world of advertising. Women found good jobs and achieved success as writers in film and advertising between 1930 and 1960 to a greater extent than in any other male-dominated profession. Their gender was sometimes deemed an asset and often marked them, which means that their status as women authors (not just authors who happened to be women) is integral to how we understand some authors.[23] But neither employment law nor intellectual property law protects the employee author or speaks to the desire to know the story behind the ad campaign that launched the VW Beetle in the United States, the invention of the silicon chip or the iPod/iPad/iPhone, the writing of a truly great presidential speech, or to know which of the many writers who worked on a film or TV show wrote the most memorable scenes.[24]

When the author of a work is an employee, one might imagine that employment law would protect some right of attribution, but it does not. The essence of authorship in twentieth-century work is not captured by copyright (who owns the work); it must be described as a sort of trademark, too (whose name can be associated with the work). Yet trademark law does not regulate the authorship claims of employees.[25] In some legal systems, copyright law protects what is known as a "moral right" *(droit moral)* of attribution, which prohibits false designations of authorship of copyrighted works and, more affirmatively, allows an author to claim authorship and so prevent the work from not being attributed to her, even if it isn't falsely attributed to another.[26] But American intellectual property law, with one exception not relevant here, does not recognize or protect moral rights. When Congress in the 1930s considered a bill to amend copyright law to recognize moral rights, the bill contained an exception for movie studios (among other entities) so that corporate employers could alter employee-produced works and also designate authorship as they pleased. As Peter Decherney explains, the Hollywood studios considered moral rights entirely inconsistent with their business model.[27] In sum, the person or entity that employs a person to create a work for hire has all the rights of copyright owners, including the right to rewrite it, throw it in the trash, produce the story into a movie or TV show, or attribute it to anyone or to no one. No statutory or common-law claims have been successful in regulating screen credit.[28]

Intellectual property lawyers tend to insist on a close relationship between copyright and patent law and an individual, literary-artistic-scientific model of creation associated with modernism in the arts and literature and with the now largely discredited notion that great inventions were the product of one or a few great minds, usually the mind of the person named on the patent. This lawyerly focus on authors, inventors, and owners has been incommensurate with the relatively small percentage of twentieth-century creative people whose efforts were rewarded largely or solely through copyright or patent ownership. Regardless of the dearth of law in the books, in workplaces, a set of social practices identify particular people with the ideas and intellectual property that they generate. Although lawyers might not initially recognize these practices as law, a law in action *does* govern the allocation of credit for creating work. Thus, the fifth major argument of this book is that modern authorship is a socio-legal concept formed not only, perhaps not even principally, by the actual work of creating or by copyright law's dubbing some person or entity as an author. Rather, modern authors created themselves through social and legal processes through which individuals and firms were *recognized as being* authors. In the workplace, *attribution* of work, rather than *ownership* of the intellectual property represented in it, defines the modern connection between creators and their work. Just as significantly, the relationship between people and intellectual property is constituted by social and legal processes of *recognition*.

By analyzing the formal (and unspoken) contractual structures of creative labor, this book offers a socio-legal history, or a historical structuralist ethnography and legal anthropology of the contracting behavior of writers on the issue of authorship. I seek to illuminate the role of what is today called "soft law" in defining the authorship of collectively created work. A main argument of this book is, thus, as follows: to understand how writers in these two industries defined authorship of work, it is important to examine their work relations and the way that they did (in Hollywood) and did not (in advertising) resort to contractually defined rules to assert claims to being recognized as the authors of their work. That is an argument about the necessarily tangled relationship between labor, copyright, and authorship in twentieth-century popular culture. It is, especially, an argument about intellectual property and labor history: we can only understand the history of intellectual property in collaboratively created works of popular culture by examining the history of labor practices. Copyright law obscures authorship. Labor practices can create or obscure it even further. But in Hollywood, union contract rules defined employed writers as authors once writers, rather than the studios, controlled the designation of screenplay authorship.[29]

Christopher Tomlins has called for an approach to socio-legal studies generally, and legal history in particular, that eliminates the old conjunctive metaphor of "law and society" and replaces it with a new metaphor of the nature of law in society as "law as . . . ." That is, instead of studying law in relation to some other distinct domain of social activity (society, history, or economics) that lies outside law, we might imagine them as the same: law as . . . , as in law as history or history as law.[30] To understand intellectual property in film, television, and advertising, one must study the history of labor relations in these industries. History—and specifically labor history—is not just an interesting perspective. Rather, the labor history is the only way to understand the operation of the intellectual property regime.

What the history of attribution practices reveals is more than just the nature and operation of a system of work relations and intellectual property. It is a perspective on what sociologist of art Howard Becker calls an "art world"—the people and organizations who produce those objects that are defined as art.[31] By insisting that film and television be attributed to people, writers and directors sought to assimilate their work to the art world, or what French theorist Pierre Bourdieu would call the field, of true art, as opposed to the commercial or business practices that advertisements were seen to be. Conversely, by obscuring the writers behind advertisements, ad agency executives distanced their work from the art world and assimilated themselves to the world of professional advisors of business.[32]

The Three Functions of Attribution and Their Relation to Intellectual Property

Corporate ownership of intellectual property and corporate employment were initially regarded as a threat to innovation and, therefore, to entrepreneurship, precisely because the good ideas and work of individual people would not be accurately attributed and fairly rewarded, and people would lose the incentive to innovate and to work. Firms avoided malaise by devising attribution schemes to reward and promote innovation. (Advertising agencies periodically confronted dissatisfied copywriters who needed recognition within the firm and the industry, even as agency leaders insisted that all light should shine on the agency and its clients. So they invented new intra-firm or industry-wide awards.) Thus, attribution became a *reward*.[33]

Attribution also serves a *trademark* function: the same novel will sell better with a *New York Times* best-selling author's name on it than with mine, and a scientific study a respected university scientist produces is generally considered more reliable than one pharmaceutical company employees conduct. Hollywood has generally preferred to market its wares under the names of actors and directors, but occasionally, it uses writers and prohibits highly paid writers from removing their name from screen credit precisely because the name will help sell the film to audiences and critics. (Since *Death of a Gunfighter* (1969), directors seized the power to substitute the pseudonym "Alan Smithee" for the director's name when they thought the studio's version of the film would tarnish the director's reputation, or when the film was bowdlerized when edited for TV.)[34]

Attribution also serves a *legitimating* function. When Hollywood studios became concerned about unauthorized duplication of DVDs, the Motion Picture Association of America commissioned a series of short films to screen before movies in theaters. Each of these infomercial-cum-documentaries featured a technical worker explaining how piracy affected his livelihood by hurting sales of motion pictures. The antipiracy spots sought to legitimate corporate copyrights in films by linking them to the efforts of "normal" people, not movie stars, marquee directors, highly paid screenwriters, or studio executives whose names are usually associated with movies and to whom authorship of films is conventionally attributed. Banking on the emotional value of an antipiracy plea delivered by a set builder in a flannel shirt—a guy who in no circumstances would ever have a claim to intellectual property rights in a film—is a persuasive rhetorical strategy because it links the sanctity of corporate copyrights to the paychecks of real people.

Norms of attribution, however, are not the same as legal ownership of the work, and they do not confer control over the work that actual authorship entails. The right to receive screen credit did not save Hollywood writers from frustration when studios allowed scripts to languish or from chagrin when their stories were changed. The grim denouement of *Chinatown* (1974) was not in the script Robert Towne wrote, and it was not the ending he wanted. (Spoiler alert: the protagonist Evelyn Mulwray—Faye Dunaway—is killed in the movie; in the script, she survives and escapes the web of corruption.) Yet Towne won a Best Screenplay Oscar and made his name on the film.[35] The screenplay for *Friendly Persuasion* (1956) was nominated for an Academy Award (and the film won the Palme d'Or at Cannes), but the film had no screenplay credit because the writer, Michael Wilson, was blacklisted as a communist sympathizer in 1952 just a year after having won a Best Screenplay Oscar for *A Place in the Sun* (1951). To avoid the embarrassment of awarding a Best Screenplay Oscar to a writer the Academy was pretending did not exist, the Academy changed its rules to remove the screenplay from the ballot. (Twenty-five years later, the Academy reinstated Wilson's nomination for the film, along with his nomination for *Lawrence of Arabia* from 1962 and his Oscar for *The Bridge on the River Kwai* from 1957.)

The legal fictions and cultural constructs of intellectual property—the author as proprietor, the trademark brand as corporate property, workplace knowledge as a trade secret—were recycled into an all-purpose notion that knowledge, human capital, and persona could be regarded in law and in life as an investment vehicle and an asset to be managed. In economic terms, an innovation or someone's talent or a bit of knowledge could produce two separate revenue streams: one from the intellectual property itself (the copyright, the trademark, the trade secret) and one from the attribution of the intellectual property to a person. Authors, publishers, lawyers, marketers, and others have long known that a marquee name like Virginia Woolf or James Joyce has a market value, wholly apart from the value of the books that bear their names.[36]

Claimants to the value of attribution and to commodified personas embraced intellectual property as a framework for making arguments about the value of attribution. A right of attribution is protected when the association between a company (or its goods or services) and a name, word, or image is a registered trademark, as in "a Chanel suit." But the identity of the creator need not be known to the consumer for a valid trademark to exist—it does not matter whether Coco Chanel herself designed a suit or Henri Bendel designed the hat in the Cole Porter song, "You're the Top" ("You're a Bendel bonnet, a Shakespeare sonnet . . ."). In some circumstances, the right of publicity protects against misappropriation of one's likeness for commercial purposes. Thus, when the Ford Motor Company commissioned an advertisement with a soundtrack featuring a song made famous by Bette Midler but sung by a woman who only sounded like Bette Midler, the court allowed Midler to sue for misappropriation: "The human voice is one of the most palpable ways identity is manifested. . . . The singer manifests herself in the song. To impersonate her voice is to pirate her identity."[37] But when one is employed to create a persona, the employee may not have the right to prevent use of the persona. So intellectual property hasn't been useful to employees because attribution rights are as alienable as intellectual property rights are. Bela Lugosi became the classic image of Count Dracula after he starred in the iconic 1931 film (and his face remains dominant in a Google images search of Dracula). After Lugosi's death, his heirs claimed that Lugosi's image as Dracula was Lugosi's property and theirs to inherit. But in the litigation over it, a California Supreme Court opinion insisted that the employer owned that Dracula, not Lugosi or his heirs, because Lugosi had created him while employed by a movie studio.[38]

Trademark and the right of publicity are the areas of law that recognize the value of attribution. They became the apogee of modern intellectual property when effective control of texts or images was rendered difficult through technological and cultural changes allowing rapid circulation of pirated works. And yet employee creators of intellectual property cannot trademark themselves, nor can they bring a right of publicity claim for a misattribution of their work that results in an enhancement of another's persona or reputation at the expense of their own. The legal regime under which many creators worked deprived them of the intellectual and financial independence of idea entrepreneurs. In sum, although law's imagination of authorship has many facets, including copyright, trademark, and publicity, when it comes to employees, it is at best unclear whether the employee is the author of her persona or her works. In many cases, the employee creator is not, in law, an author, even of her persona, which may in some cases feel that she is not the owner of herself. Ironically, the advertising agency employees who enhanced the value of personas like Lugosi's or Midler's, and those who sought to capitalize on them in ways that courts later found illegal, were not the "authors" (in the ownership or attribution senses) of the works that created or infringed upon that value.

Art, Commerce, and the Modern Author at Work

In ad agencies and in film and television production, as in law and in culture, those who talked about the nature of creativity imagined the relationship between a person and a creative work in two ways that existed in tension. First, there is the modernist ideal of authorship: to be an author is to conjure a work out of imagination and to exercise comprehensive compositional control over it. The work reflects the uniqueness and the individuality of its author, and the individuality of the author is proven by the uniqueness of the work. James Joyce is the author of *Ulysses*, and *Ulysses* is proof of the individual genius of Joyce. Of course, a number of canonical modernist texts borrow conspicuously and were fluent in pastiche and parody; *Ulysses* famously borrowed from classical literature, advertising, and many other sources. But modernist notions of authorship insisted upon the distinction between them and the kind of commercial authorship involved in twentieth-century forms of cultural production as exemplified by advertising agency and entertainment industry work.[39]

The modernist conception of individuality and creativity existed, as it continues to exist, alongside another. This second version emphasizes not the essential, miraculous, unique genius of the individual's perception and creations and a notion of artistic merit wholly divorced from public acceptance, but instead, the mixture of hard work, fortuity, and marketing that enables works to come into existence and those who create them to capture the public eye. This Madison Avenue notion of authorship places primary importance on the *perception* of the relation between an author and her work, and it recognizes that the perception is created by the investment of time and resources in marketing. To be an author or inventor is to be a repository of a felicitous mix of inspiration, labor, money, cleverness, and luck that enables a person and her work to seize fifteen minutes of fame. Madison Avenue knows that the genius of the author cannot be divorced from the canniness of the publicist, and it accepted an interdependence of creativity and commerce in producing all work.[40]

In the heart of Madison Avenue, right alongside the norm of corporate attribution of any ad campaign, there exists a deep faith in the transformative power of fierce originality. Both the creative people and the company managers valued some of the same qualities in agency employees that they valued in "noncommercial" writers and artists—creativity, effective use of words, compelling visual images or melodies. Many at JWT esteemed both things that could be described with the adjective *modern* and *modernism* as a movement in art and literature, and they sometimes conflated being modern (up to date) with being modernist (as an aesthetic style). They deliberately and unconsciously aligned the firm's work and work practices with all things modern, including the aesthetics of modernism.

Of course, neither the modernist nor the Madison Avenue view of the nature of authorship is a pure type. The great modernist writers and artists knew they needed to market themselves and their works, just as Madison Avenue agencies knew they needed to cultivate and recognize individual talent. And everyone knows that great creative accomplishments often reflect the assistance of many besides the named author. The reputations for great genius of many great modernist writers and artists are partly a result of successful marketing. Moreover, twentieth-century copyright law embraced both the modernist and the Madison Avenue conceptions of authorship. Lawyers seeking to expand property rights in valuable mass culture commodities like movies, photographs, or popular music frequently invoked the creator's unique and transformative vision as the basis in law for protecting property rights in the work.[41]

In the early and mid-twentieth century, modernism in literature and the arts insisted on a vision of the creative process and on a notion of the author at odds with the increasingly collaborative and commercial nature of the process by which many texts, images, and sounds were being produced. Modernism offered, according to literary scholar Paul Saint-Amour, a "portrait of the artist as a lone insurgent" creating high culture works of great artistic integrity. Modernism defined itself as being distinct from Madison Avenue; critical theorist Andreas Huyssen called it "the Great Divide" in the twentieth-century arts. Modernists harbored an "obsessive hostility to mass culture" and "insist[ed] on the autonomy of the art work." Modernist critic and modern art booster Clement Greenberg (1909–1994) wrote a famous essay, "Avante Garde and Kitsch" (1939), in which he insisted on the separation of art from mass culture. What Greenberg dismissed as kitsch—"popular, commercial art and literature with their chromotypes, magazine covers, illustrations, ads, slick and pulp fiction, comics, Tin Pan Alley music, tap dancing, Hollywood movies, etc., etc."—is where I want to explore the law and norms of authorship. What he deemed a travesty—the power of promoters, dealers, publicists, and advertisers to define or, worse, to create great artists or authors—I see as a new kind of intellectual property. Modernism defined its identity in relation to modern commercial mass culture, and in that respect, it depended on commerce for its identity and it depended on the Madison Avenue habit of defining the author by recognition and attribution.[42]

It is important and interesting to read a television show as Michael Szalay does for the symbolism, metaphor, and allegory that reflect the studio's corporate strategy.[43] Yet it takes adjustment for many to analyze motifs in *Game of Thrones* or *Deadwood* as reflecting what HBO thinks or conveys rather than what a writer thinks or conveys. Even if much literary criticism abandoned focus on authorial intention around the time that theorists announced the author was dead, we still find it more intelligible to talk about writer David Milch's vision and language in *Deadwood,* not HBO's. And until studios and networks always produce similar works, those who admire one film or television program for its writing want to see other work by the same writer. That is especially true if you're trying to hire a writer—every writer on an HBO show is not a perfect substitute for every other. So the writer's name has trademark value distinct from the studio or network name. Studios and networks want to tread a very fine line between locating the value of the show in the studio or network (an HBO show) and in the writer or director. Hiring an acclaimed writer will generate buzz at the development stage and when the project is released to audiences, even if the work is poorer than the writer's prior work. Hence, studios don't want to subsume the identity of the writer entirely into the corporate brand, and they don't want celebrity writers to be able to remove their name from projects. Yet the Writers Guild has fought for the right of writers to use a pseudonym or even to remove their name from the credits entirely and sacrifice the writer's share of the profits so that writers can protect themselves from being associated with projects that they consider harmful to their reputation. The Guild relies on legal processes to manage the conflict among these meanings and to make difficult and extremely high-stakes choices about which of its members will get the considerable financial rewards of credit in an environment in which all participants know that authorship is collective but credits name individuals.

Even in the realm of "literature" and "high art," marketing mattered; the relationship between the publisher and the author, and the dealer and the artist, was an important feature of the modernist world long before Andy Warhol famously tried to collapse the distinction between art and commerce by painting soup cans, referring to himself as a brand and his studio as "the Factory," and disclaiming authorship of some of his paintings by deflecting questions about the intent of his work to his assistants who, Warhol said, actually created them.[44] Warhol's merger of artistic talent, transformative vision, and the ability to generate hype does not make sense except against the backdrop of modernism's insistence on the separation between art and commerce. Artistic labor markets depend, in part, on reputation to determine the dollar value of creative labor.[45]

Law both facilitated and reacted to a modern conceptualization of talent as not merely inhering in a person, nor even being the product of the talented person's effort, but as reflecting the investment of the promoter and the impresario, the TV hosts, the DJs, and even the social and serendipitous relation between the artist and the crowd. As the social theorist Pierre-Michel Menger observed, one should understand the value of artistic labor as a matter of reputation as much as talent. "[T]he appraisal of art and artists varies with the organizational traits of each art world, since it reflects the cooperative and competitive activities of the various members. . . . Rather than being a causal factor, talent becomes a dependent variable, socially determined by the behavior of employers on one side of the market and consumers on the other side. This is why talent may be conceived as embodying not only artistic abilities and technical skills, but also behavioral and relational ones."[46] Attribution was, thus, a function of the labor market and the consumer market, but it was enormously valuable to the creative worker. As with other things of value, people began to think of attribution as a species of property. As intellectual property concepts of authorship permeated legal conceptions of attribution, other areas of law recycled copyright's established equation of text with property and unoriginality with copyright infringement into a new equation of persona with property and unauthorized representation with theft. Madison Avenue's marketing of pop songs and pop stars made it possible to say that when someone else on Madison Avenue chose to ask a singer to sing too much like Bette Midler it was an act of "pirat[ing] her identity."

Threat of copyright-infringement litigation prompted musicians to abandon the longstanding musical tradition of borrowing and riffing on melodies, rhythms, and passages from existing music,[47] squelched certain forms of satire and parody, and thus changed the way in which contemporary musicians negotiate their relationship to both the sounds, and the reputation, of their forebearers.[48] Musicologists and literary scholars have noted, usually with regret or alarm, that the expansive copyright protection enables authors and musicians, their heirs, and their recording or publishing companies to control the uses to which creative works are put. The control is not merely about how sounds, words, and images will be used, but also how the reputation of a past generation of creative workers will be shaped by the work of a new generation. The dogged efforts of James Joyce's heir to prevent uses of Joyce's works and correspondence that might portray the Joyce family in a light not favored by the heir are an effort to blend the copyright of the author as proprietor with the tort that treats the persona as property.[49] It is modernism harnessing the power of law to fight back against the postmodernist or poststructuralist claim that the reader, not the author, gives meaning to a work.[50]

Hollywood and Madison Avenue have been metonyms for many things; in this book, they are used to stand for two contrasting twentieth-century visions of the nature of authorship and the role of labor relations in constituting some writers as authors and others as not. But they were also, in both a figurative and a literal sense, places where creators worked for intellectual property owners and, in so doing, worked out the nature and meaning of modern authorship. They were places where the meaning of authorship mutated to emphasize the value of attribution over the value of creation and the value of nonattribution as a good in itself. But by so doing, and by modeling how and why attribution should be alienable, Hollywood and Madison Avenue created the conditions that would give rise to a backlash—the search for the real people behind the company name. In some sense, the screen-credit regime the WGA administers exists because movie and television producers consider it in their interest to shore up the romantic model of authorship in the face of its increasingly being challenged by the reality that most art, writing, and other copyrighted works were created as works for hire and that attribution of creative work could be as saleable as the work and the copyright in it.

Structure of This Book

As is perhaps fitting for a book on writers, this book has a three-act structure. The first act ("Beginnings") introduces the labor relations and attribution practices in the two industries and charts the efforts of writers to secure the legal and social rights of authors. Focusing on the J. Walter Thompson (JWT) agency in the 1930s and 1940s, Chapter 1 traces the anonymity of ad authorship to the emerging conception of advertising as a learned profession in which the agency served as an expert advisor dedicated to advancing the client's interests. JWT executives, just like white-shoe lawyers of that era, sought social status by describing themselves as professionals devoted solely to the client's interest, which led them to insist that work be attributed by clients only to the agency, not to individuals, and by the public only to the advertiser and never to the agency. The agency relied on norms of professionalism cultivated through personnel policies rather than on employment contracts or intellectual property law to define and police writer claims to authorship or ownership of their work. Chapter 2 shows that abuses of screen credit and desire for control of script copyrights were two of the most important issues that drove screenwriters to unionize in the early 1930s. Writers today tell a story of how the writers of the 1930s sacrificed ownership of script copyrights to gain the right to bargain collectively and the right to control screen credit. The evidence from the legal proceedings and from the Writers Guild deliberations of the 1930s and 1940s, however, tells a more complicated story.

Act II ("Intersections"), the middle three chapters, covers the crucial period when writers working for advertising agencies and Hollywood companies began to do the same work under different authorship norms. From the 1930s to the early 1950s, ad agencies wrote and produced radio and TV shows for their clients to sponsor, and they sometimes recruited film writers to do the work. The intersection of the labor relations of Madison Avenue with labor relations of Hollywood in the early days of TV very nearly resulted in ad agency staff gaining the author rights that film and TV writers secured by unionizing. Chapter 3 describes the first encounter advertising agencies had with writer demands for ownership and attribution of their work, which occurred in the mid-1940s when freelance radio writers employed by agencies joined the Radio Writers Guild. The contract demands made by freelance radio writers were strikingly different from the personnel practices that agencies used for their staff copywriters on the crucial issues of ownership of rights in scripts and on-air credits for writers. Chapter 3 argues that the legal categories of employee and freelancer, and the notion that writers who occupied the status of "employee" were more closely connected to the agency than those who occupied the status of freelancer, were what enabled the agencies to fend off claims for authorship. Legal statuses thus became a firewall.

The same conflict flared up again when, as recounted in Chapter 4, TV writers unionized. Ad agencies employed the same people to do the same work as production companies and television networks, but they brought to that work a very different set of personnel practices and norms of authorship. To demand attribution of authorship of the shows they wrote and produced contravened both long-established anonymity norms and, equally as important, the very notion of a loyal agent. This chapter also shows that TV writers began regularly to assume the managerial role of production executive at the same time they were still engaged in writing. It therefore sheds light on the long debate over which person—the writer, the producer, or the director—should be understood as the author of film and TV by showing that authorship is a *legal* role that has always been deeply entwined with contractual issues over which writers negotiated vigorously both in their individual contracts and, especially, in the Guild's collective agreements with the networks and studios.[51]

The magazine format that TV ultimately adopted (in which ad agencies produce commercials that were interspersed in programs that Hollywood produced, just as ad agencies create advertisements interspersed with articles written by magazine staff or freelance writers) ended the intersection of ad writing and TV writing. But the Guild's insistence on screen credit for TV writers enabled the creation of compensation through residuals and the separation of rights in scripts. Chapter 5 shows how writers gained some control over subsidiary rights as well as contract provisions requiring payment to credited writers for the reuse of their material. Those payments—known today as residuals—have been a cornerstone of writers' compensation ever since. In telling the history of the origin and early expansion of residuals tied to screen credit, Chapter 5 shows the crucial role the Writers Guild played in overcoming the considerable collective action and administrative challenges in creating residuals as a novel form of intellectual property and deferred compensation.

The book's third act ("Denouement") examines the significant legal rights to credit and the labor-relations models of the two sectors in the years after the division between Madison Avenue and Hollywood attribution practices were relatively settled. To illuminate the significance of screen credit, Chapter 6 offers a new perspective on the blacklisting of scores of writers on allegations that they were communist or because they refused to answer questions before the House Un-American Activities Committee (as it was colloquially known; HUAC). Every book on the blacklist has observed that the Guild's contractual right to determine screen credit proved to be vulnerable. What no one has ever explained, perhaps because no one today realizes, is that for those successful and talented screenwriters who continued to write and sell scripts, even as they dodged HUAC subpoenas by living in Mexico and sold their work under pseudonyms or through fronts who were credited as the authors of their work, the Guild continued to operate its own mechanisms to award credit. The Guild sometimes arbitrated credit disputes, even when everyone knew that the studio would never abide by the credit arbitrators' decision. The continued operation of the credit-arbitration machinery enabled the Guild to regain power over credits when the blacklist began to fall apart in 1960. And, in some cases, the records of these apparently useless credit arbitrations helped the Guild to restore credits to blacklisted writers in the 1990s and 2000s. Credit corrections, like every other credit determination, often pitted one Guild member against another, or the heirs of one against the heirs of another, when both were not only deeply invested in issues of reputation and authorship but also beneficiaries of the residual payments that turn on screen credit. Legal norms were essential to the Guild in making these painful and high-stakes decisions.

Chapter 7 examines the significance of Hollywood writers' employee status to their claims to credit. It also examines the culture of being a corporate employee and therefore not an author on Madison Avenue in the period after agencies had confined themselves to production of advertisements and commercials. Writers skirmished with ad agencies and movie, TV, and radio production companies in the 1930s, 1940s, and 1950s over whether writers were employees or independent contractors and labor or management. Whether writers were independent contractors or employees mattered for whether they could unionize, whether collective negotiations would violate antitrust laws, and whether they could claim ownership of their work under copyright law. The eventual resolution of the legal issue—that freelancers were employees precisely because the employing company has the right to direct the writer in the act of writing and revising—defines the legal status of employee in terms of control over writing. That control is an essential attribute of an author. The writer's lack of control, particularly when combined with the anonymity and anxiety about the quality of the work produced in the corporate-culture factories, sparked a literature about alienation and conformity in 1950s corporate writing. Today, the shorthand name for that period is drawn from the title of Sloan Wilson's 1955 novel, *The Man in the Gray Flannel Suit,* but there were a dozen other post-WWII novels about the alienation of ad agency copywriters and other corporate creatives of the 1950s. Lengthy debates by office memo at JWT explore what agency leaders and copywriters said about the norms of anonymity and loyalty to agency and sponsor and the problem of alienation. The alienation of the corporate writer stemmed from a series of legal and personnel choices about whether the agency should make writers more closely identified with their work or less, more like modern authors or more like modern professionals.

Drawing on interviews I conducted with thirty working television writers in Los Angeles in 2013 and 2014, the Conclusion explores the significance of the different laws and norms of attribution and what contemporary television writers say that unionization has accomplished for them. There are many reasons for the wide gulf in the work and norms of advertising and film and TV writers since the 1960s, but one of them is that Hollywood writers remained unionized. What they say about their experiences suggests possibilities for collective representation of white-collar workers in the twenty-first century entertainment and knowledge industries.

Act I

BEGINNINGS

1

The Cloak of Anonymity and the Literary Gunman

If a copywriter cast aside his cloak of anonymity and placed his signature on the ad, it would look as though a sort of literary gunman had been hired to do the job.

—*Printers' Ink* (1930)

In late 1932, the advertising agency N. W. Ayer & Son made an oral agreement with Vernon Grant, a thirty-year-old artist and illustrator who had just scored a commercial art coup when his drawing of an elfin Santa Claus appeared on the cover of the December 1932 issue of the popular magazine *Ladies Home Journal*. Ayer hired Grant for one year to provide paintings, drawings, and sketches of gnomes and elves for use in advertising. The advertising director of Kellogg must have loved the work, because Grant produced a number of art works over the six years he worked for the Ayer agency on behalf of Kellogg, and his elves, Snap, Crackle, and Pop, became regulars in ads for Kellogg's Rice Krispies cereal.

Grant and Ayer did not have a written contract and never explicitly discussed the rights to the drawings. According to the court that eventually heard the copyright-infringement claim that Grant brought against Kellogg, in the first year, Grant simply promised not to sell art to Kellogg's competitors, and after that time, Grant was free to sell to other clients so long as he didn't sell the same images or characters. Neither Grant nor Ayer copyrighted his drawings, although Kellogg in some cases copyrighted entire advertisements containing Grant's drawings of Snap, Crackle, and Pop. Ayer paid Grant per drawing, not on a salary; Ayer issued purchase orders to Grant to acquire particular drawings, and Grant invoiced Ayer for payment. Ayer paid Grant varying amounts for his drawings, depending on the use to which they were put. After the first year, in which Grant agreed to provide his work exclusively to Kellogg, Grant sold his art to other agencies and advertisers, as well as to magazines for use as covers.

Grant's drawings were popular, so Ayer and Kellogg hired him to produce other work. He drew dozens of posters and an illustrated Mother Goose book, both of which Kellogg sent as premiums to consumers who mailed in cereal box tops.[1] Kellogg sent him on a publicity tour to promote his work and their products in 1934. For each of the premiums, Kellogg (through Ayer) paid a royalty to Grant for each copy Ayer sent to consumers.

Grant and Ayer were casual about ownership of the rights in his work, but Grant exercised the kind of aesthetic control that artist-owners did. In 1933, and again in 1934, Ayer hired a lithographer to enlarge Grant's drawings for window decoration. The lithographer asked Grant to sign the enlargements, but he refused, insisting that the quality was poor. So Ayer hired Grant to do the enlargements. For a decade, Grant was the only artist who drew Snap, Crackle, and Pop. In 1938, Ayer hired Grant to do twelve drawings of Snap, Crackle, and Pop to be reduced for use as package advertising and to be printed at full size as a premium, and Ayer agreed to pay Grant a fee for each drawing plus a royalty for the full-size prints.

J. Walter Thompson (JWT) took over the Rice Krispies account from Ayer in 1938. The relationship with Grant soured, and in 1942, JWT terminated its dealings with Grant. When JWT went on using Grant's art work and employed other artists to do drawings of Snap, Crackle, and Pop, Grant filed suit against Kellogg over ownership of the characters and Grant's art.[2]

The court ruled that Kellogg owned the rights to the characters and to all the drawings. Under the copyright work-for-hire doctrine, the court explained, Grant "was employed or engaged by contract, whichever may be the case, to prepare and submit art work for Rice Krispies advertising. He did what he was engaged to do, and what he did belonged to the one who employed him or with whom he contracted."[3] (Technically, the employer was Kellogg, even though Grant was actually hired and supervised by Ayer. Like other agencies, Ayer was careful to have the client hire the talent, at least on paper, and the agency paid the talent's wages and billed the client for the cost plus the customary 15 percent agency commission.) But the facts as stated by the court make it seem that Grant was not an employee; he was rather (as the court put it) "engaged by contract." If he was a seller of drawings rather than an employee, the absence of a clear, written employment contract stating that Kellogg had commissioned the work could have been fatal to Kellogg's claim. It certainly would be fatal today: under the 1976 revision of the Copyright Act, one who specially commissions work from a contractor (not an employee) is the author and owner of the copyright only if a written agreement specifically so provides.[4]

Yet the court thought justice required that Kellogg own the drawings and the characters. Kellogg could not be obligated to pay Grant for later uses of his work because to do so would enable Grant to "control the advertising policy of defendant" and deny the company "the benefit of six years of advertising, in which it has invested millions of dollars." And Kellogg also must own the characters because: "They had not been publicized except to forward Rice Krispie sales, and never had any personality or characteristic except as Rice Krispie salesmen. They lived no life like Mutt & Jeff, Buster Brown and his dog, Jiggs, Superman, Betty Boop, Sparkplug, and other inhabitants of the comic strip world." To give Grant control over the characters would mean that "Grant's defection, voluntary termination of service, or expulsion, or even death" would prevent Kellogg from continuing the ad campaign, which, the judge said, would be "contrary to the authorities, against the weight of the evidence, and entirely unreasonable."[5]

But it was not clearly contrary to law at that time. Because Grant was not an employee, of either Ayer or Kellogg, but rather sold finished works to Ayer, who acted as Kellogg's agent, his drawings were arguably not works made for hire of which Kellogg was the author under the copyright law. Until the turn of the twentieth century, the law was unclear as to whether the patron who commissioned a work owned the copyright in the work, particularly if the artist had tried to register the copyright himself. By the 1930s, a few courts had held that artists did surrender the copyright to a patron who commissioned a work, but Grant insisted he had sold only the right to use his images of the elves, not the copyrights in them.[6] Nor was it clear then (though it later became clearer) what relationship the characters bore to the specific representations of them in his work, and whether sales of drawings also constituted sales of the rights in the characters. Ayer's and Grant's lack of attention to copyright issues is astonishing by contemporary standards, at least for parties as sophisticated as Kellogg and Ayer, but not unusual for advertising agencies in those days. What was unusual was that Grant sued for what he considered unauthorized use of his art.

As this chapter will show, most words, images, and music used in advertising were written anonymously, as they still are. The *Grant v. Kellogg* court's ruling reflects the general practice of agencies and their employees or freelance talent about ownership, and the absence of a written agreement between Ayer and Grant reflects the general practice, too. Ayer was not unusual in hiring an established artist on a contract basis; ad agencies had been doing so since the late nineteenth century, recruiting artists and illustrators like Maxfield Parrish (who did beautiful art for ads for cameras, tires, and other products), N.C. Wyeth (whose cowboy ads for the national Cream of Wheat campaign evoke the same nostalgic images of the American West that he used in his fine art), and, of course, Norman Rockwell.[7] While some successful artists had long-term arrangements and a degree of autonomy to choose projects or deadlines, others complained (as N.C. Wyeth did) that contracts were "a blight" on one's "artistic ardour" and rendered the artist "too much of a machine."[8] J. Walter Thompson boasted in a 1919 house ad promoting itself to prospective clients that it had twenty-three artists on staff and "an index of six hundred outside artists . . . with complete information on their type of work and their rank in their particular field."[9] Although advertising agencies relied mainly on their own staff to write copy, they regularly worked with freelance artists, including lithographers, photographers, illustrators, and printers for the artwork in print advertisements. And an agency's success depended in part upon its ability to recruit and manage freelance talent.

The unusual aspect of the Kellogg case, other than that it resulted in litigation, was that Grant became known to the public as the artist behind Snap, Crackle, and Pop. Occasionally, agencies hired artists whose style and name were already widely known. (Painters Georgia O'Keefe and Stuart Davis did art for advertisements.) But mainly ad agencies insisted the anonymity of ads was integral to the emerging conception of advertising as a learned profession in which the agency served as an expert advisor dedicated to advancing the client's interests. The business model of advertising agencies was that they would purchase space in newspapers, magazines, and other media on behalf of their clients and then design advertisements to promote the clients' products in the media space they had purchased. The agency charged the clients the cost of the space and the freelance labor (e.g., outside artwork and printing), plus a commission of 15 percent that covered the agency staff costs and a profit. As agents for advertisers, and as self-proclaimed professionals who in the 1920s emulated lawyers in seeking to enhance their social status by defining their work in elite disinterested terms, advertising executives felt they needed to promote the clients' interests single-mindedly, not their own interests in being recognized in the trade as creative. They therefore insisted that work be attributed by clients only to the agency, not to individuals, and be attributed, when presented to the public, only to the advertiser and never to the agency. Agencies relied on norms of professionalism cultivated through personnel policies rather than on written employment contracts or intellectual property law to define writer and artist claims to their work.

The Modern Advertising Agency of the 1920s

Over the course of the 1920s and 1930s, the rise of radio and the corporate mergers that brought company finance and governance to Wall Street centralized national advertising in New York City. The growth and concentration of the advertising industry led Madison Avenue in the 1920s to become a metonym to refer to the business. One of those New York agencies, founded by James Walter Thompson in 1876, hired a young man named Stanley Resor to open the agency's Cincinnati office. Resor brought with him Helen Landsdowne, a copywriter he had met while working on ads for Procter & Gamble. Lansdowne had begun her career right out of high school, working on ads at Procter & Gamble's advertising department to sell the company's soaps and personal-hygiene products to women. After working for a few years for Stanley Resor as the sole copywriter at the JWT Cincinnati office, Landsdowne transferred to the New York office, as Resor had recently done. When Resor bought the agency and took over its management in 1916, he left Landsdowne and the women she recruited to the firm in charge of writing copy for many of the products aimed at female consumers. (And Landsdowne and Resor married in 1917.) Women were thought (apparently by both themselves and the men who ran JWT) to have special insight into the female consumer, and later in her career, Landsdowne was celebrated for introducing emotion and sexuality into advertising; her work included the famous "A skin you love to touch" slogan, which she wrote for Woodbury Soap in 1911.[10]

Before 1920, advertising was not a high-status occupation. It attracted people right out of high school (like Landsdowne) or those who had worked in sales or for newspapers, but few considered it a suitable job for college-educated men. Stanley Resor, a Yale graduate, disagreed. He believed that creating an agency as a "community of scholars and experts" would bring greater "precision and rationality" to advertising and also would bring legitimacy to a business that had been regarded as a bit unseemly. So JWT recruited a staff of young copywriters from Harvard, Yale, Princeton, and other elite colleges. As JWT's longtime personnel director said, hiring college men along with a few university professors was part of Resor's vision that making advertising a learned profession would allow the agency to speak with authority to its clients and to the public. JWT frequently touted the academic credentials of its agency's staff to clients and competitors, and at any given time, Resor could count precisely the number of college graduates and PhDs on the staff.[11]

Resor and the other self-declared elites of the New York advertising business wanted to raise the status of ad work, and to do so, they pursued the strategy New York corporate lawyers adopted at the same time. First, both the ad men and the lawyers declared their occupation a profession and increased the length and rigor of the education required to enter it. (Both law and advertising in the nineteenth century had plenty of practitioners who had, at most, graduated from high school.) Also like elite lawyers, Resor and his cohort hired only people who had attended the "right" colleges and had the social background they favored. And, third, like their college classmates who became the New York and Chicago lawyers who founded a trade group (they preferred the term professional association) to raise the stature of the profession by inviting only those who met their standards to join (for lawyers it was the American Bar Association, or ABA), Resor and his peers founded the American Association of Advertising Agencies (the AAAA). Just like the ABA with its 1908 Canons of Professional Ethics, the AAAA promulgated a code of ethics that defined the elite's business practices as the ethical gold standard and branded as unethical the kind of business-getting tactics that were necessary for the less well heeled and socially connected. Condemning as "not in the interest of the public, the advertiser, or the agent," the AAAA ethics rules prohibited "speculative preparation of plans, copy or art work, in the solicitation of business," and "hiring of a man from an agency or any other source because of his control or personal influence over a prospective account." Professionalism, as the elites defined it, was necessary to render the business trustworthy to clients and to the public, and also to maintain the social status of the practitioners in the field. Professionalism, as the elites in both advertising and law defined it, required avoiding the appearance of undue competition in soliciting business, maintaining financial independence from clients to the extent possible, and ensuring the agency had the resources to enable its leaders to make their own judgments.[12]

A related strategy for pursuit of status was to hire elites and pay them enough to act like elites. And JWT did exactly that. In 1935, two-thirds of JWT's New York copywriters had domestic servants, nearly half had never been to Coney Island or recently visited any of the "remoter sections" of the United States, and none belonged to a lodge or a civic club (the social groups favored by middle-class men). JWT executives worried a bit that the strategy of hiring a "better sort" had succeeded all too well; their copywriters were out of touch with the mass of middle-class consumers who were the audience for their work.[13] But the homogeneity and "clubbiness" of the New York elite had the advantage of binding the copywriters to the agency and convincing them that their interests were best served by unswerving loyalty to clients.

Another strategy for claiming elite status and recruiting talent involved the firm celebrating the difficulty of the craft of writing and the intelligence required to do it well. They delighted in the quote of Aldous Huxley, who at one point worked in advertising, that "the advertisement is one of the most difficult of modern literary forms." They embraced the notion, as expressed in a 1926 trade publication, that copywriters "dealt more with humanity than with merchandise," "wrote advertising dramas rather than business announcements," and served their clients' interests in selling goods by "also sell[ing] *words*. In fact, we have to go further: we must sell *life*." This self-aggrandizement assured agency leaders and their clients that it was unnecessary to focus too closely on the intellectual property rights in their work because, as professionals in the close-knit community of Madison Avenue elites, they would not dream of breaching a duty of loyalty to clients by claiming too much credit for work or ownership of the copyrights in it.[14]

Anonymity and the Costs of Professionalism

The more that agencies extolled excellence in the craft of writing, the more sharply copywriters felt the divide between literary writing and selling soap. It was not just that copywriters doubted the social or artistic merit of their work; it was also that they longed to be recognized for their work when it was really good. Addressing the Sphinx Club in New York in 1909, the prominent copywriter Claude Hopkins said advertising men were known by their works but not by their names: "Perhaps you, as I, have longed to be a Jack London. It is a happy position where one may contribute to the amusement of mankind. Such men are known and applauded. They are welcomed and wanted, for they lift the clouds of care. But those who know us, know us only as searchers after others' dollars." College men who aspired to be Jack London sometimes chafed at writing beautiful and effective prose anonymously. A few articles in the trade journal *Printers' Ink* in 1930 debated the merits of attribution of ads. One pointed out that artists often signed illustrations, even in ads, and argued that attribution of copy would enhance the satisfaction of writers and keep talent in the ranks of copywriters. Attribution would convince readers of the honesty of the ad because it would convey that a real person was speaking to the reader. Another speculated that if copywriters ever unionized, their priority in bargaining would be for more freedom in writing copy rather than shorter hours or more pay. This is, of course, a mark of the success of the professionalism project—like dedicated lawyers, copywriters were ambitious and so committed to their craft that they did not seek shorter hours, but rather wanted only recognition for their talent and contributions to their clients' success.[15]

These strategies for asserting professionalism invited debate over whether advertisements should be singled out for their literary or artistic merit rather than their effect on client sales. Ad agency leaders believed that superbly crafted work was more effective in serving the client's interest, but having defined professionalism in terms of devotion to the client's interests, they struggled to reconcile the desire for recognition with their notions of service to the client. If ads were "taken as the voice of the advertiser," to insert the name of a professional copywriter would "sound a false note" and remind the reader of the artifice of the ad.[16]

Debates over public recognition of agency staff for excellence in writing and design tended to occur in connection with the perennial argument over whether advertising should have annual awards and, if so, how excellence in advertising should be judged. In 1921, the Art Directors Club of New York began public exhibitions to demonstrate advertising's contributions to artistic excellence, and, in 1924, the advertising trade announced the creation of Harvard Business School awards for excellence in advertising, which a trade publication later described (without any apparent trace of sarcasm) as comparable to the Nobel and Pulitzer Prizes. Awards "encouraged advertising to rise to a higher level of intelligence, decency, and appreciation." Awards mattered to staff because awards signified recognition within their profession, even if the public never knew the name of the person who created a popular or celebrated ad. Indeed, awards rapidly came to matter so much that when JWT did not submit entries to the Harvard Awards in 1926, company leaders felt compelled to explain to staff that the agency was disqualified from competition that year because Stanley Resor was on the prize committee.[17]

But public recognition of the literary and artistic merit of the advertisement was sometimes condemned as disloyal because it diverted attention from the client and its products. One critic of awards suggested that agencies disregarded their professional responsibilities if they could not honestly answer the question "Shall I spend my client's money to raise the tone of the advertising business? Or shall I spend the money to increase his sales?" It was not merely that pursuit of advertising awards encouraged agencies to waste client money; it was also that advertisements were group efforts, "not a personal thing," and credit ought not go to just one person.[18]

Employees at JWT invoked the common metaphor that advertising should be like a perfectly smooth and unblemished mirror in which the consumer can see a version of herself in the client's product; it should not draw attention to the advertisement's qualities as an ad, just as a mirror should not have a decorative pattern carved into the glass that might distract the viewer from the reflected image. "It is not the purpose of advertising to be remembered, admired or liked. It is the purpose to push the product into the foreground, to make the *product* remembered and liked and thereby bought—at the risk of making forgotten the printed advertisements or the commercial itself." And the attribution of work to individuals, if a copywriter were to doff his "cloak of anonymity," would make it seem that "a sort of literary gunman had been hired to do the job." A signature would introduce a middleman between the advertiser and consumer and destroy the "direct-to-reader" tone.[19]

Yet agencies and their clients apparently could not resist adding luster to a product by hiring respected artists, illustrators, and photographers, including some whose work was known to the public, and when the work crossed the boundary from advertising to popular art, the agency and client wanted to capitalize on its popularity. Hence, Ayer and Kellogg sent Vernon Grant on a publicity tour and gave signed copies of his drawings and booklets to consumers. JWT's famous "A skin you love to touch" ad for Woodbury Soap used a signed painting by the commercial and fine artist Alonzo Kimball and offered it as a print for consumers who wrote to request one. And, although JWT commissioned the image, and the advertiser (the Jergens Company, which manufactured Woodbury Soap) paid for it, Kimball signed the painting in the ad and also copyrighted it in his own name.[20]

Whether the artist signed the work and who owned the copyright varied from one ad or agency to another. One of the most celebrated artists whose work appeared in JWT ads and who never signed his advertising images was the modernist photographer Edward Steichen, whom Helen Landsdowne Resor hired to do photographs for a Jergens lotion campaign. Steichen himself embraced the artistic merit of the work he did for JWT, taking care to include many of his advertising photos in exhibitions of his work during the 1920s and 1930s. He cropped the photos differently when they were art rather than ads, but still they were the same images—hands peeling a potato, for instance. As for fine art's supposed purity, Steichen pointed out that patronage made the artist "a glorified press agent for the aristocracy" and confessed that, having produced fine art, "wrapping it up in a gold frame, and selling it to a few snob millionaires who could afford it—after I got to thinking about it, I did not feel quite clean." But in his work for JWT, he said, "I have an exhibition every month that reaches hundreds of thousands of people through editorial and advertising pages."[21]

Law and the Norms of Authorship
in the Profession of Advertising

Agencies and their clients derived legal benefits from their equation of professionalism with anonymity of writing. Seeking status as a learned profession devoted to the client's interest, committed to excellence in the craft and to speaking for the client rather than for oneself as a creator, obviated the need to invoke law in dealings with employees or to negotiate with employees over intellectual property. The company did not require written employment agreements of its staff and did not insist on formal assignments of copyright by those it hired. Nor did it copyright work in its own name, even though it could have done so until the client paid for the ad and it was about to run, at which point the client might reasonably insist on owning the copyright itself to prevent the agency or a competitor from appropriating the images, ideas, or text for another campaign.

A great deal of legal work was done by the social norm that the agency was a collective, not a group of individuals, and it spoke with a collective voice, not the voice of individual representatives, writers, or artists. Howard Kohl, a senior JWT executive interviewed for an oral history of the firm, distilled the firm's culture in recalling a single episode about the day Stanley Resor purchased the firm in 1916. Resor took Kohl and six or seven other men from the office to lunch. When they were seated, Resor turned to them and said, "'I want to tell you that . . . now, J. Walter Thompson Company is ours.'" Kohl continued, "He didn't say 'mine,' although he could have done; because, in fact, it was. But Mr. Resor always thought of the company in terms of a partnership of endeavor. It was never 'I.' It was always 'we.'"[22] Advertisements were rarely attributed to individuals when presented to clients and never were attributed to anyone when presented to the public. JWT described authorship of its work in the passive or collective voice (JWT, or "we" or "it was felt that a survey of market conditions should be made").[23]

Copywriters were confronted on a daily basis with the awareness that the social and economic significance of authorship was not captured by copyright ownership. What mattered to consumers, to corporate clients, and to themselves as creators was whose name was attached to the product as its creator and in what contexts. Walter Lord, who left Yale Law School to work for the Office of Strategic Services (the forerunner to the CIA) and then became a copywriter for JWT (he later left advertising to become a successful nonfiction author after publishing a celebrated 1955 book on the sinking of the Titanic, A Night to Remember), recalled Resor "would never let anyone have credit for even an ad. It was a 'Company' job. The whole thing was 'Company.' No one person. The Thompson Company deliberately beclouded the matter as to who was responsible for a particular ad. Mr. Resor believed so firmly in the team idea . . . that an individual was never known as the person

who wrote such-and-such an ad. . . . Keep yourself out, if you want to get
your idea across, is the cardinal rule in dealing with the Old Gentleman."
Excessive attention to individual contributions—indeed, almost any form of
obvious self-promotion—was unprofessional and counterproductive.[24]

On Madison Avenue, where everything was a commodity that could be
sold, the norms of professionalism at JWT made some people within the firm
reluctant to commodify talent or the reputation for talent. Because the name
of the firm was valued above the names of those who worked for it, there
weren't names on office doors, and senior executives considered it gauche for
people to claim credit for their work. Henry Flower, a senior JWT employee,
described the corporate form of organization in the 1930s and 1940s as "a
picket fence" rather than a "pyramid": "That's why we depreciated titles—we
didn't have labels or titles." People didn't sign their names individually to projects; they signed their work "J. Walter Thompson." Flower added, referring to
Stanley Resor's philosophy of professionalism, "The phrase he said, 'I don't
ever want to hear you say that's your account. It belongs to the Company. It
belongs to your partners.' He kept emphasizing that over and over again."[25]

The professionalism that JWT executives sought to instill in the agency's
operations caused consternation, especially during the darkest years of the
Depression when business opportunities seemed to disappear. After a dozen
of the fifty creative-department employees met with William Day in late February 1932 to complain about their prospects in the organization, the difficulties they experienced in getting good work approved, and the quality of the
work the creative department was putting out, the senior leadership decided
to institute a weekly meeting of the creative department. Day was a JWT
executive whose theories about advertising aimed at the ordinary consumer
rested on analogies between consumers and animals: emotions and instincts,
he maintained, were the strongest levers that advertisers had to influence the
buying public; it was the job of advertising leaders to give direction to the
directionless public and to steer them to adopt new products. But when it
came to copywriters and the creative staff of the agency, Day thought that the
agency needed to treat copywriters as talented individuals. As Day explained
the problem in a staff meeting: "[I]f we become large at the expense of the
individual's pride in himself, in the perfection of his own individual powers,
we will reach a stage when the individual either is not happy in this organization, or when the organization is unable to attract the kind of individuals

necessary to its perfection. The dominance of a system over any sort of creative worker in any field of art has always resulted in the death of creative ability in that field. . . . It seems to me that if we wish to become larger, we shall have to stress individual progress, individual cultivation of individual talents, very much more than we have been stressing them during the past four or five years."[26]

The new JWT "system," as Day called it, would promote "greater contact and inspiration" among the creative workers, enable junior writers to meet more often with account representatives, and alert senior leadership to ideas junior writers produced. Day promised that creative department meetings would give people "an opportunity to give evidence of [their] thinking capacity on any problem" on any of the company's accounts and would result in a system where good ideas would percolate up to an advisory committee composed of senior leadership without anyone "tak[ing] anybody's ideas without credit," or "attach[ing] any importance to whether you are only twenty-one or . . . fifty-six." Day also promised that each week, proofs of the agency's recent or forthcoming advertisements, with the name of the writers and art directors responsible, would be posted on a bulletin board so that all creative staff could vote on the best copy and best layouts.

Day also cautioned, however, that "[i]n placing before fifty people the entire basic creative work of the Agency, we are imposing upon every one of you as individuals a confidential relationship which I sincerely hope will not be violated" because leaks to competitors could be very damaging.[27] The cultivation of the sense of professional responsibility of the staff served the role that nondisclosure agreements might in a more law-heavy workplace.

Law and Norms of Employment and Intellectual Property

JWT employed hundreds of people in the 1920s and thousands by the 1940s. In hiring, the agency relied quite a bit on reputation, on what applicants or references claimed the applicant had done in a prior job, and on the intuition of those who interviewed the candidates. Robert Haws, the longtime personnel director of JWT, said the key question was, "Is he very exciting from the standpoint of what he *may* be able to do here? Either in the form of talent or your estimate of the way he will grow in a general way." JWT recruited internally, by having account heads "come to see the personnel director and suggest names of people working on other accounts whom he would like to have" and comparing the names suggested with the personnel director's own list of promising or accomplished people. JWT also recruited externally, keeping "sort of like an executive recruiting file, internally here, of people that we know," and assigning "an intelligence team" to identify talented prospects and to vet their work and their reputation.[28] All of this required attribution of work to individuals, even though advertisements were never signed. Attribution was done in various ways, ranging from the displays of ads around the office, to the weekly meetings of the creative staff, to articles in the company's weekly newspaper profiling copywriters and artists and particular campaigns.

What the agency did not seem to worry about, though, was the terms of the agreement under which a person was hired (other than salary). They hired people to produce a full range of materials that were protectable as intellectual property, including photographs, text, symbols, music, film, and radio programs, and also things that were valuable but not protectable as intellectual property, including ideas for copy or art and concepts for ad campaigns. Yet the firm did not use written contracts for any of its employees. Everyone from the general counsel to account heads to writers and designers simply assumed that the norms of professionalism would prevent employees from absconding with the client's or the agency's ideas or intellectual property. Indeed, JWT executives considered contracts for copywriters and other employees not only unnecessary but positively undesirable.[29]

Nor does the paper trail left by the employees and in-house counsel deal much with copyright or other intellectual property law. It was generally understood that all the intellectual property and ideas the employees generated belonged to the firm. JWT made its money by selling its employees' ideas and works to its clients, and the agency treated both the intellectual property rights and the credit for creating the property as the agency's to sell. Work the client did not actually publish or broadcast remained agency property until the client paid for it. JWT's general counsel rejected the idea, initially proposed by a client, that the agency would convey the property to the client when the client *approved* the work: "Unless the client actually uses and pays for material which we have shown him, we should not be precluded at a later time from using it for another client."[30]

The agency did not, however, always claim ownership of employee-generated intellectual property. In the late 1920s, 1930s, and 1940s, when the agency wrote and produced radio programs for its clients to sponsor, the show's freelance writer might own the copyright in the script even though he or she was hired (albeit on a short-term basis) with the legal status of JWT employee. Composers of music JWT commissioned for radio programs sometimes owned the rights to the music, and JWT licensed the songs under the American Society of Composers, Authors and Publishers (ASCAP) system. Later, when JWT produced its first television shows for clients as sponsors, JWT hired writers without a written contract and simply assumed that it owned the copyrights to the scripts as works made for hire. In some cases, the writer owned the script's copyright, although the script had been written for JWT or its clients.[31]

Privately, and within the world of ad agencies, JWT did attribute work both to itself collectively (in the case of ads that were nominated for awards) and to individuals within JWT. People said that Helen Landsdowne Resor "was an A-Number 1 advertising man" because of her uncanny ability to understand what would appeal to the female consumer. Many attributed to Mrs. Resor whole concepts (the use of emotion, especially romance or sexuality in advertising, and also the perfection of the technique of celebrity and society women's endorsements of beauty products), or particular slogans ("A skin you love to touch"), or even managerial strategies (hiring and promoting women into creative and responsible positions within the firm and maintaining a separate women's department).[32]

Apart from the desire to identify authorship or talent for its own sake, the company had instrumental reasons to identify authorship. Obviously, it did so with respect to setting employee salaries. JWT's personnel director claimed the goal was "the distribution, *as nearly as possible in proportion to individual contributions,* of the total available for all compensation payments." Said the company's general counsel, "We have always determined salaries by *periodic reviews of each individual case."* Of course, both the personnel director and the general counsel were talking about individual contributions to collectively created works, and thus not about authorship in the sense in which we use it for poems or novels; still, the agency had to think about what each individual added to an ad, which is a form of authorship.[33]

The company newsletter, which was published weekly or biweekly for decades, routinely profiled individual employees and often attributed slogans, ideas, or other aspects of ad campaigns to them. In addition, the background and development of particularly successful ad campaigns—like the "Uncola" 7-Up

campaign of the late 1960s and early 1970s or the "She's lovely, she's engaged, she
uses Pond's" campaign of the 1940s—were covered in the newsletter and typically credited to a group of people, many of whom were named (and, not surprisingly, the group leaders were always named). The company maintained files
of employee accomplishments so that it could match the talents of employees to
ad campaigns it might want to launch for other clients whose accounts the
employees weren't currently working on. And, when particular commercials
garnered unusual praise, the account representative considered it gracious to
pass along the compliments to the head of the group that worked on it.[34]

Nevertheless, advertising awards credited leaders, not necessarily the
person who generated an idea. For example, when an advertisement with the
slogan "Drive a FORD and FEEL the difference" that JWT did for Ford Motor
Company in the 1940s won first prize and the gold-medal grand award, in
JWT's files, it was credited to Walter Wilkinson as the artist and Wallace W.
Elton as the art director, and to the agency as a whole and the lithography
company. Yet sometimes the client had no idea who in the agency was responsible for work it particularly liked and simply asked the account head "to
express their thanks for an excellent job to all concerned." When praise came
from highly placed people in the client organization or in the advertising
industry, anonymity may have prevented some from claiming credit they
weren't due but also prevented others from benefiting from credit they were
due. Thus, when Walter Annenberg, the owner and managing editor of *TV
Guide,* praised a 1956 commercial as "the finest commercial he had ever seen
on television," the male account head and the male department head passed
the compliment internally to Peggy King, but she would have liked to have
had Annenberg's plaudits go directly to her, as the acknowledgment would
have helped her career.[35]

Attribution and Gender Segregation

The creative workers at JWT were constrained by the conventions of advertising from making the author's relation to the work the subject of the work.
No such taboo on self-reflexiveness constrained the creators of serious art
(what art historian Michele Bogart termed "art art"). Indeed, to make
apparent and immanent the worker in the work was a crucial tenet of the
artistic philosophy of Arts and Crafts, the influential early-twentieth-century

American artistic movement. As the connection between workers and the products of their work was first challenged by the mass production of consumer goods, Arts and Crafts insisted that the connection between the creator and the consumer/user of an item must be apparent and immediate. The Arts and Crafts movement was a rebellion not only against the dehumanizing labor relations of the factory, but also against the anonymity of mass production.[36] The attribution of works to individuals, even if the individuals did not own the works themselves, was an antidote to the labor alienation that resulted from factory production in a capitalist system.

Although the work process of the studio or workshop aimed to avoid the sweating and alienation of labor typical of factory mass production, the works were often sold under the name of the founder or the organization. The craftsman ideal persisted with respect to an expectation of high quality and pride in the work, but even these organizations were acutely conscious of the value of the "brands" under which Arts and Crafts work like Tiffany glass and Stickley furniture were sold. Individual creation was celebrated just as much as romantic authorship, but its products were sold under the brand name that Madison Avenue saw to be crucial. The idea that an object was art rested on attribution of the work to the creator, not—as copyright law or most studies of the relationship between copyright and authorship would have it—on the ownership of the intellectual property rights in the work.

In many instances, gendered and racial hierarchies of empowerment surely dictated who got credit then and whose names can be recovered now.[37] But sometimes, power relations that enforced gender segregation at least enabled attribution. Women at JWT worked in a segregated "women's department," which made it easier to trace their work to their department and even to particular women. It happened, too, at the Tiffany glass studio in New York. At Tiffany, like at JWT, gender segregation prevented the effacement of women's contributions and vision within the context of a workplace that did not, unlike Hollywood, publicly attribute individual works to people. Workplace practices that mark people as distinct—whether it is the distinctiveness of a Hollywood writer as a creative person or the distinctiveness of a glass designer or copywriter as a woman—can become the basis for designation as an author or a creator.

Some of the most prized creations of the glass design studios that bore the name of Louis Tiffany were created by Clara Driscoll, the head of the women's glass-cutting department, who worked at the Tiffany Studios from 1888 until 1909. For twenty years, Driscoll designed or supervised the creation of most Tiffany lamps, including some of the most prized lamps showing natural motifs like insects and flowers. Her name was not mentioned in the Tiffany Studios' publicity.[38] Tiffany generally did not publicly disclose the names of designers. Nevertheless, Driscoll had a close working relationship with Tiffany himself. He championed her work within the firm, in the face of significant hostility from male glass designers and cutters.[39] Driscoll and the thirty-five other women who worked in the women's glass-cutting department enjoyed considerable autonomy within the firm; they worked on their own projects and made their own designs, and they successfully resisted the various attempts of the Lead Glaziers and Glass Cutters Union to eliminate them or reduce their sphere and influence.[40]

So, too, for women copywriters at JWT, who attained numbers and influence that women achieved in few other industries beyond publishing, movie acting and writing, and retail. An estimated 10 percent of people employed in the advertising industry in nonsecretarial positions in the 1920s were women, and JWT was especially aggressive in hiring women—in 1918, it trumpeted to its clients and competitors that it had a "staff of women" with degrees from Columbia, Chicago, and Seven Sister schools who did campaigns for Yuban, Libby, and other products. JWT was the only agency with a woman (Helen Landsdowne Resor) in senior management in the 1920s, and by 1939, half of JWT's employees were women, with a quarter of the women in nonclerical positions. Women were particularly welcome in research, because they could interview female consumers at home about their buying habits, and in copywriting, which typically involved no executive responsibility and was therefore, as JWT copywriter Aminta Casseres explained in an article in *Printers' Ink,* "women's happy hunting ground."[41]

Although women's success in advertising (as in film writing) was based on the notion that women were more able than men to channel the feminine voice and perspective, the segregation of women copywriters to women's products, and even in their own wing of the eleventh floor of the Graybar Building housing JWT offices after 1927, had certain advantages. The important women at JWT wore hats in the office to distinguish themselves from secretaries, who did not. Women used gender segregation precisely so that they could be, and be recognized as, autonomous authors of their work within the firm. The Women's Copy Group controlled most of the agency's crucial soap, food, drugs, and toiletries accounts. Margaret King, who went to work as a copywriter at JWT after graduating from Barnard in 1921, was quite emphatic about the success of the women's copy department and credited Helen Landsdowne Resor for inspiring women to create and insisting that gender segregation would protect women's interests. In an early 1960s interview, retired senior JWT executive Ruth Waldo, who joined JWT in a clerical position in 1915 and became the first female JWT vice president in 1944, explained why she supported the idea of a women's department, even though women newer to the firm thought of it as discriminatory:

> When a woman works for a man or in a men's group, she becomes less important, her opinion is worth less, her own progress and advancement less rapid. Then she does not have the excitement and incentive to work as hard as she can, nor, in a men's group, does she get the full credit for what she does. . . . But with the knowledge and confidence of Mrs. Resor's support, a woman at Thompson could advance in her own group without having to compete with *men* for recognition of her ability. She has greater independence and freedom; a woman's ideas could be judged on their value alone. It was one less handicap.

As another woman put it, "I think you cannot have a strong woman's department unless it is separate. . . . [O]f course the men have had women writers, over the years. But no woman writer in the men's department has ever been made group head, for instance."[42]

Gender segregation was pervasive. Men had a formal training program that cycled them through all the departments in the agency, women did not— they started as secretaries or researchers, doing their own work during the day and writing copy at night, hoping to be invited to join the Women's Copy Group. Yet, women advanced in advertising during World War II as men were mobilized, and they hung onto their gains after the war ended. By 1947, JWT had two women vice presidents and seventy women in "creative jobs" throughout its US offices. Yet the executive dining room was closed to women, although Helen Landsdowne Resor and Ruth Waldo were allowed to bring in female executives once a week, at which time men were excluded.

The executive washroom was used only by men, so the women all shared a common washroom, which became "a rather social place," in which Helen Landsdowne Resor, "elbow propped up on the cosmetic shelf under the mirrors," "would be holding forth on some subject or giving instructions to almost anyone who crossed her path." As one advertising agency president said in 1957, explaining why "women do not make good account executives," "Advertising men resent women who compete with them on their own level." So in 1957, a writer explained the role of women in the industry: "The man had the title and salary, but to get the answers you often had to ask the woman who sat at the next desk or in the next room." When JWT VP and creative director Wallace Elton urged that more public appearances be made by junior people to promote the firm's talent and creativity, among the eight people he urged for greater publicity was only one woman, who was "[a]ccepted by women *and* men as an authority [and] bursts with ideas."[43] Even relatively junior writers in the women's department were credited with the firm on important campaigns, as when Ruth Waldo said that in the early Jergens lotion campaign featuring the celebrated Steichen photographs of hands, a Miss Lewis wrote the copy that gave "the story an unusually human and moving quality."[44]

JWT thus maintained a flexible array of practices with regard to individual attributions and branding itself through its employees' creativity. Its business was to focus on promotion of the client's brand. It persuaded its clients of its fitness to do so by focusing on the abilities of its creative staff, and this in turn required JWT to promote its own brand of professionalism and polish. It prided itself on a workplace culture in which some individual contributions were lauded but no person was a brand on his or her own. It was a clever and adaptable blend of individual and collective authorship. And none of it rested on a creator's copyright in a work. Authorship was determined largely outside the purview of law and obscured for reasons of bureaucratic rationality according to a variety of management theories pervading the large twentieth-century corporation.

2

The New Story System

In my opinion, the writer should have the first and last word in film-making, the only better alternative being the writer-director, but with the stress on the first word.

—Orson Welles, 1950

In a 2013 interview at his office in Los Angeles, Matthew Weiner, the creator of *Mad Men* (2007–2015), was asked how he felt about the fact that, although he is recognized as the author of the show and most of the episodes, he does not own the copyright in it. He responded at length, first remarking on the pleasures of working collaboratively with talented people and the generous compensation he receives, and then railing against the vulnerability of writers in a world in which new methods of distribution constantly erode the writers' share of the earnings. But when he got around to production company ownership of copyrights, he said: "I hate it. I hate it, and it's the way it was set up. . . . [T]he Writers Guild gave it away a long time ago. They gave the copyright away, and they took the money." The loss of ownership and creative control in exchange for generous compensation and Guild control of screen credits is the origin myth of the unionization of writers in the 1930s. Like all myths, it contains a kernel of truth: the Writers Guild did give up the fight to get writer ownership of script copyrights in exchange for a collectively bargained minimum weekly salary that represented a pay raise for many writers (though none on the bargaining committee that actually negotiated the contract). But writers did not exactly give away the copyright; they accepted the fact that the studios would never give up ownership of the writers' scripts but were willing to allow writers to decide who would be credited as authors.[1]

Most writers in the 1920s and 1930s took for granted that studios insisted on owning copyrights, but they resented that studios used the power they had as copyright owners to manipulate screen credit. Abuses of screen credit, lack of creative control, and anxieties about unemployment were the issues that drove writers to unionize in 1933. Writers did not simply take the money and accept studio ownership of copyrights. Rather, writers used the studios' position on copyright ownership as a weapon. To be the owners of scripts, the studios had to insist that writers had the legal status of employees because if writers were not employees, then studios would not own their copyrights as works made for hire. Employees, however, are the legal category of workers who enjoy the legal right to form a union and bargain collectively under the National Labor Relations Act of 1935. Although many writers resisted the control connoted by the employee designation, they chose to embrace their legal status as employees because they believed that by unionizing they would gain power—over wages, over screen credit, and even over the conditions under which they wrote—that only the most successful writers could get in individual negotiations. While unions have been decimated by de-industrialization and the rise of contingent employment throughout the economy, they have persisted in Hollywood for reasons of tradition (what economists call path dependence) and because both talent (actors, directors, writers, and so on) and craft workers (grips, gaffers, set builders, and so on) see the benefits that unionization delivers.

When writers today tell the story of how writers of the 1930s sacrificed ownership of copyrights to gain the right to bargain collectively, they miss the nuances. The evidence from the legal proceedings and the Writers Guild deliberations of the 1930s tells a more complicated story about how writers tried to both secure the right to unionize and change what had already become an established practice that writers would sell all rights in their scripts to studios when they were hired or when they completed a script. Thus, the history of the early Guild resonates with longstanding and contemporary debates among writers about ownership, authorship, creative control, and freelance work.

The Industrialization of Film Writing in the New Story System

As sound replaced silence in films in the late 1920s, writing became more important than ever to the quality and the success of a film because plot, character, and dialogue became more complex and more crucial. Writing for silent films had involved skills in which particular writers specialized in the

1920s, and with the advent of sound, producers hired multiple writers to combine those skills so that it came to be said that "novels are written; pictures are
fabricated." A decade later, Leo Rosten (a screenwriter turned Hollywood
ethnographer) attributed serial rewriting of scripts to the fact that the "sce-
narists" of the silent era (he branded them "plot carpenters and stereotype
experts") couldn't write dialogue. Producers, Rosten said, hired playwrights
and novelists to write "beautiful lines and witty repartee" and create "three-
dimensional characters and subtle situations," but they were dismayed to dis-
cover that playwrights' and novelists' stories "did not *move*" and "groaned
under a massive load of talk." So producers began to use multiple writers,
believing that some writers could construct plots, others could create realistic
characters, others could write dialogue, and still others could add jokes.[2]

The studios flocked to Los Angeles and found steady employment, usually on
a weekly salary. The movie studios scattered across Los Angeles were large,
hierarchical, movie factories that handled every aspect of production. Each
company hired a staff of writers to adapt material for filming or write scripts
based on new ideas. Studios filmed on their own lot or on location, and they
handled post-production editing and sound-mixing. And five studios (known
as the majors) distributed the movies through studio-owned theater chains
across the country; the three others (the minors) distributed their movies
through independent distribution companies.[3]

The studios (individually and collectively) released dozens more films
each year in the 1930s and '40s than they do today, and so they attempted to
systematize every aspect of production. They imitated the assembly lines and
management techniques that were in vogue in the industrial economy and as
theorized by Frederick Winslow Taylor; in short, they tried to industrialize
story production and moviemaking. The new "story system," as Twentieth
Century Fox described it in 1930, involved the studio buying the rights to large
numbers of books, articles, plays, songs, and vaudeville sketches—anything
in which the writers or executives saw a suitable story or even just a familiar
or catchy title—and hiring a staff of writers at a flat rate of about $200 per
week to adapt material or spin a new story out of a title or an idea the writer
dreamed up.[4] MGM had a similar system: in one year in the early 1930s,
MGM's readers filed reports on over 1,000 novels or original screenplays, 500
short stories, 1,500 plays, and 1,300 works in foreign languages, all done sup-
posedly according to Irving Thalberg's "Ten Commandments for Studio

Readers." (The first commandment was to "find great ideas," most of which would be "buried under tons of mediocre suggestions." The eighth was to "prove your ability to recognize creative material by writing and submitting to us stories of your own.")[5]

Working in offices on the back lots, writers churned out stories, screenplays, and treatments, and polished plots, characters, settings, and dialogue. Producers imposed strict deadlines and working rules when they could. While some writers had the market power to force the studios to acquiesce to their desire to work at home, many worked on the studio lot from 9:00 A.M. to 6:00 P.M. or longer and on weekends. Screenwriters complained they "punched a clock, sat in cubbyholes, writing to order like tailors cutting a suit."[6]

Writers had formed the Screen Writers Guild (SWG) in 1921 as a club and as a professional association with the aspiration of raising the stature of writers in the film business and improving the intellectual and artistic pretensions of their industry in a period when intellectuals and cultural elites regarded films with disdain. The Screen Writers Guild was established as a branch of the New York–based Authors League of America, a group founded in 1912 by playwrights, magazine writers, dramatists, and novelists in New York to represent the interests of writers in the wake of the Copyright Act of 1909.[7] The Writers Guild of the early 1920s formed a "Federation of Art" with actors, cinematographers, and directors to advance the interests of "the great mass of decent people who really create motion pictures." The Writers Guild also attended to economic issues: Guild leaders wrote a "Standard Guild Contract" for its members to use in their negotiations with the studios, the Guild Executive Board scrutinized the terms on which studios contracted with writers, and it protested contracts that departed from the standard contract in ways that seemed inimical to the interests of writers. Contracts elicited protests if writers were paid too little, required to do rewrites without pay, or if the agreement did not guarantee writers "adequate mention in advertising matter and publicity notes."[8]

Early screenwriters were particularly concerned about the work-for-hire provision of the 1909 Act. When studios purchased the film rights to literary properties or hired writers to adapt existing material or write a new script, the contract of purchase or hire invariably stated that the studio would own the material as a work made for hire. As playwrights, short story authors, or novelists in New York, writers would have retained ownership of their copyrights and only licensed their work to the producer. But studios were more insistent about securing the copyright to scripts than theater producers were. Eager to work, awed by the amount of money studios offered, and uncertain that there would be any further market for a movie script (unlike a play, which could be produced in theaters everywhere), writers did not strenuously oppose selling the copyrights in their work. Intellectual property rights nevertheless became crucial to the early efforts to unionize writers in Hollywood.[9]

The writers who formed the SWG had complaints about working conditions and intellectual property rights, but they did not initially think they needed a union. Indeed, in 1922 and 1923, the SWG emphasized the elitism of its members, boasting that it admitted "no amateurs or students to membership, [did] no advertising for new members, carrie[d] on no business criticizing or selling scripts for amateurs or professionals and, in short, [was] purely a legitimate professional association." When the union that represented stage actors refused to allow its nascent Hollywood branch to affiliate with the SWG because the SWG was not a union affiliated with the national federation of trade unions (the American Federation of Labor, or AFL), the SWG made no effort to affiliate but instead proclaimed that actors could form another membership organization outside the purview of the AFL and that new organization could affiliate with the SWG.[10] Writers were deliberate in describing their organization as a guild, not a union. Some feared that if they formed a trade union, people would see screenwriting as a trade like painting or electrical work. They wanted writing to be a profession and their Guild to be a "legitimate professional association, representative of the screenwriters and authors of the country, precisely as the Authors League, the parent organization is representative of the professional authors of America." Writers did not at first seek for the SWG to bargain collectively (as unions did), but only to secure fair terms of employment, credit for writing, and some creative control over uses of their work.

Some writers scoffed at the notion that the professional and artistic stature of screenwriters would be jeopardized if the SWG were a union rather than a professional association or a club. Having seen the rough conditions endured by the working class, John Bright was one who believed writers must unionize. In the 1920s, Bright was working at a soda fountain in Chicago frequented by Al Capone, and his observations of the mob led him to write a number of stories on gangsters that were later made into movies. His breakthrough in Hollywood was the screenplay for *The Public Enemy* (1931), which was early among the gangster genre to examine the sociological roots of crime. Bright, like other founders of the SWG in 1933, had no faith that elite pretensions would help most writers. As he complained in an essay in *The Screen Guilds' Magazine* in 1934, the "principal reason for any ineffectiveness we may have as an employee organization" is that "the writer stands aloof on one hoof—spinning webs of idiotic logic about his special singularity." Writers "buck unconsciously against every attempt to unionize," fearing their status would be jeopardized if they were seen as "artists in uniform."[11] (Bright paid dearly for his sympathies with the working class. He was a communist in the 1930s, was one of many writers subpoenaed by the House Un-American Activities Committee (HUAC), and he fled to Mexico to escape incarceration for contempt of Congress rather than testify against friends and colleagues. The blacklist destroyed his career; he had no screen credits after 1951.)

The debate between the unionists and the believers in professionalization was cut short by the huge pay cuts of 1933 that disabused most writers of the idea that their "special singularity" would ensure job security.

The Son-in-Law Also Rises: Screen Credit and the Formation of the Writers Guild

One of the studio practices that most irked writers was misallocation of screen credit. Writers complained frequently about their inability to negotiate individually for contracts requiring studios to credit writers accurately or to mention them in advertising and other film publicity. Writing credit was entirely up to the studio, and studio moguls sometimes granted it to themselves, to writers who had not worked on the script but whose names had marquee value, or to moguls' family, friends, "in-laws, golf partners, or bookies." These abuses were so legendary that ninety years later, Writers Guild President Howard A. Rodman, Jr. derisively referred to the era of studio favoritism in credits by parodying the Hemingway novel *The Sun Also Rises:* when studio moguls doled out screen credits to help their relatives, "the son-in-law also rises."[12]

Even when studios tried to allocate credit on merit rather than favoritism, it could be difficult to decide which of the many contributing writers had done enough to deserve having their names on the screen. People who had written the screenplay were sometimes reduced to a credit for "dialogue by," which suggested they had just added a few zingy lines. Not surprisingly, writers schemed and fought over credit; as Donald Ogden Stewart—*The Philadelphia Story* (1940); *Holiday* (1938)—recalled:

> The first thing you had to learn as a writer if you wanted to get screen credit was to hold off until you knew they were going to start shooting. Then your agent would suggest you might be able to help. . . . It was the third or fourth writer that always got the screen credit. If you could possibly screw-up another writer's script, it wasn't beyond you to do that so your script would come through at the end. It became a game to be the last one before they started shooting.[13]

Abuses of screen credit became one of the major issues driving the campaign to form a writers' union, and studios eventually realized that having the union take responsibility for making credit determinations had advantages for the producers as well as the writers.

In the early 1930s, the Guild wrote and disseminated a code of fair practices requiring that writers be credited accurately. The Guild also drafted a standard form contract for writers to offer studios as an individual contract of employment, and it also contained a writer credit provision. But neither the code nor the model contract was binding on the studios. Writers occasionally sued over denials of screen credit, but lawyers were expensive and could accomplish nothing for writers who had not specifically negotiated for a credit provision in their contract of employment or contract for the sale of original material. Even when writers navigated those obstacles, damages were difficult to prove. Walton Hall Smith (an obscure writer with only two credits in his career whose other claim to fame was developing a Florida park known as Weeki Wachee) sold Paramount a story called "Cruise to Nowhere" based on his script adapting a J. M. Barrie play about class division when a group of aristocrats are shipwrecked on an island. His contract required screen credit, but although Smith proved that the Paramount film *We're Not Dressing* (1934) was based on his script and omitted credit to him, he was awarded only $7,500 of the $50,000 in damages he claimed was attributable to the lost publicity. Whether he collected the judgment, and the amount of attorneys' fees he paid to litigate the case, is not known. Although he received a "story by" credit, it was not enough to salvage his writing career. Experiences like his were not unusual and underscored to writers the need for the Guild to take control of writing credits.[14]

Through the SWG, writers considered a number of different ways to ensure that writers received credit. In 1922, some Guild members proposed "it would be a good thing—and a great advertisement for the writer, incidentally—if the Guild would take a page advertisement in some trade journal every month advertising pictures written by the members of the Guild."[15] But a Guild advertisement in *Variety* would not be nearly as effective in promoting the interests of writers as a contract requiring the studios to list the actual writers in the screen credits and movie posters at every theater where the movie screened, and to put the writer on the set when the film was shot and on the red carpet when it premiered.

Writing on Sand with the Wind Blowing

Another major complaint of writers in the studio system was lack of respect for their craft and lack of creative control in the production process. The pace and budget of production and the collaborative nature of filmmaking meant that writers did not expect to control their own creative process or its results as if they were novelists or playwrights. Nevertheless, the endless rewriting seemed unnecessary. Writers complained bitterly in 1930 when Fox hired more than a dozen people to rewrite each other in adapting Mark Twain's *Connecticut Yankee in King Arthur's Court*. The amount of rewriting and the absence of creative control frustrated even successful and highly paid writers. Frances Marion—founding president of the SWG in the 1920s when she was the highest paid writer in Hollywood—complained that writing a screenplay was "like writing on sand with the wind blowing." Writers at Paramount described an "assembly line" run by producers "who doled out dramatis personae, one each to a team of five writers—the writer was then instructed to supply 'his' character with lines of dialogue but to avoid consultation with other members of the team: the idea, so far as anybody understood it, was that the producer would 'assemble' the five contributions, jigsaw style, into a final script." One such writer later quipped that he "considered himself fortunate to be given 'a sailor with a parrot': at least *his* character had someone to talk to." Writers sought greater responsibility for their work "from its inception to its ultimate presentation on the screen" and sought to be given "a hand and a voice in the actual production of the picture."[16]

When producers and several leading actors and other talent formed the Academy of Motion Picture Arts and Sciences in 1927, writers initially thought it would be a good forum in which to raise issues about the status of writers. Although the Academy is known today primarily for the Oscars, it was founded with a broader set of purposes, including representing writers, directors, and actors in collective negotiations with producers. From the start, the studios controlled the Academy and used it to thwart independent union organizing. Membership in the Academy was by invitation and was conferred only on the basis of distinguished accomplishment in film production, which meant it would be unlikely to reflect or represent the interests of the struggling writer. Nevertheless, in the 1920s, some writers hoped the Academy would be the organization through which writers could gain greater respect from studios. The Academy obtained a few concessions for writers in 1932, including one week's notice before termination of a writer's employment and an agreement that producers would give all the writers who worked on a film twenty-four hours to decide on screen credit. But the agreement empowered producers to decide writing credit in the event that writers could not reach unanimous agreement on one or two names. Writers had good reason to fear that the Academy was not the forum for redress of their concerns, but the prestige of its members made it difficult for writers to reject the Academy's leadership.[17]

That changed abruptly in 1933, at the depths of the Depression, when MGM and other studios called an emergency meeting of all writers, actors, and directors and announced a 50 percent pay cut. The ostensible reason for the pay cut was the crisis facing the banks, and the studio executives claimed that they simply lacked enough money to make payroll. The Academy acquiesced in the pay-cut plan, and word leaked out that the cuts were not uniformly applied and that many producers were exempt. And, of course, the craft workers who had a union contract were not subject to the pay cut, which made writers realize that having a union contract offered protection that their individual contracts did not. Writers had proof of their vulnerability, even in a studio like MGM, whose legendary head of production, Irving Thalberg, had been known as a great believer in writers and who had generally not laid off writers between pictures. Even if they were the most important people in Hollywood, as Thalberg said, they were expendable.[18]

Some writers, meanwhile, had been talking about transforming the old Screen Writers Guild, which was affiliated with the Authors League but was really a cross between a social club and a professional association, into an organization that could effectively represent the economic and legal interests of writers. Writers had been discussing this idea before the wage cut, but after the cut, the effort had new urgency and many more writers became interested in the Guild. Some of the original organizers of the SWG were veterans of the New York writers' struggles that had created the Dramatists Guild in the 1920s, and they envisioned a similar strategy and possibility for success in the west. The National Industrial Recovery Act of 1933 granted rights to unionize and bargain collectively, and both writers and actors took the chance to form independent unions: a group of actors formed the Screen Actors Guild and, at the same time, writers revived the defunct Screen Writers Guild. On April 6, 1933, John Howard Lawson was elected SWG president by acclamation. Because the National Industrial Recovery Act, like its 1935 successor, the National Labor Relations Act (NLRA), granted only employees the right to organize and bargain collectively, writers overcame their qualms about embracing the employee status, realizing that whatever status they might lose by calling themselves union members and employees would be compensated for if they could secure acceptable salaries and other terms.[19]

In early 1935, the producers renewed their effort to revive the writers' branch of the Academy, hoping to use it to weaken the support for the newly militant SWG. The Academy drew up a new basic agreement and writer-producer code of practice. One problem with these codes of practice and fair competition is that they explicitly aimed to reduce salaries and also to prohibit one studio from luring talent to another by offering high salaries. Among the most galling provisions to writers was the proposal that producers would determine credits based on an assessment of substantial contributions. A writer who disagreed could appeal to the Writers Adjustment Committee of the Academy, but even if that body found that the producer had improperly allocated credit, the producer was not obligated to change it. Writers branded the provision as "puerile and meaningless," an "empty gesture." Nevertheless, many writers supported the writers' branch of the Academy, and the SWG struggled to gain recognition from writers or producers.[20]

On April 4, 1935, a group of screenwriters met at 8 P.M. at the Hollywood Athletic Club on Sunset Boulevard to elect new leadership of the Screen Writers Guild. The newly elected Executive Board met two weeks later at the Guild office on at the corner of Hollywood Boulevard and Cherokee Avenue (and it continued to meet every other Monday night for decades). One of the first items of business at the meeting was launching a campaign to persuade writers to resign from the Academy and join the Guild instead. Each board member committed to lobbying his or her acquaintances, especially successful writers, to resign from the Academy and join the Guild. The SWG Board meetings of 1935 usually included a report of the Guild's treasurer and efforts to increase membership and get members delinquent in their dues to pay up. The Executive Board also decided on applications for associate and full membership (as writers began working in the industry) and resignations from membership (as writers took jobs as producers or agents or left Hollywood writing entirely).[21]

Labor organizing among writers involved more than cocktail parties and conversation about left politics (although there was plenty of that). The Guild proved its worth to members by advocating for their interests, and one of their most important interests was screen credit. Writers often said at Guild meetings that they wanted to be recognized as authors, just as New York playwrights were. As Dudley Nichols put it in a 1936 article in the *Screen Guilds' Magazine,* film writers "were paid wonderfully well. They were supplied with typewriters, charming stenographers, luxurious homes, and parked cars." But there were "certain joys that even poverty had not denied them, but which Hollywood certainly did." One was credit, and another was creative control. If control over one's work and the ability to refuse even "really silly" writing assignments were among those joys that writers in Hollywood could not expect, at least they could get screen credit.[22]

Although the studios were not bound by the law or, in most cases, by contract to correctly credit writers, nevertheless, in its first few months of existence, the Guild made a bit of progress in trying to bring fairness to the system. It formed a conciliation commission that in June 1935 reported successful arbitration of eight complaints over screen credit and six cases in which the commission collected unpaid fees or salary for writers, and in August 1935, it reported conciliating ten disputes over screen credit, two cases of unpaid fees, and two disputes between writers and their agents. But that was just a start.[23]

Guild Executive Board and membership meetings involved extended debate over writers' goals in unionizing. One was to be paid royalties. Payment on a royalty basis rather than a fixed salary would protect writers against unilateral salary cuts. As Lawson later recalled, this "could best be done by embodying in a standard writer's contract a minimum percentage of the gross revenues of the picture, the writer to have a specified drawing account against such royalties."[24] Moreover, Lawson insisted, payment on a royalty basis also recognized that "The *writer* is the creator of motion pictures."[25] Many writers wanted to be paid a percentage of the returns on the film in addition to their weekly rate, but only some were able to negotiate such arrangements. Each individual negotiation involved difficult questions, such as whether the studios should calculate the writer's share as a percentage of gross returns or net, and how royalties should be calculated and paid. Lawson insisted collective action was necessary to secure a right to royalties.[26]

Writers also wanted advance notice of termination. Even in good times, writers wanted notice so they could find a new job quickly, but notice was a particularly serious problem during the Depression when studios summarily fired many. In addition, writers on long-term option contracts wanted the right to accept other employment when idle and unpaid at their studio. Writers also demanded "an equitable practical deal on credits" and "an end to the system whereby the writer gives up every idea even if it's unused that comes into his head while under contract," and "not to give up every conceivable undiscovered right in the sale of original material."[27]

The year 1936 proved to be a pivotal one. Writers left the Academy in favor of the Guild, and by early March, the Guild claimed 840 members.[28] Guild members protested the Academy's failure to address their grievances by boycotting the 1936 Academy Awards. The SWG scored a publicity coup when loyal Guild member Dudley Nichols, one of the highest-paid writers in Hollywood, won the Oscar for best screenplay for *The Informer* and publicly turned down the award in a letter that rebuked the Academy for failing to respect the writers' choice of bargaining representative.[29] The SWG benefitted from the fact that the agreement between the Dramatists Guild and stage producers expired at the end of February 1936. Dramatists demanded 100 percent of the sale of screen rights instead of sharing them with the producer/manager, who in many cases was sympathetic to the film studios. Writers insisted that movies had been financing Broadway but that screen rights had been sold too seldom and for too little money, and writers demanded more control over the sales and a bigger share of the profits. The formation of a united front of Hollywood and Broadway writers under the aegis of the Authors League suggested that writers had real bargaining power.[30]

But forming and maintaining a united front was difficult. Political disagreements among writers shaded into disagreements over union strategy and governance, and a group of writers who thought the SWG leaders were too socialist formed a separate union, the Screen Playwrights ("SP"). The producers supported SP in the hope that it would drain members from the more militant SWG, and they gave the SP power to determine screen credits. Some writers believed the SP favored its members over SWG members in credit arbitrations. In the summer of 1936, the SWG all but collapsed as writers defected to the SP because it was the one studios favored and it used its power among producers to award screen credit to reward SP members for their support.[31]

Becoming the Writers' Bargaining Representative

In the spring of 1937, however, writers came back to the SWG as they realized that the SP would be no more effective than the Academy in addressing their concerns about credit, notice of termination, or creative control. By July, the SWG claimed a large majority of writers. Dorothy Parker, the noted wit, intellectual, *The New Yorker* writer, and founding member of the Algonquin Round Table, had a foray as a Hollywood screenwriter and was an early and determined supporter of the SWG and other progressive causes. Parker gleefully reported at a July 1937 Guild meeting that the Guild had 409 members, of whom 269 were working in the studios, while the SP had only 67 members working in the studios. (Parker became a socialist in the 1920s after the Sacco and Vanzetti trial, and like many other SWG founding members, paid a price for her devotion to left politics by being blacklisted in 1950. When she died in 1967, her will bequeathed her estate to Dr. Martin Luther King, Jr.)

Confident it represented a majority of writers, in July 1937, the Guild filed a petition with the Los Angeles regional office of the National Labor Relations Board (NLRB) and demanded recognition from the studios in August as the exclusive representative of Hollywood writers, as provided under the

National Labor Relations Act. The NLRB and NLRA had just survived a constitutional attack in the Supreme Court three months earlier. Filing the petition commenced a year-long legal process, beginning with a seventeen-day hearing before the NLRB regional office in Los Angeles in October, followed by an appeal to the Washington, DC office in December, and then another hearing in May 1938 in Los Angeles. On June 4, 1938, the NLRB ruled in favor of the writers.[32]

The studios resisted the Guild's request for NLRB certification by arguing that screenwriters were not the kind of employees who should have the right to unionize. Because this is a legal issue that came up repeatedly in the 1930s, 1940s, and 1950s for writers in radio, film, television, and advertising, and arose under copyright, labor, and antitrust law, I devote much of Chapter 7 to an examination of the law and social context of fights over whether writers were employees. Here it is enough to note that the NLRB rejected the studios' arguments that screenwriters were "artists" and could not belong to a labor union, and it decided that screenwriters were employees within the meaning of the NLRA because the studios often exercised the contractual power to direct when, where, and what writers wrote. The NLRB found unimportant that some writers were employed on a "free-lance basis under contracts providing for a week-to-week continuation of the employment or for the completion of a certain piece of work at a specified aggregate compensation," because "there is no essential difference between a free-lance writer and a writer working under contract for a term in the manner in which they performed their work and that the only difference between the two is one of length and tenure of employment."[33]

Once the NLRB determined that writers were employees eligible to form a union, it scheduled an election for writers to vote on whether they wanted the SWG, the SP, or neither as their bargaining representative. The SWG won the election, but that did not by itself give the SWG real power. Litigation ensued about the continuing validity of the SP contract with the studios, and a particular bone of contention was the SP's authority to determine screen credits. The SP still had the studios' blessing in determining screen credit, and the SP still used it to benefit its members.[34]

Meanwhile, the SWG set up its own committee to arbitrate disputes over screen credit under a provision in the Code of Working Rules it drafted and urged as a sample contract for all its members. It began arbitrating credit disputes in 1937, even before the SWG won the NLRB's sanction of its right to represent writers. The SP retained the power to arbitrate credit disputes until 1939, so for a few years, both the SWG and the SP arbitrated credit disputes and the studios resolved their disagreements.

Dual unionism presented a variety of practical issues for SWG members, especially (but not only) for credit determinations. Mary McCall, a successful writer who had fourteen screen credits by 1938 and served two terms as president of the SWG, first in 1942–1944 and again in 1951–1952, reported that it was sometimes difficult to get a studio to let the writer cross out a clause in an employment contract requiring arbitration under the SP system—she said MGM had refused to let her strike out the SP clause, so instead, she had signed the contract and sent a letter of protest.[35] The SWG insisted that it violated SWG ethics rules to accept any arbitration except under the SWG system, that members already under contract should refuse arbitration by the SP, and that if forced by the studio into SP arbitration, they should do so only under protest.[36] This problem did not finally disappear until the SP faded away and studios after late 1939 no longer included in individual employment agreements a provision requiring SP arbitration of credit disputes. SWG members also wanted a legal right to join the union of their choice because studios occasionally fired writers for joining the more radical SWG. Dalton Trumbo, for example, was fired less than seven months into his contract with Warner Bros. because he refused to resign from the SWG. He went to work at MGM, where he stayed until 1947 when the blacklist drove him first from MGM to a tiny start-up independent studio, then to federal prison, and finally into writing through fronts and under a pseudonym.[37]

The First Collective Agreement for Writers

The SWG fought for over three years after winning the NLRB election to get the producers to accept an agreement. The prolonged negotiation process began in 1938 when, after deliberations of the Executive Board and meetings of the entire membership to set priorities, the Executive Board appointed a negotiating committee. Then, as now, many writers thought it an advantage to have a bargaining committee of illustrious writers because the studio executives would simply have a harder time saying writers should be paid less or made unimportant contributions to films if they had to say it to writers whom they respected and who were not easily replaceable by a young novelist or magazine writer fresh out of college or off the train from New York. And so, when the studio leaders finally sat down to negotiate, they faced a who's who of writers, all of whom had many screen credits and either had been or would be nominated for Academy Awards.[38]

The Writers Guild has always faced a considerable challenge in developing cohesion and negotiating for the common interest of a group of writers with widely disparate skills, careers, reputations, and incomes. Some have been very wealthy, but a significant percentage of the Guild's membership is unemployed at any given time. Budd Schulberg's classic 1941 novel, *What Makes Sammy Run?*, makes drama of the impossibility of reconciling the disparate interests of writers, and the Guild's survival in the face of the extreme disparities is astonishing. One of the crucial practices underlying the Guild's early accomplishments and long survival was established at the beginning when the original negotiating committee fought for some issues that affected its members personally (screen credit) and others that did not. The minimum weekly wage they negotiated was far below what any member of the negotiating committee earned, but it would be a raise for the significant number of writers who earned less than $125 a week (about $2,100 in 2015 dollars). This situation has remained unchanged, as many members of the negotiating committee in the run-up to the 2007–2008 strike were negotiating for residuals in new media that they could easily have negotiated individually but wanted to secure for everyone. All unions face the problem of finding a common interest among members with different interests, but the disparities among writers are especially great.[39]

One of the priorities that writers urged was that they should be paid royalties for the use of their material or have some form of profit sharing. In the face of studio opposition, the negotiating committee decided to abandon the effort, focusing instead on a minimum wage, advance notice of layoffs or termination of employment, union security, arbitration of contract disputes, writers' control over screen credit, and a right to repurchase unused original material at the price the writer had been paid. Although the negotiating committee and Executive Board apparently believed that the Guild was putting aside royalties or profit sharing only "for the present," it proved to be decades before writers secured that kind of deal.[40]

The SWG won some of its demands. In early 1942, pressure to mobilize for the war effort finally prompted the producers to resolve the few outstanding issues with the Guild and sign the Minimum Basic Agreement. It was time, said one producer, to "sign this goddamn contract and make pictures for the boys."[41] The agreement was very short. In its five pages, it did little other than give writers a minimum wage, notice of termination, and Guild control over screen-credit determinations. The producers had agreed to SWG determination of screen credit for writers shortly after collapse of the SP in 1940, but the provision languished on the bargaining table as the studios resisted other Guild demands. All disputes arising under the MBA would be subject to a Guild-studio conciliation process and, if conciliation failed, would be resolved by arbitration rather than litigation or use of strikes or lockouts. Thus, the MBA created two arbitration processes: one for credits (which the Guild handled unilaterally) and one for all other contract breaches (such as failure to pay writers), which operated like many other grievance-arbitration processes negotiated by labor unions and companies. The MBA prohibited writing on speculation and established a minimum wage of $1,500 ($25,000 in 2015) for flat deals to write major motion pictures, $1,000 ($16,800) flat deals for westerns, or a minimum weekly salary of $125 ($2,100). It also provided for one week's advance notice of layoff, prohibited intermittent layoffs during the term of a writer's individual contract of hire, and required writers be notified when others were assigned to the same material.

But the SWG did not get two of the most important things that writers wanted. Layoffs and reassignment of writers were not restricted, which meant writers could be hired, laid off, or fired on a producer's whim unless the writer negotiated an individual contract for a term of months, and writers did not get ownership of their copyrights or the right to prevent rewriting by someone else. These conditions meant that writers had little or no job security and no control over the uses of their work. They remained "pencils for hire," as they sometimes called themselves, not authors.[42]

In an effort to regulate writing other than through collective agreement, the Executive Board adopted rules of ethics for its members. These rules predated the MBA and continued after its adoption, as the Guild (like every union) imposed membership rules above and beyond the contract rules enforced by the employer and by the union and employer jointly through the arbitration process. The Guild's 1938 Code of Fair Practices, which it proposed should be the basis for all individual hiring contracts, contained provisions about minimum wage, notice of layoffs, screen credit, and arbitration, and the SWG hoped to include all these in a collective bargaining agreement.[43]

So writers had experience with guidance from the Guild about terms on which they should negotiate individual employment contracts before the first MBA was signed. Five of the eight ethics rules concerned credit and public claims of authorship. Advertising the writer's accomplishments was prohibited, as was receiving screen credit on a picture "to which you have not contributed a substantial part of the ideas, construction, or dialogue as finally filmed." Both of these were considered unseemly self-promotion and tended to foment discord among writers. For similar reasons, the Board adopted rules prohibiting a writer from accepting credit that misrepresented the nature of the writer's contribution or stipulating for sole credit unless no other writer "has made substantial contribution to the picture." In addition, the rules prohibited either being or hiring a ghost writer. Other rules prohibited working on any material when the writer knew another Guild member was working on the same material without notifying the other member and being "a party to plagiarism." The last ethics rule required Guild members to "keep all contracts in spirit as well as letter."[44] Collectively, these rules articulated a vision of the screenwriter as autonomous, as a person known for her work, but only for her own work, and as a responsible professional who would not dream of excessive self-promotion or breaching a contract.

The Board debated but did not adopt a rule prohibiting working for free (known as writing on spec). This issue proved to be a longstanding problem for the Guild. On the one hand, writing for free had a long tradition and unknown writers could hardly insist on being paid in advance of producing work. On the other hand, the Writers Guild, like every other union, had to protect its hard-won minimum standards against being undercut by desperate writers willing to work for less than the union's minimum wage, and they knew that producers would eagerly exploit writers by asking them to write for free. Writers today, even established ones, still observe that they are often asked to do free rewrites and that it is virtually impossible to refuse.

Early Administration of Credits

The Guild began arbitrating credit disputes in July 1937, just as soon as it was revived in the wake of the SP dispute, a year before it secured recognition from the studios, and three and a half years before it secured its first MBA. The process used then was similar in essence if not in details to what it has been ever since: a few writers acting as arbitrators would read all the literary material and scripts and compare them to the final shooting script to decide which writers had made the most significant contributions to the film that was ultimately made. They did so using a process and rules developed by the Guild's membership and the Executive Board.

By the end of 1939, while the Guild was still negotiating with the studios for a collective agreement, it had conducted arbitrations without contractual authority in about twenty credit disputes. For the most part, the Guild succeeded in getting the studios to adopt the arbitration award, but it did so by cajoling the studios and not because the studios had any legal obligation to honor the Guild's credit determination.[45] In the absence of any contractual requirement, the Guild found that not only did the studios not always accept its credit determinations, its members did not either. In July 1939, Adele Buffington, Richard Collins, and Bradford Ropes arbitrated a credit controversy on the Warner Bros. film *On Your Toes* (1939), which was a film adaptation of a Rodgers and Hart musical about a vaudeville singer turned composer who joins a Russian ballet and falls in love with the lead ballerina. The arbitrators originally thought screenplay credit should be shared among Jerry Wald, Richard Macaulay, Sig Herzig, and Lawrence Riley, but they reached a compromise to give Herzig and Riley a shared "adaptation by" credit instead. Wald and Macaulay were furious that Herzig and Riley received credit, and Warner Bros. refused to give an "adaptation by" credit. Faced with criticism from the writers and a refusal of the studio to abide by the arbitration award, all the Executive Board could do was to threaten disciplinary action against the writers. The Executive Board then decided that the arbitration committee's credit should be modified slightly to give a "story by" credit to Herzig and Riley, and that if Warner Bros. refused that, then the credit would simply be shared among all four writers. In the end, Warner Bros. capitulated, the movie was credited according to the first committee compromise, and the dispute fizzled.[46] It was a lesson about the importance of getting Guild arbitration of credit into the MBA and subject to binding arbitration with the studios.

The credit rules were not in the MBA, but in a separate document, Schedule A, which was drafted by an ad hoc committee appointed by the Board to study credits. After the Board approved the first version of Schedule A in June 1942, it directed its lawyer Morris Cohn to commence negotiations over it with counsel for the producers. And as the years went by, revisions to Schedule A were negotiated both as part of the MBA and in the interim by the Guild and the producers.[47]

The credit-determination process of the first Schedule A formalized what the SWG had been doing since 1939: when a film was in post-production, the studio would make a tentative determination of writing credits and send notice of it to the Guild and to all writers who had done substantial work on the final shooting script. The substantial-work determination could be controversial. The Guild eventually forced the studios to send the notice to every writer ever employed on the film. The notice enabled writers to assert their claim to credit, studios to avoid belated claims from angry writers, and the Guild to check the correctness of the tentative credits. The tentative credits became final unless a writer objected within about a day. If a writer protested, all participating writers had forty-eight hours in which to get the final script from the studio and read it. If a writer requested arbitration, the Guild would ask three writers (ideally from the same studio, for the sake of convenience) to read all the materials to determine who deserved credit. (Today, because writers are no longer on the staff of studios, the three arbiters are chosen for their experience in the film genre.)

Then and now, the three arbitrators read all the literary material, including the final shooting script, and determine which writers made the most significant contributions to the film as it was finally shot. In evaluating the significance of contributions, the arbitration committee considers plot, characters, scenes, and dialogue. The Guild has always insisted, and my study of decades' worth of credit arbitrations confirms, that arbiters generally do not assess the significance of a contribution by counting lines in the script, but rather through an informed and qualitative judgment about the importance of each successive writer's changes to the original script. The arbiters' decision is final.[48]

Establishing the Guild's Authority to Determine Credits

An important and distinctive feature of the Writers Guild's fight for control over screen credits was its long effort to establish *exclusive* control. Obviously, the Guild did not want the studios to decide credit, for reasons noted above.

But equally, the Guild did not want courts to intervene. Plagiarism charges came up every couple of months in the early Guild Board proceedings, and often the aggrieved writer threatened to sue the Guild, the credited writer, and the studio. The Guild always asserted to both inquiring writers and studio executives that it had and should exercise the power to handle such charges through the contractual-grievance mechanism. The Executive Board looked for ways to expand the Guild's authority. In July 1942, at a time when the MBA covered employment of writers but did not cover the sale of original material written by those not employed by a studio, two writers sold an original story, "Venus Ascending," to a studio (the movie was never made). The sales agreement said that one writer would waive screen credit. The Executive Board obtained the legal advice from its longtime lawyer Morris Cohn that it had jurisdiction to investigate the situation and opine on whether the waiver of credit was permissible because the Guild's Code of Working Rules prohibited members from accepting credit that misrepresented the writer's contribution, even though the MBA did not cover the sale. The Board accepted the writers' agreement but warned that it intended to look thoroughly into all agreements to waive credit in the future. In the second MBA, the Guild made clear there was to be no exception from Schedule A for stories not written under employment. This stance became significant when the number of writers hired as employees declined with the collapse of the studio system after 1950.[49]

The Board also paid close attention to plagiarism cases filed in courts and occasionally filed briefs as *amicus curiae*. Plagiarism suits by one writer against another and against a studio usually asserted causes of action for breach of contract (against the studio), theft of ideas (against the studio and the writer), and/or copyright infringement. Plagiarism suits were expensive, their outcomes were unpredictable, and they posed a constant threat for writers and studios in a world of collaborative work. They were between writers, or brought by one disgruntled writer against another, or brought by or against a story editor (a studio employee, often a former writer, who hires writers and supervises the development of scripts). In a plagiarism suit brought by a story editor at MGM over another movie that was never made, the Guild instructed its lawyer to file a brief arguing that if, in the absence of an employment contract, a writer writes a story at the request of a producer on speculation, the producer does not own the story and that if the producer contributes some ideas, the story does not belong to the producer. In sum, writers, studios, and the Guild all had reasons to want rules governing the use of, and credit for, scripts and story ideas.[50]

Although the credit-arbitration system and the minimum wage were the major achievements of the first MBA and SWG credit arbitration rapidly became established practice, neither was immune to challenge. In June 1942, not five months after signing the MBA, the studios proposed that credits be suspended for the duration of the war "in order to conserve film." Representatives from the Directors and Writers Guilds met to discuss a response—was this a genuine conservation effort or a ruse to back away from the agreement the studios had just signed? Directors and writers noted that the studios had not proposed to eliminate credits to actors, presumably because publicity for movie stars enhanced the market for the film. When the directors announced they had no intention of relinquishing screen credit, writers decided they, too, would not. Each Guild could inform the Hollywood Committee for Film Conservation that the studios could conserve film by making fewer prints or other ways "not detrimental to the creators in the industry." And, periodically, the Guild's Executive Board dealt with complaints from writers that studios' credits violated this or that rule, as by giving minor credits major attention (such as by putting an "added scenes by" or "additional dialogue by" credit on a card near the main writing credits), or that a studio's advertising violated the MBA provisions by failing to include the writer along with the stars and director. The Guild typically notified the studio of the violation and its intent to invoke the conciliation procedure. Yet over the first several years of the MBA, the Guild control over credits became established, and by 1945, the Guild arbitrated about fifty credit disputes a year. The Guild bore the cost of administering the system, which occasionally prompted the Executive Board to propose that the Guild should negotiate for the producers to share the expense.[51]

In the early years, at almost every meeting of the Executive Board, a Guild member asked the Board to fight with studios for its rules to be observed. Republic Studios, for example, routinely listed writing credits at the end of the film, along with technical credits, rather than at the beginning along with the stars, the producer, and the director. And so the Guild protested this practice, even though it recognized that it was "not yet established that this is a violation of Schedule A."[52] On *Shadow of a Doubt* (1942), for example, the Guild informed Universal that its proposed credits (screenplay by Thornton Wilder, original story by Gordon McDonell, dialogue by Sally Benson and Thornton Wilder, and continuity by Alma Reville) did not comply with Schedule A since there were to be no separate credits for dialogue or continuity.[53] Universal changed the credits to give Wilder, Benson, and Reville shared screenplay credit and McDonell story credit.

The reality was that the Guild had limited power to force the studios to observe the credit rules, and writers knew it. In April 1945, Lester Cole complained to the Guild Executive Board that Cagney Productions was violating the MBA by placing the credits as determined by the Guild Arbitration Committee in such a way as to give major attention to an "added scenes" credit, thus diminishing attention to the screenplay credit. The Board wrote a letter to the company insisting that the film not be shown without changing the credit card; the letter imposed a three-day deadline for the company to notify the Guild that it would change the credits and stipulated one week to make the change. But if the company refused, the Guild's options were limited. It could threaten to put the studio on the unfair list, but it could do nothing further except invoke conciliation. The Board told Cole that he was free to take whatever action he wished as an individual against the company. Yet the studios generally did follow the decisions of the conciliation committee established under the MBA, and particularly in credit matters, they seemed willing to have the Guild assume responsibility for resolving fights among writers over credit. The Guild regarded screen credits as an important economic issue for all writers, and therefore published the credit rules in pamphlet form for distribution to all Guild members, story editors, and others, so they would follow them and not sign contracts that did not include a provision incorporating the terms of the MBA on credit.[54]

Still Writing on Sand: Rewrites, Credits, and the Multiple-Author Problem

Writers never obtained the power to eliminate serial rewriting, much as they loathed it for both its effect on film quality and the fact that it made authorship difficult to discern. On *Gone with the Wind* (1939), Hollywood legend has it, seventeen writers were hired, performed writing services, and then were fired.[55] Serial rewriting has continued ever since, and usually writers simply live with it. Occasionally, someone sues, but rarely do suits accomplish much. The first *Pirates of the Caribbean* movie (*The Curse of the Black Pearl* (2003)), for example, has screen credits to four writers (two for the screenplay and two more for the story), but a fifth writer filed two unsuccessful copyright infringement suits against Disney.[56] So the Writers Guild struggled to decide whether or how to credit every person who wrote on a picture. Over time, the multiple-writer phenomenon raised interrelated problems. How many writers should be credited? If multiple writers were to receive credit, whose contributions should be prioritized—the first, the last, or the one who made the most significant contributions, and how should significance be assessed? Even if every writer is credited, what should be done in a situation like *The Pirates of the Caribbean: The Curse of the Black Pearl* (2003), in which multiple people worked on separate projects that eventually merged into one movie? The Guild resolved all of these problems through its internal deliberations over credit rules and its administration of the credit system.[57]

Although studios in the 1930s hired many writers to work on the same film, they generally credited only one or two people. As the Academy of Motion Picture Arts and Sciences said in the 1932 Writer-Producer Code of Practice, the "central idea" ought to be that "the screen author should be publicly recognized along with the director and the producer as a co-partner in the creation of the photoplay."[58] The Academy suggested this was to be done by "concentrating the recognition of one or two writers for each picture, by exploiting the term 'Screen Play' as a summarizing phrase to make it the equivalent of authorship of a play or a novel, and by giving the Screen Play credit a better position on the title cards than the credits of the technicians."[59]

When the Guild took over the administration of credits, it continued the practice of crediting only a few writers. In the first Guild credit rules, credits were divided into "top" credits, "joint" credits, and "additional" credits. The top credit would usually go to the first writer hired. To obtain a joint credit, a writer would have to show that he or she had written 50 percent of the final shooting script. An additional credit would be awarded to a writer who could prove having written 30 percent of the final shooting script.[60]

The Guild decided to concentrate authorship in one or two writers by limiting the number and types of writing credits and requiring that writers must make a substantial contribution, as measured in percentages of the final shooting script, to get credit.[61] In addition, when crediting more than one writer, the early credit rules distinguished (as the current rules still distinguish) between writers who worked independently (their names are joined by "and") and those who wrote as a team (their names are joined by "&"). As with all other forms of credit, this denotation is a signal about the nature of creative contribution. The order in which writers are credited is another signal of the nature of the creative contribution: the person who wrote the original script is usually listed first.

In 1938, the Guild membership and Executive Board debated ("thoroughly," the minutes reveal) and voted that screenplay credit be limited to three names (or a maximum of four, if ordered by the arbitration committee) and that no other credits be permitted on the screen other than original story credits. It recommended that names be listed in alphabetical order in the credits, but the order of names was so contentious that the Executive Board decided to poll the membership on it. The poll revealed that sixty-two members voted in favor of alphabetical listing and fifty-two opposed it, and so the membership decided to table the matter until more members could be polled.[62]

In 1947, an ad hoc committee of writers appointed by the Executive Board to study the credit system recommended that the additional credits be eliminated, and the Executive Board approved the proposal. The proposal was controversial, and at the annual meeting of the Guild's entire membership on February 19, 1947 at Hollywood Roosevelt Hotel, the members voted to refer the matter back to the Credits Committee for further study. In the discussion, among the suggestions made were that the credit "in collaboration with" be substituted for "additional dialogue by" credit. After further study, the decision to limit credits prevailed only in part. The Credits Committee recommended and the Executive Board approved that the "additional scenes" and "additional sequences" credits be eliminated, but the "additional dialogue" credit was included in the newly drafted Screen Credits Manual of 1948.[63]

Although the 1948 Screen Credits Manual allowed the additional dialogue credit, it nevertheless insisted "fewer names and fewer types of credit enhance the value of all credits and the dignity of all writers."[64] A "screenplay by" credit "will not be shared by more than two writers, except that in unusual cases, and solely as the result of arbitration, the names of three writers or the names of writers constituting two writing teams may be used." The number of eligible writers was (and still is) limited by the requirement that a writer must contribute more than a specified percentage to the final script. For example, a writer "whose work represents a contribution of more than 33 percent of a screenplay shall be entitled to screenplay credit," except "[i]n the case of an original screenplay, any subsequent writer or writing team must contribute 50 percent to the final screenplay." The 33 percent provision has been in the Screen Credits Manual since 1948. In 1948, the manual said that the order of names was subject to arbitration due to "the tendency on the part of certain studios to give term contract writers first credit even though another writer has been a major contributor to the script."[65]

A "screen story" or "adaptation by" credit was also introduced in 1948 to distinguish when a writer had written an original story from when she had adapted a story written by another. The screen story credit in 1948 was defined as appropriate when the screenplay was based upon both a story and source material and the story was substantially new or different from the source material. The difference between the screen story and the adaptation credits in 1948 turned on whether the producer was obligated to give story credit to the author of the source material in connection with the source's contract with the studio, in which case the second writer would be given "adaptation by" credit. The "screen story" and "adaptation by" credits were originally said to be interchangeable, but they were given their current distinct meanings in 1956. These credits referred to writer(s) who incorporated more than 75 percent of the work from a novel or play or writer(s) who remade a movie, respectively. The 1948 rules also allowed a "suggested by a story by" credit when the screenplay did not follow the original story but was unmistakably derived from it. The Guild specifically objected, however, to a "from an idea by" credit.

This entire regime for parceling out credits rests on subjective determinations about the significance of various writers' contributions. The Screen and Television Credits Manuals specify the criteria arbiters are to use in assessing the degree of contribution. For example, to receive credit, a first writer must have contributed more than 33 percent and a subsequent writer must have contributed more than 50 percent of the four important elements of the screenplay, which are specified as dramatic construction, scenes, characterization, and dialogue. But the manuals recognize that the "percentage contribution made by writers to a screenplay obviously cannot be determined by

counting lines or even the number of pages to which a writer has contributed. . . . It is up to the arbiters to determine which of the above-listed elements are most important to the overall values of the final screenplay in each
particular case." Arbiters get to decide what measuring device to use to distinguish between a 33 percent and a 50 percent contribution to a screenplay.
(Arbiters never find that no one contributed more than 33 percent of the final
script, even when multiple writers contribute.)

The commitment to concentrate credit on the few rather than the many
has led the Guild to prohibit its members from claiming credit contrary to the
final determination. The credit rules today advise "it is in the best interest of
all writers that certain facts relating to any particular credit determination
should remain confidential."[66]

Over the years, the Guild made changes to the credit rules trying to bal-
ance fairness to multiple writers with the goal of limiting credits to make it
appear that the writer, like the director, is the author of a film. In 1956, the
additional "dialogue by" credit was eliminated so that writers are credited
only in the front titles (before the film) and not in the long list of credits that
scroll up the screen at the end of the film. Since then, the Guild has not had a
rule allowing additional writers to be credited in the end titles, although it has
periodically made proposals to reintroduce additional writing credits, either
in front titles or in end titles. Occasionally, however, writers have been given
other types of credits, often known as a "consolation" credit. Robert Towne,
for example, was credited as a "special consultant" on *Bonnie and Clyde* (1967)
because Warren Beatty, as the star and producer, wanted him involved as an
on-set script doctor. The Guild sometimes challenges this type of credit as
prohibited when given to studio-favored writers who lose credit arbitrations.
A few arbitration awards have disallowed such credits.

Another rule the Guild adopted to define writers as the authors of films
concerned protection for the first writer on a film. The challenge in devising
credit rules regarding first writers was to distinguish the situation in which
the first writer develops an original vision that others only revised, in which
case the first writer should get a first credit, from a situation in which a first
writer wrote only a generic sort of story and the distinctive aspect of the
film was created by the rewrite. In 1980, first writers in film received protection through a rule providing that subsequent writers on an original screenplay must contribute more than 50 percent to the final screenplay to receive

screenplay credit. In the same year, an irreducible story credit for the writer of an original screenplay was introduced. This provision, as it exists today, provides: "in the case of an original screenplay, the first writer shall be entitled to no less than a shared story credit."

While the Guild was still establishing its authority over screen credit in films in the 1945, the Board began to consider questions from Guild members over what rules would apply in television. During the long struggle over the Guild's right to represent television writers, the Guild revised its Screen Credits Manual in 1948. The revised manual acknowledged that some TV writers might negotiate individual contracts to provide more credit than the Guild was able to negotiate collectively. In television, the rules protecting first writers adopted in the first Television Credits Manual in 1956 were less stringent than subsequent rules. In 1962, the Television Credits Manual increased the standards for subsequent writers to receive credit. In 1967, a provision was added to address the division of credit between first writers and subsequent writers. It provided, in part, that a "writer who is the original writer . . . of a teleplay shall be entitled to teleplay credit unless a second writer is determined to be entitled to a sole credit. . . . As a general rule for a second writer to receive credit his contribution must consist of changes of a substantial and original nature that go to the root of the drama or comedy, characterization, and content of a teleplay and constitute substantially more than the contribution of the first writer." The rule then identified the most important elements in a teleplay as being "Construction or structure, i.e. the ordering or internal structuring of scenes so as to affect dramatic values (the ordering or structuring of scenes affecting basic narrative line"; "Point of view, style or attitude"; "Characterization or character relationships"; and dialogue. The Television Credits Manual in 1956 stated that the MBA were minimum conditions and that writers might negotiate more favorable conditions such as "audio as well as visual credit," "credit to be given next to the producer or director," or "parity with the producer or director."

In 1949, upon recommendation of the Credits Committee, the Board adopted a more formal procedure for credit arbitrations. The arbiters would not know the identity of other arbiters, and each arbiter would be required to render his or her decision in writing. If the arbiters were not in agreement, the Guild office would appoint a credit consultant to help three arbiters reach agreement. If the arbiters still were not unanimous, it would be reported to the studio that the decision was not unanimous. A participant in the arbitration could seek review by a Review Board, consisting of three members of the Credits Committee. The Review Board would never itself read the material or reverse the arbitration committee, but it could review the procedure the arbiters used and ask them to consider additional evidence. In extreme cases, the Review Board could appoint a new arbitration committee.[67]

Today, the credit-arbitration system still adheres to the same general system. The studio sends a "Notice of Tentative Writing Credits" and a copy of the final shooting script to each participating writer and the Guild. If no one protests, the studio's proposed writing credits become final. A written protest from a participating writer triggers the arbitration process. The WGA selects three volunteer arbiters from a list it maintains of WGA members eligible to serve as credit arbiters, which are those who have been WGA members for at least five years or have received three screen credits. At least two of the three arbiters must have served as credit arbiters at least twice before. Participating writers may peremptorily strike arbiters from the list before the three are selected, but once the three are chosen, their names remain confidential. The names of participating writers are not revealed to the arbiters or the other writers.[68]

Each participating writer is entitled to prepare a written statement for the arbiters explaining why he or she should receive screen credit. The arbiters also review all the literary material, including scripts, stories, and treatments that have been verified by the Guild, the studio, and the participating writers as being part of the project. Each arbiter then reads all the material and makes a decision based on the Credits Manual guidelines for determining credit. Each arbiter makes an individual decision, but when the arbiters are not unanimous, they conduct a conference call to discuss their decisions in an effort to achieve unanimity. If the arbiters are unable to agree, the majority prevails. Each arbiter must confirm his or her individual decision in writing with a summary of the reason(s) for it.

Any participating writer may seek review of the arbiters' decision within twenty-four hours by the Policy Review Board, which is composed of three members of the Guild's Credits Committee. The function of the Policy Review Board is to determine whether the arbiters deviated from the Guild's policies or procedures; the Policy Review Board is prohibited from reading the literary material involved for the purpose of judging the writers' contributions and may not reverse the arbiters' decision in matters of judgment about the participating writers' relative contributions.

Screen Credits and Production Executives

The history of how the writing credit rules evolved for production executives reflects the challenge of treating fairly writers who also work as producers or directors ("hyphenates"), without opening the door to the kinds of abuses by production executives that led the Guild to insist on controlling credit in the first place. While some frustration is inherent in any collaborative creative process, the power relations between writers on the one hand, and producers and directors on the other, often exacerbate the tension. Writers who wish to have greater creative control have occasionally become entrepreneurial as writer-producers or writer-directors, thus leaving, in some sense, the ranks of labor and joining the ranks of management. (The social position of directors as labor or management is murky in Hollywood; in film, directors have considerable power over writers, but in episodic television, directors have little power over writers. But their legal position is clearly that of labor. Because they are hired and fired by producers, they are labor and have the legal right to bargain collectively through their Guild, just as writers do.)

A production executive is one who receives credit as the director or producer. A production executive of a film is defined in the Screen Credits Manual as the director or anyone who works in a producer capacity. In television, the current definition of a production executive is broader and includes any employee of the production company customarily hired for, or engaging in, activities considered part of the managerial part of the company's business, which includes story editors, story supervisors, or any other person who represents management in dealing with writers. The original MBA prohibited production executives from receiving writing credit unless the production executive was the only writer. The need for such a provision was obvious to writers, given their experience with studio moguls abusing credit for self-aggrandizement. The easiest solution to producers overreaching was simply to ban production executives from receiving writing credit at all. But even in the days of the studio system, the Guild's Executive Board occasionally struggled with the divide between writers and producers when a valued writer and

Guild leader took a job as a production executive and offered to resign from the Guild. For example, in August 1935, Nunnally Johnson (*The House of Roth-schild* (1934), *The Grapes of Wrath* (1940)) offered to resign his Guild membership because he had taken a job working as a producer; but because he continued to work as a writer, the Executive Board declined his offer. As the Guild secretary explained to him in a telegram, it would cause the Guild no "embarrassment" for Johnson to retain his office because, under Guild bylaws, producers who could not be Guild members did not include "writers who supervise their own work even though incidentally they may employ other writers to work thereon."[69] Johnson was credited as a producer dozens of times beginning in 1936, many times, although not always, on films he had written. He later wrote and directed his own movies, including *The Man in the Gray Flannel Suit* (1956)—a story that, as explained in Chapter 7, is all about the liminal position of ad agency and TV writers and the alienation of the creative worker in a corporate setting.

The rule that prohibited writers who employed other writers from con-tinuing as Guild members was changed ten years later to allow, as a matter of policy, what the Board had allowed Johnson by special agreement. The Board decided in 1945 to amend the Guild constitution to allow writers who pro-duced their own work to remain in the Guild. Advocating for the change, one Board member said such a writer-producer "has the type of control over his material which the Guild would like to have for all its members" and the posi-tion of the hyphenate "is really only an extension and enlargement of the writing function." Moreover, hyphenates "are not in a position to determine Producer policy in the sense that we use Producer when we mean producing company." The Guild noted that it benefitted from having hyphenates con-tinue as members because they supported the Guild financially (they were paid well), they shared a community of interest with writers, and they needed the Guild's protection, too.[70]

Writers considered the hyphenate rule especially unfair to writers who directed or produced films they had written, a practice that became increas-ingly common after the decline of the studio system. So beginning in 1948 and continuing over time, the barrier to production executives receiving credit was steadily lowered. However, production executives were and still are held to a higher standard to prove they were significantly involved in the writing. In addition, the Guild adopted procedural protections, including arbitration in any case in which a production executive is proposed for credit and a requirement that production executives notify writers of the intent to claim credit.

Guild leaders realized in the early days of television that the rules for credit for production executives were a problem because then, as now, writers often worked both as writers and as production executives. In 1955, the Board recognized that the working rule requiring production executives to notify the Guild and other writers of the intent to take credit was not administrable because the production executive often did not know in advance whether writing would be necessary on a script another writer submitted. The requirement of automatic arbitration whenever a production executive took credit would save the writer the risk of alienating the production executive by asking for arbitration, although it would require lots of arbitrations. The Board decided to waive the working rule requiring advance notice, but insisted that the automatic-arbitration rule be strictly enforced and that the production executive be required to supply written evidence of his contribution to the script.[71] The greater power writers have enjoyed in television labor relations led to a different approach to credits for hyphenates. Television currently has no heightened contribution requirements for production executives to receive credit because directors do not claim to be the authors of TV series nor do most producers, except for writer-producers (showrunners) and senior writers.[72]

Writers negotiated not only for Guild control of credit determinations for writing but also for what came to be known as the Parity Rule: that in the screen credits and in all advertising and promotion of a film, the writer be accorded credit equal in prominence to the credit for the director and producer. The Guild hoped to enhance the stature of writers through MBA provisions requiring parity of writer, director, and producer credits. And, when the studio violated the Parity Rule (as studios did many times over the years), the Guild would invoke the conciliation mechanism of the MBA, which was jointly managed by the Alliance of Motion Picture and Television Producers (AMPTP) and the Guild. Thus, for example, when Warner Bros. ads for *Streetcar Named Desire* (1951) and *Force of Arms* (1951) failed to mention the screenwriters (the *Streetcar* ad credited Tennessee Williams only as the playwright and not for the screenplay, and the *Force of Arms* ad mentioned no writer at all), the Guild asked repeatedly for a Guild-AMPTP Conciliation

Committee meeting, by which time the advertising (sans writer name) was already ubiquitous.[73]

A Film By [Writer or Director?]: The Possessory Credit

When critics and cinema scholars in the United States in the 1960s began writing that films, like books, have an author whose artistic vision is reflected in the work, they followed the French practice and credited directors as the auteurs of film.[74] It became common among critics to write about "a Hitchcock film" or "a film by Godard," almost always referring to the director, attributing the creation of the film to the director—the film became "his" film just as a novel belonged to the novelist. This "possessory credit" (as it somehow became known in the 1970s) suggested the film was the director's, even when the director was not the writer of the film. After the popularization of auteur theory in the United States in the 1970s and the increasing use of the "film by" credit by directors who had not written the script, writers had a theoretical framework to understand their status grievances, but the conflict between writers and directors over authorship of films dates back to the 1930s, at least.[75]

In 1940, the Writers Guild tried to bar anyone but the writer from claiming authorship of a film, but it failed to secure an express contractual provision limiting the possessory credit. The Guild occasionally expressly agreed to allow a director to claim authorship, as it did in November 1940 in allowing a credit for "Screenplay and Direction by Preston Sturges."[76] It did not object when films were advertised as "A [Director Name] Production," as was *A Streetcar Named Desire* (1951). Nor did the Guild object to Alfred Hitchcock's use of the possessory credit, as in *Rear Window* (1954) or *Notorious* (1946), even though Hitchcock did not receive writing credit. But the Guild did sometimes object when directors not known for their distinctive vision claimed the "film by" credit. When *The Man with the Golden Arm* (1955) was dubbed "A film by Otto Preminger" and the poster omitted any mention of the writers (Walter Newman and Lewis Meltzer, based on the Nelson Algren novel), the Guild's Executive Board insisted that Preminger had violated the spirit of the MBA. The Board could do nothing, however, because the MBA had not been violated, so it wrote to all members of the Guild's East and West branches to explain why the possessory credit harmed writers who worked for Preminger.

In 1963, the WGA did get a contract term in the MBA prohibiting use of the possessory credit by anyone who had not written the script. In 1967, the Directors Guild of America (DGA) insisted to the AMPTP that the WGA's control over the possessory credit violated directors' rights, and even initiated inconclusive litigation against the AMPTP and the WGA over it. In 1970, the WGA agreed to permit some directors to use the possessory credit, believing that its use would be limited to a handful of extraordinarily accomplished and marketable directors, such as Alfred Hitchcock. Whatever the intent of the parties in 1970, the use of the possessory credit expanded dramatically in the years that followed. In 1981, the DGA got AMPTP to agree that directors would be given a "film by" credit in outdoor advertising if the ad contained more than six credits. As the years went by, the WGA came to believe that a possessory credit could be claimed by, as one irritated writer put it, "any film school grad who could bargain for it." So in negotiations for the 2001 MBA, the WGA tried unsuccessfully to limit the possessory credit.[77]

When producers began in the 1990s to routinely claim the credit, the DGA began to express concerns about the proliferation of possessory credits by producers, but ultimately, the WGA, the DGA, and the companies were unable to reach an agreement that respected the DGA's desire to institution-alize the use of the possessory credit for directors, limit and regulate its use by producers, and sharply limit it, as sought by writers. In 2004, the DGA unilat-erally overhauled its own credit guidelines to limit when a first-time director could receive a possessory credit and eliminate the outdoor advertising rules. Many in the WGA believe, however, that the possessory credit is still unfair to writers, is claimed too often by directors, and that the 2004 changes did not fix the problem. But the WGA cannot prevent the DGA and the AMPTP from using it. In an effort to convince the DGA to rein in the use of the credit, the WGA continues to study the use of the possessory credit, showing that between three-fifths and three-quarters of all films under WGA jurisdiction released since 1990 have possessory credits, and it is very rare that the writer gets the film by designation.[78]

Paths Taken and Not Taken

From the beginning, the Guild recognized that the expansion of media raised questions of the Guild's jurisdiction and, in a larger sense, the types of writers with which screenwriters wanted to make common cause. Over the course of just a month in October and November 1938, the Guild Executive Board made a few decisions that reflected both farsightedness and a lack of imagination. In October, the Board voted unanimously to advise seven writers at Disney studios that cartoon writers were not within the Guild's jurisdiction and to refund the membership dues they had paid.[79] Thus, it missed the chance to organize the writers who worked on animated classics, including *Snow White and the Seven Dwarfs* (1937), *Pinocchio* (1940), *Dumbo* (1940), and *Fantasia* (1940). And animation writers are, with some exceptions, still not Writers Guild members, although the WGA and the Animators Guild cooperate.[80]

In a number of meetings in 1938 and 1939, the Executive Board discussed at length the importance of working with the Radio Writers Guild on television. The Guild recognized that screenwriters' work was already being used on radio, and indeed, Dalton Trumbo complained about studios turning over scripts to radio producers without giving credit to writers.[81] The Executive Board also thought writers should be compensated for reuse of scripts and predicted reuse would soon be "an acute problem" for screenwriters.[82]

The Guild was right about the looming problem of television, and it soon discovered that its reluctance to organize animators was shortsighted, not only because of the importance of animated screen entertainment but also because organizing writers working in allied media became essential with the advent of TV. In the decades since Hollywood writers first unionized, changing technology and changing business practices have presented the biggest challenges for writers. Early Guild leaders were prescient about the need for writers to form common cause and the ways that writers could do so notwithstanding the disparate economic and work situations between freelancers and staff writers and between the most and least successful. One way they did so was by making authorship a core union issue. Yet even they struggled to see how to unite writers across sectors of the entertainment industries, and that remains a struggle for writers to this day.

Act II

INTERSECTIONS

3

Agency-Built Storytelling

In those days, JWT wrote all of the material their stars used on the air. . . . The writers and directors [got] no credits on the air or in the trades. Ours was an anonymous society, and our only accolade, after a particularly fine show and one which "broke new ground," was an orchid, which we would find on our desks the morning after.

—JWT Executive Colin Dawkins

R adio was the first major point of intersection of the Hollywood style of corporate writing and the Madison Avenue style. Some writers free-lanced for both film and radio in the late 1930s, and some screenwriters had seen studios resell their scripts to ad agencies for radio broadcast (without compensation or credit for the writers). Hollywood studios used radio to advertise their stars and their films from 1928 onward (although they also in 1932 temporarily prohibited contract stars from appearing on the air, but the ban lasted for only a month). And radio and film companies had close ties: the giant Radio Corporation of America (RCA), which manufactured radios and created the National Broadcasting Company (NBC) networks, established the Radio Keith Orpheum (RKO) movie studio in 1929, the same year Paramount and the Columbia Broadcasting System (CBS) merged.[1] But for all the con-nections between radio and Hollywood, the labor relations of writing for radio and for film remained largely distinct until the end of World War II. Ad agencies made scripted radio comedies and dramas because their clients were willing to pay for the development of content to gain the brand recognition and customer goodwill that sponsorship would provide. For reasons of tech-nology, business model, and the failure of regulators to insist on public radio, someone besides the audience or the taxpayer had to pay for content develop-ment, and corporate advertisers had deep pockets. Air time was purchased by ad agencies for their sponsors just like space in newspapers and magazines and on billboards had been, and ad agencies then generated the content for radio just as they had been doing for print media. The business model for movies was, of course, quite different, and as Chapters 1 and 2 showed, the two sectors had very different labor relations.

Advertising agencies first confronted writer demands for unionization, regular air credit, and ownership of the rights in their work shortly after New York radio writers formed the Radio Writers Guild in 1937. Freelance radio writers employed by agencies joined the Radio Writers Guild and demanded adherence to its code of fair practices and, later, to a minimum basic agreement. The contract demands made by freelance radio writers were strikingly different from the personnel practices ad agencies used for their staff copywriters on the crucial issues of ownership of rights in scripts and air credits for writers.

As radio dramas migrated to TV in the postwar period, ad agencies started producing filmed and live TV shows and hiring experienced film writers who could write a script for a visual medium. They also began hiring film actors and directors, so they had to deal with the guilds representing them and comply with the talent contracts. Independent production companies began contracting with ad agencies and networks to produce television shows, which they sold through the agency to the advertiser as a package (hence, they were called packagers). With industry changes the labor relations of the two formerly distinct industries began to intersect. And in that intersection occurred a collision of norms and employment-contract provisions about credit and intellectual property rights.

The unionization of freelance radio writers put the agencies in the position of drawing fine distinctions between freelance writers and their own staff writers because unionized writers demanded the same kinds of attribution that the guild contracts had guaranteed film writers. However thin the distinctions were, they wound up having a huge impact on the rights and self-conception of the writers, as well as on the labor relations in Hollywood and on Madison Avenue after the agencies got out of the business of producing radio and TV shows in the mid-1950s. Although some ad agency leaders, including the general counsel of JWT, eventually decided that freelance writers could unionize without a significant threat to the business model of ad agencies, most agencies disagreed. As a consequence, the consortium of agencies that bargained with the Guild stalled negotiations for two years asserting that (1) freelance writers working on agency-built shows were not employees eligible to unionize under federal labor law and (2) collective bargaining violated the antitrust laws. The prolonged negotiations over unionization of radio writers reveal the difference in legal strategies and norms about ownership and attribution of this kind of writing. Writers of scripted radio (and later television) remained unionized and entitled to credit and compensation for their work, while writers on Madison Avenue did not.

Radio Writers in the 1930s and Early 1940s

The major nationwide commercial-television networks of the twentieth century—NBC, CBS, and ABC—began in radio in the 1920s. The National Broadcasting Corporation (NBC) was launched in late 1926 with two networks, Red and Blue. The Columbia Broadcasting System (CBS) created its own network in 1928, and Mutual formed a network in 1934. (NBC Blue was sold and became the American Broadcasting Company (ABC) in 1944. Mutual's assets were sold to various media companies, and it finally dissolved in 1999.)[2] Radio schedules included news, music, and variety shows, but also many dramas and comedies that required the kind of writers who worked in movies and theater. A handful of early radio writers worked for networks, but most worked for ad agencies or the independent production companies ad agencies hired. Most were labeled as freelancers (and were paid by the week), while others were staff (and paid a salary). But whether freelance or staff, radio writers worked for ad agencies either directly or indirectly because the ad agency hired the packager and controlled the content on behalf of the sponsor. Some radio production was local, while some was national, although even on national shows, the production was geographically dispersed (mainly between New York, Chicago, and Los Angeles).

Ad agencies were crucial in the early development of radio shows. The radio networks during the 1930s and 1940s served as conduits for advertising agencies and sponsors that purchased air time and produced shows. Ad agencies, not the networks, controlled the creation of the shows that aired during the most popular hours. Radio was, thus, quite different from movies. Whereas movie studios produced the content and controlled the distribution, when it came to scripted radio shows (as opposed to news or music), radio networks largely distributed the content that the ad agencies generated.[3]

As the largest ad agency in the United States, JWT quickly became involved in radio. JWT programming helped NBC achieve financial stability in the network's formative years, and JWT continued writing, producing, and directing radio shows through the 1940s. Ad agency purchases of time became the core of the broadcast model and remained so for decades, even when agencies had ceased producing shows and instead confined themselves to purchasing thirty-second or sixty-second spots. Very early in the history of radio—by the mid-1930s—almost all evening programs were originated and produced by sponsors and ad agencies. As a consequence, the business model and labor relations of the advertising business, rather than the movie production business, dominated content generation in radio.[4]

Although much important programming remained centered in New York, by the late 1930s, the desire of sponsors to have film stars in their shows had led agencies and packagers to move some radio production from New York to Hollywood. Once in Hollywood and dealing regularly with studios and film writers as they adapted film scripts for radio programs, ad agencies and packagers grudgingly adopted some of the labor practices of the movie business.[5] But through the 1940s, the ad agencies that effectively controlled radio adhered to the nonattribution practices that had long been core to their conception of writing. JWT crowed within the firm and to its clients and competitors about the ratings of its shows, but it did not credit particular people as writers, not even in the company newsletter.[6]

All of this presented logistical and legal challenges for radio writers in organizing a union. Although some ad agency staff writers worked on radio shows, most of the demand for unionization and most of the success the Radio Writers Guild achieved were with network staff writers and freelance writers, and these writers were hired either by independent production companies who created shows as a package and sold them to agencies or by agencies themselves when they created the shows. Freelance writers were treated as ad agency employees for tax purposes, but they were not staff of the production company or the agency. Their liminal status as freelancers—they were not employees in the ordinary sense of the word—also created unique legal challenges.

For ad agencies and writers, creating radio shows was an exciting business prospect and creative challenge. In magazines, which had been the dominant advertising medium, the advertiser controlled only the ads. But in radio of the

1930s and 1940s, there was no separation between the editorial content and the ads. Rather, the ad agency created the entertainment content and the commercial message. The agency and the freelance writer, in consultation with the client's advertising department, developed the concept of the show. The agency hired the performers and additional writers, and it negotiated with the network for the day and time of the show. The terms on which radio writers were hired could be quite exploitative. Freelancers were expected to write "audition" scripts for free; an audition script was essentially a pilot episode of a show, and the agency or network would acquire all the rights in the script and its ideas and characters with no provision for profit sharing to the writer. Don Quinn, for example, wrote a pilot script called "Fibber McGee & Molly," which he sold outright to an ad agency. The script spawned a hugely successful radio series and two spin-off series, and Quinn received no share of the profits. Conditions for network staff writers were also grim: staff writers often were paid little; everything they wrote on or off the job belonged to the network; they got no air credit; and they had no job security.[7]

Ad agencies hired screenwriters, playwrights, short story writers, and others as freelancers, but they also relied on agency copywriters to write scripts. Agency creative directors, as well as the client's advertising director, supervised script development. And commercial announcements interspersed in the script were always written by agency copywriters, even if a freelance writer wrote the script. As a consequence, radio writing was a collaborative process between agency staff, sponsor, and freelance writers. The script would be reviewed by the network's censor, although the sponsor's advertising department had already censored anything it deemed offensive.[8]

Although ad agencies and Hollywood writers collaborated on the production of radio programs, agencies created the fiction that an on-air celebrity host, like Cecil B. DeMille on *Lux Radio Theatre*, was the show's creator. If the story was adapted from a Broadway play or a popular film, the agency wrote scripts for the host, making it appear as if he were the editor and curator of stories he selected. The involvement of JWT staff in writing or rewriting scripts for *Lux Radio Theatre* was hidden so carefully from the public that even Hollywood writers whose scripts were repurposed for the show appeared to have no idea who was responsible for the use of their work. In June 1942, Charles Brackett (*The Lost Weekend* (1945), *Sunset Boulevard* (1950)) complained to the Executive Board of the Screen Writers Guild that three scripts he had written with Billy Wilder had been used on *Lux Radio Theatre* without air credit to them, and he reported that he had protested the lack of air credit to Cecil B. DeMille but had not received a satisfactory answer. Brackett wanted the Screen Writers Guild to do something about studios selling scripts for use on radio without air credit to the writer. Even a sophisticated Hollywood writer like Brackett apparently had no idea that JWT really controlled what DeMille said on the show, or at least he and the SWG overestimated DeMille's ability or willingness to challenge JWT's policy on credits.[9]

Writers had no legal recourse, however, because they sold their scripts outright to the studios or the studios acquired the scripts from writer employees as works for hire under copyright law. The credit provisions of the screenwriters' MBA applied only to movie studios and to the exhibition and advertising of the movie, not to other uses of the script. Nevertheless, the SWG Board promised Brackett to "check with the Radio Writers Guild and find out what their agreements are in connection with air credit," and send a letter to DeMille "indicating the attitude of the Guild to the practice of giving proper air credit to writers." The SWG letter had no effect, and in December 1942, the Executive Board again discussed complaints by George Oppenheimer and Paul Jarrico that *Lux Radio Theatre* had broadcast edited versions of their scripts for *The War Against Mrs. Hadley* (1942) and *Tom, Dick and Harry* (1941) without credit to them. The Board wrote another letter of complaint to DeMille, to which DeMille responded saying that the matter "more properly came under the Legal Department rather than the Production Department" of *Lux Radio Theatre*, and that credit was up to Danny Danker (JWT's Hollywood producer) and subject to the terms of the agreement by which JWT purchased the rights from the studios. Because agencies seldom gave air credit to writers, there was nothing SWG or writers could do. Both Oppenheimer and Jarrico were successful and well-known writers. Oppenheimer (1900–1977) had been a publisher before coming to Hollywood in 1933, where he worked on several hit movies for two decades before leaving the industry to become a drama critic for *Newsday*. Jarrico (1915–1997) won an Academy Award for *Tom, Dick and Harry* in 1941 and was very successful until he was one of the first writers to be blacklisted in 1947. So they were aghast at SWG's inability to do anything about uncompensated reuse of their work.[10]

While film writers expected to be rewritten and were alarmed primarily by uncompensated and uncredited reuse of their scripts on radio, novelists who wrote for radio found unauthorized rewrites distressing. Pearl S. Buck became a literary celebrity with her prize-winning 1931 novel, *The Good Earth*, which had been made into an Academy Award–winning movie in 1937. When she wrote a radio script that was broadcast with unauthorized changes, she complained about the changes to Erik Barnouw, the president of the Radio Writers Guild, whom she had known since she took his radio-writing course at Columbia. He explained that radio writers never had control over their work. He may have mollified Buck by saying he himself had become uncomfortable about how "cavalierly" he had treated freelance writers when he was working at an ad agency in the 1930s, now that he had become active in the RWG and was "seeing writers' problems more and more from a writer's point of view."[11] But the RWG had no more success than the SWG had had in preventing rewrites in cases when the original author of the script lacked the market power to protect herself.

Ad Agencies and the Radio Writers Guild

The wide gulf between the two Guilds and the worlds of film and radio writing revealed in the SWG's uncertainty about the terms of RWG agreements on air credit persisted into the 1940s. The Radio Writers Guild had no agreement with ad agencies, and individual radio writers who worked for agencies or networks did not have individual contracts requiring air credit. The Radio Writers Guild had in 1940–1941 gotten the American Association of Advertising Agencies to agree to a Code of Fair Practice, including a model individual employment contract, but it was not binding (a RWG pamphlet joked that the Code "was printed and framed to be hung on the walls of executive offices" but "was never observed"). In any event, it did not prevent uncompensated and uncredited reuse of film scripts. In 1945, the RWG tried to get ad agencies to agree to a minimum basic agreement for freelance writers employed on "agency built" shows like *Lux Radio Theatre*. The RWG wanted a contract covering all writers on all shows, whether produced by a network, a packager, or an ad agency.[12]

Radio writers and the agencies fundamentally disagreed about a fair approach to ownership and remuneration for the writers' work. John Reber, JWT's longtime head of the radio and TV department, recognized that radio writers wanted "to be known and treated as craftsmen who produce a commodity without which the radio program couldn't exist." And he recognized that one of the goals of the Radio Writers Guild was to negotiate for its members the same kinds of contractual protections of ownership and air credit that the Screen Writers Guild had negotiated for its members. The film agreements recognized, Reber said, writing as "an essential creative contribution which comes from the writer's own self." But he thought the world of advertising was fundamentally different from the world of film. As Reber explained to the JWT executive in charge of producing an Al Jolson radio show: "The advertising business, especially in a company like ours, conditions us to the general idea that anything that is written is the net result of the work of a great many individuals" and it is "difficult for us to concede that an advertisement written in a J. Walter Thompson Company office was the property of any one writer." (Reber here meant that attribution to a writer would be like saying an idea was his property, even though writers did not claim to own the ads or radio scripts and only wanted credit as authors.) This was true even in radio, which Reber acknowledged was a bit like film production, and Reber knew that a very different attitude toward attribution of writing prevailed in film. Reber described the agency philosophy as "a basic resistance to our being able to consider a radio script as something which is not the net result of the work of practically the whole organization."[13]

However much advertising agency employees celebrated the creativity of ads, the origin of their business was as agents who purchased space, hired people to write copy, and charged the client the costs of space and production plus a 15 percent commission. This situation did not change, even as the complexity and creativity of content generation grew with the advent of radio and television. They were professionals selling expert advice and service to clients, a self-conception of their role as corporate authors quite different from movie and radio producers, who saw themselves as content creators (in modern parlance), as corporate authors responsible for creating and selling stories. Thus, ad agencies registered copyrights in their clients' name for everything from scripts to musical compositions used as jingles to leaflets, package inserts, and posters. As Reber said, after JWT produces a script, it "becomes the property of the advertiser."[14] The ad agencies' view of authorship was thus more like the law of trademark than the law of copyright: under trademark law, no matter who created the trademarked brand name, logo, or slogan, the trademark rights belong to the producer of goods or services associated with the trademark, not to the person who created the mark.

The difference between the agency conception and the corporate-author conception was laid bare when ad agencies encountered the Hollywood model on a massive scale with the postwar expansion of the radio model into television. To the extent that the Radio Writers Guild succeeded, it was because the structure of production enabled the norms of Hollywood to prevail at independent production companies without requiring wholesale change in how advertising agencies managed their own staff. Packagers could adhere to union contracts requiring attribution. Even the agency could do so for the occasional freelance writer it employed because the agency had long insisted that the client really employed the talent, even though the agency hired, fired, and supervised talent. Freelancers were already quite distinct from agency writers in workplace culture and legal culture. For one thing, while copywriters might work for years at the same agency, freelancers came and went. And freelance writers had written employment contracts modeled on the studio contracts, whereas JWT copywriters did not. JWT's in-house counsel and head of its radio department both "emphatically" believed that contracts with employees were undesirable and unnecessary.[15] By contrast, no studio executive would have insisted on hiring a writer to produce copyrightable material without an employment contract. The administrative separation of freelance radio writers from the agency's permanent writing staff allowed it to have two different sets of labor practices and, with them, two diametrically opposed approaches to attribution.

Reber and other JWT executives insisted that nonattribution of writing recognized that the agency's primary loyalty was to its clients. This conception of a duty of loyalty was not, however, a complete abnegation of agency authorship. Indeed, it became the basis for agencies to insist that they, and only they, should control the content of the radio and television shows they produced. It was in the name of the agency's duty as an author on behalf of the client that Reber resisted NBC control over the content of *Kraft Television Theatre* in the late 1940s because he thought it compromised agency loyalty to the client. Moreover, he refused to give any agency employee air credit, allowing it only for star actors, and occasionally directors and freelance writers, thinking credit would detract from audience identification with the show's sponsor. The agency insisted on its control over the content to discharge its obligations as an agent. Yet in refusing to allow its own staff to be credited and in recognizing that the sponsor, not the agency, would own the rights in the work after it was completed, the agency simultaneously asserted the control aspect of authorship while relinquishing the author's attribution and ownership claims.[16]

The Unionization of Radio Writers Begins

The unionization of different types of workers in radio occurred fairly quickly, from many sources, but writers were the last group to unionize. First, the American Federation of Musicians (AFM) in 1924 demanded that broadcasters recognize it as the union of staff orchestras employed by the stations to fill unsold time on the air.[17] The National Association of Broadcast Employees and Technicians (NABET) formed next, in the 1930s, to represent technicians. The union of stage actors, Actors Equity, set up committees to organize radio performers in New York and Los Angeles, and those committees, which became the American Federation of Radio Artists (AFRA), won the right to represent radio performers in the late 1930s. The Radio Writers Guild was formed (in New York in 1937) as an affiliate of the Authors League at the same time other radio talent unionized, but it did not finally win a contract until 1947, more than five years after film writers did and, significantly, almost at the same time that TV began to supplant radio as the most remunerative and significant form of scripted broadcast entertainment.

The RWG's first contract was for network-employed writers, but they were a minority of radio writers. The real challenge, said Erik Barnouw, was to win a contract for freelance writers, who were the majority of RWG membership, who wrote the sponsored programs that dominated network radio, and who worked for the ad agencies (the agencies' clients, technically).[18] Unlike the movie studios and the radio networks, both of which had been dealing with unions since the 1920s, ad agencies had never had unionized employees and were, with a few exceptions, extremely hostile to the idea.

Worse than the agencies' lack of union experience was that the climate for labor had changed radically since the 1930s, when the SWG was formed. During the Depression, both President Roosevelt and Congress supported labor's legal right to organize and millions of workers in all occupations saw a labor union as an essential protection against economic catastrophe. By

1947, however, a strongly antilabor Republican Party had taken over Congress for the first time since 1930. A huge postwar wave of strikes led to public-opinion surveys showing that a significant segment of the public identified labor strife as the most pressing policy problem of the day, the Republican Congress enacted the Taft-Hartley Act of 1947, which sharply limited the rights of workers to unionize, and both the Screen Writers Guild and the Radio Writers Guild were under attack for alleged communist influences. Undaunted, the RWG proposed to the agencies a minimum basic agreement for writers that was consistent with what the SWG planned to demand for film writers when the film MBA came up for renegotiation in 1949. The RWG asked for lease rather than sale of shows, changes to the standard copyright release form, and a minimum scale of payments depending on the length and type of show. The agencies flatly refused to negotiate with the RWG.[19]

Only one agency broke ranks. Young & Rubicam, which employed five staff (not freelance) writers on a show called *We the People,* negotiated a contract with the RWG for the staff writers on the show in late 1946. According to JWT's lawyer Ed Wilson, who followed the negotiations closely because of the similar situation facing JWT, the Young & Rubicam *We the People* negotiations over pay were not especially difficult. The Guild thought that the terms were "rather favorable," though not every writer agreed. Wilson thought the terms were "no better than the present situation of these writers," which surprised him because, he said, "the function of a labor union is to improve their situation," not just preserve the status quo.[20]

All the other agencies resisted bargaining with the Guild for years. Their resistance was not about the money at stake because most agencies, especially for sponsored prime-time shows, paid writers more than the RWG proposed as a minimum.[21] They resisted because they refused to accede to Guild demands for air credit or writer ownership of rights. So the agencies used a number of tactics to stall bargaining. First, they insisted that their clients (the sponsors) did not give them authority to negotiate any agreement. Later they said freelance writers were not employees at all, or, if they were, then they were employees of the sponsors, not the agencies (even though the agencies hired, supervised, paid, and fired them).

After months of fruitless efforts to negotiate with the agencies, an exasperated Barnouw wrote to the president of Standard Brands—a major radio program sponsor—complaining about the agencies' intransigence. Many sponsors had unionized workforces in their manufacturing operations, and Barnouw thought they would be open to unionization of writers and other radio talent and therefore might intervene with their advertising agencies to prod them to negotiate. Barnouw explained to Standard Brands that a contract for radio writers "would stabilize conditions in the radio industry, and recognize certain rights of authorship which are basic to the whole principle of copyright." And if that didn't persuade the company, Barnouw raised the specter of a public-relations problem: "We doubt that you would wish to engage in public controversy with a handful of creative people" where the "the basis on which your hired advertising agents deal with writers of your advertising programs is not a large question, financially speaking." But the appeal changed nothing, as sponsors left it to the agencies to negotiate with writers, and most agencies remained adamantly opposed to writer unionization.[22]

Ownership of Rights in Scripts

The most divisive issue in the RWG-agency negotiations concerned the division of ownership of rights in radio scripts. Radio writers wanted what screenwriters had requested but not gotten in the 1942 collective agreement with movie studios: a provision stipulating that employers would not acquire the copyright in scripts, but rather would license scripts for the purpose of creating a film and the writer would retain the right to develop the script for another buyer if the studio didn't use the script and also would retain rights to subsidiary uses (such as for novels or short stories).[23] While the RWG was prepared to give up on a number of its demands (a guaranteed term of employment, the right of the first writer to do all rewriting, restrictions on asking prospective writers to prepare a spec script for free), the RWG was adamant about writer ownership. The RWG also insisted on the other badges of genuine authorship: writers would not be asked to rewrite each other's work, writers would be paid for material ordered even if it was not used, and writers would be given air credit. On these issues, the RWG was putting up a united front with the SWG, which also planned to make writer ownership the do-or-die issue in its upcoming negotiations.[24]

Negotiations between the agencies and the RWG broke down repeatedly over the issue of script ownership. Wages were not the problem; rather, "the real issue was property rights," reflected Ed Wilson, JWT's General Counsel, at the end of the negotiations in December 1948.[25] The agencies, sponsors, and their lawyers identified all sorts of problems with writers retaining rights in their work. They feared that a serial might have to be discontinued if a writer ceased to be employed. They feared having to pay a reuse fee every time a gag line was used if it became a regular part of a show, as "Ain't this a revolting development" became on the popular show, *Life of Riley*. The network agreement the RWG negotiated in August 1948 addressed these issues, but still the agencies feared the worst. At the end of the negotiations, Wilson mused that freelance writers wanted to insist on property rights in part because freelance writers wanted a "feeling of . . . belong[ing], of having each man's voice count in some place," and owning the rights in a script represented that.[26]

In January 1948, the RWG offered the network agreement as a pattern for freelance writers employed by agencies. It did not require that writers share the proceeds of sales of rights in series programs as it had in the network agreement. (The network agreement did not require splits of the proceeds from sale of episodic or serial rights.)[27] The proposed agreement dealt with the ownership issue by establishing exclusivity periods. A writer would grant the employer the right "to use the script on AM, FM, television, etc., during the period of exclusivity . . . with the writer agreeing not to license the use of the script" for other purposes during the period. The employer would obtain reuse rights by payment of another fee and could extend the exclusivity period indefinitely into the future by payment of successive fees. Writers would not ever sell "subsidiary rights," that is, the right to publish the script in book form, or make it into motion pictures, or to record for home use.[28]

To get agencies to agree that writers would sell only broadcasting rights proved to be a struggle. The negotiating committee of advertising agencies refused to agree that writers would own their scripts because the agencies feared the effect of writer ownership of copyrights in a labor market in which freelance writers switched from one agency and one sponsor to another. The agencies also had long existed in a world in which ideas that an agency developed but did not use for one client might be recycled to use for another client or another campaign, and agencies did not want freelance writers to do what the agencies themselves did because the agencies believed *they* owned the freelancers' work. Agencies feared "writers changing sponsors or agencies might have the right to use old scripts over again or to turn out another program of the same name," and "producers might not have the right to use running gags if the original writer is no longer in their employ." Moreover, agencies conceptualized the value they created for their clients (if the client owned the program), and for the owners of the copyrights in films or other materials used in the shows that client sponsored (if the client did not own the copyright in the program), in terms that are recognizable in today's transmedia world. As an advertising executive explained it, "performance of the script on the air gives value to theatrical, screen, literary, and other rights."[29]

Ad agency executives believed the purchaser (the sponsor, not the agency) typically cared more about having complete control over the script and the show developed from it than it did about profiting from other uses of the script. Ed Wilson explained to an employee in JWT's Hollywood office the agency's and sponsors' thinking on ownership and reuse. The Hollywood office had asked whether the Wrigley Company, the sponsor of the Gene Autry singing-cowboy *Melody Ranch* radio show, would be able to purchase rights in a script from a writer who wished to retain the rights to sell to a movie studio. Wilson explained that, where networks or sponsors purchased all rights in a radio script, individual writers sometimes negotiated agreements whereby the buyer (usually the sponsor) would give the writer "a percentage, as high as ninety percent, on the non-radio income from the artist's material. In other words, if the broadcasting company sells movie rights, it only retains, in the usual case, what amounts to a commission."[30] Occasionally sponsors did profit from scripts that they hadn't used themselves, but those instances were rare.[31]

Agencies and sponsors were relaxed about copyrights in scripts because they didn't perceive much reuse value in them. Songs were another matter. Everyone knew a song written for a radio show might become popular and therefore a valuable source of revenue. The American Society of Composers, Authors and Publishers (ASCAP) had been founded early in the century to facilitate licensing of the public performance of songs and collecting copyright royalties for every public performance at a concert, a bar or restaurant, or on the air, so that the owners of songs would be paid and those who performed, recorded, or broadcast a song would be assured of the right to use the music. ASCAP thus protected copyright owners' right to payment for broadcast or performance and had a licensing system to collect and disburse fees to owners. ASCAP had first asked for payment for music broadcast on radio in 1923 and sued successfully to enforce the rights of song owners, and so broadcasters had paid an annual license fee for use of music. Agencies occasionally had to abandon use of a song in a radio show or an advertisement when a songwriter appeared and demanded royalties or alerted ASCAP to the failure of the advertiser to pay.[32] Thus, ASCAP existed as an established model for use of songs on the air, and RWG thought it could perform a similar role for use of scripts.[33]

While some sponsors were relatively relaxed about intellectual property rights in their advertising, DuPont was not; it was extremely controlling about every aspect of its history series, *Cavalcade of America*. The show, which premiered in 1935, began as an effort at damage control during a US Senate investigation of DuPont for munitions profiteering during World War I. DuPont's ad agency, Batten, Barton, Durstine & Osborn (BBD&O), wrote and produced the show for radio and, starting in the early 1950s, for television.[34] DuPont tightly controlled the topics covered; the stories emphasized "individual achievements in scientific research and the quest for a better life." (Absolutely taboo subjects included labor history and race relations, because DuPont executives were quite reactionary on those issues. The safest way for a writer to get a script approved was to acquiesce in the company's unstated view that, except for advances in science, "history tended to end in the nineteenth century."[35]) According to a 1954 BBD&O analysis, the agency "jealously guarded" DuPont's rights in *Cavalcade* with the result that the show would have value for use as educational programing or could be sold to other sponsors for reuse on television.[36] DuPont had become fairly aggressive in protecting the patents and trade secrets in its innovative chemical products in the late nineteenth and early twentieth centuries, so its lawyers and executives thought of *all* intellectual property, including *Cavalcade* scripts, as being sources of company value, not just the intellectual property rights in the products it developed and sold.[37]

Eventually, JWT concluded that agreement with the RWG was in their own interest, as well as that of their clients, because "most writers of any prominence are Guild members," so recruiting talent required dealing with the Guild. Plus, they recognized the RWG wouldn't be a big deal because only about ten writers on the five radio shows they produced for their clients would be covered. And even for those five shows, adopting most RWG terms, even writer profit participation, would not dramatically change the way JWT worked. For example, on *Red Ryder* (a popular radio show based on a comic strip), the writer, Paul Franklin, already had a deal giving him and Slessinger, the creator of the comic, a share in the royalties resulting from sales of the program in syndication outside the California, Oregon, and Washington territory that was of greatest interest to the sponsor, Langendorf Bakery. Franklin and Slessinger retained television rights, and the contract with Slessinger recognized his ownership of the copyright in the comic strip and gave him the right to incorporate new radio characters into the strip. If all of these terms were occasionally negotiated individually, JWT recognized they could be negotiated collectively.[38]

Air Credits

The biggest change that recognizing the RWG would have for the way agencies did business, besides profit sharing and rights sharing, was in air credit to writers. Yet agencies understood why credits mattered to writers, since they themselves looked at credits when hiring. For example, when the 46-year-old George Faulkner was hired as a freelance writer to write a script for *Cavalcade of America* in 1949, BBD&O sent his bio with a long list of credits to the manager of DuPont's in-house radio advertising department. His credits mattered to BBD&O and to DuPont: these credits convinced both parties that his work would be up to the standards they set for *Cavalcade*. BBD&O highlighted his achievements, boasting to their picky and important client DuPont that Faulkner had worked in JWT's radio department from its formation in 1929 to 1939, when he decided to work freelance with "notably successful results."[39] Before hiring him, BBD&O could have relied on its contacts at JWT to confirm Faulkner's uncredited roles on the *The Rudy Vallée Show* (*The Fleischmann's Yeast Hour*) or the *Chase and Sanborn Hour* in the 1930s, which JWT produced for its clients, and his freelance work on JWT-produced shows, including an early episode of *Kraft Television Theatre* in 1949. But air credits would be especially important to confirm what writers had done as freelance work or where the agency or package producer did not have the network of contacts to confirm the accuracy of an applicant's résumé.

So in the draft RWG collective bargaining agreement, RWG proposed that air credits would be required "to at least one writer on all comedy and dramatic shows (once a week if show broadcast 3 or more times a week) when 50% or more of program" consisted of scripts covered by the agreement. On all other shows, credit would be given "when excellence, etc., of writing warrants it." Finally, the RWG was prepared to do something that the SWG was not: allow individual deals to waive credit or to grant it when the contract would not otherwise allow doing so. The decentralized nature of radio production made individual deals less of a threat to minimum standards than in movies, where all the deals were negotiated in Los Angeles.[40]

Agencies asserted two major obstacles to granting air credit. One was that crediting writers on some serials would destroy the illusion that the stories were real. This was said to be especially problematic on the daytime melodramas targeted toward women homemakers; sponsors often used these programs to reach consumers of household products and soap.[41] This obstacle was eventually overcome when the owners of the company that produced a large number of these "soap operas" agreed to recognize the Guild in October 1948.

The other major obstacle was the attitude of advertising agencies, which had a major impact on what sponsors would agree to. To agree to a minimum basic agreement with writers that would require air credit required a change in the ad agency way of doing business. In the early days of JWT's move into radio advertising, the company's handling of credit was consistent with its general culture of anonymity:

> As you look back at the credits for writing, directing and producing these and other JWT shows another striking thing stands out. The credits look like a roster of JWT Radio Department talent. . . . In those days, JWT wrote all of the material their stars used on the air. The stars might be getting five thousand to seventy-five hundred dollars a week, and the writers and directors might be getting that much a year, and no credits on the air or in the trades. Ours was an anonymous society, and our only accolade, after a particularly fine show and one which "broke new ground," was an orchid, which we would find on our desks the morning after—from John Reber.[42]

Although ad agencies acted in the early negotiations as if unionization of writers would be a major change in their way of working, behind the scenes,

some agency executives recognized that the honest answer to the question
writers posed—What difference would the unionization of freelance radio
writers make?—was "not much." In the short term, all it would really change
would be air credit to the writer, which had not been done on most agency-
produced shows.[43] But it was done sometimes, with no discernible problems.
Air credit to radio writers was negotiated individually on *Meet the Meeks,*
which was produced for JWT by an independent company, and air credit was
given to writers on *Cavalcade.*[44] On the *Red Ryder* show, Ed Wilson said, the
union contract "could be signed and, with the possible exception of giving air
credit to [Paul] Franklin once a week, life would go on just as in the past."[45]

RWG Negotiations Drag On

Although by 1948 JWT and Young & Rubicam were willing to recognize the
union and enter a freelancer collective agreement, a majority of the agencies
were not.[46] Representatives of ten agencies met after their first meeting with
the RWG in the 1948 round of negotiations to decide what to do. According
to Wilson, "as a stalling tactic," "[a]ll but two of the agencies indicated that
they would recommend against negotiating with the Guild unless it was
certified by the NLRB." Wilson, however, said JWT and Young & Rubicam
were the two agencies "having a different point of view."[47] In the end, JWT's
position did not carry the day and the agencies informed the Guild in February that they would refuse to negotiate until the Guild was certified by the
NLRB as the representative of freelance writers working on agency-produced
shows. Wilson feared that requiring the Guild to obtain certification would
give the Guild the excuse to unite its members behind the leadership and
thereby to strengthen the Guild's ability to call a strike, but he speculated that
a strike might not succeed because the shows could get scripts written by
either the regular writers or others.[48] A number of advertisers and agencies
were convinced that "members of the Guild are such individualists that they
could never be united in a successful strike," although some worried that
"many members of the Guild, particularly the more successful writers who
feel they are championing a good cause, are rather fanatical."[49]

It seemed to some that the agencies were all but daring the Guild to call
a strike. The negotiating ploy that most exasperated the RWG was the
agencies' refusal to agree to the definition of *employee* in the RWG-network

contract, refusal to identify any problems with it, and refusal to offer an alternative. As Erik Barnouw explained the results of a fruitless mediation conducted by the Federal Mediation and Conciliation Service, the conciliator "likened this attitude to that of a small girl stamping her foot, and abandoned his efforts at conciliation." The ability of radio writers to strike was tested, at least a bit, beginning in the summer of 1948 when the Guild leadership got its members to vote to authorize a strike.[50]

As spring turned into summer, and summer headed toward fall with the threat that a radio writers' strike would paralyze the new season, the internal memoranda at JWT grew increasingly candid about Ed Wilson's frustration with the intransigence of other members of the agency committee toward recognizing the Guild. All the freelance writers working on JWT shows were paid more than the proposed RWG minimum. He worried that advertisers and agencies "should not appear to be strike-baiters." He worried, too, that agencies and advertisers were not prepared to withstand a strike. Without a reliable cadre of writers, performers, and technical employees who would cross a picket line, shows would go off the air. If an agreement were signed "on threat of strike, we undoubtedly will take just about what the Guild offers," which would be less advantageous than what could be gotten through reasonable negotiation. Looking at the rest of the entertainment industry, Wilson thought unionization was inevitable because AFRA, AFM, the Screen Writers Guild, and the Dramatists Guild had already secured contracts for writers, performers, and musicians working in stage, screen, and some radio jobs. Most important, the network agreement that RWG proposed as a pattern was not bad from the agency or sponsor point of view since it allowed "acquisition of title, character names, etc., of a serial if the network and writer agree that the excess (or some part of it) over the minimum fee is used for that purpose," and, in most cases, "sponsors have already given away more rights than would be required under the network agreement."[51]

Although ad agencies and sponsors had gotten quite upset over the prospect of writers retaining ownership of the rights in their scripts, Wilson thought the RWG-network contract went "no further than to specify certain specifically defined rights which the sponsor agrees not to acquire *in toto* from the writer." As Wilson explained in a document intended to get JWT executives to persuade sponsors and other agencies to moderate their stance, the sponsor could acquire the title of the show and the characters and obtain the rights to reuse a script in a show simply by paying a reuse fee. As for the fear that the writers' retention of subsidiary rights would cause a problem, Wilson admitted it would vary from show to show, but that the problems could be solved through individual negotiations.[52]

Negotiations grew increasingly testy in the fall of 1948. Barnouw wrote to the chair of the advertising-agency negotiating committee that the agencies' "only reason" for refusing to compromise "appears to be that 'our problems and those of the networks are not the same.' In what ways do the problems of employing free-lance writers for such series . . . covered by our network Minimum Basic Agreement . . . differ from the problems of an advertising agency in employing writers for very similar programs? You have never explained this difference. In view of your rejection of our offer, we can only refer the problem to our membership." By which Barnouw meant the Guild would ask the writers to make good on their threat to strike.[53]

The membership did strike. The RWG appealed to the SWG to cajole its members to honor RWG picket lines. The SWG Board passed a resolution supporting the RWG's efforts, noting the importance to all writers of better conditions and supporting the RWG efforts to secure licensing (rather than sale) of material.[54] A mediator was called in, and then the agencies finally turned seriously to negotiating a contract in November after daytime soap opera producers recognized the Guild in late October, which weakened the resolve of the other packagers and then the agencies and sponsors. By December 9, 1948, the agencies, who at the last minute were joined in negotiations by package producers, reached agreement with the Guild on substantially all issues, and in the spring of 1949, the agreement was drafted and circulated to all the sponsors for approval and to the Guild membership for ratification on June 28, 1949.[55] The Minimum Basic Agreement was dated 1949, but it only went into effect in 1951 after prolonged legal skirmishing under the Taft-Hartley Act. As Erik Barnouw later recalled, the "writers' strike of 1948 was no great labor crisis. But in the business affairs of American writers it marked a fateful turning point." The Guild won "precious rights for radio writers: to receive writer credit; to be present at rehearsals; to be paid for repeat uses; to be paid for adaptations to other media; and, in case revisions were needed, to have the first chance to make them." This change gave writers some of the power and respect they deserved, but it came at the cost of writers accepting that they were employees whom the networks, studios, agencies, and sponsors had the right to direct in dictating the form and content of their work. Radio writers, like film writers before them, reluctantly agreed to call themselves employees because only by acquiescing in that title—which connoted a lower status than some wished to occupy and which meant their works belonged to their employer—could they gain the right to unionize and bargain to regain some of the intellectual property rights they lost under the 1909 Copyright Act's work-for-hire rule.[56]

In the end, the agencies and sponsors took a slightly different approach to the vexing issues of air credits and writers' property rights than had been taken in the network agreement with the RWG. Air credit was provided for two writers a week, with the Guild agreeing to create a committee to grant exceptions. Agencies and sponsors had less interest in owning scripts for one-time shows or "unit series" shows—such as *Lux Radio Theatre* or *Cavalcade of America*—other than protection against competitive use of the same script within a reasonable time. But it was on these types of show that writers had the most grievances. So for one-time or unit series shows, the writer retained ownership but agreed not to authorize another radio use of the script for forty-four weeks after the initial broadcast and thirteen weeks against television use. On the other hand, on episodic series and serials where the characters and stories continued over time, the rights depended on whether the writer had the power to negotiate for ownership (some did). The agencies and sponsors agreed with the Guild that the sponsor would generally own the scripts but would license to the writer the use of "extricable material" that the writer wrote (only after fifty-two weeks from the date of broadcast or sixty-five weeks after the series or serial went off the air) and would pay a fee for reuse of scripts and, if the script were sold for use outside of radio and television, the writer would receive compensation. (Extricable material was dialogue elements and plot, but not character names, characterizations, identifying devices, or general story line.) If the writer owned the script, the writer and producer would agree to restrictions on the writer's ability to license others to broadcast the series or serial.[57]

The agencies had handled the entire Radio Writers Guild negotiations badly, at least in the estimation of JWT's lawyer, Wilson. He thought they "lost hours upon hours of costly time" in negotiating and did not gain much from the delay, except possibly that the agencies joined forces with the package producers in the negotiations, which could have been worked out anyway. Most important, the agencies' insistence that freelancers could not unionize was a frivolous legal position, as far as Wilson was concerned, and one should "never rely solely on a technicality in an effort to forestall negotiating with a union."[58]

Though Wilson was dismissive about the agencies' intransigence, it was quite an accomplishment for the Radio Writers Guild to get as much as it did, and it was fortunate for writers that the agreement was negotiated before the full effect of the blacklist of communists was felt in late 1948 and for more than a decade thereafter. While political, income, and status differences within the RWG and SWG membership had always challenged efforts to establish solidarity, the postwar attack on communists, their friends, and anyone imagined to be a communist was catastrophic. When Congress enacted the Taft-Hartley Act in the middle of 1947, one provision in it required all union leaders to sign affidavits that they had no communist affiliation. The agencies used this provision of the law as an excuse to postpone negotiating with the RWG, and RWG leaders, for their part, refused on principle to sign the affidavits. Even as the blacklist gathered steam in 1948, the noncommunist affidavit issue was, as Wilson put it, another "technicality" that the agencies used to forestall negotiations, not an actual concern because sponsors did not yet feel pressure to ensure that the writers on their radio shows (who were mainly anonymous to the public because air credit was not common) were not communists. (As Chapter 6 details, that issue became a big concern for sponsors just a year or two later.) For most of 1947, the RWG could focus rather on how the unionization of writers could transform writers into authors of radio.

Writers as Authors of Radio

When Erik Barnouw reflected later on the achievements of the Writers Guild he had led in these crucial years in the history of American broadcasting, he focused on the work-for-hire rule of copyright. Work for hire, in his view, subverted what he considered the constitutional rights of writers and inventors. At least by unionizing, radio writers got some of the rights of authors: "to receive writer credit; to be present at rehearsals; to be paid for repeat uses; to be paid for adaptations to other media; and, in case revisions were needed, to have the first chance to make them." But what writers could not get, even by unionizing, was control over the final form of their work.[59] Nevertheless, attribution mattered.

Of course, no sooner was the ink dry on the radio agreement than it became clear that television would supplant radio as the mass medium for broadcast storytelling. DuPont, for example, discontinued radio advertising in 1952, moving *Cavalcade of America* from radio to TV, even as its budget for advertising and its in-house advertising staff continued to grow.[60] Storytelling started to vanish from radio, leaving music, news, and sports, which did not require the kind of writers who had made a living in radio, film, and advertising. The Radio Writers Guild disappeared when it merged into the Writers Guild of America in 1954. The advertising agencies found themselves involved with labor negotiations for television, as the next chapter tells. The RWG negotiated a limited form of script ownership rights in its agreement with ad agencies, although it was different from what the Writers Guild negotiated for TV writers in the 1950s. But it was one strand in the twisted skein of efforts of unionized writers to negotiate for attribution as authors and ownership of the intellectual property rights in their work.

4

The Revolution Will Be Televised

If J. Walter Thompson were to give air credit to the producer, director, and story editor of, for example, Lux Video Theatre, and the named people "acquire a following," does not the client have a more valuable property? Or in the alternative, does not the fact that credit will be given enable us to attract personnel of higher caliber?

—JWT executive John Devine (1955)

As World War II wound down, while radio writers fought to unionize and get the author protections screenwriters had won before the war, attention in Hollywood and on Madison Avenue turned toward television. As TV writer Richard Murphy said at a Writers Guild Executive Board meeting in September 1951, "television is a new medium of distribution, and if we miss participation on this medium, we're through forever."[1] The labor and authorship fights in TV overshadowed those in radio, although they were similar, because everyone saw TV as the technology that would revolutionize entertainment. Television presented even more complicated labor law and intellectual property issues for writers, studios, ad agencies, and independent production companies than radio did because TV shows were more expensive to make and involved more creators. TV needed writers who knew how to write scenes that worked on film, and the anonymity norms that ad agencies had transmuted to radio could not easily be imposed on the people who were used to screen credit in movies. Although screenwriters knew their scripts were adapted for radio in the 1930s and 1940s, most didn't see radio writing as a job they wanted or as a medium that would replace movies. But TV was an entirely different matter: TV was eroding movie audiences and therefore eroding film writing jobs, and TV writing had an appeal that radio writing did not.

The fight over ownership and attribution of work was ultimately a fight over the labor market for writers at a time that film production was declining, television production was expanding, and scripted dramas and comedies were moving from radio to TV. The first decade of television—from 1945 to 1955—was pivotal in the history of attribution because Hollywood and ad agency writers were doing not just similar work (writing collaboratively in a highly commercial medium) but *the same work* (writing scripted shows to appear on the screen) for the same entities (sponsors, ad agencies, and the production companies hired by them) when it was entirely unclear whether the contractual rights, labor relations, and attribution practices of Hollywood or Madison Avenue would prevail.

Although television technology existed in the 1930s, and the radio networks were poised to develop their television networks, World War II caused the commercial development of TV to be put on hold. But in 1945, just as soon as the need for war materiél declined, RCA (which established the NBC radio and television networks) and other electronics companies began making television sets as fast as possible, and people began buying them. The demand for something to show on them was there, but the economics of producing content were entirely unsettled because it was unclear how the costs of production could be recouped. America chose not to follow England in charging a license fee for every TV sold, which is how the British Broadcasting Company (BBC) was funded, and instead adopted the advertising-sponsored model that had been used in radio. Although in the beginning ad agencies produced television programs and resisted both the labor relations and attribution practices that writers had secured in film, after about five to eight years, they gave up producing television shows themselves, at first hiring independent producers to do so and then confining themselves to thirty- or sixty-second commercials interspersed in programs that the networks controlled. But while TV writers were employed by ad agencies or packagers hired by agencies, it was not at all clear that writers would win the legal protections they had secured in film or that today's sharp distinction between attributed TV writing and anonymous ad writing would emerge.

The Early Days of TV Work in New York and Hollywood

In the 1930s, the networks quickly adapted for TV the methods they had been using to generate content for radio, and writers found jobs in all types of production. Ad agencies bought time and produced shows for clients to sponsor, in many cases by migrating a popular radio program to a TV format, and so former radio writers became TV writers or people with experience writing film scripts worked freelance for ad agencies or packagers. Network news began with the networks simply hiring industrial film and newsreel production companies to supply film footage to illustrate radio news scripts. So writers with experience in newsreels and industrial films found work. And, of course, many recognized that television was a place where studios could generate profits from their film libraries beyond the lucrative theatrical reissue market that studios had cultivated in the middle 1940s, although the full development of TV as an outlet for old movies took a little while. But still there was a need for more content.[2]

The way ad agencies approached content for television was, as with radio, different from the way entertainment companies did. Hollywood companies saw themselves as content creators and as the corporate owners of all the content they created. Ad agencies, in contrast, saw themselves as working on behalf of clients to produce shows clients owned. To demand attribution of authorship of the shows the agency's staff wrote and produced contravened both long-established anonymity norms and, equally as important, the very notion of a loyal agent.

The power of writers was also limited when the Federal Communications Commission (FCC) decided in late 1948 to stop issuing new licenses for television stations, giving the one hundred existing stations a monopoly. The television freeze lasted for three and a half years and allowed companies with licenses to consolidate their leading position in the industry. The consolidation and monopoly of a few networks weakened the ability of writers to negotiate with some producers or networks for better conditions than the established ones would offer. Some cities had multiple stations—New York and Los Angeles each had seven. Other cities—such as Austin, Little Rock, and Portland, Oregon—had none. The concentration meant writers needed to deal with the industry leaders, who were the ad agencies and their sponsors and the networks, because there would not be the wide array of outlets for, and financial support for, creative work that television theoretically could have offered.[3]

The challenges for writers negotiating the new world of television were increased by the decline in jobs for film writing. Studios made money during the war and immediately after by reissuing old films, which filled screens and generated revenue for studios without offering a penny to writers. The situation for writers worsened in May 1948, when the Supreme Court found antitrust law to prohibit the distribution practices of the five major film studios that controlled the distribution of their films through subsidiary theater chains (Paramount, Loew's, RKO, Warner Brothers, and 20th Century Fox) and the so-called independents (Columbia, Universal, United Artists). The challenged practices had enabled studios to ensure profitable distribution of their bigger-budget films (the A-list films) and their low-budget films (B movies). The studios reacted by drastically reducing production, especially of B movies. Reissues in theaters, declining movie attendance, and the *Paramount* case led to layoffs of film writers, while the FCC moratorium on new television stations stunted the growth of new writing jobs in TV.[4]

TV grew in the same years that film studios had begun shifting from the integrated-factory model of production to the outsourced-production model of today. When studios began financing and distributing independently produced feature films in the 1950s, even the most successful film writers became less likely to be employed for an extended period directly by a studio and to work on a studio lot. Film writers became freelancers like never before, while TV writing offered the longer-term staff writer jobs that studios had once offered. Moreover, in contrast to the blockbuster-movie model, in which expensive independent productions (many filmed away from Los Angeles) offered the possibility of huge payoffs but tied up large portions of studio funding for up to two years of pre- and post-production work, television production offered a use for the Los Angeles back lots and sound stages and the promise of meeting the expenses of studio overhead and improving cash flow.[5]

Writers Guild leaders struggled to figure out what approach to take toward television. Many regarded television as jeopardizing the dominance of screenwriters in the union, screenwriters' livelihood, and the credit and compensation rules that the Guild had fought to establish in the 1942 Minimum Basic Agreement. Moreover, they confronted the advent of TV at a time when the Guild was tearing itself apart over the hunt for communists, which made it difficult to negotiate from a position of strength.[6]

Madison Avenue executives saw television as a major business opportunity, and as an expansion of the radio and magazine format that they knew, and so they began to produce content to fill the TV airwaves in 1946 and 1947.

J. Walter Thompson, for example, had experimented with TV in the 1930s—
preparing and airing a commercial television program in Chicago in 1930 and
a variety show in 1940—but it began regular, weekly, hour-long sponsored
television production in 1946 with *The Hour Glass* for Standard Brands, and a
regular, weekly, hour-long dramatic program in 1947 (*Kraft Television Theatre*).
By 1951, JWT had 254 people working in radio and TV, including forty-seven
writers, many based in Hollywood.[7]

The Writers Guild tried initially to include advertising agency staff writers
who worked on television programs with the group of writers protected
under the collective agreement the Guild was trying to negotiate with the network or the producer, but that strategy failed. In the end, ad agencies did not
adopt for their own staff the labor practices and norms that structured writer
labor relations with studios and networks. They nevertheless agreed to abide
by the collective agreements for their non-staff writers. In various negotiations
in the late 1940s and early 1950s between networks and production companies
and guilds representing actors, directors, and writers working in television, ad
agencies generally participated as observers rather than principals in the negotiation. Once the agreement was finalized, each agency would sign a letter of
adherence for some of the freelance talent it hired when it produced shows.[8]
When the NLRB decided in 1953 that agency employees were not in the unit of
unionized writers who had a right to bargain with agencies and producers, the
SWG's lawyer insisted that it was not a major defeat for the Guild because the
number of actual agency employees working directly on shows as writers was
relatively small. Most writers were freelancers, so as long as the agencies
adhered for its freelancers to whatever agreement was negotiated with the
producer, the union would achieve its major goals, even though it meant
agency writers would not get the residuals, separated rights, and other attribution and ownership rights guaranteed under the MBA.[9]

Yet the Screen Writers Guild leadership remained anxious about how television would affect the job market and working conditions for writers well
into the 1950s. Each new vision of the possibilities of the medium presented
both opportunities for more writers to get work and opportunities for producers to erode minimum standards for which the Guild had fought hard in
the 1930s and 1940s. For example, in 1955, Eric Johnston, head of the Alliance
of Motion Picture and Television Producers (AMPTP), invited SWG President Mary McCall to testify before the FCC, the federal agency that regulated

broadcast TV and radio, as an expert witness on behalf of the motion picture and television industry in connection with the industry's request for twelve UHF channels for "theater television." The Executive Board considered the SWG position on authorization of new TV channels to be so explosive that it scheduled a special meeting devoted entirely to the question whether she should appear before the FCC and, if so, what the Guild's position should be on theater TV. Would theater TV kill the movies? Or would it generate new writer jobs? The Board eventually decided that it needed to study the economic and professional impact of theater television on Guild members before it could go on record "as favoring this new method of distributing entertainment to the public" and, therefore, that McCall should not testify.[10]

In short, writers and the organizations that represented them—the SWG, the RWG, the Dramatists Guild, and the Authors League, as well as the Television Writers Association, an organization formed specifically to represent writers in TV because many writers felt that neither the SWG nor the RWG was up to the task—confronted very unsettling conditions at the time when television began to expand. The choices writers and their unions made in adapting to the new technology and the new business model had longstanding consequences for writers as authors.

How Ad Agencies Produced TV Shows

Television production resembled both radio and movies: some programs were broadcast live (like radio) and some were filmed in advance (like movies). Although live TV based in New York dominated in the late 1940s, by about 1950, filmed television programs proliferated for a variety of reasons, including the growth of an international market for American-made television shows.[11]

Television programming was made by different entities in different ways, and the business changed rapidly in the late 1940s and early 1950s. Some television programming was made by networks, but most of the shows broadcast during prime time were made either by ad agencies for their clients to sponsor or by packagers who contracted with ad agencies on behalf of sponsors. In deciding whether to make the show itself or contract with a packager, labor relations and authorial control were the agency's crucial considerations. Agencies considered the disadvantages of lack of creative control against the advantages of avoiding legal liability for the conditions of work.[12]

Sponsors exercised ultimate authority over any aspect of a television show they wished to control. The kind of creative control that DuPont exercised over the telling of American history in *Cavalcade of America* became relatively standard. The control also extended to who was hired and fired to work on shows, particularly in the red-baiting period that began in late 1947. For example, Young & Rubicam, which produced *The Aldrich Family,* announced in August 1950 that it had cast film star Jean Muir to play the mother in the new TV version of the long-running radio show. Someone complained to General Foods, the show's TV sponsor, that Muir was listed in *Red Channels,* a publication that existed for the purpose of spreading rumors about supposed communists. Young & Rubicam promptly fired Muir, as directed by the "highest echelons" of General Foods. She denied affiliation with some of the organizations, and her actual affiliations and actions— such as signing a cable of congratulations to the Moscow Art Theatre on its fiftieth anniversary because she was a student of the Stanislavski acting method—were hardly subversive, even by the standards of the day. General Foods did not care; it only wished to avoid controversial people. Ad agencies vetted names of actors, writers, and directors, and both in-house producers and package show producers had to run every name past the agency vetters.[13]

An ad agency producing a show hired freelance writers or, less often, used the agency's own staff to write a script. Agencies typically relied on the network to supply the technical people necessary to operate the cameras, lights, and sound equipment. Some agencies (including JWT in 1954) built their own in-house studios to make filmed commercials. By the mid-1950s, JWT had hundreds of people in its New York and Hollywood offices working in writing and producing radio and TV. JWT supervised seventy local live shows in sixty-two markets, and boasted its TV group "actively participates in the production of the program and . . . designs, invents, and builds sets and props especially for the client involved."[14]

In hiring for TV, agencies partly searched for talent as they always had, especially for writers, and also relied on casting directors to sort through the piles of résumés listing credits that writers, actors, and directors had compiled in working in radio, vaudeville, theater, film, and early TV. Résumés listed not only the shows on which the person had worked but also the ad agencies that had produced the show, the network on which the show had aired, and the companies that had sponsored it. The absence of air credits meant that agency personnel offices had to rely on word of mouth to check the accuracy of a résumé. Agencies also looked at an applicant's prior work, including newspaper or magazine advertisements, radio or television programs, or broadcast commercials; it is difficult to know how they decided who had contributed what to the material they reviewed. But the one source of information agencies (or at least JWT) refused to consider was unpublished work, for fear of later being sued for taking an idea and passing it off as their own. When an agency was interested, they might consider a spec script, but would do so only if the writer signed a contract giving the sponsor all rights in the script, the ideas, and the characters.[15]

As TV programs became too expensive and complicated to produce in house, agencies increasingly relied on independent production companies. When production was outsourced, the agency supervised the writing, casting, and filming. The independent producer was usually paid a per-program lump sum, a "package" price, and the sponsor paid that plus the time charges for the network and the agency's standard 15 percent commission.[16] Writers often considered working for an independent producer preferable to working for an advertising agency. As veteran radio writer and RWG president Erik Barnouw explained, a producer is "a specialist in television rather than in advertising," and if the producer had market power and prestige, it could perhaps protect writers "from the more foolish whims of sponsors and their agents." As Jack Warner said in resisting sponsor and agency script review on Warner Bros.'s initial foray into television (the western *Cheyenne*), "They're going to tell *us* how to make pictures?" But most writers had many bosses on a single show. DuPont advertising department employees offered extensive notes to its agency (BBD&O) and to the writers and producers hired by the packager the agency hired to produce *Bat Masterson*. The notes did not just stick to how DuPont and its products were portrayed, but included detailed suggestions about character, dialogue, setting, and plot. Not surprisingly, writers often found the notes process annoying. Rod Serling, creator of the acclaimed show *The Twilight Zone* (1959–1964), said while writing *Noon at Doomsday* (1956) for the *U.S. Steel Hour* that he was in "at least two meetings a day for over a week, taking down notes as to what had to be changed" from the independent producer, the ad agency, the sponsor, and the network. (*Noon at Doomsday* was very loosely based on the story of Emmet Till, a black 14-year-old boy lynched in Mississippi for allegedly flirting with a white woman. Notwithstanding extensive notes from the agency, sponsor, and network, and the complete absence in the script of any reference to race, the episode caused a firestorm of controversy when it aired in 1956.)[17]

The Unionization of TV Writers

Guild leaders began discussing television in late 1938, recognizing that it presented employment opportunities for writers but also that it was a risk to future writing jobs since screenwriters' film scripts would be reused on TV.[18] Although the Guild recognized it would be some years before TV would become widespread enough to have a serious impact on writers, the Guild saw an immediate threat in radio, where film scripts would sometimes be reused as radio stories without either compensation or credit to the writer.[19] But because the United States entered World War II just as the Guild finally secured its first collective bargaining agreement with the studios, and the commercial exploitation of TV technology was put on hold during the war, the issue of compensation for reuse of writers' work on radio or in any other format also seems to have been put on hold for the duration.

In the spring and summer of 1945, the Executive Board of the Writers Guild turned its attention to television in a serious way for the first time. It was, one Board member said, terra incognita—unknown territory. The Executive Board asked the most basic questions of its lawyer and a committee set up to explore TV: Did the Guild need to amend its constitution and bylaws to seek representation of TV writers? (No, said lawyer Morris Cohn.) How many writers were there, or would there be, in TV? (No one knew.) Would TV writers outvote film writers in membership meetings? (Maybe. Indeed, by 1951, over half of the people newly applying for Guild membership were writing for television at least some of the time.) And enforcing minimum salaries was going to be a challenge; it would require the SWG to quickly organize writers and pressure TV producers to curtail the emerging practice of paying less than the Guild minimum. The SWG Board responded to member queries about whether they could write on speculation (for free), which was prohibited in film, saying, "while the Guild has not yet established jurisdiction over the field of television, it would advise the writer against writing to order on speculation."[20]

As the number of screenwriters working in television grew and questions of this sort began to mount, the Board appointed a committee of members to consider whether the Guild wanted to include television within its jurisdiction and, if so, how to "make that jurisdiction stick." It was a challenge to convince writers working in TV that the SWG was better able to protect their interests than individual negotiations would be and that the SWG was a more effective union than the Radio Writers Guild, the Dramatists Guild, and the Authors League, all of which sought to represent TV writers.[21] Because some TV was live and some was filmed, the Radio Writers Guild and the Screen Writers Guild both saw protecting television writers as an extension of their mission, and for a few years, writers working on live television broadcasts were represented separately from writers working on filmed TV programs. Indeed, it took the SWG a little while to realize that its members even had an interest in representing writers working on live TV, and initially they concluded it mattered only because some shows, such as Red Skelton's, were both live and filmed. An additional complication was geography. The Authors League, the Dramatists Guild, and the Radio Writers Guild were based primarily in New York where book publishing, theater, and radio dominated, and they had support among New York TV writers. While the SWG had strength among TV writers in Hollywood, it was not obvious until the 1950s that TV production would be centered there. In New York and Chicago, the average weekly salaries for TV writers were considerably lower than the MBA minimum weekly salary in film writing.[22]

Although SWG leaders constantly said it was important to move quickly to resolve the question of who would represent TV writers, between 1945 and 1950, endless meetings between the SWG, RWG, Dramatists Guild, and various committees of television writers affiliated with the Authors League did not produce agreement over the matter. Controversy simmered over which organization would bear the organizing expense and how a television writers' guild would be governed.[23] In 1949, the various Guilds and the Authors League established a National Television Committee, which began negotiations with the networks in New York in September 1950. The negotiating committee consisted of two SWG writers, two RWG writers, two Dramatists Guild writers, and one representative each from the Authors Guild and the Television Writers Group. Eventually, on July 13, 1951 at a New York meeting of all the Guilds and groups with claims over writers in TV, the jurisdictional claim of the RWG was rejected in a contentious vote; an eastern and a western branch of the National Television Committee were established with jurisdiction over all writers in TV. The situation was further complicated by the formation the next year (1952) of the Television Writers Association, which claimed jurisdiction over all television writers. It was necessary to negotiate over writers working for networks, ad agencies, studios, and independent television producers, and also for staff writers on salary and freelance writers who worked week to week. At the same time as the struggles over television writers were going on, the SWG was negotiating for a new MBA for writers in film, first to replace the MBA that expired in 1949 and then to replace the MBA that expired in 1952.[24]

The jurisdictional struggle among the guilds that delayed resolution of writer representation in television was further complicated by the blacklist and by the Taft-Hartley Act's new requirement that union leaders sign affidavits of noncommunist affiliation. Some SWG leaders were reluctant to sign as a matter of principle, even after the purge of the current, former, alleged, and friends of communists in November 1947, and the RWG and Authors League leadership flatly refused to sign (in 1950, the Authors League finally relented). Some TV writers were, as Miranda Banks notes, concerned about joining an organization that had turned on its own members in participating in the blacklist. Moreover, under the Taft-Hartley Act, even after workers voted for a union as their bargaining representative, a separate election had to be held on whether the union could negotiate for a union security provision in a contract. (A union security provision is one that requires each employee the union represents to either join the union or pay a fee to the union for the worker's share of the cost of contract negotiation and administration services that the union is required to provide as the employee's recognized exclusive representative.) The SWG won that election overwhelmingly in the early autumn of 1950, but the process consumed time and resources.[25]

The fight over jurisdiction to represent TV writers dragged on for years, divided on the lines of geography, industry, and ideology. The SWG, which had its base of strength in Hollywood, was terribly anxious that the RWG— which was based largely in New York—would gain too much control over television in the west and would undermine the strength of the SWG. It also feared too much control by the New York–based Authors League, both for geographic reasons and because SWG leaders were convinced that the

Authors League was inept, indecisive, and financially weak. The SWG had better-paid members and therefore a larger financial base on which to collect dues, and it was experienced with the business of film production. And, of course, each group wanted control over member dues, and the SWG worried that its dues structure (one percent of earnings), which was higher than what the RWG or Authors League charged, would put it at a disadvantage with its members. Moreover, no one wanted writers to have to pay dues to multiple organizations. At a meeting among Authors League, SWG, and RWG people in New York in June 1953, it became apparent that the Authors League and the Dramatists Guild also "have had their hands as full of television problems as the Screen Writers Guild over the past year or so and will be as glad as we to settle the matter on a practical equitable basis," but that the SWG felt it was threatened more than they were by the advent of television because of the "interchange of film being used for theaters and television."[26]

Whatever the SWG's original reservations about admitting TV writers to membership had originally been, by 1951, they were overcome, and the Executive Board established criteria for membership, initially only for writers working on filmed TV programs (a few years later, with the reorganization of the guilds to create one Guild for all film and TV writers, the rules applied to all writers). One could become an associate member by having written three produced scripts or being employed in the TV film field. Active membership required either having produced three one-hour scripts, six half-hour scripts, or twelve quarter-hour scripts, or an aggregate of fifty-two weeks' employment. Yet debate continued through 1952 about whether the TV membership rules were laxer or stricter than the membership requirements for film writers.[27]

The SWG Executive Board also extended the other rights and responsibilities of Guild membership to TV writers in 1951. It opened the script registry to TV scripts (so that TV writers, like film writers, could register their scripts as protection against idea theft) and created "working rules" for TV writers just as it had for movie writers. As with working rules for movies, writers were required to file a copy of their employment contract with the Guild, to not work below the Guild minimums, to insist on screen credit, to reserve all separated rights other than those for release in the United States, Canada, Hawaii, and the Philippines (Hawaii and the Philippines were essentially US colonies at the time). But it would not be easy to enforce these requirements.

Television stations needed to be monitored constantly to find out who was writing the material that aired. Television writers did not work just in New York and Los Angeles, but also in smaller cities that did not have a Guild presence. Moreover, some agents did not understand the complex jurisdictional claims over TV writers.[28]

In some respects, the negotiations over TV writers echoed the recently concluded negotiations over radio writers. The freelance versus staff writer division remained challenging, and writers wrangled with the employers over the definition of employee covered in the agreement; the employers wanted to limit the coverage of the agreements to exclude as many freelancers as possible. (Eventually, the employers gave up this idea, just as they had with radio.) Of much greater significance was the writers' insistence on retaining ownership of scripts, or joint ownership between the writer and the producer, and that the only rights transferred would be for use of a script on television and that all other rights (for motion picture, dramatic, radio, book publication, and other commercial exploitation) would be reserved to the writer. Writers also insisted that compensation be in the form of a minimum advance against a royalty of between 5 and 8 percent of gross receipts. The producers refused to consider any compensation scheme giving the writers a percentage of the gross.[29]

Notwithstanding the divisions among writers, the National Television Committee negotiations with the networks went well for the writers. In part, this success was because there was a shortage of material for television in the summer of 1951 and in part, because the television networks were not as unified a group as the movie studios were. Writers reported that the networks were prepared to agree to a much shorter period of exclusivity for TV than they had for radio in the RWG contract. But there were difficult issues, especially the writers who would be covered by the proposed MBA, the payment for reuse of a writer's material using characters the network owned, and subsidiary (separated) rights.[30]

Between 1948 and about 1953, some branch of some guild of writers was constantly in negotiations over some aspect of the industry. Everyone knew aspects of any agreement with studios, independents, and networks would be a pattern for others, and that made it risky for anyone to agree to any provision that might create a precedent for another negotiation. The timing of the multiple negotiations was tricky. In January 1952, the RWG asked the Authors

League Council to instruct the SWG to postpone the SWG TV negotiations until after the RWG had concluded the New York network negotiations. The SWG objected on the grounds that the SWG anticipated having to negotiate with independent film producers in early 1952 "and it is imperative that we establish the royalty principle with the independent TV producers before it becomes necessary to open negotiations with either the Independent Film Producers or the Majors." As an alternative, the SWG invited representatives from the RWG to sit in on the television negotiations then being conducted by the Television Negotiating Committee.[31]

In the end, writers thought it necessary to have a national union with jurisdiction over film and television writing for a variety of good reasons. Writers moved back and forth from the west to the east, and between film, TV, books, and theater, and it was necessary to work together to solve common problems and prevent one form of distribution from undercutting the other.[32] After a long struggle, in 1954, the various groups representing writers in all the broadcast and film media merged into a single organization. The Writers Guild of America (which is actually two separate but affiliated unions, the WGA East and WGA West), took over the negotiation and enforcement of the various collective bargaining agreements that had been negotiated with the networks, studios, independent production companies, and other entities making film and TV.[33] And in the 1950s the writers—after prolonged negotiations, a strike, and a second threatened strike—eventually secured compensation for TV writers, including separated rights for writers working in television and revenue percentages for writers who wrote films that were later shown on television.[34]

An Ad Writers Guild?

Of all the divides among writers—between those working in the east or the west; in radio, TV, and film; for ad agencies, packagers, studios, or networks; and between leftists, centrists, and anticommunists—none remained as significant beyond the 1950s as the divide between agency staff and Hollywood freelancers. All of these divisions made it hard for writers in one sector to unite with others to pursue their common interests in pay, credit, and creative control, but all eventually saw their common interest. The occupational and legal divide between Hollywood film and TV writers and ad agency staff was never bridged. The SWG leaders knew, of course, that some ad agency staff and freelancers were writing TV shows, but the SWG made only the most half-hearted efforts to form common cause with them.

As ad agency staff looked at the gains writers employed on agency-produced TV and radio shows made through collective bargaining, some began to wonder whether they should unionize. A group formed the Advertising Guild as a branch of Local 20 of the United Office and Professional Workers (CIO), a white-collar employees' organization based in New York City. But the Advertising Guild described itself as a professional association, not a union. In appeals to prospective members, the Advertising Guild identified postwar layoffs of advertising agency staff as a major issue. The Advertising Guild pointed out to copywriters that Young & Rubicam had laid off ninety-one staff in a year, yet "handles tens of millions more billing than before the war." A leaflet appealing for new members listed a seven-point program: "(1) cost of living increases for all advertising people; (2) equal pay for equal work; no discrimination against veterans; (3) job security to protect employees against unjust layoffs; (4) ample severance pay, based upon length of service; (5) a 35-hour week, with overtime to start after 35 hours; (6) longer vacations to make up for the strain of advertising; (7) promotion opportunities for all qualified employees."[35]

The Advertising Guild appealed to the Screen Writers Guild's Executive Board in Hollywood for support. The SWG leadership debated whether to encourage its members to actively participate in the Advertising Guild's organizing campaign, but ultimately, it just wrote a letter of support to the Advertising Guild explaining how union organization benefits writers. The SWG Board was not keen to be seen as supporting the efforts of the Advertising Guild to organize ad agency writers.[36] Writers found it easier to see their common interests when they worked for different entertainment companies.

Madison Avenue in Conflict with Hollywood

The ad agencies recognized that the negotiations over various forms of TV (live, filmed, packaged by a producer, or made by a network) would, as JWT's lawyer Edward Wilson said, "affect the whole future of television,"[37] and also the nature of the agencies' relationships with their clients. As the negotiations over television writers commenced in earnest in 1950, with the agencies in the role of observer rather than of principal, the question arose whether writers would be treated as employees of the agency or the sponsor. Writers who were not salaried employees of the agency had been treated as employees of the sponsor in part so that the sponsor would own the intellectual property rights in their work. But it was more than just a matter of intellectual property. Agencies had worked hard to establish themselves as "a professional organization" and, therefore, "an extension of the client's own organization." "The relationship of mutual confidence which must exist between agency and client is a delicate one and might easily be upset should we, in any area of our relationship with the client, seemingly become a seller of 'goods.'" If the agency became akin to a "packager of radio and television shows," it could compromise the agency's "interest in selecting the best possible media for a client's advertising," with greater responsibility for the content but without the kind of artistic independence independent production companies enjoyed. And this practice might spread to other areas of advertising beyond just radio and TV.[38]

Television challenged the advertising agencies' way of managing employees. As the American Association of Advertising Agencies (AAAA) watched the negotiations with the Writers Guild in 1952 over ownership of television scripts, the AAAA canvassed its members about their practices with respect to writers. This was sensitive information because agencies competed with each other to get the best writers. JWT reported that they hired writers mainly as employees but sometimes as independent contractors for weekly series dramas and daytime serials. JWT did not use written contracts with them, instead relying on "the principles governing employer-employee relationships" to attain the rights to use the stories writers developed, with the understanding that writers could not use scripts on other programs.[39] And in many cases, the writer retained the rights in the scripts, licensing only TV rights, with payments to the writer for reuse, and with rights reverting to the writer after a period of time.[40]

One aspect of employment relations from the studio system did not migrate to ad agencies—the hated provision in every contract giving the studio the option to renew the contract for successive periods over and over again. These long-term contracts were used primarily to tie star actors to studios, but they were occasionally used for writers, too. Some ad agency executives with experience working in Hollywood thought that such option provisions would be a good way of allowing agencies to retain talented young writers without having to match salary offers when another agency tried to recruit talent away. Although agencies competed with each other to attract and retain the best writers and artists, the practice of tying a worker to an agency never caught on. William Howard of JWT's Detroit office wrote to Jack Devine, head of the JWT radio and TV department in New York, asking for Devine's and Ed Wilson's legal opinion about a contract another Detroit agency had with twenty-three trainees in its office. Like the standard studio contract of the era, it gave the trainees six months' employment at a stated monthly salary and gave the agency an option to renew it for five additional six-month periods at increasing salary. Howard was attracted to the contract because he thought some of the trainees were quite able and he might want to hire them. Wilson wrote that the contract was "legal all right, but not [the] right philosophy." And Devine wrote back to Howard, "From a practical point of view, an employee who remains with a company only because legally bound to remain probably will not be a very good member of the team." But he added "one word of caution. Before we hire any young man who has been employed under a contract such as this, we must be sure that he is completely free from his contractual obligation. We must not be in a position where it could be charged that we induced such person to breach his contract of employment."[41]

Screen Credit for Commercials?

As shown in Chapter 2, ad agencies, especially JWT, believed the advertisement should never call attention to itself as an art form distinct from the its role in selling the product advertised.[42] The Writers and Directors Guilds had negotiated for screen credits in TV, and the agencies had agreed in negotiation with the Radio Writers Guild in 1949 to give air credits to freelance writers. In the summer and fall of 1955, JWT began to re-evaluate its position on credits for agency staff. Networks and packagers had begun to use star directors and writers to draw audiences.[43] As JWT's radio and TV department head Devine acknowledged in one of many interoffice memoranda on the topic of air credits, the JWT program *Screen Directors' Playhouse* credited directors and used celebrity directors to draw an audience. Devine thought it unlikely that giving screen credit to JWT people would detract from the identification of the advertiser because a "great many air credits are given on *Ford Theatre,* for example, and yet the total sponsor identification is not affected appreciably, if at all." And, Devine mused, if JWT credited the producer, director, and story editor of, for example, *Lux Video Theatre,* and the named people " 'acquire a following,' does not the client have a more valuable property? Or in the alternative, does not the fact that credit will be given enable us to attract personnel of higher caliber?" Devine acknowledged that giving air credit could drive up costs by making credited talent more recognizable to audiences, which "might increase the opportunities offered to such a person elsewhere." But Devine pointed out that many JWT producers and writers already "are known to the people in the television business." Devine acknowledged that it would be difficult to draw a line between credited and uncredited people. "To date, the Director, and, in at least one case, the story editor, have not pressed fully for air credit only because they recognized the Thompson attitude against air credit for *any Thompson* employee. Once any Thompson employee receives air credit, these people will be unable to see any logic in excluding them," which "could have a disruptive effect on our efforts." Ultimately, Devine concluded that as air credit seemed to be gaining in importance in TV, it might be necessary to give credit to attract and retain top talent. But decisions on whether to credit talent would require "client approval of course."

Devine acknowledged the possibility that there is "inconsistency between the giving of credit to Thompson employees and our fundamental philosophy that the end purpose of our activities should be the promotion of the client's goods and services and not per se the promotion of the J. Walter Thompson Company." To this notion, the memo said credit to the writer would not detract from the promotion of the client's product if "the persons so credited are directly identified with the sponsor." Devine suggested a credit reading

FOR LEVER BROTHERS COMPANY

Executive Producer:	Stanley Quinn
Producer:	H. Calvin Kuhl
Director:	Buzz Kulik
Story Editor:	Dick McDonogh

In essence, the memo proposed that the agency remain invisible to the public even as the employees got credit.

Devine's arguments were persuasive, and in October 1955, Howard Kohl sent a memo to the heads of various departments saying that "Mr. Resor has approved a change in our point of view regarding air credits for Company employees on JWT produced shows." Credit could be given to the Executive Editor, the Executive Producer, the Producer, the Director, the Editor (story editors) and even, on occasion, the "Adapter" (the writer who adapted a novel, short story, or movie script for TV). Kohl's memo also recognized "by adding these names we will automatically have to give credit to certain technical men employed by the networks." And, thus, JWT staff writers got credit on some shows alongside freelance directors and others on JWT shows. Some of those who were proposed for credit—such as George Roy Hill, who worked as a director on a few JWT shows including *Lux Video Theatre* and *Kraft Television Theatre* (and who later directed *Butch Cassidy and the Sundance Kid* (1969) among other movies)—received Hollywood credit even as they worked for an advertising agency.[44]

Apart from the policy arguments, it was also a matter of the union practices. The Writers' and Directors' Guilds both had contracts with the Alliance of Television Film Producers requiring television air credits. The 1954 agreement with the networks for freelance directors required a director's credit to appear immediately before or after the most prominent credit to the producer, the writer, the star, the title of the program, or the entertainment portion of the program. Even after advertising agencies had largely gotten out of the business of producing entire shows, still the issue of credit was one the directors cared about. In November 1960, after the Directors Guild negotiated a new provision for television credits, the Alliance negotiated with the American Association of Advertising Agencies for "a troublesome new provision for directors' credits," which required that the director be credited "either before the beginning or the first credit following the end, of the picture, with no commercials or other material intervening," which problem was "complicated by the fact that the writer's credit must be immediately adjacent to the director's credit."[45]

The centralization of writing for filmed television programs in Los Angeles helped writers assert claims to credit in TV. The credit system was well established in Los Angeles and only required getting studios and packagers, and then agencies, to adhere to the credit norms. Even before TV writers were organized and the inter-Guild squabbles over jurisdiction were resolved, the SWG had begun handling a few arbitrations over TV screen credit. Between November 1951 and November 1952, the Guild's Credits Committee oversaw eighty-two arbitrations, sixty-one of which were from the major studios (including four for TV), and twenty-one from independent production companies (including one for TV).[46] Although an early draft of a National Television Committee–proposed contract for freelance writers in TV did not cover air credits, the Executive Board of the SWG suggested that a provision be added requiring that writers get the same type of air credit given to the producer or director.[47]

Differences in the norms of television writing between west and east complicated efforts to administer the credit structure. During the live television negotiations in February 1955, the Writers Guild East said they felt the West's "credit structure is unnecessary because of practices in the East—one man usually does the whole show," and where a writer rewrites, "he usually rewrites it all." So credit arbitrations in TV seemed unduly cumbersome to them.[48]

Advertising agencies were only in the business of producing entire television programs in the earliest days of television and, by the mid-1950s, had largely gotten out of making shows and confined themselves to producing commercials. As with magazines, ad agencies made the ads and networks interspersed them in what was known as the "entertainment" portion of the schedule. Pat Weaver of NBC, who had worked for the Young & Rubicam ad agency before becoming the vice president of NBC in 1949 and its president in 1953, believed that the magazine format would diversify and improve the quality of the content of TV, attract more and smaller advertisers, and make TV less suspect as a medium by making it more like magazines and movies. The gains in quality didn't materialize; when no one sponsor controlled the whole show, no one felt quite as responsible for content. But it did end the practice of crediting agency staff.[49]

As the magazine format gained traction, agencies and networks negotiating with the guilds representing television talent began to draw a distinction between credits for contributions to the entertainment portion of a program and credit for the commercials. The actors' collective agreement provided for screen credits for "performers who speak more than 5 lines" but "only for appearances in the entertainment portion of the program." Following that pattern, writers got credits only when they wrote the entertainment portion.[50] The SWG Executive Board and TV Committee decided that writers of

TV commercials were eligible for associate Guild membership because they did "creative writing and characterization" and also because it was better to have them as Guild members than to have them join NABET, which was organizing TV employees.[51]

When the "magazine format" for TV took hold in the late 1950s, it ended the possibility that a practical merger would occur between the work of writing commercials and the work of writing shows. And thus it ended the hopes of ad agency staff writers that they would become the authors of their work. Without screen credit and without the right to be paid for reuse of their work—the two crucial rights of film and TV writers—ad agency writers became the forerunner of today's videogame writers, web designers, and many other freelance creative workers. They were paid a good salary and they often had good jobs, but they were writers only, not authors. Some people continued to work in both industries, and they do today. But when they worked as Hollywood writers, they had the contractual protections and expectations to have some of the rights of authorship. When they worked for Madison Avenue, they had—and expected to have—none, except where they negotiated them individually.

The Writer-Producer and Television Writers' Room

With the division between advertising and film and TV writing solidified by division between the entertainment portion and the advertising portion of a TV broadcast, the struggle of Hollywood writers to secure their rights as authors did not end; it just changed. And one of the major changes they confronted is one that remains significant today: how could writers secure control over what happened to their scripts? To gain that control, one needed to become a producer or director as well as a writer. That was rare enough in the movies during the studio era, but it was possible in the much less hierarchical world of television production. However, the idea that writers would work simultaneously as writers and as producers presented a number of challenges for the Guild, even as most writers celebrated the possibility that television could be controlled by writers—a writers' medium—in a way that movies seldom were.[52]

The organization of television writing, in which a senior writer functions as a producer who supervises a writing staff, emerged early in the history of the medium. Today, this labor and creative structure is known as the "writers' room," referring to a conference room in which all the writers on a show sit around a table to develop plots, settings, characters, and dialogue and to critique drafts. But even before the institutionalization of the writers' room as a place and as a part of production culture, writer-producers hired and supervised other writers in developing shows. And that structure raised complex questions for the Writers Guild in considering whether supervisors were still functioning as writers, as labor, and also how to treat the most junior writers who gained entry to the business by working in a sort of apprentice role.

In July 1953, the Guild's Executive Board encountered an early version of the contemporary writers' room. Sam Perrin, a writer on *The Jack Benny Program,* wrote to the Guild to inquire how credit should be handled for writers working on another show Perrin had just gotten a deal to create. Perrin claimed to have transferred to TV the radio technique of a group of writers collaborating on a script. He explained that he had hired three writers to collaborate with him on writing scripts, that it was impossible to know who had contributed what, and that he himself did not want screen credit, as he had a deal with CBS and they did not want his name to appear on any shows other than the ones he wrote for them.[53]

The Executive Board was alarmed by the phenomena of group writing and unattributed writing by a writer-producer like Perrin, seeing in both a threat to "a system built up over many years" and also a pressing need to adapt to "the new system in TV of head writers and collaborators." Schedule A precluded credit to more than two writers without arbitration, and arbitration was impossible without a record of which writer had contributed what. Moreover, Perrin's refusal of credit "is contrary to our whole philosophy on credit," but as he was acting as a producer, any claim he might make to credit was subject to automatic arbitration and he would have to prove that he contributed more than 50 percent. The transfer of "loose radio techniques" to television, some Guild Board members felt, would jeopardize the credit system for motion pictures. Ultimately, the Board decided to refer the matter to the Motion Picture and Television Credits Committee for study and recommendation. A month later, the Credits Committee decided, and the Board agreed, that automatic arbitration was infeasible and that waivers should be granted to allow credit to more than two writers where they collaborated, so long as all participants agreed in writing in advance. The Guild's working rules were amended to require writers performing duties as production executives to tell the Guild and all other writers in writing in advance if they intended to claim writing credit. In January 1955, the Board adopted an amendment to this rule to punish writer-producers who violated the notice rule by fining them an amount equal to "any and all rerun payments, whether for television or theatrical release," and recurrent violations would be punished in addition to a fine not to exceed $1,000.[54]

Writers were excited by the prospect of gaining control over their work by becoming producers. As Miranda Banks explained, writer-producers in early TV—like Jess Oppenheimer *(I Love Lucy)*, Jack Webb *(Dragnet)*, David Dotort *(Bonanza)*, and Gertrude Berg *(The Goldbergs, The Gertrude Berg Show)*— set an example for screenwriters about gaining "new forms of power through dual, even triple roles," because in the content-heavy medium of television "writer-producers soon became not just necessary but also valued."[55] Jess Oppenheimer—whom Lucille Ball credited as "the brains behind" *I Love Lucy*—is still subject to debate because *Lucy* writers did not receive residuals for the show, though Oppenheimer's contract with CBS made him a 20 percent owner of it and he said he gave 5 percent to the writers Madelyn Pugh Davis and Bob Carroll, Jr.[56] It was difficult to tell when writer-producers were still working as writers and when their collaborative work arrangements deprived staff writers of the credit and compensation they deserved. The Guild Executive Board got many requests from members who had become producers to approve exceptions from the usual rules for screen credit, and the Board was skeptical about them.

For example, George Oppenheimer got a deal in 1953 to deliver twenty-six scripts for a Topper series for producer John Lovton. Oppenheimer proposed to hire what he called "apprentice writers" to write scripts based on plot ideas and a formula that Oppenheimer would provide to each writer. He said he would pay $200 for each three- to four-page treatment, but he did not want to do credit arbitrations "because if the writer were to win he would have to pay the writer repayment percentages" which he insisted were "impossible" under his deal with Lovton. When the Guild told Oppenheimer that he could protect himself against losing credit arbitrations simply by outlining the plot for each script in writing before assigning the writer to insert the shot sequences, Oppenheimer insisted that it would be too time-consuming and he wanted to just dictate the plot to the writer rather than to a secretary to type up and give to the writer. The Executive Board and the MBA Enforcement Committee were unimpressed with Oppenheimer's arguments, finding that he wanted to create a "disastrous precedent" for writers. Rather, they voted that "Anybody who has the power to hire and fire, even though it is limited, shall for purpose of contract enforcement be considered a production executive who must therefore abide by the MBA" and that "the contribution of a production executive must be in writing to be considered for credit."[57]

Just a year before, another variation on the conflict between a writer-producer and his staff arose involving a staff writer described as a "secretary." Stanley Meyers, producer of *Dragnet*, asked SWG president Mary McCall what he would have to pay his "secretary" (who the Guild later learned was Kitty Buhler, an associate member of the SWG) for writing on the show. Although the producer insisted that the writing was quite minimal—simply inserting "motion picture directions" into old radio scripts so that the old scripts could be reused to film TV episodes—the SWG insisted that adapting scripts for TV was the work of a writer and that because the show cost about $25,000 per episode to make, the $250 weekly minimum pay scale must be followed.[58]

By early 1955, collaboration between lead writers and writing staffs was becoming more and more common in TV. Douglas Hayes, a writer-producer on *Rin-Tin-Tin*, came to meet the Guild Executive Board because he had "heard there was some dissatisfaction" among writers with whom he worked. He said he did not have an official title but started by giving a freelance writer "the story," the freelancer wrote the first draft, and Hayes then revised so that "the stories follow a pattern and are uniform." Some episodes were credited to Hayes alone, others to the other writer, and most were split. The Executive Board, and its lawyer Gordon Stulberg, were concerned that this form of collaboration would destroy minimums and the Guild would end up with jurisdiction over the teleplay writer only but not with freelancers staffing series. The Board decided that, "at the risk of wrecking negotiations" they should seek to reopen negotiations with the studios to develop a formula to stop this practice.[59]

Throughout the history of television, writers became producers while still working as writers and writer-producers collaborated with other writers. Over the years, the WGA negotiated for better protection for TV writers in terms of credit and compensation, and then worked hard—and occasionally struck—to extend those rights to the new versions of TV that came along. That is the story told in Chapter 5. But by the mid-1950s, the fundamental rule was clear: writers of the entertainment portion of TV were entitled to screen credit and compensation turning on it, while the writers of the advertising portion were not. Nothing in the evolution of scripted screen entertainment has changed that practice.

5

---·◆·◆·◆---

The Writer's Share

Our industry is one of the few in the world where talents and skills of
its workers, preserved on strips of celluloid, can be used repeatedly
without any remuneration to the possessors of those talents and
skills.

—Lester Cole, "The Writer's Share" (1947)

Television writers joined the Writers Guild because they decided that
unionization would better protect their claims as authors than would
adherence to the professional norms that prevailed in advertising agencies. As
the last two chapters explained, the Guild's first successes in radio and then
TV were to enforce its rules about minimum payment and on-air credit. But
the Guild's other major fight—and it is one that has been waged over and over
again every time technology changed the way that screen entertainment was
distributed—was one about payment for reuse of the writers' work. As Hollywood moved steadily away from the ad agency model of semipermanent
salaried staff and ever more toward the freelance model of intermittent work
punctuated by periods of unemployment, writers realized that their economic security depended on being paid for later uses of their work. The
system of residuals writers developed (that actors and directors emulated) has
been crucial. As entertainment lawyer Jonathan Handel wrote, "the industry
needs residuals because talent—especially actors, writers, and TV directors—
survive on them between gigs. In fact, residuals make up on average about
one-third of the typical SAG actor's income. Without these payments, the
industry's professional talent base would evaporate." This chapter explains
how the Writers Guild developed that system. It also points out that the
Guild's early proposals for compensation for reuse would have avoided
some of the problems that exist in the current system. In particular, today's

mind-bogglingly complex and expensive-to-administer system was the Guild's fallback position when the studios resisted a much simpler system—which today is advocated as the desirable reform—of paying talent a percentage of *all* of a project's gross revenue from all platforms. That is, instead of paying different percentages for different types of reuse (and reuse is becoming a meaningless concept in the world of streaming), talent would get a percentage of all revenue from all sources of income.[1]

In August 1947, eminent screenwriter Ring Lardner, Jr. published an article in *The Screen Writer,* the magazine of the Screen Writers Guild, with the title "One Percent of the Gross—An Economic Primer of Screen Writing." Lardner observed that writers received as payment about one percent of the box office revenue from films. Lardner asked: "Does it seem preposterous to argue that we actually provide as much as, say, two percent of what the movie goer gets for his money?"[2] The question was rhetorical; Lardner argued that Hollywood writers were both underpaid and underappreciated for their contributions to films. Writers had made the complaint from the earliest days of the film business, but the explosive growth of radio in the 1930s and 1940s, the transformation of the film business immediately after World War II, and changes in the print industries made the complaint even more apt than before.

The disputes over copyright, credit, and profit sharing that were at the core of the screenwriters' successful drive for unionization in the 1930s resurfaced in the late 1940s as writers prepared to negotiate their second MBA with the movie studios and their first agreement covering television. Lardner's article in *The Screen Writer* was part of a concerted nationwide effort by writers to change the terms of the debate over the financial and creative share that writers would have in all media. They did not achieve nearly all the financial gains they sought, and they did not succeed in convincing the public that film and television writers are the authors of the stories viewers see on the screen. But they did establish a system of profit sharing (residuals) and writer retention of rights to write sequels or novels or stage plays based on their movie scripts (separated rights). Residuals transformed the way that writers were paid, and separated rights gave film and TV writers some control over future uses of their work. Disputes over sharing the revenue generated by copyrights in film and television have been the source of labor unrest in Hollywood from the early 1930s through the long 2007–2008 writers' strike. Today, the two most significant functions of the WGA involve the administration of two forms of contractually negotiated quasi-intellectual property rights that are unique to Hollywood: screen credit and residuals.

Residuals were and remain a unique and interesting form of compensation since the Writers Guild inaugurated them in the early 1950s. They resemble a copyright royalty, in the sense that a residual is a payment for certain reuses of copyrighted material. But they are not quite like copyright royalties in that the writer does not own the copyright, the writer is entitled to a residual only if he received screen credit, and the right to receive a residual applies only to reuse of the material (as when a theatrical movie is shown on TV or streamed over the internet), not to the initial use (as when the movie runs in US or international theaters) or to every use (as in movie previews). But one might think of residuals as a kind of intellectual property—the right to be paid for some uses of intellectual property that the worker participated in creating. And, in that sense, they are the only form of intellectual property that workers acting through their labor union invented and perpetuated. Writers had to strike to persuade producers to accept residuals. They have struck several times in the sixty years since to protect them as distribution through new technologies (cable television, home video, and the internet) threatened to undermine the system.[3]

The Writers Guild was crucial in overcoming the considerable collective action and administrative challenges in creating this novel form of intellectual property and deferred compensation. Quite simply, had writers not unionized, they would probably be paid a salary, an hourly wage, or a flat fee for their services just as all other employed intellectual property creators are today, in sectors such as video game and website design, computer programming, and advertising. Writers with market power, or those working on indie projects where the producer could not pay a reasonable salary, would negotiate individually for a share in the ownership and profits of the project, and some writers do that today. But residuals are a collectively bargained benefit to which all credited writers are entitled, regardless of their bargaining power, the amount of their salary, or the script fee paid for their work. In a sense, residuals make every credited writer like a partial owner who shares in the financial success of a movie or TV show that has a long life in reruns, syndication, downloads, or streaming. Writers' demand for residuals challenged the political, social, and economic boundary between labor and capital and the legal boundary between employee and independent contractor. And it was part of the writers' effort to secure their rights as authors.

This chapter tells the story of the origins of residuals and separated rights for writers. After explaining how residuals and separated rights operate today, the chapter then examines the major episodes in the post–World War II effort of the Screen Writers Guild and other writer organizations to negotiate for some form of payment for, and control over, reuse of scripts. Screenwriters were not the only group interested in negotiating some form of profit sharing—the quest for reuse payments was the primary goal of every writer group in the 1940s, and also actors and directors, who have a right to be paid residuals today as well. The chapter concludes with reflections on how residuals changed the significance of screen credit and how they had other long-term consequences for the status of writers in Hollywood.

The Rules of Writer Ownership and Profit Sharing Today

The Minimum Basic Agreement (MBA) today provides writers three types of partial ownership and profit sharing in the scripts they write: separated rights, residuals, and script fees (in television). In addition, film writers can negotiate individually for a bonus payment if they receive screen credit for a film (a credit bonus), and any writer as an individual can negotiate to own all or part of a film or TV show, in which case the writer shares profits with a production company. All of these forms of compensation are in addition to the writer being paid for the labor in writing the script in the first place (either in selling a completed script written while the writer was not employed by the buyer or the script fee and/or salary paid to writers who work as employees of the studio that will produce the project). The nature of the rights and the formulas for calculating them are extremely complex, but to understand the history of their development, it may help to understand what writers ultimately worked out.

Today, separated rights for writers of original film stories (not adaptations of someone else's novel or book) include the right to publish the script or book(s) based on the script subject to a waiting ("holdback") period. The company may publish a novelization in conjunction with the release of the film, but it must give the writer the option to write the novelization and must, in any event, pay no less than the WGA minimum for the right to publish it. The writer is entitled to produce a stage version of the material, to receive payment for any sequels or series made based on the film, to do the first rewrite of a script, and to meet with a production executive before being replaced as a writer. Finally, a film writer with separated rights is entitled to buy back unproduced material from the company within five years at the price the writer was paid for the script or the writing services, which is very important because it ensures that writers profit from the resale of unproduced scripts rather than studios profiting when they sell scripts to each other without the writer's consent or participation in the profits.[4]

In television, the separated-rights provisions are slightly different and, as in film, are quite complex, but they are more comprehensive and more protective of writers. The company has the exclusive right to produce the material for a period of years after which the right to produce the material becomes a nonexclusive shared right between the company and writer. The writer has the right to buy back unproduced material after a period of years. The writer credited as the series creator has the right to sequel payments (in addition to residuals) for each episode of a series that is produced, and if the company does not produce a series within the exclusivity period, then the series right reverts entirely to the writer. As in film, a television writer with separated rights enjoys the right to a compensated rewrite; to produce the material for the stage, motion picture, or radio; to publish a book; and to create interactive programs. In both film and television, when writers share the qualifying credit ("written by," "story by," or "screen/television story by"), they share the separated rights. Separated rights have been extended to material created for or used in new media, including the internet.[5]

From the standpoint of companies, one function the Guild plays in simplifying separated rights is coordinating which writers are eligible to claim them. If it were not for the fact that separated rights are tied to screen credit, and that screen credit is determined only when a project is finished and is limited to two writers, production companies would have a very complicated set of individual negotiations with writers at the time of hiring. Each writer would presumably negotiate for separated rights. A project that hired multiple writers might find itself very limited in its ability to attract talent late in the writing process if the separated rights had already been allocated to an earlier writer. Even if the producer could persuade a sixth or tenth writer to sign on with the understanding that he or she would be sharing the separated rights with many previous writers, the various writers (and the production companies that might later contract with them to exercise the separated rights) would find themselves in a complicated negotiation over whether or how each one could exercise the right. It is possible that separated rights could be treated like joint ownership of copyrights, which allows each joint owner to independently exploit the copyright so that all the writers could write and sell, say, a novelization of a movie. But publishers and writers might find the value of the novelization limited both by the possibility of multiple similar novels being published and the possibility that the least talented or industrious of the joint owners might be the first to market, thus damaging the value of the "brand" in the eyes of later publishers and consumers. Moreover, if the most significant separated right is the right to reacquire an unproduced script so that the writer can sell it to another studio rather than have one studio sell it to another, it seems logical to limit this right to one or two people, lest multiple different versions of the same story be available from different sellers; however, none could be produced if they were similar without the resulting movie infringing the copyright in a version of script held by a studio that refuses to sell.

Residual payments for reuse of material are more economically significant for most writers than are separated rights. Residuals were originally designed as a payment for each time a theatrical film was shown on TV or a TV program or made-for-TV movie was rebroadcast on TV after the initial broadcast. Today residuals are less significant because they are only payable after an initial period in which material is streamed or available for download, which means that writers earn less in residuals, even for wildly successful shows, than they once did. Like separated rights, residuals are extremely complex and the WGA has been indispensable in designing and administering them. In 1953, the WGA first negotiated an agreement requiring the payment of for reuse of material written for television, and in 1960, the residuals requirement was extended to the reuse of film material shown on television. At the time, residual payments were considered quite innovative by lawyers and legal scholars because they were not royalties for use of a copyrighted work paid to the copyright owner, but were instead payments for services rendered in making a product, calculated based on product sales. Over time, residuals became an established feature of the industry and are perennially important in collective negotiations. Securing residuals for TV was the Guild's top demand in the 1959–1960 negotiations, and residuals for new media was a principal issue leading to the 2007–2008 writers' strike. As with separated rights, the right to residuals depends on being awarded screen credit.[6]

Residuals are foundational to the Hollywood labor market, and the residuals system depends on the WGA to function. By negotiating uniform terms of eligibility, the WGA simplifies individual hiring negotiations. This simplification is particularly important when multiple writers have worked on a project because the division of residual rights among the writers would be a difficult task for individual writers to arrange in their separate negotiations with the production company. (Of course, it would be easier for a studio to pay residuals to a dozen writers on the same film than to negotiate with a dozen writers over the sale of an unproduced script or the right to write a novel based on a script, but still it's beneficial for both writers and the studio to limit the number of people who share the residuals.) More important, writers benefit from the WGA's calculation and collection of residuals. The Guild investigates claims of nonpayment or underpayment, and it arbitrates claims to collect them. Individual writers could not administer the system on their own because they lack the technical ability to track reuse of their work. The WGA solves the problem by handling residuals on a collective basis, reducing transaction costs for the writer and the production company. Essentially, the WGA does for film and TV writers what ASCAP and BMI do for songwriters and composers—collectively monitor uses of the work and administer the payments for those uses. But, unlike ASCAP and BMI, which are performance-rights organizations that simply handle permission for public performance of copyrighted works on behalf of the copyright owners (whether that is the songwriter, the publisher, or someone else), the WGA represents writers (who are not the owners of the copyright in their work) to ensure compensation for use of their work other than through copyright licenses.

In a market in which the earnings on work are likely to be received over a long period (as is the case with the reuse of TV programs and movies), it makes good sense to design a compensation scheme that allows the buyer of the creative work (or the employer) to pay the creator (the writer) over a long period. Moreover, particularly when the buyer/employer cannot predict whether a work will become popular and generate revenue over the long haul and/or the buyer/employer does not have enough cash to pay a generous salary at the time the work is done, future payments measured by product sales are thus a sensible compensation scheme. Also, the writer cannot easily predict the likely success of the film and set a price for the sale of the script tied to the project's eventual profits. Equally as important, residuals smooth out the irregularities in income associated with the fact that few writers are continuously employed.[7] While this approach benefits writers, it also benefits employers because residuals allow writers to stay in the labor market rather than leaving the industry and taking their considerable industry-specific human capital with them.

A third way in which credited writers receive additional compensation—one that looks less like a form of intellectual property than separated rights or residuals do but that is nevertheless financially significant to film writers—is the credit bonus. A credit bonus is a provision of an individual hiring contract stating that the film writer will receive a bonus if the writer is awarded screen credit. (Credit bonuses exist only for movies; in episodic TV, credited writers are paid a script fee that is collectively bargained by the Guild.) In essence, if the movie script is not substantially rewritten during the production process, the writer will be paid a bonus. The purpose of the credit bonus is to reward the writer whose script is good enough that it does not need significant rewriting (or who is fortunate enough to work on a project in which the production executives decide not to drastically revise the script). Unlike residuals and separated rights, credit bonuses are controversial among writers. But because they are popular with producers, they exist, and the Guild facilitates their use.[8]

The evolution of these forms of compensation and division of rights occurred over successive negotiations between the Guild and the studios and production companies between 1949 and 1960. The full history is quite involved; what follows is a brief synopsis.

The Long Fight over Licensing and the Writer's Share

From the beginning, writers recognized the costs of studios that insisted on outright ownership of all scripts. Even in the 1930s, scripts had uses besides just in making a movie for a single release. Homer Croy, a novelist who adapted some of his own work for the screen in the 1930s and 1940s, knew how the multiple uses of a novel or script could profit writers. He observed in *The Screen Guilds' Magazine* in 1936 that "dribbles of radio money are beginning to flow into the pockets of screen writers" because radio companies "are perfectly willing to buy a screen story a year after it has been released, when presumably it has slipped from the screen." That is why, he said (in italics), *"All screen writers should reserve radio rights to originals."*[9] But in the postwar period, the practice of reissuing movies and the growth of television brought special urgency to writer demands for greater ownership or profit sharing in their scripts.

Writers occasionally negotiated as individuals to reserve radio, stage, or novel rights when they sold scripts to studios. Especially when working for small independent production companies, some writers negotiated individually for compensation based on the film profits. Most of the time, however, writers sold their scripts outright and were paid either a flat fee or a weekly salary. At the end of World War II, as writers began planning to negotiate for a new MBA covering film and to negotiate for an MBA covering television, they were determined to negotiate for payment on some kind of profit-sharing basis and to retain some of the rights in their scripts. These goals eventually led to the residuals and separated rights provisions in the MBAs of the 1950s and since. But it was a long road to get there.

When World War II ended, the Guild began to develop its priorities for a new collective bargaining agreement. The issue of profit sharing was a logical one to raise in 1947 because the rapid growth of television, the studios' drastic reduction in the number of movies made, and the studios' increased reissue of old films were causing widespread unemployment of writers. The SWG Executive Board received a report showing that only 466 writers were employed in July 1947, down by 80 since the year before and 100 in two years. At the same time, writers knew their old scripts were being reused as radio dramas and anticipated that studios would soon license their huge catalogues of films to be shown on TV. Writers felt entitled to share in whatever wealth the studios made from the reuses of their work, in a way that theatrical reissues and radio already offered and television promised.[10]

Some form of profit sharing, as well as payments for reuse or reissues emerged as priority issues in 1946 when the Executive Board began considering its bargaining strategy for a new agreement. Some writers had negotiated profit sharing in their individual contracts, usually turning on whether the writer's contribution was a significant portion of the final shooting script. SWG President Mary McCall, who had a productive career of about two or three movies a year for twenty years between the 1920s and 1940s, described her deal to the Executive Board in 1945 as a model. Her contract gave her

$15,000 for a script (almost $200,000 in 2015 dollars). If the final script was less than 75 percent her work, the $15,000 was her total compensation, but if it were more, then she would receive 5 percent of the producers' share and the $15,000 fee would be considered an advance against her percentage of the profits. The Board wanted to see if some form of percentage could be negotiated on a collective basis for all writers. So it appointed Lester Cole, who had been one of the founders of the SWG in 1933 and was a very successful writer, to chair the Economic Committee, which was assigned to develop the Guild's goals and strategy with respect to economic issues. Cole's committee proposed that the Guild negotiate for a percentage of profits to be paid in addition to salaries and for payments to be made to those receiving screen credit on all reissues and remakes.[11]

That same year, the Guild appointed Ring Lardner, Jr., as chair of the Committee on the Sale of Original Material. His committee made the same proposal as Cole's committee. It is not surprising that Cole and Lardner—who would in the following year be blacklisted as communists—proposed that writers should act more like capitalists. They recognized that writers and their scripts were the means of film production and were simply urging that workers should own them. Lardner urged the Guild's Executive Board and the Authors League to

> substitute a limited licensing agreement for the current system of outright sale . . . . It is our belief that this action would be one of the major landmarks in the history of the League, and that there is no moral or practical reason why the same general concepts of copyright vested in the author, reversion of rights and control of subsidiary rights should not obtain in the motion picture field as have been won during the past three decades in other fields. Though present practices vary with the type of material purchased and in the bargaining power of the individual author, picture studios remain alone in the extremes of ownership and control which they demand in their purchases. The introduction of television . . . gives increased urgency to this reform.[12]

The committees offered many examples of writers who had launched but never profited from hugely successful stories because they sold outright the ideas and characters in audition scripts (as they were known in radio) or spec scripts (as they were known in film and later TV). One example was *Fibber McGee & Molly*, the wildly popular radio show that grew from an audition script that Don Quinn had sold to an ad agency. Companies had made millions from the show, but Quinn had not. In sum, Cole and Lardner and their committees agreed that the Guild should negotiate not only for minimum wages (as before) but also for a percentage of profits above the minimum salary, and for payments to those receiving screen credits in the past on all reissues based on a percentage of the salaries received in making the original and revenues received on remakes.[13]

The SWG joined every other Guild representing writers—the Radio Writers Guild, the Dramatists Guild, the Authors League, and various committees of writers in television—in making profit sharing and licensing, rather than sale of scripts, the writers' top priorities in bargaining for new collective agreements for writers in every medium. The idea—which the Guilds all phrased as a bedrock principle from which they would never deviate—got a great deal of attention in the trade press, in the mainstream press, and from the studios, ad agencies, and television networks.

The American Authors Authority

The challenge was to design a system to administer the licensing of scripts on behalf of writers because everyone realized that it would be very complicated for thousands of authors to negotiate individually with hundreds of radio, film, and TV employers and exhibitors over uses of scripts. Moreover, as novelist and screenwriter James Cain realized when talking at a Guild committee meeting with Cohn and Lardner, it might be necessary to create a system where it would be impossible for writers to sell their copyrights outright because "[t]here is a profound difference between what a man is forbidden to do, but may do, if enough money is shaken in his face, and what does not lie within his power to do." In 1946, *The Screen Writer,* the magazine of the Writers Guild, published an article proposing the idea of creating the American Authors Authority (AAA), which would own the copyright in every form of literary material produced by writers for all media. The AAA would be to writers somewhat like what ASCAP and BMI were to composers and song writers: the AAA would obtain the copyright in all written material and would license it and collect royalties for each use and would transmit the royalties to authors. As the AAA proposal was debated, critics wondered how the AAA would decide to whom to license a work and whether to license it exclusively or not, and the AAA's defenders insisted that the AAA would not have the power to act as a censor in granting licenses.[14]

Cain, the article's author, drew on his experiences as a novelist, short story author, and screenwriter who had struggled to make a career as a writer until finding success at age forty with the publication of *The Postman Always Rings Twice* (1934), and whose short story "Double Indemnity" was adapted into a successful movie in 1944. Cain published essays presenting the AAA idea in several publications. Ring Lardner, Jr., with assistance from the long-time SWG lawyer Morris Cohn, on behalf of the SWG's Committee on the Sale of Original Material, advanced the same idea in other publications. Cain and Lardner and Cohn argued that writers were forced to accept inequitable contracts in every market for their work—book publishing, magazines, film, radio, and the stage.[15]

Cain argued, based on his own experience, that writers were undercompensated for the subsidiary rights in their work (serialization in magazines and newspapers, paperback editions, stage, film, and radio adaptations, translations and foreign editions). Income from subsidiary rights were crucial to an author's fortunes, yet writers routinely were required to sign them over to publishers, radio producers or networks, or film studios. Even writers who managed to keep these subsidiary rights often found it difficult to track profits from their exploitation. More important, he argued, book publishers acquired the rights to control sales of, for example, trade and paperback editions and then negotiated extremely unfavorable (to the author) deals. Cain, for example, got only half of one cent for each twenty-five-cent pocket paperback copy of *The Postman Always Rings Twice*. Knopf (his publisher) would get one quarter of all stage royalties and MGM (which bought the movie rights) would also get a third, which meant Cain received less than half of the normal author's royalty for the play he wrote based on the novel he wrote. In sum, Cain argued that the literary marketplace had grown extremely complex and writers were not keeping up and getting their fair share of the wealth that their creativity produced for print, radio, stage, and screen media.[16]

Reaction from the business community was vociferous and negative. The industry trade paper *Variety* characterized it as "the most radical action ever taken by a talent organization" and as giving "the outfit a virtual monopoly in American literature." A column in the *New York Sun* insisted the American Authors Authority "would do to thought and its expression" what ASCAP had done to music: compel every writer to submit his work to the control of one entity that would exercise monopolistic control. The proposal to enable an organization of unionized writers to control which materials would be sold was "a device to get around the Constitution" because it would force writers to "submit to" a "one-man authority." "But the most important right of an author is self-expression, to say what he pleases. . . . A writer is not a drummer. He is a creative person with something in his mind and heart, as willing to risk the garret as to accept the emoluments and plaudits that come to him for his work. Maybe, it is the preoccupation with rights and deals that has reduced American literature to its current vulgarity."[17]

The insistence by commercial publications that the proposal would doom American letters was cynical; the owners of *Variety* and the *Sun* apparently did not see their ownership of copyrights in their employees' work to be the threat to freedom of thought and speech that they prophesied from writer ownership. Risking the garret was something that executives of movie studios and newspaper owners could celebrate as essential to political and artistic freedom since they themselves never had to do it. The vehemence of the opposition surely stemmed from the editors' recognition that their own business model was based on corporate ownership of the copyrights in works produced by staff and freelance writers and that the creation of the American Authors Authority might mean that newspapers would have to purchase the right to print reporters' stories and could not rely on the work-for-hire doctrine to secure the rights at low cost.

The key for the Guild was to design collective management of the rights in scripts and other forms of writing that did not arouse the ire of every newspaper, magazine, ad agency, and other corporation that depended on acquiring the copyrights in works their staff produced. One dispute over the design of the system focused on whether it would censor writers as by, for example, accepting material only from writers who were Guild members. At a SWG membership meeting on the proposal, a conservative Guild member,

Richard Macauley, proposed a resolution requiring the AAA to accept material from anyone, whether or not a member of the four Guilds that would make up the AAA. The resolution was voted down, but members did vote unanimously in support of an amendment prohibiting the AAA from discriminating against an author or work on the basis of its content.[18]

The writers who developed and advocated the AAA concept never considered that the AAA would censor. They envisioned it simply as a device to centralize licensing transactions, not as a censor of content. Nor did they worry about the opposite problem, that a compulsory license regime modeled on ASCAP would give writers too little control over uses of their work. But the business community succeeded in tarring it with the censorship brush. The timing was terrible, too. The AAA made this proposal just before the House Un-American Activities Committee (HUAC) called many of the Guild's leaders to testify about the alleged communist domination of the Guild, and many of the Guild advocates of writer ownership (but not James Cain) were shortly thereafter jailed for contempt of Congress and driven out of the United States. (Although, as Richard Fine in his history of Cain and the AAA points out, the AAA collapsed before the November 1947 HUAC hearings that launched the blacklist in earnest.) Cain himself left Hollywood in disgust shortly thereafter, and he complained vociferously in letters to friends that writer organizations (including the Guilds and the Authors League) were "invariably futile, feeble, and ineffective, at best, and crooked, hypocritical, and clique-ridden, at worst." And so the AAA idea never got very far.[19]

But film, TV, and radio writers did not abandon their effort to claim ownership of their scripts, and they turned to other ways of expressing their conviction that all writers should own the copyright in their work. In doing so, they compared writers for film, TV, and radio to novelists and playwrights, who typically retained ownership of their copyrights and licensed them for particular uses. The key was to design an entity that could manage the huge numbers of copyrights that became part of movies and the huge numbers of uses of the copyrights as films were screened in theaters and on television screens around the globe. While they never achieved anything quite as ambitious or all-encompassing as the AAA, the system designed for film and TV writing has endured, and Cain's jaundiced view of writer organizations has not been entirely accurate.

One Percent of the Gross

"One percent of the gross" was another way of expressing the same idea as the AAA, although it was less ambitious in that it would not prohibit outright sales of material. "One percent of the gross" was a way of expressing the writers' demand that they be paid a share of the gross profits, and as noted at the beginning of this chapter, writers could argue about whether it should be one percent, or two, or some other percentage. The idea was eventually embraced in the residuals formulas, which are calculated in percentages. (The devil is in the details, as "gross" is not a clear concept, and the MBA uses various terms such as "producer's gross," "distributor's foreign gross," and so on, and defines each of those terms. Depending on how the terms are defined, and the success of a film, one percent or two percent could be a substantial amount of money or a relative pittance.)

Agreeing to a percentage of the receipts was an alternative to the more ambitious proposal that authors retain ownership, because writer ownership ran into opposition from some unanticipated quarters. The Authors League was skeptical that a system of one-time leases could be implemented. In reply to Lardner's argument about one percent of the gross and the Screen Writers Guild 1947 lease proposal that began this chapter, Elmer Rice (a novelist and newly elected head of the Authors League in New York) wrote, "I do not know how many of the members would voluntarily forego a motion picture sale, in the event that the prospective purchaser refused to buy anything but unlimited rights." But "the chief problem," thought Rice, would be the Dramatists Guild, which represented playwrights in New York. "Under the Basic Agreement, the manager has an unqualified right to participate in the proceeds of a motion picture sale, and I doubt if the Guild could jeopardize that right by imposing limitations which might result in the loss of a sale and the consequent loss of revenue for the manager." The Dramatists Guild's Basic Agreement could, of course, be modified, "but I think we would have a very hard time getting the managers to accept it, in view of the fact that there is a time limitation on the manager's participation in motion picture rights and therefore he would have little or nothing to gain in the event of a resale of the rights."[20]

Nevertheless, the Dramatists Guild did subsequently endorse a formula proposed by the Screen Writers Guild regarding licensing of material and agreed that it should be included in the proposals when a new Basic Agreement was negotiated. The proposal was also approved by the SWG Executive Board to be submitted for approval at the next general SWG membership meeting. The Radio Writers Guild (also an affiliate of the Authors League) joined the effort, demanding in its 1947 contract negotiations that radio producers agree only to license material for a single performance rather than purchase rights to it, and the SWG endorsed their effort.[21]

The issue of compensation for reissues was one that could unite many otherwise opposed groups, in both the talent guilds and the craft unions. Lester Cole reported at a July 1947 meeting of talent guild and craft union representatives that of the 400 films released for exhibition in the previous year, more than 100 were reissues. Cole estimated that the 100 reissues "displaced from employment at least two or 300 writers, a couple of hundred directors and producers, and thousands of actors and skilled studio workers." Cole then insisted that the problem of reissues was not merely about unemployment, but also fair compensation:

> Our industry is one of the few in the world where talents and skills of its workers, preserved on strips of celluloid, can be used repeatedly without any remuneration to the possessors of those talents and skills. This fact must be recognized, and some plan is called for whereby compensation will be paid for the repeated use of the creative and technical work of those who make our motion pictures.
>
> Compare motion pictures with the book publishing industry. Writers of books are protected by copyright law, and when their books are re-issued, they are compensated for it. Probably the only workers who are not compensated in the reprinting of a book are the original type-setters. If new plates are made, even the type-setters are paid.[22]

After Cole spoke, all at the meeting agreed that all Hollywood labor groups deserved to share in the profits from reissues.

It helped that film and television writers could draw on the example of theater, where writers typically owned their scripts. And as writers began to make some headway in persuading people in the industry that writer ownership was important for television, it seemed possible that the terms on which movie scripts were written and sold might change. As screenwriter Emmet Lavery (*Hitler's Children* (1943), *The Magnificent Yankee* (1950)) said in 1946, once writers took the position in the first television negotiations that "licensing is to be preferred to sale and that separation of copyright is imperative at all times, the moment seems propitious to suggest that this excellent theory of operation be extended without delay to the field of motion pictures. . . . [T]here will never be a better time to achieve for the seller of material to the screen some of the privileges and protections which the dramatist enjoys in the theatre."[23]

In the lead-up to the SWG's September 1947 general membership meeting, the Guild published a number of articles in its magazine, *The Screen Writer,* presenting different points of view on the question of royalty payments for reissues and profit sharing more generally. But most of the articles were eloquent arguments for writer ownership of scripts or profit sharing in movies. *The Screen Writer* was created by the Executive Board in January 1945 as a free magazine to be distributed to all Guild members. Dalton Trumbo was chosen as its first editor-in-chief.

It was unfortunate for writers' efforts to secure profit sharing and ownership of scripts that the editor-in-chief of the magazine and the chairs of the committees that advocated writer ownership were so soon to be branded as communists, driven from their positions of Guild leadership, imprisoned, and forced to flee Hollywood. The position they advanced for writer ownership and compensation proved to be hugely important, and perhaps if they had not been hounded from the film business for ten or more years, the Guild might have negotiated an even bigger piece of the entertainment pie for writers than it ultimately got. The internecine fight over the political affiliations of the Editorial Committee of *The Screen Writer* began in May 1947, even before Cole, Lardner, and Trumbo were called to testify before HUAC. Two Executive Board discussions of the magazine's editorial content revealed that some writers were annoyed by the left-wing politics of some contributors. Some (including Lardner) defended the magazine as focusing mainly on craft problems facing writers. But others, notably James Cain—who had agreed with Lardner and Cole at least on the issue of writer ownership—said that the content "verged toward the left" and some was "definitely Communist propaganda." Cain said he resented that his money was used to put forth such a document and that it would divide the Guild to subvert the magazine in that way. Cain moved (seconded by Mary McCall) to discontinue *The Screen Writer*, but the motion failed.[24] (The Guild discontinued the magazine a few years later, citing the expense of publishing it.)

But in the summer of 1947, *The Screen Writer* was the forum for a thoughtful debate among writers and producers about how writers should be paid and whether they should sell or license the rights in their scripts. A number of articles were published under the heading "The Writers' Share: Some Comments on the Contribution of Writers to the Screen Industry and Vice Versa." It was rhetorically clever of Lardner to have opened the discussion of "the writer's share" arguing that writers were currently paid about one percent of a film's gross profits and deserved two percent. Noted writers of all political stripes generally favored the idea, and novelists who also wrote for the screen were particularly pointed in their criticism. Stephen Longstreet, a novelist and screenwriter who had just enjoyed success with the Oscar-winning biopic *The Jolson Story* (1948), scoffed in his essay on "the writer's share" that "no author in his right mind would work for two percent no matter how hungry," except of course in Hollywood. James Hilton (who wrote the hugely popular novel *Lost Horizon* and who won the 1942 Academy Award for his script for *Mrs. Miniver*) opined that "Hollywood would be a bigger and certainly a better success if writers had more share in *production* and *responsibility*—as in England. That would make more sense—and probably also more cents." Martin Field, a writer who never had many screen credits and so felt quite acutely the vulnerability of writers in the industry, published two cleverly titled essays, "Twice Sold Tales" and "No Applause for These Encores," charging that the studios' practice of reselling scripts reduced employment for writers and also reduced the demand for original stories from freelance writers.[25]

Not surprisingly, producers saw it differently. Some of the biggest names in the studios insisted that the key to Hollywood's success was the producers' ability to spot and nurture writing talent and to revise scripts to make them filmable and saleable. They objected strenuously to the idea that writers as a group were underpaid. Samuel Goldwyn insisted that the profit-sharing proposal did a "disservice to a great field of art" because it lumped all Hollywood writers with "the few capable ones." In Goldwyn's view, "it is a virtual impossibility in Hollywood to assign a writer to a script and to get from him a work that can be put on the screen." He also said that "Hollywood is hungry for new and fresh material and Hollywood still pays the highest monetary reward in the world for creative writing. But let's have more attention paid to fine ideas and vibrant words than to percentage figures." David Selznick (who claimed credit for the huge success of Gone with the Wind (1939)) agreed: "The contributions of writers to motion pictures are not sufficiently uniform, in relation to the pictures in their entirety, to warrant any arbitrary allocation of the share of the earnings as the proper share of the writers, either real or merely credited." Moreover, Selznick argued, "the earnings on a picture are dependent, to an extraordinary extent, upon such factors as star values, show-manship, presentation, distribution, and the effectiveness of and expenditures for exploitation. To none of these does the writer contribute, of course." And he could not resist pointing out that "the best writing does not necessarily mean the highest earnings."[26]

In September 1947, the Writers Guild's entire membership met in the ornate ballroom of the grand neoclassical Hollywood Masonic Temple on Hollywood Boulevard to discuss the question of what the Guild should demand with respect to payment of percentages on the gross. This was an important meeting at which the members had the chance to forever change the way they were paid and also to come up with a plan to assert the rights of TV writers to have the claims to credit, creative control, and compensation for which movie writers had fought in the 1930s. But it happened at the moment at which the House Un-American Activities Committee (HUAC) was threatening to find and banish every communist from Hollywood, and also just a couple of months after the new Republican majority in Congress had enacted the Taft-Hartley Act sharply limiting the rights and protections of unionized workers. So what seemed to some an entirely sensible and quite capitalist notion—that writers should be paid like entrepreneurs—got caught up in the emerging fight between the left and right wings of the Guild.

Ring Lardner, Jr., and Lester Cole delivered the report of the Economic Committee urging the membership to adopt as its economic program in bar-gaining a demand that writers be paid a percentage of the gross on a film. Emmet Lavery—who at the time was SWG President and leading the effort to get Executive Board members to sign affidavits of noncommunist affiliation—opposed the report. Lavery had no reason to oppose paying writers a per-centage of the gross. He was a lawyer, a writer of successful movies, and he personally would have every reason to support a proposal that allowed writers of successful movies to share the profits. But he, like other writers, was anxious about endorsing anything recommended by writers whose politics he feared would destroy the Guild. So he said that the Guild should study the matter more fully before acting and that it should determine whether the percentage of the gross be paid to the individual writers or to the Guild, which would distribute it among the members on some basis. (The irony of the moderate advocating sharing the profits equally among all workers and the communists advocating ownership by individual writers could not have been lost on many.) While the membership voted to adopt the committee report 195 to 136, the political controversy hung over the whole matter.[27]

But as late summer turned to fall while the Guild was trying to unite its fractious membership around the issue of demanding a percentage of the gross, the House of Representatives subpoenaed nineteen prominent Hollywood writers and directors to testify at a hearing investigating the alleged communist influence in motion pictures. Some of those subpoenaed proved to be friendly to HUAC's efforts to eliminate the alleged communist influence from the movies, but eleven were not. Cole and Lardner were two of those unfriendly witnesses among the ten cited for contempt of Congress when they refused to answer questions about their politics. (So was Dalton Trumbo, who had also advanced the idea of the AAA.) Immediately afterward, during the Guild's annual elections, Cole and Lardner were voted off the Guild's Executive Board and lost their role in formulating Guild strategy.

The blacklist forced the Executive Board's attention away from the economic program they had been pushing, as well as most other issues having to do with the Minimum Basic Agreement (MBA). It dramatically weakened the writers' bargaining position in the run-up to the negotiations for the second MBA in 1949. But in mid-1948, the Executive Board again turned its attention from politics to economics and confronted both the matter of reissues and forming a committee to meet with the Authors League in New York to discuss forming a Guild to represent writers in television.[28]

The Guild recognized that it was difficult to form a plan for payment on a royalty or percentage basis for movies without considering how writers would be hired and paid for TV, as everyone knew that reissuing movies in theaters would not be the only or the most common way in which writers' work would be reused. And the question of how to divide royalties was complicated by the fact that, in movies, it was common for multiple writers to work on a project—if the writers were paid a share of the gross rather than on a weekly basis or a flat deal, how would that share be divided? A Guild Committee on Royalties reported to the Executive Board at the end of December 1948 that one possibility might be that writers could be paid a fraction of the total writers' share of the gross, "except that if one writer wrote the screenplay which was used, he would be entitled to the full percentage." The Committee finally decided "to hold the matter in abeyance until the television question could be gone into thoroughly," and that the merits of different systems should be debated at a meeting of the full Guild membership.[29]

In April 1949, the Guild proposed to producers that writers be paid a percentage of the gross and retain separated rights to use their scripts in print, stage, radio, and some TV purposes. The producers were "adamant" in their opposition to leasing of material rather than outright sale, but would take under advisement the question of separated rights. The Guild proposed in June that writers be paid at least 10 percent of the gross revenue derived by producers for rerelease of film in another medium (including television and radio) and that if more than one writer had been employed on the film, that percentage would be divided in proportion to each writer's compensation (not their contribution) on the picture. Again, the producers objected.[30]

At least one of the studios tried to exploit the writers' insistence on profit sharing as a strategy for wage cuts. Warner Bros. announced in the spring of 1950 that henceforward it would pay its writers the contract minimum as a weekly salary and would pay any writer whose contract provided for a weekly salary above the MBA minimum his or her full salary when the film went into production if the writer received screen credit. Writers promptly complained to the California Labor Commissioner, the state agency charged with enforcing worker wage-protection laws. The Labor Commissioner ruled that no part of a weekly salary may be deferred. So Warner Bros. took a different tack: employ writers at the Guild's collectively bargained minimum rate for a flat deal and then pay the writer the difference between that and whatever the writer's usual weekly salary was, plus a bonus, later if the writer got screen credit. The Writers Guild Executive Board adopted a resolution urging its members not to accept employment under these conditions. This kind of deal would put the writer at risk of underpayment (they would be working for less than their usual rate), would pose the risk that many writers would expect payments that wouldn't be paid because of the limits on the number of credited writers, and would require even credited writers to wait quite a time to be paid. In another instance, Robert Blees, who wrote on *Three Steps North* (1951), was denied a deferred payment of a part of his salary because he was not given screen credit. The Executive Board wrote to the producer to complain about the treatment of Blees and to go on record against the practice of deferring compensation and making payment of it contingent on screen credit.[31]

Negotiations for a new screenwriters' agreement dragged on with the major studios between 1949 and February 1951. Along with minimum compensation, the most contentious issues were payments for reissue or reuse of work and separation of rights. The process of getting to that agreement involved the Guild revising its own working rules for writers who made sales of original material (material written neither while employed by a studio nor specially commissioned by a studio), as well as bargaining for the minimum basic agreement covering studios and writers. In sales of original material, the Guild sought to amend its rules to require Guild members to reserve separated rights in the sale and also to prohibit members from selling the television rights without the Guild's approval. The producers reluctantly agreed in negotiations in early February 1951 to give writers separated rights in radio as well as print publication and drama. In a split vote, the SWG Executive Board agreed to accept this proposal. Nevertheless, after the parties finished their negotiations, trouble arose over the Guild's working rules prohibiting writers from selling all rights to original material without separate consideration for radio, television, print, and dramatic rights. The studios insisted the rule was inconsistent with what had been negotiated, and the studios refused to sign the agreement until the Guild rescinded its working rules.[32]

Reuse Payments and Television

Having secured some forms of profit sharing and separated rights for film writers working for major studios, the Guild turned its attention to securing ownership and profit sharing in television. Independent television and film producers occasionally agreed to pay with a percentage of the profits, which writers considered one of the boons of the growth of independent production

as the studio system began its decline in 1946. Profit sharing in this little segment of the industry, at least, achieved "the long-cherished dream of screen
writers . . . to have a royalty in the earnings of the pictures they write." Mary
McCall, Jr., president of the SWG, gave a speech in early 1952 at the annual
dinner of the Society of Independent Motion Picture Producers, an organization that existed between 1941 and 1958 to advance the interests of independent producers in the studio-dominated industry. McCall advocated that
writers be paid a minimum fee plus a percentage of the gross. The next day,
one small independent, Snader Telescriptions, called McCall to say that they
were prepared to pay a flat fee of $500 plus three percent of the gross after the
company had recouped $20,000. In negotiating with Snader, the size of the
percentage was controversial, but the Guild thought it could get "what would
be the greatest gain for writers we could possibly hope for—copyright in the
name of the author as well as the proprietor." But getting the right mix of
guaranteed compensation and profit sharing and getting that agreement
accepted by all the production companies proved to be a long fight.[33]

SWG negotiations with the Alliance (the trade association of movie and
TV producers that negotiated with the talent guilds on behalf of all production company members) stalemated in the summer of 1952 over the issue of
royalties. The Guild said it would negotiate on the amount of the advance
payment, the percentage of the gross to be paid as a royalty, and the time at
which the percentage would be paid, but it would not budge on the principle.
As the demand for material to put on TV exceeded the supply of writers able
to provide it, Guild negotiators thought they were in a good position to insist.
The most contentious issue was the minimum advance against a percentage
of gross revenues. Profit sharing required allocation of risk between writers
and producers. The Guild offered a schedule of advances estimated so that
the producer would have a return on "negative cost" before any further
money must be paid to the writer, which essentially meant that writers
absorbed much of the risk. The Guild hoped that by so doing, it could establish profit participation as a principle in most cases, without financial risk to
the producer. But the television producers refused to discuss compensation
on the basis that rights remained in the author subject to a long (seven year)
lease to the producer. Instead, the Alliance proposed payment to the writer
for all reuse, but not for each reuse, and only after a certain number of reuses
or a certain period. The Guild informed its members that a strike might be

necessary because the "Guild's position must prevail—not only for the sake
of TV writers, but to safeguard the economic future of screen writers when
and if the major motion picture studios release their vast backlog of product
to television."[34]

One of the complications was that while the SWG negotiated hard for the
royalty principle for TV production in the west, writers in the east were not
negotiating for a royalty contract because at the time TV production in the
east was not profitable. In addition, the Guild could not predict the likelihood
of success of a strike. Gordon Stulberg, SWG's lawyer, explained to the Guild
Executive Board in July 1952 that the success of a strike would depend on
whether TV producers were determined just to fill air time or wanted to
improve the demand for TV by improving its quality. "If they are in the
market for first class material which only our members can give," Stulberg
predicted the Guild could successfully strike. But if producers would put anything on the air, Stulberg feared that a strike might fail as non-Guild people
would probably not honor the strike. Moreover, he added, "because of the
Communist issue some Guild members even might scab," especially those
who are desperate for work "or in the right wing of the Guild."[35]

While the Guild had its divisions, producers had theirs. Even if some
television producers were prepared to withstand a strike by going off the
air or using scripts written by scabs, some advertisers (a producer claimed
Proctor & Gamble, the huge maker of cleaning and personal-care products,
was one) put heavy pressure on their packagers and agencies to avoid a strike,
even by accepting the Guild's terms. A producer who depended entirely on
work from particular advertisers would not put up with a strike if the advertiser did not wish to.[36]

The negotiations were complicated by geography, by doubts about which
union represented TV writers, and because the SWG decided to exercise the
right to reopen the 1949 MBA with major film studios on October 26, 1952,
although it hoped to limit the bargaining to screen credit, minimum compensation, and payment for use of films on TV.[37] The multiple and simultaneous
negotiations with different types of producers over different media meant
that the gains secured by the Guild or by producers in one negotiation could
serve as a model for others. That made all parties leery of striking a deal.[38]

The diversity of companies making television programs in the early 1950s
was also an obstacle to establishing a uniform scale for compensating writers.

However hard it had been to negotiate minimum compensation in 1938–1941 with the film studios, the problem was magnified ten years later when television production was done by a larger number of companies with very different financial situations. This difficulty existed both in figuring out what should be minimum compensation and in figuring out how to calculate profit sharing. The Guild proposed different minimum profit-sharing scales depending on the producer, but it was complicated by separate negotiations with the different entities. In discussing the possibility of a strike focused just against the independent production companies (which were much smaller than the studios), a skeptical NLRB official suggested to the SWG's lawyer, Gordon Stulberg, that the so-called "principle" for which the Guild was bargaining (writer ownership and payment on a royalty basis) was not one the Guild had demanded of the major studios. The NLRB lawyer speculated, "[i]n other words, this is a strike to compel the little guys to give in so that someday you can knock over the big guys." Stulberg replied that "they don't pay the minimums in television that are paid in the majors, and we have to make up the gap by some sort of royalty principle."[39]

Although the Guild struck over the right to royalties and initially considered residuals to be a betrayal of the fundamental principle over which writers were on strike, in practice, it was sometimes difficult for writers to understand the difference. The Guild's ideal was that writers would either own or be entitled to profit sharing for all uses of their work, including the first use. (If a film was a huge success in its theatrical run, the writers would share in the profits.) What they ultimately settled for was residuals: the writers did not own their works or share in the profits from the first use (theatrical release or the original TV broadcast), but they got residual payments only for reuses (for reruns of TV programs, or when a movie was rereleased in theaters or, for movies released after 1948, when the movie was shown on TV).

In the end, the Guild got producers to agree to residuals for some reuses but gave up on claiming the right to payment for broadcast on television of pre-1948 movies. Instead, the Guild agreed that some of the money the studios made would be used to create a pension plan. In 1955, RKO became the first studio to sell its film library for TV showing, followed in 1956 by Warner Bros. and Twentieth Century Fox. This was a huge source of revenue for the studios, and the writers got none of it in residuals.[40]

For TV, the Guild secured a contract with independent television producers that became effective in part in November 1952 and in full in February 1953. The three-year agreement provided a complex schedule of minimum payments for different kinds of writing and required additional payments for rewrites and polishes. The agreement required automatic credit arbitration for a teleplay based on original material that had not been published or produced in another medium. It provided screen credits and gave writers the right to see the final shooting script and to view the rough cut and answer print, and it required notice to all writers employed on the same material as a way of limiting simultaneous or sequential rewriting and also to enable writers to dispute credits.[41] The agreement provided a complicated set of rules for separated and reserved rights.[42]

To enforce the right to residuals, the Guild recognized that it would have to assume responsibility for monitoring uses of material and keeping track of how much writers were owed and whether they were paid. The Guild studied and debated for months in 1955 how to monitor reruns, and it anticipated substantial struggles with major studios over how to police reuse of material. It was important to secure the cooperation of actors' and directors' unions to set up a national monitoring system, as all of them shared an interest in residuals. At one point, the Guild committee tasked with enforcement of residuals requirements considered the reliance on auditing the producers' records and also trying some variation of the ASCAP system of monitoring broadcasts.[43] The Dramatists Guild had done this for its members. Monitoring broadcasts was necessary not only to calculate residuals but also to ensure that credits were not clipped at the end of the program so writers would get the credit for which they bargained. Of course, if the industry had adopted a percentage of the gross formula instead of residuals for reuse, it would have been unnecessary to monitor broadcasts except to protect credits. On the other hand, it wasn't all bad for the Guild to have the responsibility for tracking residuals. As the Board recognized, it would empower the Guild to demand studios to say "what is being paid and how it is being paid; and it will give the Guild a chance to police contracts."[44]

The SWG was not alone in reconsidering lease versus sale of original material in the late 1940s. The RWG also launched an effort to restructure the terms on which writers sold their work to studios and networks. In 1946, the RWG proposed to the American Association of Advertising Agencies (AAAA) that leasing of one-time rights to radio scripts be the only method of acquiring rights to them. The AAAA had instead proposed that one-time lease would be "a satisfactory method of operation in many cases," but that "there were many others where it is desirable to buy scripts outright." The AAAA had been drafting form contracts for its member agencies to use, and the form could be changed to stipulate that scripts would be licensed rather than sold. JWT's lawyer, Ed Wilson, was concerned that the RWG effort to eliminate outright sales of scripts was an unnecessary and undesirable effort to change "the recognized industry custom." An advertiser needed "the complete protection" of script ownership because "we expect to be in business for many years and expect to put on many radio shows. We certainly want to be free from claims that we have 'lifted' from somebody's script which we once used years before."[45] Another agency member feared that lease of scripts would allow writers to recycle ideas or characters in scripts written for other clients. "It should not be possible for the writer to make a second sale of [a] script by changing the name of the central character [from 'Dr. Christian'] to 'Dr. Anderson.'"[46]

When negotiating about employment on TV (as opposed to reuse of material on TV), producers were much more amenable to payment on a percentage basis, largely because TV was not yet profitable. Writers, as the Guild's Executive Board said, were "gambling on the percentage part of the deal" but thought that their proposal (a percentage of "gross receipts" not "net profit") "was a revolutionary idea and applicable also to the motion picture field." "If and when there are profits, we should have a piece of it," the Board explained, but it should be a percentage of the gross, not the net.[47] In 1955, the Board was asked to approve a waiver for a deal in which a producer asked a writer for a script in exchange for one-third of the producer's share of the package with the stipulation that all rights in the script would revert to the writer if the package did not sell and that the writer's compensation, when paid, would be above the minimum. The Board approved the waiver, while insisting that its decision not be considered a precedent, that the deal must guarantee the writer at least the MBA minimum, and that the rights in the script must revert to the writer within one year.[48]

With the principle of payment for reuse (as residuals were initially known) established, every round of contract negotiations for film and TV, with the majors, the independents, the networks, and (in the beginning) for live and filmed TV, invited a new opportunity to tweak the formula. And discussions of the credit rules then always implicated the payment of residuals.[49]

How Residuals Changed the Debate over Credits

Once compensation began to turn on screen credit, the Guild had to debate all over again a fair system for dividing up credit, which was especially difficult in the collaborative writing culture of TV. Two different points of view were in tension, as reflected in proposals of the Credits Committee in the autumn of 1955. On the one hand, the writers wanted to limit the number of writing credits in TV to make it more like film and thereby enhance the writers' prestige by identifying them as the authors of TV. On the other hand, the Committee suggested it might be necessary to give additional dialogue credits on some shows, particularly situation comedies, because "a script is often given to a writer who can put humor into it and make it playable," and "such a writer should get credit in order to share in residuals." In August 1955, the Board settled for restricting the number of credits making it the same formula as for screenplays: teleplay by, or teleplay and story by. The Board did allow a special material credit in a variety show. As for rewrites in comedy shows, the Board recommended a change in the arbitration standards rather than in the allowable credits, urging the Credits Committee to consider whether it was possible to revise the one-third rule "so that it is not always on a mathematical basis" and therefore the comedy writer who contributed a significant amount of the humor in a comedy would be found to have contributed the one-third necessary to get a shared teleplay or story credit.[50]

Debates over removing one's name from credit after having been rewritten were also complicated by residuals. In 1955, the Guild considered the matter of Paul Franklin, who in 1954 had written a teleplay called *Dead to Rights*. The producer, Gross Krasne, then hired Robert C. Dennis to rewrite the teleplay, and when Franklin saw the revised version, he asked that his name be removed from the credits. On the third rerun of the teleplay in 1954, however, Franklin's name was somehow added as a story credit, and under the MBA, therefore, Franklin was entitled to a residual of $50. Franklin decided he wanted the money, apparently as a form of damages for the harm done to his reputation by using his name in connection with a picture from which he had tried to disassociate himself. When the Guild asked Gross Krasne to pay Franklin,

Krasne's lawyers insisted that the addition of Franklin's name was a clerical error, the residual had already been paid to Dennis, and paying twice would be unfair to the producer. And, alternatively, the MBA required residuals to be paid to all credited writers and provided no remedy to a writer who believed his name had been used in error.

This matter flummoxed the Board, both in the individual case of balancing the equities between Dennis and Franklin and as a general policy. As for the equities in the case, the Board felt "that Mr. Dennis had a right to rely on Mr. Franklin's withdrawal [from credit] as a guarantee to Mr. Dennis of full payment of residuals, and the Board therefore [could] not at this late date deprive Mr. Dennis of half the residuals in order to compensate Mr. Franklin for the damages he feels he suffered by the incorrect use of his name on this picture." Some felt that the issue was not a Guild problem and that Franklin should simply pursue a claim for damages against Gross Krasne. Some thought the solution was for a writer to use a pseudonym so that a poor quality script would not ruin his reputation but the writer could collect a residual. But allowing writing under a pseudonym was controversial in the mid-1950s because of the blacklist, and so the Board decided that if pseudonyms were to be permitted there would have to be a policy allowing their use only in the case of "mutilation" of material. Yet the Guild recognized it had no easy way to distinguish actual mutilation of material from improper uses of a pseudonym, other than by arbitration, which was not intended to resolve this sort of dispute.[51]

Negotiating for Separate Rights to Control Other Uses

The Guild secured for writers not only residuals but also rights to use a script or the characters or ideas in it for purposes other than to make a movie. The negotiation for separated rights began in the 1930s when some writers opposed the practice of writers selling the copyright in their script. They thought writers ought to lease their scripts to the studios so that the writer would have the right to develop a script that the studio decided not to put into production. One legal problem with this strategy was that studios believed that copyrights were not divisible. (Technically, until the Copyright Act was revised in 1976, a copyright was indivisible, meaning all the rights in a copyrighted work could only be assigned from one owner to the next, though the owner could license it for multiple purposes and multiple times.) Studios feared that purchasing only a license to use the copyrighted script for a movie might void the copyright in the script and the studio would be unable to prevent other studios from making a similar movie from the same script. In the 1951 MBA, the Guild negotiated the predecessor of the separated rights provisions. That first version allowed writers to negotiate as individuals to retain book publishing rights and provided that separate consideration would be paid writers for publication, stage, and radio rights. But it did not provide a rule that would give all writers separated rights in publication, stage, and radio rights as a matter of course. In 1960, the WGA sought and obtained separated rights in media other than book, stage, and radio. The separated rights provision has remained without substantial change since.[52]

In the 1930s and 1940s, dividing up the rights in a script was less threatening to studios than it later became. Although the studios owned the copyrights to the work, the business model of motion picture production at the time did not demand total control over the ideas or characters in it. Motion picture production did not then entail possible sequels or tied-in marketing campaigns of novelizations and merchandising, so the main aspect of controlling a screenplay was complete at the time the picture was filmed. Similarly, early television production envisioned a one-time use of the script rather than the uses in related series. Some of the major writers in both film and television had successful careers writing plays, short stories, and novels, and they could negotiate to protect their own reputations and the literary rights to the material they wrote for the movies or TV. However, a case occasionally arose about whether a later work infringed a copyright to a film, such as the litigation over whether a radio show that Dashiell Hammett created based on the Sam Spade character from his novel *The Maltese Falcon* infringed the copyright to the movie based on the novel. The contract between Warner Bros., Hammett, and Knopf, publisher and owner of copyright in the book, did not prohibit Hammett from granting CBS the right to use book characters in a radio show. (In litigation over that contract, the court suggested in dictum that the sale of the copyright to a story containing a character does not foreclose the author's later use of the character unless "the character really constitutes the story being told." The court clearly wanted to allow Hammett to keep writing Sam Spade stories, but rather than interpret the contract to allow that, it went on to suggest that Spade wasn't copyrightable at all because he wasn't "the story being told.") In general, however, sequel rights and character rights were not considered crucial at that time.[53]

Sequel and character rights became hugely important, however, with the rise of the blockbuster in the 1970s and 1980s, which could be promoted by tied-in marketing and could generate the desired return on the massive investment of production costs through an emphasis on sequels, franchises, novelization, and merchandising. In the same era, technological change multiplied the number of formats or media through which a motion picture or television show could be disseminated. These major economic changes increased the possibilities for mining the ideas in a single script for use in spin-offs. The number of sticks in the bundle of rights represented by the copyright in a screenplay for a motion picture or a television show grew, as did the entrepreneurial opportunities for the copyright owner. In the 1950s, a television production company might be willing to allow the writer to keep all rights except the use of the script on a single TV show anticipated to be shown only once. By the 1980s, possibilities grew for conflict over the use of the script or its ideas in multiple formats.

The principle of separated rights and the fights over ownership of characters occurred before production companies began regularly to use trademark law to claim an exclusive right to use the title, characters, character names, and other distinctive elements of a film. The individual and collective contracts of the 1950s and before did not contemplate how writers could exercise separated rights if doing so would infringe the studio's trademark in the characters and so on. As studios sought to use trademark to protect an exclusive right to all the distinctive elements of a film or TV program, opportunities for writers to profit from separated rights declined, at least if the studio objected to collaborating with the writer on how those rights would be exercised.

Authors and Owners of Film and TV

It is ironic that the period between 1945 and 1955, when the Writers Guild organized television and pioneered residuals and separated rights and thus ensured its own survival and the financial well-being of many of its members and some writers' claims to be authors of their work, was also the time when the Guild was nearly destroyed by the blacklist. Reading the Executive Board minutes and the Guild magazines during this period is an almost surreal experience of seeing a union deliberate about the relationship between writers and their intellectual property rights and how to adapt to a radically changing entertainment industry, while at the same time figuring how to purge its ranks of communists and whether to cooperate in which aspects of the whole misguided witch hunt. Each of these topics appeared to consume equal amounts of energy and thought of the Guild's Board. One nearly destroyed the union, and the other saved it. Many of the ideas for how the Guild should protect writers through licensing rather than outright sale, profit sharing, and separation of rights originated with writers—John Howard Lawson, Lester Cole, Dalton Trumbo, Ring Lardner, Jr.—whom the Board seemed willing to allow to be driven out of Hollywood.

The history of residuals is inextricably linked with the quest of Hollywood writers to achieve greater recognition of their role as authors of motion pictures and television programs. Almost every discussion about what writers ought to demand, whether in Guild deliberations or publications or by students of Hollywood, tends to intermingle the issues of compensation with attribution and creative control. What makes the history of the Guild's campaign for residuals so fascinating is its effort to reconceptualize the role of the writer as a proper author entitled to share in the proceeds of the work. The economic issues of residuals—from the earliest demands for profit sharing in the 1920s up through the last round of negotiations for a new Minimum Basic Agreement—have always been a crucial part of the writers' efforts to obtain recognition as the authors of films and TV.

Negotiation over residuals also raised issues of writers' status as labor. Writers understood themselves as allied with management and as managers of capital as they aspired to share in the profits (through residuals), have more control over uses of their work (through separated rights), and be recognized as the authors of films and TV programs (through screen credit). Yet writers understood themselves as labor when they negotiated for minimum payment by the job (as a script fee) or by the week, and they had to insist on their status as employees in order to assert their rights to unionize and bargain collectively. They thought that distancing themselves from employee status would enhance their claims to profit sharing and their control over subsidiary rights in their work. They also thought maintaining their independence would reduce the power producers had over working conditions. Ironically, writers had to insist on their status as labor in order to gain power as entrepreneurs entitled to profit sharing in their work.

Act III

DENOUEMENT

6

--- ◆ ---

The Blacklist

The public is not to be protected from my work, however beguiling and subversive it may be. The public is only to be protected from my name.

—Paul Jarrico

Only a decade after its founding, the Screen Writers Guild confronted an existential crisis when studios blacklisted hundreds of its members on allegations that they were communists or because they refused to answer questions before the House Un-American Activities Committee (HUAC). The blacklist was a spectacle of legal process—hearings, subpoenas, alleged breaches of the collective agreement and individual employment contracts, and invocations of the First and Fifth Amendments—in service of a gross injustice. It revealed to writers that people actually noticed writing credits. (Otherwise, who would care about the politics of the writer since writers were a good deal less visible than actors, producers, and directors?) More important, it also revealed the vulnerability of the Guild's contractual right to determine screen credit. The blacklist tore the Guild apart at the crucial moment when it was negotiating its second Minimum Basic Agreement (MBA) with the studios, trying to establish the principle of writer ownership of scripts, and trying to organize television writers so they would have the same rights to a minimum wage, script ownership, profit sharing, and screen credit that had been the Guild's top demands in film for years. Studios, ad agencies, and networks embraced the blacklist just at the time that writers had become quite aggressive in their demands for a greater share of the profits from their work, and because the Guild focused on making equitable profit sharing linked to attributed authorship, it is unsurprising that the blacklist also focused on eliminating the screen credits on which compensation rested. Employers and purchasers of writers' work had very good economic reasons—whatever their ideology—for weakening the organizations of writers that were demanding more protection of writers' copyrights.[1]

The history of the blacklist is well known, but what is less commonly known is that it presented the Guild with a gruesome collision among the laws and norms that writers considered essential to their profession. The familiar legal histories are about whether the First Amendment prohibits firing employees because of their political beliefs or jailing witnesses who refuse to discuss their political associations or ideas, and about how the black-list destroyed lives and careers. The less familiar legal history is about how the blacklist nearly destroyed the Guild's contractual right to determine screen credit for those screenwriters who continued to write and sell scripts.

The Guild has been justly criticized for capitulating to the blacklist, and its unwillingness or inability to protect writers from discriminatory treatment on the basis of ideology or association. Although the Guild hired top lawyers to challenge the blacklist, the courts ruled against the writers over and over again, and in the end, the Guild grudgingly settled the litigation and agreed to modify the Minimum Basic Agreement to allow the studios to deny credit to blacklisted writers. As a result, the Guild effectively ceded for over a decade the power to control screen credit for suspected communists.

The unfamiliar legal story of the blacklist is how the legal rights to screen credit survived. It is not well known that the Guild continued to conduct credit arbitrations at the request of blacklisted writers, even though everyone knew that the studios would ignore the Guild's determination if a writer was on a blacklist. The fact that the credit-arbitration machinery continued to operate, even when it was futile, enabled the Guild to regain power over credits when the blacklist began to fall apart.

This story is, thus, about both the significance of attribution and the significance of legal processes in preserving institutional power during times of extreme political pressure.

The Guild's adherence to its legal processes facilitated restoration of credits to blacklisted writers in the 1990s and 2000s. Credit corrections, like every other credit determination, often pitted one Guild member against another, or the heirs of one against the heirs of another, when both were deeply invested in issues of reputation and authorship but also current or potential beneficiaries of the residual payments that turn on screen credit.

Legal norms were essential to the Guild in making these painful and high-stakes decisions.

Many have written excellent histories of the blacklist and biographies of blacklisted writers. My focus is on the Guild's ultimately unsuccessful use of litigation to challenge the blacklist and on the ways in which the Guild attempted to keep the credit system operating during the blacklist, which was particularly difficult because the whole point of the blacklist was to keep the names of suspected communists and sympathizers from being associated with projects. Many people's careers were destroyed, and they did not work for a decade—or ever again. And the blacklist on writers (along with actors and directors) was part of a general attack on Hollywood labor in the postwar years, an attack that hurt craft labor as much as, or more than, the better-paid talent. But some writers did continue to work, and for them, the blacklist operated as a denial of screen credit. How the Guild balanced the interests of its members—blacklisted ones, fronts, and those who tried desperately to avoid being blacklisted—both during and after the blacklist reveals the power of legal norms about authorship even in a setting like Hollywood where contractual and intellectual property law are the usual subjects of legal analysis.[2]

The Beginning of the Blacklist

Political conflict within the Guild began in its earliest years. Like many writers, artists, and other intellectuals, some influential Hollywood writers and Guild leaders were Communist Party members or quite leftist and others were not. The efforts in 1946 by writers in film, radio, television, and publishing to end the employer ownership of script copyrights and establish instead a licensing system, as the previous chapter describes, provided studios an incentive to exploit the red scare and the political differences among writers to weaken their negotiating position. The enactment of the Taft-Hartley Act in the summer of 1947 also provided the impetus for renewed recriminations within the union and from outside it. The law required leaders of unions to sign an affidavit swearing that they were not communists. The SWG Executive Board spent some time at almost every meeting from September 1947 onward debating whether the leadership should sign the affidavits and tried to postpone any action on the noncommunist-affidavit issue so the Guild's fractious membership could coalesce around bargaining demands.[3]

The Guild leadership lost the ability to postpone dealing with the issue in October 1947 when nineteen successful Hollywood writers and directors were subpoenaed to appear before the House Un-American Activities Committee (HUAC) to answer two incendiary questions: "Are you a member of the Screen Writers Guild?" and "Are you now, or have you ever been, a member of the Communist Party?" Because the HUAC chair was militantly anti-union as well as anticommunist, the question about Guild membership was almost as accusatory as the question about Communist Party membership, particularly since he believed that the Guild was a communist-dominated organization.

Ten witnesses famously invoked the First Amendment freedom of speech and association as a basis for refusing to answer directly. (They might have avoided the contempt citation and prison had they invoked the Fifth Amendment privilege against self-incrimination. But they insisted that political and union affiliations were not criminal.) They were convicted of contempt of Congress and sentenced to prison. (Ironically, two of them—Lester Cole and Ring Lardner, Jr.—went to the same prison as the HUAC chairman, Parnell Thomas, who had sent them there. Parnell, an arch-conservative stockbroker turned Republican congressman from New Jersey, was convicted of defrauding the government. President Truman pardoned Thomas in 1952.) Among the ten who refused to name names before HUAC—Alvah Bessie, Herbert Bilberman, Lester Cole, Edward Dmytryk, Ring Lardner, Jr., John Howard Lawson, Albert Maltz, Samuel Ornitz, Adrian Scott, and Dalton Trumbo—were some of the most talented and successful Hollywood writers. (An eleventh, the famous playwright and refugee from the Nazis, Bertolt Brecht, answered the HUAC questions a bit and then promptly fled to Europe.)[4]

Although initially the producers and studios had expressed reservations about HUAC's attempt to pressure the studios to blacklist suspected communists, shortly after the "Unfriendly Ten" appeared before Congress and were pilloried in the press, the studios changed their tune. Fifty top studio executives met at the Waldorf-Astoria hotel in New York in late November 1947 and issued a joint statement condemning the Ten and promising that they would "forthwith discharge or suspend without compensation [members of the

Ten] in our employ" and henceforth would not "knowingly employ a communist."[5]

In the same month, a fierce leadership battle occurred within the membership of the Guild. A moderate slate was voted in, purging the Executive Board of any writer who had communist sympathies. By the end of November, Hugo Butler, Lester Cole, and Ring Larder, Jr. were off the Board, and the economic program they had championed (writer ownership of scripts and a percentage of the gross) fell from the attention of the new Board. (The story of their economic program is told in Chapter 5.) Even with the leftists out of Guild leadership positions, the Guild did not immediately capitulate to the wishes of its most conservative members to cooperate with the blacklist or the efforts to make political litmus tests a condition of employment or union office. But the new leadership ultimately complied with the Taft-Hartley requirement that union leaders sign noncommunist affidavits. While insisting writers' politics were irrelevant to their work, the SWG also tried to protect members from rumors and innuendo that they were communists, and it struggled to respond to charges from right-wing organizations like the American Legion that the Guild was full of communists and that their ideologies had seeped into films and were ruining the reputation of Hollywood. In the end, the verdict of many scholars, as said by one, is that "the blacklist could not have been instituted, nor could it have been enforced without the assistance of the Screen Writers Guild and the other Hollywood talent guilds."[6]

The Guild's involvement in litigation challenging the blacklist began on December 8, 1947, when Cole and Lardner appeared before the new Board to plead for legal support for members cited for contempt of Congress and dismissed from their jobs. After they spoke to the Board for twenty-five minutes, they left and the Board members asked Morris Cohn, longtime lawyer for the Guild and a regular attendee at Board meetings, to leave the room, too. In his absence, the Board decided that Cohn be instructed to tell the members at the December 15 general membership meeting that Cohn "has assisted counsel for the five men suspended; . . . that the Board has taken the position that the Guild has nothing whatsoever to do with the Washington hearings of the 10 men cited for contempt and that he [Cohn] should observe this line of demarcation in his statement to the membership." A Board member moved that the Guild make legal services available to any Guild member to challenge discrimination in employment "because of race, religion, or political belief," but the motion failed. Instead, the Board decided simply to issue a statement admonishing the producers not to discriminate on the basis of political affiliation.[7]

But even the moderates on the new Executive Board were alarmed by the Waldorf-Astoria statement, and, regardless of their views on communism, they feared that a political test for writers would be disastrous for their membership and for the power of the Guild as a bargaining agent. The general membership voted on December 15 that the Guild take legal action against blacklisting. In December 1947 and January 1948, the Board decided to initiate litigation against the studios to challenge the blacklist. Although blanching at the $25,000 fee, the Board hired Thurman Arnold, the New Dealer, antitrust expert, and former federal judge who founded the elite Washington, DC, law firm of Arnold, Fortas & Porter, to file a suit against the studios challenging the Waldorf-Astoria statement as a conspiracy in restraint of trade.[8]

The blacklist quickly decimated the ranks of the Guild membership, which meant a corresponding decline in dues-payers. The minutes of the Executive Board meetings month after month in 1948 listed hundreds of members in bad standing, which was usually for failure to pay dues. Many names on the list were eminent (and formerly highly paid) writers and stalwart leaders of the Guild (including the Ten) whose dues (half of one percent of annual earnings) sustained the Guild's services to all members. Some were former Guild Executive Board members, noted writers and directors, and even members of the negotiating committee for the new MBA, who of course were forced to resign from that committee, too.[9]

The Guild was divided about how to handle the blacklisted writers. Some members felt the Guild should support them strongly, while others felt the Guild should distance itself from them to protect noncommunist members from guilt by association. This dilemma persisted through the entire blacklist period. People's names would turn up on lists of suspected communists, either because they were allegedly named by a writer under HUAC subpoena or in an FBI interview or because their names were on the American Legion's list of subversives or in *Red Channels: The Report of Communist Influence in Radio and Television,* which listed 151 radio and television writers and actors and journalists whom it branded as communists, sympathizers, or otherwise subversive. Sometimes the blacklist wasn't public—a writer would just not be rehired at the end of a contract and his or her agent would simply report that no studio had a project suitable for that writer. The inaccuracies of the blacklists were many—some allegedly subversive activities were not (such as being at a party where some people discussed Marxism or donating to the efforts to resist fascism during the Spanish Civil War), and some writers wound up on blacklists entirely in error because they had the same name as another person or the person who named them was mistaken or settling a score. Many writers wanted the Guild to create a process by which writers could clear their names. But, as members of the Board constantly repeated, if the Guild did so, it would effectively be participating in the creation of a political litmus test for employment, which was exactly what it had condemned.

Writers' Legal Challenges to the Blacklist

At the May 1950 general membership meeting, there was sharp disagreement over whether the Guild should participate in the criminal-contempt cases against writers. The Board had decided, after considerable discussion, that the Guild was nonpolitical; therefore, what to do for the targeted writers was "a matter for the individual consciences of writers as citizens." The Guild's longtime counsel, Morris Cohn, was representing the Ten and had informed the Board that he could not act as the Board's legal counsel in advising the membership how to proceed with respect to the Ten because of a conflict of interest. The Board had waived the conflict, but at the general membership meeting, controversy arose over whether Cohn could continue to represent both the Guild and the Ten. Although Cohn explained to the Board and the membership that the conflict, such as it was, did not preclude him from continuing to represent the Guild while also representing the Ten, he nevertheless offered to resign as counsel to the Guild. The Board accepted his resignation. The membership decided that the Guild should take no action of any kind with respect to the cases of the individuals charged with contempt. Thus, when Mrs. Lawson, Mrs. Maltz, and Mrs. Cole (who were active in a group of wives of blacklisted writers) asked to appear before the Board in August 1950 to seek the Guild's support for a petition for clemency for their husbands and the other writers who were serving sentences for contempt of Congress, the Board refused to see them and refused even to allow them use of the SWG mailing list to send their petition to the Guild membership, explaining that the membership had "established a definite policy that no action is to be taken relating in any way to the contempt cases."[10]

Writers among the Ten filed a series of cases challenging the studios' effort to discharge them and deny them screen credit. Although the courts ruled against them, the legal basis for the courts' rulings was dubious. Writers could be refused hire for any reason and fired at the expiration of a contract. But firing a writer during the term of employment appeared to breach the individual employment contract, and refusing to grant screen credit for a script a writer had already written clearly violated the MBA.

The studios insisted that the blacklisted writers had breached the morals clause of their contracts, which both allowed an immediate firing and absolved the studio of the duty to comply with MBA provisions with regard to the writer. The language of the morals clauses varied slightly among the contracts, but, in the end, the differences did not affect the courts' conclusion that writers could be fired for running afoul of HUAC. The morals clause of the form contract RKO entered with Paul Jarrico provided the following:

> In addition to the services of the Writer, an essential consideration to the Corporation under this agreement is the popularity and good reputation of the Writer with the public. From the date hereof, and continuing throughout the production and distribution of the Pictures, the Writer will conduct himself with due regard to public conventions and morals, and will not do anything which shall constitute a penal offense involving moral turpitude, or which will tend to degrade him or bring him or the Corporation or the motion picture industry into public disgrace, obloquy, ill will or ridicule, or which will offend public morals or decency.

The studios argued that the writers' contempt of Congress in refusing to answer questions before HUAC constituted conduct that would tend to degrade them in society, bring them into public hatred or contempt, shock or offend the community, and prejudice their employers. Jarrico's contract provided that breach of the morals clause would relieve the company of the obligation to accord credit.

Not every morals clause, however, contained such a provision. The Warner Bros. form contracts allowed the studio to cancel the agreement if the writer breached the morals clause but said nothing about screen credit. And not every writer had a morals clause in his or her contract, particularly before the late 1940s. (Dalton Trumbo said, in refusing to allow a morals clause in his contract at MGM, "when Louis B. Mayer signs a morals clause, I'll sign a morals clause."[11]) Writers had a number of arguments about why their invocation of their First Amendment rights before Congress did not breach the morals clause and why, in any event, the studios did not have a legal basis for firing them and denying them screen credit for work they had already written.[12]

The Guild and the studios had never had the occasion to test the relationship between individual employment contracts and the Minimum Basic Agreement. The Guild believed that writers and studios could not agree to terms less favorable to the writer than the MBA provided, and that view was reflected in federal labor law. The Supreme Court had ruled in a number of cases in the early 1940s that individual employment contracts could not derogate from rights negotiated collectively. But given the brevity of the first MBA (it was only five pages long), the meaning of the MBA's minimum terms was not entirely clear. Nor was it clear how claimed violations of individual contracts would be enforced. The MBA had the grievance-arbitration and conciliation process, but individual contracts did not. And many individual agreements did not say how they would be enforced, except that they reserved the right to the studio to seek injunctive relief to prevent breach of the agreement by the writer. The MBA's conciliation and grievance procedure might have dictated that the question of termination for refusing to testify should be submitted to conciliation and arbitration rather than immediate firing.[13]

In mulling over legal theories that would allow the Guild to challenge the blacklist, counsel for the Guild made a number of arguments about why the studios lacked the right to deny screen credit to suspected communists or to those who refused to testify. First, the morals clause did not trump the MBA, which did not contain any provision entitling the studio to fire or deny credit to writers based on allegedly immoral behavior. Second, the Guild pointed to an August 1951 arbitration decision involving the Radio Writers Guild and CBS, in which CBS had asserted that the morals clause of an individual hiring contract allowed it to terminate the employment of writers who did anything to offend the community or reflect unfavorably on CBS or its advertisers. The arbitrator determined that the morals clause was invalid because it gave CBS a power that the MBA did not. Third, one studio had deleted from its individual hiring contracts the provision that allowed it to deny credit to writers who allegedly violated the morals clause. This, the writers argued, showed that the studio itself did not believe it had the contractual right to deny screen credit to writers who violated the morals clause. Finally, the Guild argued that writers' political affiliations could not possibly harm the studios because, unlike actors, writers and their personal lives are unknown to the public.[14]

None of these arguments succeeded in court when the Guild or the writers presented them. In the case of Ring Lardner, Jr., the Ninth Circuit Court of Appeals found that his refusal to state whether he was a communist harmed the reputation of Twentieth Century Fox, explicitly linking his status as credited writer with the studio's reputation:

> The screen writers never have had the publicity buildups as indi-
> viduals that screen actors have had. There may have been a ten-
> dency for the ten men, all acting about alike before the com-
> mittee, to be lost in anonymity as so many screen writers. Yet the
> conduct of and the ultimate conviction of Lardner in the circum-
> stances of the case could not help but hurt Fox and everybody else
> in the motion picture business. It is true, as the record shows, that
> some people supported the ten men. But how could it be said that
> as a result of Lardner's conduct the employer sustained a net gain,
> or even held its own? Fox just necessarily suffered a net loss in
> public prestige.[15]

Lardner, who had won an Academy Award for *Woman of the Year* (1942) and had written the noir classic *Laura* (1944), was forced to spend the blacklist years in exile in England. He returned to Hollywood in the 1960s and wrote *M*A*S*H* (1970), for which he won yet another Academy Award.

While some Guild members thought the Guild should do more for the blacklisted writers, the majority of the Executive Board concluded that to defend suspected or confessed communists would harm the Guild and its members, so it largely sat on the sidelines. Specifically, Guild members disagreed on whether the Guild should pay the retainer of Thurman Arnold, the elite Washington lawyer whom the Guild had hired to challenge the blacklist. And if the Guild was to continue the suit, members disagreed about how the Guild should define the scope of the representation. This conflict raised questions over whether the Guild should ever support one side on issues of politics and whether it had a duty to represent the screenwriters Guild leaders found reprehensible on grounds of politics or morality.[16]

The battle over screen credit for suspected communists was even more threatening to the Guild and its members than was the battle over their firing. The Guild had long existed in a world in which there was no just-cause provision in the MBA governing the hiring and firing of writers. Unlike most collective bargaining agreements, the MBA did not require studios to have just cause to fire writers. Individual employment contracts often allowed the studio to lay off a writer without cause during the term of a contract but required cause to terminate a contract before expiration of the term. Individual employment contracts allowed studios broad latitude over writers. Once hired, though, writers were entitled to the protections of the MBA, and one of the most fundamental was the right to screen credit. If the studios could disregard the MBA provisions on credit for some writers, all writers were at risk. As time went on, this became an increasingly awkward line to draw. In 1951, for example, when Michael Wilson wrote an irate letter to the Guild Executive Board after Twentieth Century Fox fired him and proposed to deny him screen credit for a movie he had written which was shortly to be released, the Executive Board acknowledged both that "Fox had a perfect right to lay Mr. Wilson off under his contract," but that "the Guild is still adamant in its opposition to the blacklist," and it was "the Guild's obligation to see that Mr. Wilson receives credit on the picture he has coming up notwithstanding his subpoena by the House Un-American Activities Committee."[17]

In January 1948, the Board realized that the studios were going to deny screen credit to the Ten. An arbitration committee had awarded screenplay credit on *Smart Woman* (1948) to Alvah Bessie, Louis Morheim, and Herbert Margolis, but the producer, Hal Chester, had informed the Guild's Credits Committee that he refused to credit Bessie because of the contempt citation. The Board promptly decided to send Chester and the studio "the usual notice" of the decision of the arbitrators and postponed discussion of what to do if the studio failed to abide by the arbitrators' decision. It stuck with that position as the number of blacklisted writers grew and as studios persisted in trying to deny screen credit to newly blacklisted writers. Columbia wanted to release *The Son of Dr. Jekyll* in May 1951 without blacklisted writer Edward Huebsch's name and asked Guild permission because Heubsch was the sole writer so there was no one else to credit. The Executive Committee turned

Columbia down with a tart reminder that "credit must be given in accordance with Schedule A," but Guild leaders communicated privately to B.B. Kahane, a producer at Columbia Pictures, that the Guild would turn a blind eye to violations, and so Huebsch was omitted from the credits.[18]

Yet, as a practical matter, there was not a great deal the Guild could do if a studio refused to credit a writer. When Hugo Butler's name was deleted from the credits and advertising for the film *He Ran All the Way* in July 1951, the Guild's Executive Board simply passed a motion asking the producer to pay the Guild for the cost of running another ad with Butler's name on it in the trade papers or pay Butler the price of the ad.[19]

Some studios had begun to ask writers to sign individual agreements waiving credit as a condition of hire, and the Guild feared that individual agreements contrary to the MBA's minimum protections would undermine the whole collective bargaining system. An agent called the Guild to inquire how to respond to a studio's request that the writer sign a credit waiver. Frances Inglis, the Guild's executive secretary, responded that the Guild determined credit and the writer should so inform the studio and refuse to sign the waiver. But if a writer lacked the courage to refuse, there was little the Guild could do. In early 1949, the Guild had proposed in the negotiations for a new MBA that questions arising under individual writers' employment contracts should be subject to arbitration as well as issues arising under the MBA, in part because the Guild recognized that individual agreements could undermine the collective protections. The producers were adamantly opposed. The Guild had also proposed in negotiations for the new MBA in early 1949 that studios not discriminate in employment on the basis of race, color, creed, sex, or politics, believing this language might address the blacklist. Indeed, the SWG's lawyer, Morris Cohn, wrote to Thurman Arnold, the prominent Washington, DC lawyer whom the SWG had hired to handle the blacklist litigation, in December 1948 seeking his advice whether proposing such a term would interfere with Arnold's litigation against the blacklist.[20] Arnold's response does not appear in the files, but the Guild got nowhere in its effort to end the blacklist through a nondiscrimination provision in the MBA.

The conflict between the MBA and the growing blacklist came to a head in a fight with Howard Hughes, the irascible and reactionary head of RKO studios. Hughes—aviator, inventor, tycoon, and finally movie producer—had been successful with movies such as *Two Arabian Nights* (1928), *Hell's Angels*

(1930), and *Scarface* (1932). He gained control over RKO shortly before World War II and became keenly interested in the political affiliations of the studio's employees. After winning his battle against Jarrico, Hughes sold RKO at a tidy profit in 1955, ending his involvement in the movie business. He vanished from public life, becoming famously reclusive and the subject of speculation about his mental health and substance abuse. When he died in 1976, his heirs fought quite publicly over his estate, though many forgot about his many business and film accomplishments until the 2004 film *The Aviator* reintroduced Hughes (minus his red-baiting) to the public through the portrayal by Leonardo DiCaprio.

RKO had hired the successful writer Paul Jarrico in January 1951 at $2,000 per week to write a script for a project then known as *The Miami Story*. At the time he was hired, Jarrico had already been named (by Edward Dmytryk in an FBI interview), and he suspected he had been or would soon be blacklisted. Sure enough, just as Jarrico handed in the script, he got a subpoena. Nevertheless, RKO made the film. When it was in post-production, RKO advised the Guild and other participating writers that it proposed to omit Jarrico from the credits. RKO's handling of the matter was entirely bureaucratic on the surface. The notice of tentative writing credits looked just like any of the dozens of such notices the studios sent to the Guild each year; it simply proposed to credit two writers and made no mention of Jarrico. Jarrico requested credit arbitration. Ironically, one of the two others, Earl Felton, was a struggling writer and an old and close friend of Dalton Trumbo (who was in prison at the time). Felton on a few occasions during the blacklist allowed his name to be put on stories Trumbo had written. The Felton-Jarrico disagreement over credit on *The Las Vegas* story had little to do with politics and everything to do with the usual reasons why writers arbitrated credit—it mattered to their career. The Guild, following its customary processes, appointed three of its members to serve anonymously as arbiters to determine writing credits on the picture. The arbiters unanimously determined that Paul Jarrico and two of the others should receive the "screenplay by" credit, with a "story by" credit for the third. This determination was protested by one writer, who asked the arbiters to read a final version of what was actually filmed, which had not previously been provided to them. When RKO submitted the final version of the script, the arbiters switched the order of two names, and the Guild sent its form letter to RKO announcing the arbitration committee decision. But when

RKO released the movie, Jarrico's name was nowhere to be found, which prompted Jarrico to remark bitterly that apparently his politics did not make him unsuitable as a writer—after all, he had been hired when the studio knew he had been named as a communist. "The public is not to be protected from my work, however beguiling and subversive it may be. The public is to be protected from my name."[21]

When the Guild learned that RKO intended to omit Jarrico's name from the credits, its lawyer protested to RKO but received no reply. Advertisements for the movie appeared without Jarrico's name, indicating that RKO did indeed intend to ignore the MBA and the Guild's credit determination. The Guild invoked the conciliation and arbitration mechanism of the MBA, but RKO refused to participate. Then Howard Hughes attacked the Guild in the press for allegedly trying to force the company "to submit to the demands of Jarrico" and dared the Guild to strike to enforce the contract.

Hughes created both a legal and a public relations challenge for the Guild. The Guild could not risk the loss of all its contract rights by allowing a producer to defy the MBA with impunity, but it was leery of being seen as doing anything to support communists, and the Executive Board worried that if they invoked the MBA's dispute-resolution mechanisms, won an arbitration award, and RKO refused to abide by the award, the Guild would be forced to strike RKO, which the Board did not want to have to do, both because of the public relations problems and because a strike would be futile. At the time, RKO had only seven writers working on the lot, there was "almost no back lot activity whatever, and . . . one producer sitting with two scripts who has been waiting and begging for weeks for a go-ahead he has not received."[22]

After a tense special meeting called to discuss the RKO matter on March 28, 1952, an anxious Executive Board issued a carefully worded press release insisting that RKO had breached its contract with the Guild by refusing to abide by the credit arbitration and that matter "does not involve the political beliefs of Mr. Jarrico, however repugnant they might be to you or us." The Guild defended its involvement in the Jarrico suit as a matter of institutional obligation:

> By the terms of our corporate charter, by terms of our agree-
> ment with RKO Radio and all major motion picture studios, we
> are obligated to extend Guild membership to, and protect the

rights of, any writer you choose to employ. You chose to employ
Mr. Jarrico. We have no choice but to protect his professional
rights.[23]

The Executive Board deliberations on the Jarrico matter were anguished as
the Board debated whether to change the Guild constitution and bylaws to
ban communists from membership. Jewish screenwriter Walter Reisch said
that he had once belonged to a screenwriters' group in Germany which similarly had debated whether to change its constitution. He said he voted for the
change; in four months, he was out, in six months, the Catholics were out, in
eight months, the Austrians, and in ten months, the Czechs. A year later, the
world knew. He conceded that the litigation against the blacklist might be
unrealistic, "but the realism we had twenty years ago in Europe made it what
it is today."[24]

The Guild considered filing a suit against RKO seeking an injunction
against distribution of the film without accurate screen credit, but decided
against it both on the grounds that such relief was not available under the
contract and also that a suit "would give too much publicity to an otherwise
bad picture."[25] RKO then sued Jarrico alleging it was not obligated to accord
him credit; Jarrico counterclaimed, challenging RKO's refusal to abide by the
Guild's contractually mandated credit determination. That was litigation the
Guild could not sit out. Unlike the litigation over refusals to hire, the Guild
considered its right to determine screen credit a core protection of all writers,
so it filed an amicus brief. Meanwhile, the Guild filed an action in California
state court seeking to compel appointment of an arbitrator so that the dispute could be resolved in arbitration, as required by the MBA. But the court
refused to issue such an order.

After a bench trial in Jarrico's individual suit, in which his lawyer had
attempted to prove that Jarrico had written the substantial part of the final
shooting script and was thus entitled to credit, the court held that Jarrico's
refusal to cooperate with HUAC justified the denial of screen credit. Jarrico
argued (correctly) that screen credit is determined exclusively under the
MBA, which contained no provision governing a writer's political affiliations,
morals, or any other basis for the studio's refusal to grant screen credit. But
the court held that the refusal to testify violated the morals clause in Jarrico's
individual contract and that the individual contract's morals clause trumped

the MBA. Although reasonable minds could differ over whether being a communist violated the morals clause, the idea that the individual contract trumped the MBA had been squarely rejected by the United States Supreme Court several years before when it held that a collective bargaining agreement invalidates any conflicting provision in an individual contract of hire. To this, the court said simply (if somewhat incoherently), "the Guild is without power to prevent that freedom of contract guaranteed by the Constitution."[26]

Writers considered screen credit and adherence to the MBA important to their stature in the community and to their economic interests. Even as the moderates were loath to ally themselves in any way with the cause of blacklisted writers, for fear of facing the same fate as the blacklisted writers or tarnishing their chances of getting hired, they could not ignore the studios' refusal to adhere to the contract. In May 1952, just before a Guild membership meeting to vote on authorization of the Guild's suit in support of Jarrico and credit, fifteen blacklisted writers, including Jarrico and other members of the Ten, wrote to the members of the Guild urging them to support the Guild in its opposition to Hughes: "The Guild's right to determine screen credits is an historic right, won from the corporations after years of negotiation. If we surrender this right to RKO, we surrender it to every company in town. Our Board's efforts to enforce our contract in the courts will be supported by every screenwriter who remembers the abuses before Schedule A was won." The letter then reminded the membership that capitulation to RKO in the case of Jarrico would not save writers who thought they could distance themselves from communists, invoking the primacy of the notion of authorship to oppose the blacklist:

> It has been a long time since that producer spokesman appeared at our Guild meeting and pled with us to accept the blacklisting of ten men. Remember? It was the fall of 1947. 'Give us these ten men,' he said in effect, 'and here it will end.' The ten became twenty, the twenty fifty, and the fifty became a hundred. Each new group of blacklisted writers has warned, 'It will *not* end with us.' Yet when the House Committee on Un-American Activities wound up its sessions here last September, one could hear again the sigh of relief: 'Now it is finished.' Hughes thinks it has hardly begun.

It is in no spirit of we-told-you-so that we now warn again: Blacklisting is aimed not only at those it excludes from the industry but that those who remain in it. Its purpose is to intimidate our entire membership. The Blacklist cannot be contained by surrendering to it. . . .

Our case is strong. Today we preserve our elementary right to have our names on the screen. Tomorrow our Guild will gain other rights of authorship, not only in TV but in motion pictures. No matter what the patrioteering pretext of our adversaries, we shall not yield our goal—the recognition that we, not the corporations, are the Authors.[27]

After Jarrico released the letter to the trade paper, the *Hollywood Reporter,* the Guild Board feared that anticommunist writers would feel that supporting the Guild's position in the Jarrico suit was tantamount to supporting communists, as Hughes had insinuated. The Board purchased an ad in the trade papers responding to the letter, chastising the blacklisted writers for extending "the simple, clear-cut issue of a contract breach into the realm of politics" and reminding industry members that "the Guild's functions are economic, professional and nonpolitical."[28] The membership passed a resolution at its May 21, 1952, meeting in which it "reiterate[d] its historic stand against communism and communists within and without the Guild" and emphasized that it was "pressing the Thurman Arnold case to establish protection for those innocent of communist belief or affiliation, who may be carelessly or inaccurately identified as being in the communist camp."[29]

When RKO won both the individual suit against Jarrico and the litigation with the Guild about whether denial of credit violated the MBA, many Guild members felt the Guild had run out of options. They were unwilling to challenge the power of studios to deny screen credit to blacklisted writers, fearing that any sympathy toward suspected communists would leave them vulnerable to blacklisting themselves. The fear was sufficiently widespread that some writers seeking a new employment contract wrote to the Guild asking for a letter certifying that they had not signed petitions supporting members of the Ten for election to the Guild Executive Board or taken other stances within the union that would suggest communist sympathy. They hoped such a letter would persuade studios or ad agencies to hire them.

Advertising agencies periodically received threatening letters from anti-communist activists complaining about a suspected communist who appeared in a TV commercial or program and threatening a boycott of the sponsor or advertiser, and so they began vetting the names of every freelancer that they proposed to hire for a radio or TV show to make sure the person was not a suspected subversive. Writers perhaps hoped that having a letter would allay concerns of skittish producers, agency executives, or sponsors and convince them that the writer's name had been included on the right-wing list in error.[30]

Many writers complained about being unfairly labeled a communist based on the most innocuous memberships or activities, and others complained about being confused with another writer with a similar name. For a time, the Guild talked with other talent guilds and with producers about forming a committee of the Motion Picture Industry Council (an anticommunist organization of which Ronald Reagan was the secretary) whose purpose was to decide who was a communist and who was not. Although the Guild ultimately voted to oppose the plan, the debate over it was contentious. Thurman Arnold called the Guild's Executive Secretary to express grave reservations about any Guild involvement in such a committee:

> I am really concerned about the attitude of your Guild. I have had
> a feeling every meeting I have attended that the Guild was getting
> more and more worried about the public relations involved in this
> suit. . . . All I can say is if you set up some kind of tribunal to pro-
> tect the innocent, then you can't complain about the motion pic-
> ture companies because that is what they wanted done from the
> beginning. . . . [I]f I had it to do all over again I would not have
> brought the suit because the Guild is terrorized and I feel I have
> no more clients. . . . That makes it pretty tough as a suit when
> your clients don't stand with you.[31]

The End of the Legal Challenges to the Blacklist

Negotiations to settle both the Guild's involvement in the Jarrico matter and the Thurman Arnold blacklist suit dragged on through the fall and winter of 1952–1953, at the same time the Guild was fighting hard for its first television contract and fighting an endless internal battle with the Radio Writers Guild, the Authors League, and the Television Writers of America (a dissident group of former Radio Writers Guild members) over jurisdiction to represent writers in television. All of it was exhausting to the Executive Board and other Guild leaders. Having purged the blacklisted writers from leadership, the Executive Board considered the blacklist more a matter of principle than a crucial economic issue for most of its members. In one of the marathon Monday-night Executive Board meetings that ended in the early hours of Tuesday, one writer said that settling the suits would be "selling Jarrico down the river," to which another said "he has his own suit in court" and can defend his interests there.[32] The Board simply tabled further discussion to the next week.

In November, SWG President Mary McCall, along with Guild lawyers, met over lunch with producers to discuss various issues in the industry. McCall (1904–1986) had been a journalist, short story writer, and novelist until Warner Bros. hired her to adapt her novel *Revolt* for the movies, thus launching her long and successful career in the industry. She became the first woman president of the SWG in 1942 and was elected to two terms, stepping down in 1952.[33] (Frances Marion had been vice president of the SWG in 1933 and president in the early 1920s.) The producers proposed that a clause be introduced into the MBA giving producers the right to refuse credit to any writer in violation of the morals clause. McCall and the other SWG representatives at the lunch protested that it would give the producers "entirely too much leeway," but that the Guild would consider granting waivers in instances in which the producer could show that the writer had falsely asserted in writing to the producer that he was not a communist. Thereafter, the producers threatened that the arbitration clause be revised such that the principle of what had come to be called "the Jarrico situation" would be that the MBA arbitration provision would not cover any breach of the MBA that was also a breach of the individual contract of employment. This would mean that "only four to five provisions in the Agreement" would be enforceable. As an alternative, the producers offered that the MBA be revised such that the Guild would waive Schedule A (covering screen credit) only with respect to writers who were communists or refused to testify, and other alleged violations of the morals clauses of individual contracts would remain subject to arbitration.[34]

At the same time, the producers also offered to amend the MBA to commit the studios to join the Guild in creating procedures "to help clear people who are under suspicion," and so the Executive Board asked Arnold to postpone filing a brief in the blacklist case. This offer was tempting to many writers who had been unemployed for unusually long periods and feared, but could not ascertain, that they had been blacklisted and lacked any way of proving their innocence. In late January 1953, a delegation of writers met with the Executive Board to plead for the Guild to adopt some system to allow them to clear their name, professing that they had originally opposed the Motion Picture Industry Committee plan but saying that the Guild had to do something. Yet the Guild's Blacklist Committee struggled for several months in 1953, but it could not devise a feasible system for clearing writers' names. In the end, the Executive Board decided to establish yet another committee to contact individual production companies to be advised of whether writers had been accused and to convey to the affected writers the nature of the accusation so that they as individuals could do whatever they could to clear their own names.[35]

In February 1953, the Guild membership voted to settle the Thurman Arnold blacklist suit based on a statement from the producers that they would not conspire and never had conspired to blacklist writers. The settlement was, as Arnold himself put it, hardly even a face-saving gesture because everyone knew that the blacklist existed. But it was all Arnold could get once the Guild's membership lost the will to fight the blacklist. As part of the settlement, the Guild agreed to an amendment to the MBA permitting the producers to refuse credit to any member of the Communist Party or any writer who declined to answer questions about communist affiliations before federal or state legislative bodies. At the same time, the Guild also secured an amendment to the MBA that reaffirmed the Guild's right to make credit determinations, which had been called into question by the RKO action toward Jarrico and in other cases. A new Article 6 was added to the MBA stating that if a writer refused to state or falsely stated whether he or she was a communist, the producer was relieved of its obligation to accord credit to the writer. The membership voted to approve the changes, although members stayed away from the meeting in droves, as proxy votes outnumbered actual votes.[36] Meanwhile, some blacklisted writers settled their individual and collective suits for breach of contract against the studios for sums ranging from nothing to the writer's annual salary.[37]

Fronts, Pseudonyms, and Ghost Writing

In light of its capitulation on the blacklist, the Guild then faced a number of technical issues. One was whether to crack down on the use of pseudonyms because that was the basis on which blacklisted writers could keep working. The Guild had not prohibited pseudonyms or ghost writing until writing through a "front" (as it came to be known during this era) became an issue in the blacklist. But at the same time, pseudonyms also became controversial because their use would enable writers to work during the Guild's first-ever strike over residuals and television. Thus, in January 1951, the Board considered two rules to prohibit members from participating "either as an employer or employee in any arrangement for ghost writing" and also from accepting credit "which misrepresents the member's contribution to a picture as finally filmed." When screenwriter Leo Townsend faced Guild discipline in late 1951 after admitting to HUAC that he had fronted for Lester Cole and Dalton Trumbo, the Guild disciplinary committee and Board ultimately dropped the charges on the ground that fronting was not at that time prohibited by Guild rule. (Townsend had a long career writing popular but not challenging movies in the 1940s and 1950s and TV—mainly westerns and sitcoms, with a few action and mystery shows—in the 1960s.)[38]

Using a pseudonym, a front, or a ghost writer are not all the same. A pseudonym is a fictional name; writers used (and, as described in Chapter 2, occasionally still do use) pseudonyms to avoid the public associating them with a script, but they do not hide the identity of the writer from the studio or the producer. A front agreement was different. During the blacklist, a writer who agreed to front for another often did so out of friendship, and some—like Michael Blankfort, who fronted for Albert Maltz on the successful and well-reviewed 1950 A-movie western, *Broken Arrow* (1950)—did not even take a share of the writer's fee. Fronts risked their own career during the blacklist since they would be blacklisted too if the fronting became known. And both fronts and "backs" (the blacklisted writer) maintained the secrecy of the arrangement at all costs, to protect the front and sometimes the producer who did not know (or at least could not admit he knew) of the arrangement. Blankfort never admitted he had fronted for Maltz on *Broken Arrow*, and Maltz did so only reluctantly in the middle 1980s.[39] Ghost writing is different from fronting, as it involves a writer who is hired and then finds someone to write for him, rather than a writer who writes and then finds someone to sell his work to a studio and pretend to have written the work (and, often, to do the rewrites and attend the meetings with studio executives about the script). But the Guild never referred to fronting by that name—everyone knew it was going on, but the Guild called it ghost writing.

The issue of pseudonyms and fronting was sufficiently difficult that the Executive Board continually postponed any decision on trying to clarify its rules to members and on whether to discipline writers for ghost writing. Ghost writing and pseudonyms were complicated for the Guild because uncredited writing had happened for years and because writers who were rewritten occasionally wanted to remove their name from credit to save their reputation. But when it was alleged at a HUAC hearing that "writing clinics had been established by communist writers who rewrote scripts for fellow writers whom they were trying to bring into the communist party," the Guild's Board debated condemning the practice to avoid appearing to coddle communists, but it ultimately tabled the matter. (Later, when the Guild learned that the only writers mentioned as having participated in a "ghost-writing school" were the Ten, the Board adopted a motion "to forget bringing these members up on charges of ghostwriting.") Wholly apart from whether tolerance for writing under a pseudonym would allow communists to continue working, the Guild leadership also worried that relaxing the rule against pseudonyms would "take credit out of the Guild's hands and leave it with the writer and producer." To accommodate the concerns of writers who were angry at how someone else had rewritten a script, as in the case of the writer of a 1956 Fox television movie, *Yacht on High Sea,* the Board approved a change to the Credits Manual to allow pseudonyms if they were registered in advance with the Guild.[40]

A related issue was whether to enforce the Guild's working rules against blacklisted writers who continued to work but did so in violation of rules requiring writers to file a copy of their contract or in violation of MBA minimum-compensation rules or in violation of the pseudonym rules. Adele Buffington, who had a long career and over one hundred credits for writing westerns for the big screen and later TV, chaired the newly constituted Working Rules Committee in 1953 and was a longtime opponent of the leftists in the Guild. Whether for reasons of her ideology, professional jealousy, or ambition, she made it a personal project to enforce the working rules against Paul Jarrico for his work on *Las Vegas Story* and both Jarrico and Michael Wilson in connection with *Salt of the Earth,* a 1954 film about racial and labor oppression in a New Mexico miners' strike. *Salt of the Earth* particularly enraged Buffington: it was made by blacklisted talent and featured nuanced and sympathetic accounts of the Mexican-American and Native-American leaders and activists in the miners' union local and also an account of the powerful role that women played on the picket line. Both Wilson and Jarrico (Wilson's brother-in-law) worked on *Salt of the Earth,* and the film in later years was celebrated (and designated as culturally significant by the Library of Congress) for the filmmakers' involving the miners in the conception and making of the film and their decision to replace white actors with actual miners and participants in the strike.[41] Buffington wanted the Guild to conduct a full-scale investigation into the two writers' activities and fine each of them, and any other writer who was found to violate Guild rules, not less than $2,000. The Executive Board's members were eager not to get too embroiled in disciplinary actions against Jarrico or Wilson, saying that "in complicated political matters of this nature, no committee should take unilateral action of any kind."[42]

Wilson defended himself against the threat of discipline for failing to file a copy of his individual employment contract on *Salt of the Earth* by arguing that it was a leasing deal, not an employment contract. The Guild's lawyer, Gordon Stulberg, and Adele Buffington were unpersuaded. Stulberg said that the producers must have had the right to request rewrites, which made it an employment contract, not just a leasing deal. And Buffington said that everyone involved with the project had agreed to waive compensation until the loans financing the production were paid, which made it writing on spec unless he was at least a one-third owner of the project, which could not be determined if Wilson persisted in refusing to file his contract with the Guild. In the end, Wilson submitted his contract, which provided that he leased only motion picture rights and would be paid 15 percent of the producer's gross but in no event less than the MBA minimum. Having determined his contract was in compliance with the MBA, the Executive Board duly voted to thank him for submitting his contract. Adele Buffington dissented, obviously miffed. She promptly tried to resign from the Working Rules Committee, complaining that her report on Wilson had been leaked to the press and she had become a "controversial member." Although the Board initially declined to accept her resignation, after another contentious meeting, it eventually accepted it.[43]

The matter of discipline was part of the larger struggle between the left and the right. Buffington was absolutely convinced Wilson was a communist and wanted him out of the Guild. And some were obviously furious at the use of the Working Rules Committee as a way to harass leftists, which may explain why the matter was leaked to the press. In an angry three-hour special joint meeting of the Executive Board and the Working Rules Committee three weeks after Wilson won the fight over discipline, Buffington and the Committee were charged with libeling the Board by accusing it of sympathy to the left, and the Board insisted that since Wilson's contract was in compliance with the MBA, the Guild had no basis for disciplining him.[44]

Thus, while conceding the power of the producers to deny credit to communists and those who refused to testify about their political affiliations, the Guild wanted to guard its power to control credits. As the number of writers called to testify before HUAC grew relentlessly, studios confronted a problem. When a writer refused to name names, the studios suddenly faced a situation in which the writer on a film in production could not be credited without risking the ire of the conservative American Legion. In March 1952, Marguerite Roberts agreed with MGM studios to waive credit on two pictures she had written. *Ivanhoe* (1952), which was nominated for three Oscars, was one of them. In exchange for a reported payment of $210,000, Roberts waived credit and promised to use her best efforts to persuade the Guild to waive its rights to determine credit. The Executive Board acceded to the request. To waive credit was a major comedown for Roberts, who after her success writing on *Sailor's Luck* (1931) had signed a contract with MGM making her one of the highest-paid screenwriters in Hollywood. She was blacklisted from 1951 to 1960, and unlike many blacklisted writers, managed to return to work in the 1960s. Her biggest post-blacklist success was the screenplay for *True Grit* (1969), a popular movie in which a young woman reluctantly enlists the assistance of a cowboy, played by John Wayne, to avenge the death of her family.[45]

It is unclear how the Guild knew what she'd been paid, or even if she had, and it was equally hard for the Executive Board to know whether writers were in fact blacklisted. In Roberts's case, as in a number of other appeals to the Board by writers who sought to withdraw from the union without paying dues because they could not find work and believed they'd been blacklisted, the Board wanted some evidence that the writer really could not find work to ensure that he or she wasn't simply seeking to avoid paying dues. The Board wrote to aggrieved writers suggesting they come before the Guild's Blacklist Committee to prove they were blacklisted. The hardship on writers of the blacklist was also a topic of Guild Board meetings at this time. Roberts, who did not have another credit until 1962, asked to go on withdrawn status without paying her dues and also asked whether she could continue on the Guild's group health insurance policy even though she was out of the business. The Executive Board decided that members could go on withdrawn status without paying back dues after proving financial hardship and promising to pay from the next assignment and allowed members to continue in the group insurance plan.[46]

Credit Arbitrations and the Normalization of the Blacklist

The Guild considered the orderly operation of its credit process so important that it conducted credit arbitrations at the request of writers whom the Guild knew would never be given credit by the studios. Melville Nimmer, as counsel for the Guild, wrote to Albert Maltz, a member of the Ten, explaining the MBA provisions denying credit to writers who refused to state whether they were communists or who falsely denied it: "As a matter of policy, the Guild continues to determine credit pursuant to its usual credit determination machinery in all circumstances where it may properly do so, even if such credit may not ultimately appear on the screen." The Guild conducted a credit arbitration *whenever* a writer who had been employed on the picture challenged the denial of credit, and it made no exception for blacklisted writers. Because the arbitration process was anonymous, the arbiters did not know (or at least they could pretend not to know) they might be deciding to award credit to a blacklisted writer (unless, as may often have been the case, they knew through the gossip network who had worked on the film and knew which version of the script was written by a blacklisted writer and decided to award credit to that person). And many blacklisted writers could not get hired or, if they did, they would not claim credit. Nevertheless, in those cases where writers did seek credit, when the arbiters finished, the Guild's long-time credits administrator, Mary Dorfman, would translate the arbiters' decision

("Writer A should receive 'Screenplay by' credit") into its usual form letter, stating in a few sentences that the arbitration committee had decided what form of writing credit to give and to whom. After the Guild approved the MBA amendment allowing denial of credit to suspected communists, the Guild's usual form letter to the studio announcing the results of the arbitration simply included an additional sentence: "We understand that [name of writer] will not be given credit on the screen pursuant to the provisions of the second paragraph of Article 6 of the Producer-Writers Guild of America, West, Inc. Amended Minimum Basic Agreement of 1955." In this respect, the Guild did—though there is no evidence that it did it at his urging—what Dalton Trumbo had said people ought to do in *The Time of the Toad,* his manifesto about resisting the blacklist: First Amendment freedoms "must exist not only in law but in life itself; for it is only in the day-to-day actions of living men that law achieves reality."[47]

As the blacklist became a way of life, some of the opposition to certain aspects of it seemed to weaken. When the new Television Writers Board took the helm of the TV division of the Guild at the beginning of 1955, they agreed to sign the noncommunist affidavit without the second paragraph that the SWG had insisted on when the affidavit was first adopted, no longer feeling it essential to state "Deep in the conviction that the Guild is a nonpolitical and professional organization, we will resist any motion to impose on the Guild's general membership any loyalty oaths not required by law." At least the Board decided it was unnecessary to require the Guild staff to sign the noncommunist affidavit.[48]

In the 1955–1956 negotiations for a new MBA with the networks, the Guild wanted to negotiate for the same arrangement that it thought the RWG had gotten through arbitration some years before in which the morals clause was deleted from individual employment contracts. The networks insisted, however, on the morals clause being inserted into individual employment contracts. The networks were not concerned about short-term employment contracts but only about contracts of two to four years. The WGA East (based in New York) did not oppose addition of a morals clause, and so the WGA West (in Hollywood) set about drafting one believing "it would be better for the writers who are presently faced with the stringent clause proposed by the networks."[49]

The refusal to credit blacklisted writers mainly resulted in a front or a writer who had done minor writing on a film being credited. But every so often, a film is written only by a single person, and for whatever reason, the writer did not have a front. Michael Wilson had written the script for *The Friendly Persuasion* (1956) in 1947 before he was blacklisted. The studio finally released the film after Wilson was blacklisted, and so it informed the Guild that it would give writing credit on the film to the producer-director's brother and to Jessamyn West, the author of the short stories on which the film had been based. Wilson objected, and the Guild's arbitration committee determined that Wilson should receive sole screenplay credit and that West's credit should be "from the book by." Immediately after receiving the Guild's notice of the credit determination, a studio executive informed the WGA that the film would have no writing credit at all.[50]

The studio's strategy backfired, and it proved to be one of many embarrassing incidents in 1957–1960 in which blacklisted writers were nominated for or won Oscars. As Wilson recalled many years later, after the film was nominated for five Oscars, won the Palme d'Or at Cannes, and won a WGA award for best adapted screenplay, "my noncredit on the film gained me more recognition than I would have received had my name been on it." Under the Academy bylaws, the writing achievement could be given an award, even if under the bylaws Wilson himself was not eligible to receive it. However, because there was no other writer on the project and there would be no one to receive the award if the film should win, the Academy ordered Price Waterhouse not to list the nomination on the ballot for voting. Thus, in 1957, there were only four nominees instead of the usual five for Best Adapted Screenplay. (*Around the World in Eighty Days* won.)

In the same year, the Oscar winner in the category for Best Original Screenplay was also a blacklisted writer, Dalton Trumbo for *The Brave One;* in his case, the writer listed was Robert Rich, who was the nephew of the producer who hired Trumbo to write during the blacklist and who had no connection to the film industry. As soon as Deborah Kerr announced that Robert Rich had won the Oscar, Jesse Laske, Jr., vice president of the Writers Guild, jumped to his feet and went to the podium to accept the gold statue "on behalf of Robert Rich and his beautiful story." Rumors swirled about who the mysterious Robert Rich could be, making it obvious that Rich was a pseudonym for a blacklisted writer. It was widely rumored at the time that Trumbo had written the script, which also added notoriety to the omission of the nomination for *Friendly Persuasion.*[51]

A year later, *Bridge on the River Kwai* won the Academy Award for Best Adapted Screenplay. Although Michael Wilson had written the script, the screen credit was given to Pierre Boulle, the author of the novel. When Boulle spoke in accepting the award, it became obvious to the world what everyone in Hollywood knew—Boulle could not speak English. Yet again, people knew the writer must have been blacklisted.[52]

Embarrassments such as these led the Guild to believe that the blacklist might be vulnerable and so, in 1959, the blacklist was a top priority for the Guild's negotiating team, along with getting paid for movies rebroadcast on TV and the extension of separated rights. It helped that in early 1959, when yet another film written by a blacklisted writer—*The Defiant Ones*, written by Nedrick Young (blacklisted) and Hal Smith (not blacklisted)—was winning acclaim and threatened to cause an Oscar embarrassment for the third year in a row, the Academy Board of Governors voted to remove the ban on black-listed writers winning Oscars. The Academy explained that the rule was "unworkable" because "control over the engaging of talent for films does not rest with the Academy." Nevertheless, when the Best Screenplay Oscar was given to the film in March, it was announced for Ned Young's pseudonym. In June, the Guild negotiating team tried to get the producers to agree that they would not invoke Article 6 (the denial of credit provision) when the producers knew at the time of hiring that the writer was a communist. After discussion, it was suggested that the clause should prevent producers from denying credit when they "knowingly hire" a communist, but the meeting adjourned with the Guild committee asking for the producers' negotiating committee's definitive proposal. At the Guild's urging, Article 6 was finally removed from the MBA in 1966 without discussion.[53]

The fact that the credit-arbitration machinery continued to operate, even when it was futile, paved the way for the Guild to regain power over credits when the blacklist began to fall apart in 1960 and some producers began to credit blacklisted writers. At that point, the law governing credit was an uncertain amalgam of the formal Guild processes, which continued to govern writing credits for nonblacklisted writers and producers' discretionary denials of credit to certain writers regardless of the Guild's determinations, discretion which they exercised only for blacklisted writers.

The rules governing credit, thus, had an overlay of two individual contracts on top of the collective agreement. One was the writer's individual contract with the studio. A second was the secret contract between the writer and his front or his producer if he wrote under a pseudonym. As Dalton Trumbo said in January 1959, when he admitted he wrote *The Brave One,* he would honor his contracts that called for writing under a pseudonym, "But once I have [finished them], I will never again write anything for anybody without using my own name." And then, by 1960, some entertainment lawyers began to say that the secrecy surrounding writers raised issues of fair trade practices and false advertising and "the public interest against deception" meant that waivers of screen credit should be troublesome. Director Otto Preminger echoed the theme of honesty when he explained his intention to give screen credit for *Exodus* (1960) to Trumbo: "if someone is employed and that fact is hidden, it constitutes cheating the public."[54] In this respect, Preminger capitalized on a reputation for valuing honesty and freedom that he had cultivated after fleeing Austria in 1936, and he found success in challenging the norms of Hollywood by including taboo themes in some films, including rape in *Anatomy of a Murder* (1959) and homosexuality in *Advise and Consent* (1962).[55]

Credit Corrections

Decades later, the Guild retrospectively corrected the record. The Guild formed a committee of former officers and writers, including some who had been blacklisted, to conduct inquiries into the correct attribution of dozens of films produced between 1947 and 1966. The process raised complex issues for the Guild, because correcting credits often required taking credit away from one Guild member, who may have worked on the film and done a favor for a fellow writer by serving as a front, to give it to another. Reputations and feelings were hurt. Moreover, blacklisted writers and their descendants often had difficulty finding evidence to prove who had really written which scripts. Committee approval was often the first step in getting studios to change the writing credit on new prints and video rereleases, which paved the way for the Academy to change its records. However, since the WGA was reluctant to rearbitrate old credit disputes, the authors, their fronts, or their descendants were required to come forward with definitive evidence of blacklist credit. For pseudonyms, the Committee recommended a credit change "when there is sufficient information to identify a writer with a pseudonym and confirm that the writer used the pseudonym because of the blacklist." Since the black-list did not have an official end, some writers kept using their pseudonyms in the 1960s. For fronts, the Committee relied on information from individuals with firsthand knowledge and other documentation to support its recommendations. Ultimately, the Guild issued corrected screen credits for ninety-four films, including some that had been produced outside the Guild's jurisdiction by blacklisted writers who were forced to work in Europe or Mexico.[56]

The Academy also got on board and bestowed Academy Awards on screenplay writers that had originally gone to writers who had served as fronts. Thus, for example, Dalton Trumbo was finally recognized as the writer of *Roman Holiday* (which won an Oscar for Best Screenplay in 1954). The screen credit and Oscar were originally given to Ian McLellan Hunter, who fronted for Trumbo until he himself was subpoenaed and blacklisted. The *Roman Holiday* credit correction was complicated by the fact that when Hunter, through his agent, sold Trumbo's script to Paramount for $35,000, Paramount paid Hunter an additional $5,000 to revise the script. Hunter wrote on the project and then Paramount hired screenwriter John Dighton to revise it again. (And writers Ben Hecht and Preston Sturges worked on it between Hunter and Dighton.) So the Guild actually corrected the credits twice—first to give Trumbo "story by" credit in 1992, and then again, following a credit arbitration, in 2011 to add Trumbo's name to Hunter's and Dighton's for a shared "screenplay by" credit. The Academy changed its records in 1992 and awarded the Oscar posthumously to Trumbo in 1993, presenting the gold statue to Trumbo's widow, Cleo.[57]

As the Guild began correcting credits from the blacklist era, studios inquired whether acceptance of the Guild's recommendations regarding new credits would also require the studios to change the persons to whom they paid residuals. In 1996, after consideration, the Guild recommended that residuals be paid according to the corrected credits going forward, but the Guild decided not to pursue residuals for blacklisted writers prior to the time credits were corrected. The Guild concluded that collecting past residuals presented problems with the statute of limitations and also that being liable to pay residuals to new people would dampen both the willingness of the studios to cooperate in credit corrections (if they had to pay all the back residuals) or the willingness of people to come forward and admit they had fronted for a writer if they might have to repay money received over many decades to a studio or to the blacklisted writer or his heirs.[58]

The Blacklist and the Significance of Credits

The economic importance of credit in Hollywood was underscored to both the industry and the public by the fact that the blacklist operated because of and through screen credit. The credit regime proved to be as vulnerable as were the civil liberties of the Hollywood Ten and blacklisted writers. Neither the courts, nor the First and Fifth Amendments, nor the Guild and its credit determination process could withstand the hysteria over communism. Yet the Guild's insistence on continuing to operate the credits process for all writers, regardless of the blacklist, enabled it to retake control of credits quickly once the producers abandoned the blacklist. The bureaucratic processing of credits for all writers kept the contract rules alive, preserving the system in an amber of Weberian rationality until the blacklist collapsed, the amber cracked, and Guild credit determinations were once again regarded by the studios as obligatory.

7

Pencils for Hire and Mad Men in Gray Flannel Suits

> *Don Draper:* That's the way it works. There are no credits in commercials.
> *Peggy Olson:* But you got the Clio!
> *Don:* It's your job! I give you money, you give me ideas.
> *Peggy:* But you never say thank you!
> *Don:* That's what the money is for!
>
> —"The Suitcase," *Mad Men*, written by Matthew Weiner

Commentary on work relations in the early twenty-first century tends to imagine educated, white, male, white-collar employees in the mid-twentieth century in long-term employment, moving up promotional ladders in corporations with a sharp division between labor and management. As generalizations go, this depiction is reasonably accurate about men working in mid-century finance, insurance, law, management, or research and development, and even about many ad agency copywriters. But writers working in film and radio experienced a work world a bit more like the so-called gig economy today—they needed to be entrepreneurial to build a career out of a series of short-term jobs punctuated by periods of unemployment. Rather than thinking of themselves only as individual entrepreneurs and professionals—the strategy of their education and social class peers of today—film, radio, and television writers dealt with the uncertainty of their labor market by embracing their legal status as employees and forming a union. It wasn't just leftists who thought writers should unionize. Charles Brackett, a successful screenwriter of the 1930s, did, even though he was (according to his frequent collaborator Billy Wilder) "a right-wing Republican conservative, of the Truman Bracketts of New York, a formal man, always impeccably dressed." Brackett testified at the 1937 National Labor Relations

Board hearing on the right of the writers to unionize about why he wanted to join the Guild: Unionization, he explained, would dignify the profession of writing by giving writers control over their work and protection against retaliation. They unionized because they were writers; they described themselves as "pencils for hire."[1]

Hollywood writers have bargained collectively for more than seventy-five years, notwithstanding the economic power the successful ones sometimes enjoy, and notwithstanding the fact that some writer-producers work simultaneously in a supervisory role as well as a creative role. Even successful and powerful writer-producers or writer-directors would remain in the Writers Guild because they recognized that the real power lay not with who managed a movie or TV set but with who controlled the finances. That power was concentrated in the upper echelons of the studios. Directing or producing a TV show or film does not impossibly compromise the writer's loyalty to labor, nor does belonging to the Guild impossibly compromise the writer-producer's loyalty to the studio. But it does create conflicts that are played out most dramatically during every strike. That the conflicts have not either fractured the union or prevented the studios and networks from putting shows on the air or movies in theaters does not mean there isn't always a struggle for their loyalty.

The WGA thus gives the lie to two of the dominant canards in American labor law and business commentary on labor relations. Highly paid and highly educated white-collar workers who work autonomously want and can benefit from unionization, and companies can run quite well when many of their supervisors are unionized and, indeed, in the same union as the workers whom they supervise. Moreover, as applied to creative industries, writers could seek power as authors without completely undermining the claim of the corporation to creative control or to the validity of the corporate copyright.

Madison Avenue writers, in contrast, embraced their status as professionals, and they counted on their social power and the profitability of their firms to protect their interests as writers. Like Hollywood writers, they emphasized the importance of individual genius and hard work, but they believed that professionalism was inconsistent with individual self-promotion. The optimists among them believed loyalty to the client and to the firm would be rewarded by promotion. Eventually, the successful men would become partners in the firm, and they would all share in the success. The cynics in the industry described ad agency writers as unhappy men in gray flannel suits.

The causes and consequences of these very different workplace cultures and legal and social strategies are the subject of this chapter.

The experience of mid-century writers sheds light not only on the role of unions representing so-called knowledge-economy workers, but also on the emergence of the legal distinction between labor and management and the reasons why workers occupying a liminal position between labor and management pushed, or were pushed, into one legal category or the other. As Jean-Christian Vinel explains in *The Employee,* his 2014 legal and political history of the legal status of the employee, to be an employee is at once a legal status and a political and social position in the hierarchical workplaces that dominate American capitalism. Many film and TV writers were and remain, as showrunner Ed Bernero (*Criminal Minds,* 2005–2011) put it in a 2013 interview, "not kind of [but]—definitely" both labor and management. Being "labor" to someone else's "management" is a cultural stance with very important legal consequences, and nowhere is that clearer than when being an "employee" means the writer is not the legal author of her works but is entitled to unionize, bargain collectively, and strike for better terms on which copyrights will be sold and profits will be shared in the form of residuals.[2]

Writers' experience in Hollywood shows that labor law and labor relations can accommodate unionization and collective bargaining by white-collar professional employees in short-term jobs doing nonstandardized mental work with minimal supervision giving companies flexible, just-in-time labor practices. So, too, for workers in supervisory capacities. Not only can business accommodate this kind of unionization, it benefits from it. At a conceptual level, my argument is that writers had to embrace their status as employees—the exact legal category that renders them not authors of their writing—to gain some of the characteristics of authors: public attribution and some rights of ownership. At a practical level, my argument is that the Madison Avenue model that companies insist is the only model on which white-collar workers can profitably be employed is not the only model.

Ironically, Hollywood writers gained control and limited forms of ownership over their work by allying themselves with labor, and Madison Avenue writers relinquished control over their work by imagining themselves as professionals. Writers in Hollywood and on Madison Avenue ascribed substantial economic, cultural, and psychological power to a legal status (being an employee) achieved by signing a legal document (a contract). Employment contracts and the legal status of employees recurred repeatedly over the course of writers' efforts to secure their status as authors between 1930 and 1960. Hollywood writers embraced their legal status as employees to form a union and bargain collectively, and they negotiated a contract that defined a writer as an employee whenever the producer had the right to demand revisions. The employer's contractual right to demand revisions—which was written into the Minimum Basic Agreement even though it was one of the most aggravating experiences many writers had—became the defining feature of the legal status as employees that entitled them to unionize and bargain collectively to regain some of the rights they lost as employee writers at work.

Ad agency writers, on the other hand, downplayed their status as employees and most definitely rejected their characterization as labor because they thought it undermined their status as professional writers with a duty of loyalty to the client who owned the rights in their creation. The J. Walter Thompson agency did not have written contracts with its staff writers, and the agency used written agreements with freelancers only sometimes. As explained in Chapter 1, for example, Vernon Grant, the artist who developed the Snap, Crackle, and Pop characters for Kellogg's Rice Krispies cereal campaign in the 1930s, had no written contract governing ownership of the characters and drawings he created for Kellogg and JWT or the other ad agency that handled his work. The absence of written contracts became a mark of respect and professional stature for all JWT staff copywriters and even some freelancers. JWT's general counsel preferred to rely on the professional decorum of its copywriters, artists, and other staff to manage intellectual property rights and other obligations between the firm and its staff. The notions of professionalism and independence did a huge amount of conceptual work in reconciling advertising men to their role as salaried writers, and it kept them from seeing themselves as "pencils for hire." As one agency owner explained in an advice book distilling the experience he gained in his career, an advertising man's dignity depends on his independence from the client; to be a "mere employee" meant the advertising man was "no longer master of [his] own fate"; and to become too dependent on a client would lead him to lose "a large part of [his] objectivity and even professionalism."[3]

This chapter begins with a look at the cultural significance attached to writers' status as corporate employees in mid-century. The title character of the novel and film *The Man in the Gray Flannel Suit* was a copywriter, and a forgotten aspect of the novel that spawned that familiar trope of 1950s corporate blandness, like all the other novels by and about advertising in the 1950s, was the labor alienation inherent in anonymous writing. Most copywriters weren't alienated in the sense in which they punched a clock. On the contrary, they were deeply invested in the craft and in the success of their work. They believed some ads were genius, and they wanted even an apparently pedestrian ad to be successful in increasing sales. And they were paid well. But those who got angry about being unappreciated, or those who left the business to write novels, expressed their frustration in the same terms.

The legal history of conflicts between writers and ad agencies and film, radio, and television production companies over whether writers were "employees" has been alluded to several times in this book; this chapter explores it further and, more important, shows what turned on that legal status. The preceding chapters have already told what film and TV writers gained by embracing their status as employees and bargaining collectively for screen credit, residuals, and so forth. So the third section brings advertising writers back into the story by showing how advertising writers and agencies responded to the very different authorship norms that resulted in their industry when writers worked as employees without the contractual rights of credit and compensation that film and TV writers won.

Brains, Inc.

In *White Collar*, C. Wright Mills' 1951 sociology of the American middle class, the title of the chapter on intellectuals ("Brains, Inc.") argues that corporate bureaucracy—"a new patronage system," of "Hollywood and the Luce enterprises," and "Young and Rubicam"—"increasingly sets the conditions of intellectual life and controls the major market for its products." (Luce published *Life, Time, Sports Illustrated,* and *Fortune* magazines and, with radio and newsreel production, had a hugely influential multimedia news company; Young & Rubicam was a large New York advertising agency.) A major theme of

White Collar, as suggested by Mills' portrayal of intellectuals working at "Brains, Inc.," was the loss of independence of the American middle classes. Dismayed at the intelligentsia's quiescence and timidity, which Mills attributed to dependence on corporate employment, *White Collar* devoted several pages to salaried writers in radio, film, television, and advertising. He accused them, along with professors and journalists, of having lost "the optimistic, rational faith" of intellectuals in the 1930s. Writers for hire who depended on corpo rate employment held "more tragic views of political and personal life," and "[e]ven craftsmanship, so central to intellectual and artistic gratification," was not always a consolation of the work because some advertising and TV writing was truly terrible. Exhibit A in Mills's case against corporate writing was "the predicament of the Hollywood writer. Unlike the Broadway play-wright who retains at least some command over his play when the manager, director, and cast take it over, the Hollywood script writer has no assurance that what he writes will be produced in even recognizable form." The writer's "major complaint," Mills lamented, "is not that he is underpaid, but that while he has responsibility for his work he has no real authority over it." The writer of radio dramas and television scripts, Mills said, "merely fills an order, and often he will not write at all until he has an order, specifying content, slant, and space limits." He is "the employee of a business enterprise, not a personality in his own right," and magazines and radio shows "are not so much edited by a personality as regulated by an adroit formula." Three para-graphs later, Mills lamented a "large expansion of ghost-writing," speculating that the "chance is probably fifty-fifty that the book of a prominent but non-literary man is actually written by someone else." "Yet," Mills concluded, "perhaps the ghost-writer is among the honest literary men; in him alienation from work reaches the final point of complete lack of public responsibility."[4]

Alienation there was, but film and TV writers, and even their peers in the ad agencies, refused to be utterly alienated. Vernon Grant's fight for Snap, Crackle, and Pop, like the Screen Writers Guild's fight for movie screen credit in the 1930s; the Radio Writers Guild's (RWG) fight for radio air credit in the 1940s; the JWT writers' and Writers Guild's fight for TV screen credit; and the Guild's fight for separated rights and residuals in the 1950s are all evidence that writers resisted alienation, and sometimes they did so successfully. And, as Mills observed, writers felt that though they had "responsibility for [their] work [they had] no real authority over it." This was the battle against serial rewriting waged (continually but unsuccessfully) by radio, film, and TV writers over the decades, and also the notion of professionalism embraced by advertising agencies that they must exert control over the content of the advertisement to discharge their responsibility to their client.

Most troubling to Mills was that writing, especially in the hands of the ad men ("the Young & Rubicam mentality"), had been reduced to an "adroit formula" and the formulaic nature of writing, combined with anonymity, meant writers had a "complete lack of public responsibility" for their work. Yet advertising writers at JWT did not complain about a lack of responsibility; on the contrary, they expressed (at least in office memos) great responsibility for their work and for whether their work served their clients' needs. In the eyes of their critics (like Mills), they may have been alienated and doing soulless corporate work, but they didn't describe it that way when they were at work. Those who left the business to write novels about it did, and a progressive sociologist like Mills worried, but those doing the work celebrated the difficulty and importance of what they did.

Mills was hardly alone in excoriating anonymous writers guided by "adroit formula" who spread the "Young & Rubicam mentality" across the land. Between the end of World War II and 1960, at least a dozen novels about Madison Avenue, many by former copywriters, told a story of alcohol-soaked creative frustration and alienation in writing for hire. The dysfunctional families, postwar psychological trauma, and suburban anomie for which the novels are also remembered seem to be both cause and consequence of corporate work. The title of one of the best known of the novels—*The Man in the Gray Flannel Suit*—came to be shorthand for conformity and anonymity. Alfred Hitchcock (or perhaps Ernest Lehman, the writer, or the costume designer) put Cary Grant, an ad man, in a gray suit in every scene of *North by Northwest* (1959), as if to suggest that ad men never wore anything but gray flannel.[5]

The corporate writer may have changed his gray flannel suit for more casual attire in the decades since, but anxiety about creativity and anonymity remains a pervasive theme about writing on a corporate payroll. In Season Four of *Mad Men,* the Emmy-winning episode "The Suitcase" depicts copywriter Peggy Olson confronting the agency's creative director Don Draper while the two are working on a commercial for Samsonite suitcases. Peggy makes a caustic remark about having to work with Danny, a mediocre writer whom Don had to hire to head off an idea-theft suit after Don stole Danny's idea for a cereal ad. Don retorts:

> Don: By the way, I know it kills you, but there is no Danny's idea. Everything that comes in here belongs to the agency.
> Peggy: You mean you.
> Don: As long as you still work here.

Peggy then refers to a commercial for Glo-Coat floor wax; in a previous episode, she had suggested the idea, the agency won a Clio for it, but Peggy wasn't even invited to attend the award ceremony at which Don accepted the award:

> Peggy: You know what? Here's a blank piece of paper. Why don't you turn that into Glo-Coat?
> Don: Are you out of your mind? You gave me 20 ideas and I picked out one of them that was a kernel that became that commercial. . . .
> Peggy: Which you changed just enough so that it was yours.
> Don: I changed it so that it was a commercial. . . . That's the way it works. There are no credits on commercials.

And from there the scene continues with the exchange that is the epigraph to this chapter. The exchange between Don and Peggy speaks both about the frustrations of anonymity and attribution in writing advertisements, but also about similar frustrations in collaborative TV writing.

Mad Men creator Matthew Weiner has said that the Don Draper character represents, as creative director of an ad agency, the role of the showrunner in contemporary television, who is sometimes himself—"Do I see myself as Don Draper sometimes? Yeah, in my fantasy." Weiner (who got the sole "written by" credit for "The Suitcase" episode) has also said that the exchange between Peggy and Don reflects how he felt as a young writer working on The Sopranos for series creator David Chase. But he also said that scene represents how he feels about work relationships and credit: "There's a lot of negotiating in the show, and it's always about that—about who made what." When I asked about Peggy's demand for credit, Weiner immediately responded, "Credit is amorphous to me."

> *CF:* But residuals turn on credit.
>
> *MW:* Well, yeah, but she wants more fame. She wants love.
> And you're paid to do your work. That was what that was
> about.

Although he didn't refer to it, he may have surmised that I asked about Peggy and Don's argument over credit in part because of the widespread rumor in the TV writing community that Weiner violates the norms of television authorship by insisting on sharing screen credit with the writers on his staff on most of the episodes of the show. In interviews I conducted in 2013–2014 with thirty showrunners and staff writers, they told me that it is the job of the showrunner to revise what staff writers produce and that showrunners ought not take screen credit except on episodes that the showrunner wrote alone because splitting credit entails splitting script fees and residuals. The conversation between Peggy and Don, therefore, can be read as Weiner's justification for his practice of putting his name on almost every episode. Weiner, of course, got the last word about authorship. At the end of the episode, Peggy naps on the couch in another office while Don thinks up the idea for the suitcase commercial.[6]

The alienation that is a theme in the Madison Avenue novels was rooted in the anonymity and lack of writer psychic investment in collaborative work. Marx recognized the importance of people seeing themselves—or, more specifically, their work—realized in the world. The alienation of labor that was so core to Marx's theory was the separation of workers from the recognition of the products of their labor as being theirs. In the nineteenth century, the "art" of a worker was the particular skill and learning that defined respectable occupations and the people who performed them. Possessing an "art" conferred worth on the people who labored in those tasks, made them independent and useful, and, therefore, valuable members of society.[7] The social status of labor stemmed not only from possessing an art but being recognized as possessing one. In the twentieth century, what had formerly been the art of the skilled worker became the human capital of the workforce, and, simultaneously, the human assets of the firm. In *The Man in the Gray Flannel Suit*, the title character is assigned to ghostwrite a speech for the head of the public relations department of a television network. He suffers acute alienation and despair when his boss repeatedly rejects different versions of the speech and ultimately substitutes one of his own. Similarly, in *Blandings' Way,* after the aptly named title character spends a Sunday afternoon reading drafts of unfinished literary works he wrote before taking a job on Madison Avenue, he goes to work on Monday and persuades a junior copywriter not to quit his job to write a novel. That distasteful task complete, "Mr. Blandings turned a troubled gaze out the window and stared at the enormous Knapp's Laxative sign suspended over Broadway to the west. The three words on it were his own creation; they were responsible for the first gold medal he had received to mark him as a leader in his profession. They had made an incredible success; he was completely identified with them and they would no doubt go on his tombstone. He did not think he wanted them there." As John Kenneth Galbraith complained in his review of several of the Madison Avenue novels, copywriters-turned-authors used the novels to vent their feelings about the repellant nature of the business. Blandings is disgusted about his failure to publish his novel, about talking his junior writer out of quitting to write his own, and about winning accolades for writing three words to sell laxatives, and he fears both being known and not being known for those three words.[8] JWT's spokesmen apparently harrumphed in *Fortune* magazine at the salacious sex, backstabbing, and alcoholic anomie depicted in the advertising novels, but they had nothing to say about anonymity or alienation; JWT protested instead that between the fictional agencies "and the solid actuality of J. Walter Thompson there is a wide gulf of manners and procedure."[9]

C. Wright Mills, John Kenneth Galbraith, and the fictionalized accounts of ad men in gray flannel suits notwithstanding, writing for hire in advertising, film, and television was a good job, as measured by money and prestige. The sources of alienation—writers did not own or control their work and their work was crassly commercial but hugely profitable for its owners— became justification for being paid handsomely. Writers described the money as compensation for the loss of many of the attributes of authorship, especially independence, creative control, and recognition. As Leo Rosten's ethnography of 1930s Hollywood put it, "It is the story-carpenters of Hollywood—tough-skinned, pragmatic—who mock their colleagues in a refrain which is famous in the movie colony: 'They ruin your stories. They massacre your ideas. They prostitute your art. They trample on your pride. And what do you get for it? A fortune.'" In a more serious vein, veteran screen writer and WGA President Howard A. Rodman, Jr., explained the significance of money differently: "there's a sentence of Karl Marx which I really love which is, 'No matter the fluctuations in the price of beef, the sacrifice remains constant for the ox.' . . . I think of writing in that way: . . . the work is the same whether we're well compensated or badly compensated." If copyright owners are making a fortune, writers deserve one too because writing well is hard work.[10]

Being an employee was an argument for writers' efforts to gain adequate compensation. If they were not recognized as authors, especially not by the public, then they should be paid like the corporate professionals they and their employers understood them to be, rather than like the artists that their more literary novelist colleagues were. For the most part, this book has shown, film and radio producers and ad agencies both assumed and insisted writers were employees, at least for purposes of copyright law, so that the corporation would own the copyright in their work. Writers of film and, later, radio and TV resisted until they realized that their right to bargain collectively turned on their claiming to be employees not contractors. Being an employee connoted a loss of autonomy, a legal and social status irreconcilable with their social status as authors.

Pencils for Hire: Law and the Status of Being an Employee

Writers and other Hollywood talent are among the few highly educated, highly paid, white-collar American workers who are also relatively committed unionists. Writers call their organization a Guild, not a union, for a reason— they have often thought of it as protecting their interests as professionals, as highly intelligent, highly paid, and quite autonomous masters of a craft. And whenever they have had to strike to secure protection for their rights as authors—in 1948, 1952, 1959–1960, 1973, 1981, 1985, 1988, and 2007–2008, always involving compensation for reuse of their work in new media—they expressed awkwardness about resorting to a strike and picketing. They take pains to distinguish themselves from people who "work on a loading dock" (as TV writer Bob Barbash said about the 1960 strike) or farmworkers (as writer and showrunner Neal Baer *(Law & Order, Under the Dome)* said about the 2007–2008 strike). But they still have to act like labor to protect their rights as authors because the law deems them to be employees and, therefore, labor.[11]

Legal disputes over whether workers are employees arise only in the context of particular laws creating rights or prohibitions. The most important such law in the early history of the movie and advertising business was the Copyright Act of 1909, which made the employer the author of any work an employee created. Being the owner at the moment of creation freed the studios from having to demand a formal assignment of the copyright once the script was complete, and it also affected the studio's ability to apply for a renewal of the copyright. Thus, studios and ad agencies insisted that writers were employees. No one spent much time trying to figure out what employee meant under the Copyright Act—a writer who was paid to write was assumed to be an employee. And although screenwriters in the 1920s and early 1930s chafed at the low-status connotations of the employee title and at the loss of ownership of the copyrights in their scripts, they went along with the employee designation because it was the price of getting work in Hollywood. But when the opportunity to negotiate collectively for more control over their work, advance notice of layoffs, a minimum wage, and control over screen credit arose with the enactment of the National Labor Relations Act (NLRA) of 1935, Hollywood writers saw that embracing the legal label "employee" was the key to collective action. And they decided, both for good economic reasons and in the general enthusiasm for Popular Front politics, to become employees and unionize.

The right of the studio (and, later in radio and TV, the sponsor and its advertising agency and packager) to *control* what the writers wrote became crucial to the ability of writers to bargain collectively under labor and antitrust law. The lack of creative control that so galled writers—but that seemed to be inevitable in studio-dominated filmmaking and sponsor-dominated radio and television production—became the crucial legal weapon that secured the rights of writers as authors in every respect other than creative control. And underlying that lack of control were employment contracts and the legal status of being an employee.

In March 1936, screenwriter Seton Miller signed a one-year employment contract with Warner Bros. at the rate of $1,250 a week (in 2016 dollars, $21,425 per week, or $1.1 million for the year). Miller had been working in Hollywood for fifteen years, having arrived shortly after graduating from Yale to work as a bit-part actor and consultant on a silent movie about Ivy League football. By 1936, Miller had about thirty-five screen credits, many for character-driven dramas about war or crime, including *Scarface* (1932). (The writing of the acclaimed script for *Scarface* is attributed today mainly to Ben Hecht, who is said to have adapted Armitage Trail's 1929 novel in only ten days. Hecht got "story by" screen credit. Miller shared a "continuity and dialogue" credit with two other writers.) Miller had been nominated for an Oscar in 1931 (for *The Criminal Code*), and he later won one (for *Here Comes Mr. Jordan* (1941)). During his time at Warner Bros., he wrote on a number of popular action and adventure films, including the hit *The Adventures of Robin Hood* (1938). He also served as an officer of the Writers Guild.[12]

Except for the salary (which was high, although not the highest), Miller's was a standard writer's contract with a studio. He promised to "conscientiously perform the services required of him hereunder solely and exclusively for and as requested by the Producer," to do so "whenever and wherever the Producer may request or deem necessary or convenient," and to "promptly and faithfully comply with all requirements, directions, requests, rules and regulations made by the Producer." Miller promised not to write or work on "any stage, radio, dramatic, or motion picture production" other than for Warner Bros. or to allow his name to be used to promote any production except by Warner Bros. Miller agreed anything he wrote or dreamed up during the contract term belonged to Warner Bros. as a work made for hire. He promised to execute a standard certificate of authorship stating that Warner Bros. was the author of all his work in any medium. Warner Bros. had the right, with seven days' advance notice, to lay Miller off without pay for twelve consecutive weeks during the contract year, and if it did so, Miller had the right to work for another producer and to allow his name to be used by that employer in connection with whatever he wrote during the layoff term. Warner Bros. had the right to renew the contract several times for up to seven years, but Miller did not have the same option to renew if Warner Bros. didn't want him. Miller's contract differed in only some details from contracts at other major studios in that period. Even as the old studio system was in decline, Warner Bros. continued to use similar year-long or longer contracts for television writers up to 1960.[13]

Although the language in Miller's contract was boilerplate, it was not one of those legal documents that nobody pays any attention to. The power it gave to Warner Bros. was real; as anthropologist Hortense Powdermaker said, the agreement established a feudal relation, as it bound the worker to the studio for years.[14]

While Miller was working for Warner Bros. under that contract, Leo Rosten—who worked as a screenwriter after earning degrees in social science at the University of Chicago and the London School of Economics—brought a team of social scientists to Hollywood to study the movie business under the auspices of the Carnegie Corporation and the Rockefeller Foundation. They surveyed hundreds of writers, directors, actors, and producers (and some craft and technical workers) and gathered data from studios about payrolls, production costs, and demographics. Their principal finding about writers was that their legal status had a significant effect on their working conditions and self-conception. Rosten said, based on his research as well as his own experiences as a screenwriter, that being an employee was "the key to many of the problems, dilemmas, and agonies of the writer in Hollywood"—"He is handed collaborators whom he dislikes. He is ordered to introduce a tap dancer into a story about an African safari. He is asked to 'add a few jokes' to the scene he fought to keep poignant; or to 'speed up the story' at precisely the point where he wanted to develop the characters; or to invent a 'smart' but unnatural opening, or a 'sock' but phony climax. *He is an employee.*"[15]

Ten years after Rosten's study was published, Hortense Powdermaker's ethnography, *Hollywood, the Dream Factory,* concurred in many of his observations about the labor status of writers. Powdermaker had worked as a labor organizer between college and graduate school, and before coming to Hollywood, she had written a major ethnography about black people and their work in the rural Deep South. So it is no surprise that she, like Rosten before her, was determined to understand the film industry through study of work relations. A "bon mot in the community is that 'writers in Hollywood do not have works but are workers.'" Because they neither owned nor controlled what they wrote, they did not "have works." But she found they did insist on their status as labor and as union members. Though Rosten's and Powdermaker's field work was separated by a decade (his in the late 1930s and hers in the late 1940s), they both saw labor relations and the network of contracts linking talent (including writers) to studios as crucial to the power relations and work culture in the industry.[16]

Contracts like Miller's—which gave the studio the right to control every aspect of what writers wrote, one-sided renewal options, the work-for-hire doctrine, the power to lay off, and unfettered discretion to control every aspect of the writer's work—made it logical that even people as highly paid as Miller or "a right-wing Republican" like Charles Brackett would describe themselves as labor. Though some writers did so as a political statement, many did so as a legal strategy to gain power over the conditions and products of their work. Radical writers embraced the idea of writing for a wage as a political stance because of the membership it was imagined to confer in the working class. But in embracing their status as labor, film writers had to distance themselves from the critically lauded literary writers with whom they sometimes wished to identify. Since at least the middle of the nineteenth century, literary success has been understood to require an embrace of autonomy that is antithetical to salaried employment. As sociologist Pierre Bourdieu wrote, the basis of literary success lies in an economy of cultural production "according to which investments are recompensed only if they are in a sense thrown away, like a gift, which can only achieve the most precious return gift, recognition, so long as it is experienced as a one-way transaction . . . as with the gift, which it converts into pure generosity by masking the expected return gift."[17] Neither film nor advertising writers embraced the gift economy described by Bourdieu, in part because money was the recompense for the loss of autonomy and in part because film and advertising writing could be quite factory-like. Just as writing for the popular *McClure's* magazine was satirized in 1899 ("Every morning the foreman goes from bench to bench and gives an idea to each author. Just before noon he passes along again and carefully examines the unfinished work, and late in the afternoon a final inspection is made, after which the goods are packed and sent down to the wharf for shipping"), so too did screenwriters at Paramount in the 1930s jest about writing on an "assembly line" run by producers "who doled out dramatis personae" to teams of writers and who would "assemble" the dialogue "jigsaw style, into a final script."[18]

Writing by committee made it plausible for Hollywood writers to see themselves as labor in the 1930s, especially because, in those days, nearly everybody was thinking about or trying to form or join a union. But still, it required an attitude adjustment for writers to embrace the legal label "employee." Highly paid writers jested about convening Marxist study groups in Beverly Hills, discussing dialectical materialism at the pool, and asking the famous Beverly Boulevard restaurant Chasen's to serve vichyssoise on the picket line. But writers knew that those who earned huge salaries had all but won a lottery and that if they were not employees, they would own their copyrights and be in a better position to prevent the mutilation of their work in the production process. Studios would never concede that screenwriters, like New York playwrights, could veto changes to the script and could not be banished from the set during filming. The status of employee was, thus, about more than just copyright ownership or the right to form a union. It was about creative autonomy, about whether they were more like literary writers or more like ad agency copywriters.[19]

Writers weren't the only ones adopting a delicate and contradictory position with respect to their legal status as labor. While resisting giving writers creative control and insisting writers were employees for purposes of the copyright work-for-hire doctrine, studios opposed writers' efforts to bargain collectively by arguing to the National Labor Relations Board (NLRB) that the writers were not employees eligible to unionize. Writers, the studios said, performed services that were "creative and professional in character, whereas the Act applies to the more standardized and mechanical employments." Unions were for "wage earners in the lower income brackets." Screen writers were not employees because they were not required "to observe regular office hours or to maintain office discipline," nor "to produce any fixed amount of work," and they were "free to develop screen material in accordance with their own ideas."[20] The employers renewed this same argument with respect to radio writers in the 1940s, TV writers in the early 1950s, and freelance film writers in 1959 when writers struck over payment for reuse of material on TV. The argument consistently failed because studios insisted on control over what writers wrote.[21]

When studios in 1937 raised the argument about writers not being employees, the NLRA defined employees entitled to unionize to "include any employee." There was no exclusion for highly paid workers, professionals, those who were not closely supervised, or those who did mental rather than manual labor. During the drafting process, Congress omitted a proposed provision requiring that a worker must be under the employer's continuing authority to qualify as an employee. So writers pointed to their individual employment contracts, which, like Seton Miller's, gave studios control over the time, place, and content of their work. Writers testified that producers exercised that control in assigning writers to particular stories or parts of stories, moving a writer from one project to another, and requiring writers to attend story conferences and demanding writers follow the producer's "very definite ideas as to the changes to be made in a script."[22] The NLRB decided screenwriters were employees because producers had the power (even if it was not always exercised) to dictate the content of writers' work, assign parts of stories, and stipulate where writers were to write. The power that studios insisted upon in individual employment agreements like Seton Miller's made writers their employees. The Board noted, but found unimportant, that some writers were employed on a "free-lance basis under contracts providing for a week-to-week continuation of the employment or for the completion of a certain piece of work at a specified aggregate compensation," because "there is no essential difference between a free-lance writer and a writer working under contract for a term in the manner in which they performed their work and that the only difference between the two is one of length and tenure of employment."[23]

In radio, the story was a bit different. When radio writers tried to unionize in the 1940s, the major legal issue was whether they were employees within the meaning of the antitrust law, not, as with screenwriters, whether they were protected by the National Labor Relations Act. If they were not employees, then collective bargaining would be illegal under anti-trust law. The RWG decided they were and that it was a union, and so did some of the agencies, at least behind the scenes; but the agencies took the public position that many freelance writers were independent contractors and doggedly resisted the Guild's proposed definition of employees covered by any agreement.[24] The agencies proposed that the RWG should go to the NLRB to be certified as a union representing employees, presumably hoping that the Board would decide that freelance radio writers were not employees, or at least not employees of the agency. The RWG's lawyers advised against going to the NLRB for a definition of freelance writers because it was too hard to predict what the Board might do, as there "are not many precedents in literary fields on which the NLRB can go in deciding a dispute of this sort."[25]

In addition, the effort to unionize and negotiate for air credit and ownership of rights in radio scripts occurred primarily among freelance writers and network staff writers, not among the writers who wrote scripted dramas at ad agencies. All the entities that employed freelancers—networks, ad agencies, and packagers—asserted at one point that freelance writers were not employees under the National Labor Relations Act, and they also insisted that they were not employees under the antitrust law. The legal status of radio writers as employees or independent contractors became the most divisive issue between the Radio Writers Guild and the ad agencies, and it was also the key to the debate over writer versus employer ownership of scripts. The same arguments about control and writers' intellectual autonomy were repackaged as reasons why, under the Sherman Act, collective bargaining by writers would be an illegal conspiracy in restraint of trade. Thus, as radio writers claimed the right to bargain collectively, they needed to insist that they were employees (at least for purposes of labor law), not independent contractors, lest their efforts to negotiate minimum terms be an illegal conspiracy in restraint of trade. On the other hand, claiming to be employees meant that everything they wrote would be a work for hire and, thus, not their property. It took years of negotiation and deliberation to resolve the employee issue.[26]

The announced purpose of the antitrust law was to target the corporate monopolies in the production or sale of sugar, tobacco, oil, and a host of other products. Although Congress did not intend to include labor unions and collective bargaining agreements within the statutory prohibition on conspiracies in restraint of trade, the Supreme Court held them to be so in *Loewe v. Lawlor*, a 1908 decision arising out of a long effort of a group of hat makers in Danbury, Connecticut, to improve their working conditions through unionization.[27] When Congress amended the federal antitrust law in the Clayton Act of 1912, labor secured a specific statutory exemption for labor organizations and collective bargaining. The Supreme Court once again resisted the congressional protection for unions, but ultimately, the Court read the antitrust law to allow workers to form unions under the specific statutory exemption and unions and employers to engage in collective bargaining under what the Court had termed a nonstatutory exemption.

But how the statutory and nonstatutory exemptions applied to writers was not clear. In 1945, the influential federal court of appeals in New York handed down a decision suggesting that the Minimum Basic Agreement between the Dramatists Guild and New York theater producers was a conspiracy in restraint of trade. The suit, *Ring v. Spina*, was filed by a producer of a play, *Stovepipe Hat*, who got into a dispute with the playwrights over allegedly unauthorized changes in the play. When the playwrights invoked arbitration under the MBA and terminated the production contract, the producer sued the play's three authors, their agent, the Dramatists Guild, and the Authors

League, alleging that the Minimum Basic Agreement violated the federal antitrust law. The Dramatists Guild asserted it was within the labor exemption from antitrust liability. In the Dramatists Guild's view, the agreement between it and the theatrical producers was a labor agreement like that between screenwriters and the movie studios. It set the terms on which writers would sell their labor in an industry dominated by an oligopoly of relatively few employers. And concerted action was necessary among the writers in order to counteract the producers' oligopoly power.

The court of appeals did not see it that way. The court thought "none of the parties affected are in any true sense employees." The court reasoned that an "author writing a book or play is usually not then in any contractual relation with his producer." And "[i]f and when he does contract, he does not continue in the producer's service to any appreciable or continuous extent thereafter." "The minimum price and royalties provided by the basic agreement, unlike minimum wages in a collective bargaining agreement, are not remuneration for continued services, but are the terms at which a finished product or certain rights therein may be sold. And no wages or working conditions of any group of employees are directly dependent on these terms."[28]

Ring v. Spina did not spell the end of the Dramatists Guild. Later iterations of the litigation avoided definitively ruling that bargaining agreements between dramatists and theater producers were unlawful antitrust conspiracies, although at various points, both playwrights and producers accused each other of violating the law by conspiring to set the price of labor. The Dramatists Guild renegotiated the MBA on the same essential terms over the decades since, and bills to clarify the law have been introduced in Congress but never passed. Meanwhile, playwrights own the copyrights in their scripts and have creative control of stage productions of them. Producers pay playwrights a minimum percentage of the box office, share earnings beyond the minimum, and split receipts from sales of film rights.[29]

But the language of *Ring v. Spina* about who was an employee and who could unionize and bargain collectively was of intense interest to the advertising agencies and radio networks. The agencies wanted to use the decision to argue that radio writers were sellers of intellectual property like dramatists, not employees and sellers of labor like screenwriters, and therefore, collective bargaining would be illegal. In the beginning, the radio writers' reluctance to identify themselves as employees trying to organize a labor union played into the ad agencies' hands.

When the Radio Writers Guild met with the American Association of Advertising Agencies in June 1945 to negotiate a minimum basic agreement, they presented themselves "as an association of independent contractors, not as a union under the Wagner Act." But after the ad agencies insisted that, if they were independent contractors, the agencies had no legal duty to bargain under the labor law and any agreement with them would possibly be a restraint of trade made unlawful under antitrust law, radio writers had to choose which legal status to claim. So radio writers decided they would be employees. To get the entity that effectively controlled their terms of employment to the bargaining table, they needed to insist that the ad agencies were their employers, not the sponsors. And, because staff writers at networks also supported unionization, the RWG negotiated both for staff writers and freelancers. As to staff writers, the networks could not use the legal ploy that they were not eligible to form a union, and the RWG suspended negotiations over staff writers for a period to secure recognition of freelancers.[30]

The agencies continued to resist, arguing that radio writers were independent contractors, not employees, and therefore the agencies were under no legal obligation to bargain, any collective agreement about terms of employment would violate the antitrust law, and any agreement negotiated by a committee of advertising agencies would not be binding on the shows' sponsors, who, the agencies believed, were the actual employers of the people who wrote their shows. As Erik Barnouw, president of the RWG, later recalled, the agencies gave writers "a skillful runaround" for almost a decade.[31]

It was indeed a runaround because what the agencies asserted in negotiations differed from what at least some of their lawyers believed. JWT's in-house counsel, Ed Wilson, concluded that JWT radio staff writers and freelancers were employees of the agency because JWT controlled what and when they wrote. On *Lux Radio Theatre*, for example, Wilson privately conceded that the head writer, Sanford Barnett, who had a desk in JWT's Hollywood office and worked with JWT staff in adapting plays or movies for radio, was "subject to supervision by the client, through us." On *Kraft Music Hall*, Wilson described working conditions for writers that looked a bit like film and a lot like what quickly became standard in TV and that were enough to establish writers as agency employees:

A JWT representative or director would meet with the writers in what they refer to as a premise meeting. At this meeting the writers would be told who the guest artist would be the following week and our representative and the head writer would attempt to work out the situations around which the scripts would be written. Each writer would then go off and prepare the portions which were assigned to him. Their efforts would be turned in and coordinated by the head writer. If their material was okay, they had nothing more to do. However, if the whole thing did not shape up all the writers including the head writer would be called in and they would work together until they completed the script. Each writer would get [paid] the same amount each week, no matter how much work he had to do.[32]

In a legal memo prepared for JWT clients, Wilson concluded "the script writers on your shows are employees,"[33] later adding that they were "undoubtedly employees of the sponsor," but because the agency "act[s] for the sponsor in supervising them, it seems clear that we should handle all matters relating to their work and should, therefore, do the negotiating." JWT did briefly consider the possibility of restructuring its relationship to its clients such that the agency would employ the freelancers and sell or lease scripts to the clients, but ultimately decided not to.[34]

As a matter of legal doctrine, freelance writers did not easily fit into a box. On the one hand, they worked independently. In the 1937 NLRB hearings on the right of screenwriters to unionize, some writers testified that they wrote at home or on the golf course, at the hours they wanted, without supervision over their work, at least until the script was done and a producer asked for revisions. Many writers proposed their own topics, and the structure of the finished work was dictated more by the conventions of the medium than by the employer. On the other hand, every media company insisted (then as now) on the power to force the writer to rewrite. Rod Serling was forced in 1955 to rewrite a story about the Emmet Till lynching to remove even the slightest hint of race. John Howard Lawson recalled that although RKO bought his play in the 1930s with the promise that it would not be changed, the studio insisted that the leading characters must not be Jews, and although he "had always known that the play would be cheapened in the film version, but the Jewish theme was clearly the heart of the play." But, he said, he "had no choice but to accept the conditions imposed and to salvage what [he] could from the original work." And that power to demand revisions became crucial.[35]

When radio writers negotiated with advertising agencies, they were not writing on an entirely clean slate because the Radio Writers Guild had already negotiated with networks over the conditions of the relatively smaller number of staff writers employed by the networks. Networks appeared to exert more control over their writers than the agencies did over theirs, but conditions varied and the resolution of the question of who would be covered by the network agreement provided a useful pattern. The RWG proposed that a freelance writer not on the staff of the agencies would be covered by the collective agreement if the writer satisfied the definition of employee in its network agreement, which covered a writer "where the company has the right by contract to require him to perform personal services in making revisions, modifications or changes." The RWG also proposed to copy the network agreement's specific exclusion of independent contractors, who were corporate purveyors of material or "any individual who sells or licenses to the company rights of use or ownership of 'material' without contracting to perform personal services with respect to revision, modification or change."[36]

When the agencies finally offered an alternative definition, their definition also focused on the power to dictate revisions. But the agencies wanted to narrow the category of writers to which the agreement would apply even further to exclude a vague category of "independent contractors," without being able to explain who was an employee or independent contractor since the agencies insisted on the right to demand revisions from anybody. The agencies' inability to define the scope of their proposed exclusion ultimately proved fatal to their negotiating position. One journalist covering the negotiations lampooned the agencies' position and suggested the Guild should reject it on the "aesthetic (as distinct from the legal) grounds that any writer, . . . or simply a man with a typewriter and an urge for self-expression would jeopardize his immortal soul" in crafting such a sentence. The agencies suggested the agreement "shall cover and apply only to free-lance writers (as distinct from writers on staff) who are employees of the company while engaged in employee activities (as distinct from independent contractors) and are employed to render personal writing services in preparation of 'material' (as hereafter to be defined) for radio programs including but without limiting the meaning of the term 'employee' as used above, any such employee-writer as to whom the company by contract shall have the right to direct and control the performance of such writer's personal services in making revisions, modifications or changes in material originally prepared by such writer."[37]

The RWG refused to accept a deal that excluded an ill-defined category of writers, and so informed the agencies: "Our lawyers tell us frankly they do not know what it means. Since the intent must have been clear to the committee which drafted it, we are turning to you for help." The agencies were unable to articulate which writers its proposed definition of employee would exclude from the protections of a collective agreement, which angered writers no end. Since the agencies had stalled for several years in even commencing to negotiate by insisting that radio writers were not their employees, and sponsors insisted that the writers weren't their employees either, the Radio Writers Guild thought the effort to exclude an ill-defined group of freelancers was close to bad faith. So the exchange over the definition of employee concluded with the Guild threatening a strike: "writers have been talking with you since 1942 and are tired of talk."[38]

The fight over the legal status of freelance writers was repeated in 1952 in television, but more briefly. One advantage television writers had was the producers' desire to declare that writers were employees for some purposes (copyright law) and not others (labor law and tax). Production companies preferred to declare everyone an employee as a way to benefit from the work-for-hire rule of copyright but to treat as many writers as possible as freelancers to avoid having to withhold income and other payroll taxes. Writers threatened that if the producers insisted television writers were employees only for copyright purposes, "we should sic the Internal Revenue people on them" because the producers had not withheld tax.[39]

In the end, the definition of employee writers covered by the RWG agreement was resolved by minor tweaks to the language in the network MBA, but it kept the original notion that an employee was a writer who could be required to make revisions, modifications, or changes.[40] To this day, employees under the MBA are those who "write literary material . . . where the Company has the right by contract to direct the performance of personal services in writing or preparing such material or in making revisions, modifications, or changes therein." As Erik Barnouw later reflected, the lack of creative control—an issue that galled many radio, film, and TV writers—proved the key to their ability to bargain collectively for the rights of attribution, partial ownership, compensation, and respect that they had secured in the MBAs in radio, film, and TV writing. It was the power of the employer to force the writer to make revisions—the right of control—that defined who was an employee.[41]

Control and Autonomy: Writers as Employees

Although being deemed employees allowed writers to win the right to bargain collectively, the most subtle but the most pervasive effect of writers' legal status as employees was in their self-conception. Reactions varied, but most focused on their inability to control their time, ideas, and work product. Sometimes writers made light of it and insisted they were paid a great deal to do little work, and others chafed a bit more at the control, but all recognized the problem. British novelist P.G. Wodehouse described his experience when MGM brought him to Hollywood in 1930: "When I get a summons from the studio, I motor over there, stay for a couple of hours and come back." The actual work, he said, was "negligible." "The system is that A gets the original idea, B comes into work with him on it, C makes the scenario, D does preliminary dialogue, and then they send for me to insert class and whatnot, then E and F, scenario writers, alter the plot and off we go again. I could have done all my part of it in a morning but they took it for granted that I should need six weeks." Nathanael West told a different story about his experience at Columbia in 1933. "This stuff about easy work is all wrong," he said. The mandatory working hours were onerous and irritating: "My hours are from ten in the morning to six at night with a full day on Saturday." Like Wodehouse, though, he found the story assignment process to be irksome and idiotic: "They gave me a job to do five minutes after I sat down in my office—a scenario about a beauty parlor—and I'm expected to turn out pages and pages a day. There's no fooling here. All the writers sit in cells and the minute a typewriter stops someone pokes his head in the door to see if you are thinking." The Guild tried repeatedly, though unsuccessfully, to reduce writing by committee, by requiring producers "to notify a writer of the assignment of other writers to the same material at the time they are assigned." But the practice continued.[42]

Studios varied in the extent to which they exerted the power they had under contracts to dictate when, where, how, and on what writers wrote. RKO in its early years did not ask writers to work by committee, and writers were on the set when their script was shot. Warner Bros. and Republic, however, insisted writers keep regular office hours and retaliated against writers who refused to work on Saturdays. The Writers Guild insisted repeatedly "that a writer's work can only be judged by the script he writes and not by the number of hours worked per day; that the work of a writer is unique and extraordinary, etc." In 1948, the Guild tried to get the MBA revised to prohibit specific office hours for writers unless it was written into the individual contract. As the distinction between staff and freelance writers became clear in the early 1950s, writers insisted that the distinction be used to define when production companies could force writers to keep regular hours.[43]

Whether or how studios asserted their contractual rights to dictate when, where, and what writers wrote, and how they changed or revised what they wrote, were all variations on the theme of control and autonomy. Acquiring status and power, often measured by what one was paid, became synonymous with acquiring the right to force producers to listen. As SWG President Mary McCall, Jr., said, she wanted a big weekly salary "not because I need it" but because it would "give me authority. Then when a producer says, 'Look, sweetheart, I have a terrific angle on this opening; we fade in on a bed,' I can say, 'That's silly,' and he will listen to me because I will be so very expensive. I say 'That's silly' now, but he rarely listens to me."[44]

Assembly-line writing and fights over creative control or working hours were expressed in terms of employment contracts and pay because that is how writers and employers exerted economic and creative power vis-à-vis one another. Writers fought for their status as *authors* by invoking two legal concepts: the notion of *contract* as a source of rights and constraint on power, and notions about who was an *employee* and what being an employee meant.

Contracts remain of central importance in the way that writers conceptualize their rights and their status as workers as in their work. Glen Mazzara said about the two years he spent as the showrunner of *The Walking Dead* (2011–2013) that in disputes between the network, the studio, and the writer of the books on which the series was based, "My contract's with the studio—the network can say all they want, but I'm working for the studio." In the same moment, he also noted that contracts not only determine control but also ownership and that ownership matters: "I'm signing that my work is owned by the studio." Ultimately, Mazzara explained, resolution of issues of creative control is a matter of the contract of hire: "What am I actually being paid for? What is my contract for?"[45]

What Rosten observed about the 1930s, Mary McCall complained about in the 1940s, and Glen Mazzara was resigned to in 2013 was what Hortense Powdermaker said about writers working but not having works. McCall aspired to the economic and social power to force producers to listen and so that she might come closer to having her *work* be *her* work. Successful television writers like David Milch *(Deadwood)* and Stephen Bochco *(Hill Street Blues)* profess to have gotten to the point in their career that studios and networks no longer give them notes. But even celebrated writers with recognizable names— Rod Serling *(The Twilight Zone),* for example—often complained that notes were part of the job and writers could do little to resist. Serling recalled being told by an ad agency to change "American" and "lucky" to "United States" and "fortunate" because the show's sponsor competed with American Tobacco's Lucky Strike cigarette brand. Serling complied but took his name off the script, "the only thing a writer can do in television in the way of a protest." Thus, when real control failed, all that was left was to become anonymous and, as C. Wright Mills put it, to embrace the "final point" of alienation by insisting on "complete lack of public responsibility" for their work.

Size, Organization, and the Creativity Problem

The Madison Avenue novels of the 1940s and 1950s reflected that the lack of public responsibility entailed in being an employee could not be ameliorated by the advertising copywriters' longstanding strategy of insisting on being a professional. Whereas Hollywood writers turned to their Guild, to screen credit, and to residuals and separated rights for recognition of their status as creators, Madison Avenue writers embraced rigor, thoroughness of research, devotion to craft and to the interests of clients, and their niche as high-status professionals like the executives and lawyers who ran their clients' businesses. The problem for advertising copywriters, though, was that the self-conception of an author as a business professional was in tension with the conception of an author as a creator and the master (if not proprietor) of the ideas and words he produces. The tension between business managerialism and authorial creativity became acute in the 1940s, and it became the subject not only of the many Madison Avenue novels but also of a blizzard of office memoranda at J. Walter Thompson in the 1950s.

In the 1950s, many in the ad business lamented the lack of creativity and the dullness of ads, as well as that few of the best campaigns of the 1950s were produced by the major agencies. *Advertising Age,* the advertising industry's trade paper, in 1952 worried that "[t]oo many advertisers are refusing to explore new paths," and Whit Hobbs of BBD&O advertising agency said in 1959 that "[t]he creative man has lost the chip on his shoulder, the fire in his eye. Success has made him courteous, obedient, cautious. Thin tie, thin skin. He has moved to the suburbs, bought a boat, which he is careful not to rock." The "magazine format" of television, by limiting agency writers to thirty-second commercials produced for the approval of corporate sponsors, distanced agency writers from TV writers and consigned the former to thinking up three words to sell laxatives or floor polish and annoying TV writers with notes on episodes of shows for which their clients were major advertisers.[46]

JWT executives debated how to structure the huge agency to recapture the reputation it had once had for being the best in the business as its much-vaunted market research no longer assured it the position of industry leader and the trade press insisted that the most creative work was being done at the smaller agencies. Although JWT "has unquestionably done more than any single factor to elevate the business to the status of a profession," as an internal company document crowed, senior executive Norman Strouse warned in a 1957 speech to the Association of National Advertisers: "We must encourage young people coming into our business to have confidence in their imaginations and their enthusiasms, so that they will believe that there really are more creative worlds to conquer, and are not squashed under the foot of cynicism, captiousness or submissiveness on the part of their elders." Yet when JWT ran a house ad in the trade press and in *Time* magazine in 1956 featuring a half-page photo of five men posed with TV cameras and a head-line, "These men help give *network* quality to *local* live TV," the men themselves were not identified by name because at JWT, only the agency's name mattered. The smaller agencies prided themselves on having no meetings, no memos, and no bureaucracy to get in the way of the creative people. But at JWT, there were lots of meetings and memos, and one of them, written in 1957 by Howard Kohl, articulates the problem.[47]

At JWT, an industry leader in an economic sector in which the firm's "assets ride down the elevator every night,"[48] executives like Kohl insisted the key to success was the wise management of creativity. JWT's pioneering management idea of the 1930s was the account representative—the man (they were mainly men) in charge of relations with the client who was to coordinate the work of writers, artists, and market researchers to design an overall ad campaign—who "should be a buffer between client and agency, should serve as a filter of the client's subjective points of view." But not everybody agreed there should be a buffer, especially as smaller agencies had captured the fancy of clients because of the creativity of their writers. So some people at JWT had started putting "creatives" (copywriters and art designers) into direct touch with clients. Kohl's memo warned against this "tendency of Representatives to use creative people and specialists in daily and regular contact work with our clients" because it would undermine the company's ability to present clients with "our completely objective viewpoint," and because "the fine work of a creative man or specialist can, on occasion, be rendered ineffective or unusable because of personality problems." Division of labor, with writers focusing on writing, would be more efficient and maximize production. Finally, the representative would "reduce his value to that of a messenger boy if he places on others the major responsibility in presenting the agency's work." Three years later, JWT again attempted to impose managerial oversight on creative employees by instituting a detailed procedure (the memo called it a review board system) to follow in developing an ad before revealing it to the client, giving more control to department heads and representatives and less to writers and artists.[49]

By assimilating the manufacture of ideas, text, images, and sounds into the dominant system of automobile manufacture or managing finance, Kohl's memo and the review board system embraced the classic management theory of the twentieth-century office or factory. To be a professional, even in the world of writing and design, was to remove the idiosyncrasies of personality and individual point of view from the work process and product; to be a creative professional was to equate the "author" with "the firm" by attributing all individual work to the firm. Moreover, efficient workplace management demanded a sharp division of labor between creativity and management, and the success of the firm depended upon managers maintaining control over the creative workers.

But to those who feared that the size, profitability, systematic market research, and professionalism of a big agency still couldn't make up for the loss of creativity, these systems and memos hit just the wrong note. Bureaucratic management of the creative process, employees complained, reduced them to churning out ideas, artwork, or texts that disappeared after being placed in the out box on their desk each day. A report listing the "pros and cons of J. Walter Thompson" identified "integrity," "a professional approach," and "pioneering leadership" as the three main pros and "the submergence of creativity" and "the fear of being 'lost'" as cons. Worried that bureaucratic employment practices could not easily be reconciled with individual creativity in writing and art, one executive proposed that especially talented staff were "deserving of greater publicity," while another proposed that public recognition of creative staff could reduce alienation and improve the company's reputation for creativity. Wallace Elton, who had been an art director in the 1940s and 1950s but had become an executive vice president, a member of the firm's executive committee, and the chairman of the New York operations committee, complained "about the lack of attention on creativeness and the seeming willingness to compromise the creative effort with a profit motive." The director of the JWT TV Art Group lamented in his 1956 end-of-year report that his job had become simply making everyone think and write faster, as he had come "to preside over a normalized storyboard factory." His staff, he insisted, needed to "be allowed time to think, not just to estimate like a shoemender, how long it will take to whack off fifteen frames, four to the sheet, and then settle for half the time, because the representative says he has already made his appointment with the client." So the company adopted new systems to generate ideas and cultivate talent. In 1956, prompted by the trade press fanfare over the use of "brainstorming" sessions at another agency, JWT developed a "springboarding" group to allow creatives to toss out ideas without the usual review process, and the group grew from a handful to 179 participants by the end of 1957. But still, office memos expressed anxiety about how to reconcile creativity with corporate control.[50]

Ownership and control of ideas were at the heart of the ad agency management model and were the words writers used to describe their alienation. At Doyle Dane Bernbach—the agency that had become the darling of the trade press for sparking a "creative revolution" in advertising with a "looser management style" that produced the pathbreaking Volkswagen ads that launched the Beetle in the United States at the end of the 1950s—the creative team regarded their work as "their property." "They own it," Bernbach said, and "they walk with pride." But ownership was metaphor; clients owned the completed ads, and agencies owned the works in progress. Agencies occasionally sued employees who quit to start or join other agencies if they took ideas with them. Although copywriters often switched jobs and new agencies had long been started by defections from established agencies, a high-profile case involved the 1952 Duane Jones agency, which sued and won a huge verdict against three employees who had quit and taken a major client to the new firm they founded. The theme of preventing employee departures and start-ups through litigation emerged in advertising novels of the era.[51] And so JWT's general counsel struggled to figure out how to give clients the impression that the agency was open to new ideas while prohibiting staff from considering any unsolicited idea from nonemployees. He hit upon the strategy that the firm should "not distribute any general memorandum to the staff stating that it is our general policy to reject idea material" because "our clients might misunderstand and think that we should not close ourselves off from suggestions."[52]

As self-declared leaders, indeed founders, of advertising as a profession, JWT executives insisted they deserved to be considered as a profession because of the independence and intellectual nature of advertising. What they considered a loss of professionalism is what film and TV writers blamed on ad agencies and timid studio or network executives—killing off good ideas through notes and suggestions that undermined the independence of the writer. JWT leader John Monsarrat wrote and circulated among his colleagues a twenty-five-page memo on "Professionalism in Advertising Agency Practice" in 1964 in which he lambasted what he perceived as the decline in independence of his agency. Advertisers meddled too much in the work of their agencies, and they squelched good ideas "through the attrition of a long succession of compromises . . . in order to accommodate the whims and personal opinions of layer after layer of middle-management executives with the right to *disapprove* but without the professional qualifications to *improve*." Such tweaking is "discouraging or stultifying to the agency copywriter" who knows "almost with predictable certainty, that no matter how carefully he plans his work, it will be subjected to the need for compromise after compromise." Agency creativity thrives in "the certainty that a good idea, carefully conceived and painstakingly executed, has a clear channel to prompt and respectful consideration by top management in the client organization."[53]

Institutionalized acknowledgment of creativity became the strategy to encourage excellence. In the 1960s, to respond to the problem of alienation among agency workers no longer content to accept just the money, or a note of thanks, or an engraved plaque, the ad industry increased recognition through awards. In 1959, the Clio Awards (perhaps the best known of contemporary advertising awards) were founded to honor excellence in television commercials. In the mid-1960s, Clios were created for excellence in international TV and in US radio, and then in print and a number of specialty awards in the 1970s. They were quite explicitly compared to Oscars in film, Emmys in TV, Tonys in stage, and Grammys in music. But in a hierarchical and bureaucratic workplace like an ad agency in which there was no regular system for attributing work to individuals, annual awards like the Clios became another moment in which writers experienced their alienation.

At JWT, even when an agency won an award, the actual award (the trophy) belonged to the client. Thus, JWT's Wallace Elton received the Best Commercial Emmy in 1956 for the Ford TV campaign for which he was the creative director. (Company memoranda say Winfield Taylor had done the writing.) Although Elton signed the agreement with the Academy of Television Arts and Sciences saying that he agreed not to sell, transfer, or convey the statue without first offering it to the Academy, JWT actually gave the trophy to Ford.[54] Most copywriters had to settle for thanks or, sometimes, not even that. A few years before JWT won the Emmy for its Ford campaign, Winfield Taylor's Ford copy was acknowledged in a thank-you note simply saying the client had liked it and "a hand-made plaque, properly embellished and inscribed."[55]

But that had its problems too. One was that they sometimes rewarded the wrong people—perhaps Don did not after all deserve the Clio for the Glo-Coat commercial—and made the people whom they were supposed to motivate even more cynical. Another was that they drew too much attention to ads as artifice—"too often they are given for technique alone, ignoring the objective of the advertising," which is to increase sales for clients (the Clio included in the judging criteria whether an ad is "an effective piece of sales communication," but appeared to make no serious effort to measure effectiveness). And a third was that there were just too many awards so it wasn't all

that special to win one. By the late 1960s, executives at JWT concluded that
the proliferation of awards "was getting out of hand." The agency executives
decided, as a matter of corporate policy, to prohibit creative people from submitting individual entries to awards competitions and that the agency would
submit entries only to select European festivals and to the Art Directors Club
Awards in New York and Chicago. As writers had decided about screen credit,
fewer mentions to fewer people would enhance the status of getting any
credit at all. But, of course, the difference between screen credit and the JWT
policy about award nominations is that the former is up for debate among
affected writers, but the latter was a company policy dictated from the executive suite.[56]

Attribution and Gender Segregation

One informal form of attribution of work that persisted in advertising agencies into the 1960s was the same one that JWT had pioneered in the 1920s: a
separate women's department. Women had been able to find jobs writing
for film and advertising in the 1920s and 1930s when other elite occupations
were almost entirely closed to them, and women advanced in advertising as
men were mobilized for World War II. In 1944, Ruth Waldo became the first
female vice president at JWT, and Jean Wade Rindlaub became Batten, Barton,
Durstine & Osborn's first woman VP in the same year. Unlike in some other
occupations, where women were forced out to make room for men returning
from war, women hung onto the gains they made in ad agencies, and between
1945 and 1960, many agencies appointed their first female vice presidents.[57] By
1947, JWT had two women vice presidents and seventy women in "creative"
jobs in its US offices."[58] Mary Wells attracted attention when she became one
of the first women in the 1950s to found (and be a partner in) an agency, Wells,
Rich, Greene (her partners Rich and Greene were Jewish men; Jews had also
experienced discrimination in hiring at many of the major ad agencies).

The scarcity of women in senior positions at agencies also meant that
their achievements were considered especially noteworthy, just as copywriter
Helen Landsdowne's campaigns for Lux and Jergens had been considered
path breaking in the 1920s. Shirley Polykoff, after working in retail advertising, got a job as a copywriter at Foote, Cone & Belding in 1955 where she
wrote the Clairol ad, "Does she or doesn't she? Only her hairdresser knows

for sure." She was thus credited with sparking the huge increase in the number of women who colored their hair. Anecdotes of which copywriter coined which trademark or slogan abound in the trade press and popular histories of Madison Avenue, but attributions to women seem to have particular reliability because the women were segregated so it is easy to trace accomplishments to particular people.[59]

Although the number of women in advertising grew in the 1950s, at JWT, women retained the separate women's department. Indeed, the women's copy group lasted at least until Title VII of the Civil Rights Act of 1964 made policies of gender segregation illegal. As a 1964 *Advertising Age* obituary for Helen Landsdowne Resor explained, her being "a militant exponent of women's place in advertising" was the reason JWT's New York office still maintained a women's editorial department "separate but co-equal with the men's copy groups, where women's talents could not be submerged."[60] But the trade press decided JWT lost reputation as the most hospitable agency for women in the 1950s to McCann Erickson, which by 1960 boasted that six of its 100 VPs were women, "the highest proportion in advertising."[61]

Women who led the efforts to train and mentor other women recognized that a woman, as the saying went, had to be twice as good to be perceived as half as good; they could promote women's accomplishments against the headwind of sexism by attributing excellent work to women and hoping their accomplishments would speak for themselves. So, at JWT in 1958, copywriter Lucene Fergus wrote to Hastings Foote, who was running copy seminars to train aspiring writers, offering information on women who had signed up for his copy seminar and who had previously participated in the Women's Copy Study Group. The memo offered praise for most of the women, but it did not offer unqualified praise for any. Fergus wanted the women in the women's group to succeed in the men's world, but she also did not want to undermine the importance of the women's group as the very best training ground for women, and therefore, she proved the rigor of the training program for women by sharing the harsh criticism that women made of other women's work.[62]

The markers that sometimes marginalized women were also a form of attribution, although that kind of attribution could hurt a career as much as it helped. A 1960 JWT presentation seeking to recruit Sunkist Growers as a client proposed that the person who would be assigned to the campaign, if

Sunkist chose JWT as its agency, was "Mrs. Jean Simpson": "Since Jean is a woman, and a very active as well as attractive woman who has been in the advertising business since her graduation from college, it is not at all surprising that all of that time has been spent working on ideas for products sold to women and to be used in the home." She was described as a successful cookbook author who "has won recognition from her own sex by being elected president of the Women's Advertising Club of Chicago." Gender thus became a marketing device to attract clients, while stereotypes about women's voice, women's fashion, and the women's ambitions limited women's options.[63]

Thoughts on the Legal History of Writing for Hire

Writers' debates about their employment status open a new vista on contemporary academic and policy discussions about work in what is sometimes called the "gig economy," the "on-demand economy," or, more generally, the "new economy." Poor labor standards exist at companies with a labor "sharing" model (such as Airbnb), a crowdsourcing of work model (such as NASA is reported to have used for some innovations), a freelance model (Uber, Lyft, taxi service, and increasingly journalism, professional services, graphic design, and so forth), disaggregated businesses (as where truckers and delivery drivers are nominally independent contractors even though they perform the core work of a package-delivery business), and in supply chains (as where farm workers are not employees of the agricultural companies whose business is to grow fruits and vegetables, much less of the restaurants that depend on their labor). Most legal protections for workers—protections of the minimum wage and premium pay for overtime, eligibility for employer-provided health and retirement insurance, protections against status-based workplace discrimination and harassment—turn on whether a worker is an employee (as opposed to an independent contractor). Some insist workers do not want the stability of being an employee because they want the independence and flexibility of owning their own business and working only when and where they want. Others see the decline of the middle class and exploitation in these models, which provide flexibility and security to the company, and put all the risk of illness and economic downturn on workers. Whatever the case may be, Hollywood writers have been working in the gig economy for more than half a century, while their peers on Madison Avenue insisted that their independence, even though they were salaried, came from adherence to professional norms.[64]

Writers have long experience with the advantages and disadvantages of the world of independent production. As Mary McCall, Jr., the president of the SWG said in 1946, it would benefit writers to move away from the "old model of business," with the comfort of guaranteed studio deals, toward "a freelance model that would allow writers to better control their own work," through the lease not sale of scripts, payment of royalties, and the possibility of working as both a writer and a producer or director. Other writers agreed: the advantages of independent production included a "larger market for writers' work, less supervision, and profit-participation." The Guild has spent more than half a century devising strategies to address the disadvantages of the gig economy. It has responded to independent producers' constant refrain that they did not have money to pay writers up front, the difficulty of collecting deferred compensation when projects succeeded, the unwillingness of independent producers to train new writers, and the efforts of producers (and the willingness of writers) to expect work beyond that for which the producer had specifically agreed to pay. Then and now, building a reputation and a career from short-term and irregular work, multiple employers, minimal (or electronic) supervision, performance-based compensation, and the other hallmarks of new economy work was the labor market challenge that the Guild worked to solve.[65]

Conclusion

> You aren't writing for the love of it or the art of it or whatever; you are doing a chore assigned to you by your employer and whether or not he might fire you if you did it slackly makes no matter. You've got yourself to face, and you have to live with yourself. You don't—or at least, only in highly exceptional circumstances—have to live with your producer.
>
> —Dorothy Parker

A writer, I have argued, is a person who writes as a vocation or at least as an avocation. To be an author, however, means something more. C. Wright Mills suggested authorship connotes public responsibility for the work. Responsibility as an author means both recognition (in the sense of credit or blame) and ownership of the work (in the sense of being the one who is responsible to steward its uses). To be a writer is to be a creator, but to be an author is to be a creator and, at least under American copyright law, an owner. The Copyright Act of 1909, which codified a legal development that had been in the works since corporations had been hiring writers on a big scale, deems the author to be the person or entity that owns a work, not necessarily the one who wrote it; under copyright law, the corporation that employs the writer is the author of a work made for hire. In American law, then, people employed to write are not authors; they are writers only. To be an author is thus a logical impossibility: corporations are fictions and they cannot actually write themselves, but they are authors. Legal fictions are the authors of all the fictions we see on the screen and many we read in magazines.

Yet, for all the twentieth-century literary theory talk about the death of the author, authors actually have refused to die because writers won't let them. I mean that not in the sense in which we persist in talking about what the writer of our favorite film, TV show, or book meant by this or that aspect of a story, but more importantly, in the sense that writers for hire have fought to retain some of the rights and status of authors. They want to be recognized publicly and in the industry as authors, but they also want some of the benefits of ownership of their work.

This book has told the legal history of what happened after corporations came to be the legal authors of film, TV, advertising, and radio, and, more specifically, how writers resisted and sometimes embraced their effacement as authors. It has shown how it came to be that movies and TV shows have credited authors and advertisements do not. And it has argued that work relationships—along with individual employment contracts and collective bargaining agreements—are where authorship is constituted.

The book has made five arguments. First, copyright law and the conditions under which writers worked producing popular culture in the mid-twentieth century divorced writers from the protections they wished to have as authors. Hollywood writers unionized to claw back some of their rights as authors, and they did so through control over screen credit and collectively bargained separated rights and residuals. Advertising writers pursued a different strategy: they declared themselves professionals and developed internal labor markets within their firms through which they hoped by rising to the partnership or to the position of creative director to secure some of the control of authors. And they collectively eschewed authorship of advertising by insisting that their fiduciary duty of loyalty to their clients required that the client own the rights in their work and be the only name associated with the work in the public's mind.

The second argument is that in the fissured economy of today, in which internal labor markets are rare and short-term employment is endemic, there is much to recommend the Hollywood union model. For all its many failings, the Writers Guild of America (WGA) survives because it provides WGA-represented writers some of the credit, compensation, and control that writers in nonunion sectors do not enjoy. Among people who are employed by large corporations to create intellectual property, those who work in Hollywood are relatively unusual in belonging to a union. Creators of video or online games, websites, and computer code may be demographically similar (highly educated and creative) and do similar work as that done by Hollywood talent, but they often are paid much less, and whether their name is publicly attached to their work is a matter of corporate policy rather than enforceable legal right.

Third, I have argued that screen credit is among the most important rights that the WGA secured for writers. Screen credit affects the labor market for writers, the product market for films and TV shows, how critics and the public interpret works, and what writers get paid. Screen credit is a form of privately negotiated and enforced intellectual property right, and it is a right only because writers have a union to fight for and administer the system and the union has adhered (with the catastrophic exception of the Blacklist) to the rule of law in enforcing credits. When I argue that screen credit is a private intellectual property right, I thus contend that focus on copyright and trademark as the two most important forms of intellectual property in the entertainment industries is, in part, misplaced. We should look to the labor practices surrounding screen credit to really understand authorship of movies and TV.

The fourth argument of the book is that the different attribution norms in film and TV and advertising emerged from the different labor practices in the two industries. Hollywood and Madison Avenue are both actual sites of creative labor and metonyms for different visions of creative labor. Because writers in Hollywood unionized, and writers in Madison Avenue never did, very different intellectual property regimes and attribution norms developed in the two industries. The reasons for that have to do with the different self-conceptions of what it means to be a creative professional (what a tired phrase!). The consequences of the different labor practices have been enormous.

Finally, the most abstract argument of the book is that authorship is a socio-legal concept formed not by copyright nearly as much as by the social and legal processes by which people at work seek recognition, control, and compensation for uses of their work. To understand film, TV, and advertising as intellectual property one must understand the labor history of the efforts of writers to become authors. Attribution practices are so integrated in work culture that to understand how attribution works requires uncovering the history of the labor and employment relations in Hollywood and on Madison Avenue and of the effort of writers in film, radio, and TV to unionize. While this book has not aspired to be a history of the WGA or the J. Walter Thompson Company (JWT), I have had to say a lot about workplace relations and these two organizations to tell the history of attribution.

Almost everybody receives some credit for the work they do, and the way that credit is noted—a plaque on the wall of a workplace, a byline on a story, a name stamped on the bottom of a paper bag, a note in a file, a reference given by phone during a job search—varies from one workplace or industry to another. JWT tried, with varying degrees of success, to hide attribution from the public. Hollywood is at the other end of the spectrum of recognition: film and TV writers are unusual in receiving very conspicuous public attribution, working under an elaborate system of writer-controlled rules governing credit, and having their compensation depend on screen credit. Credits have become the norm such that even nonunion-produced TV includes writing credit. My favorite example: During the 1960 writers' strike, episodes of the TV shows *77 Sunset Strip, Hawaiian Eye, Colt .45,* and *Bourbon Street Beat* were created by nonwriter Warner Bros. staff who recycled old scripts by switching characters or locales, or turning a Western into a detective episode. Each of these corporate-written episodes had a credit reading "Written by W. Hermanos" (W. Brothers in Spanish). That was surely a dig at the Guild and the striking writers, not an actual effort to credit work for the benefit of the audience. But other nonunion screen entertainment has credits today.[1]

Authorship designations may influence how we perceive work. Whether we watch in a theater, on a TV, or on a computer, we can view and interpret a movie or TV program as being authored by someone, and we can compare and contrast movies or shows by author, just as we can compare and contrast novels, plays, photographs, or paintings. The commercials that precede or interrupt the movie or program are not authored products, and so only those in the industry can approach them as the works of identified people. So, too, with print and online magazines, newspapers, and blogs: the stories usually have a byline and a photo credit, but the text in advertisements never does and the photos rarely do. Although the unionization of Hollywood writers did not initiate the practice of giving screen credit to writers, the WGA has perpetuated the practice, has made credits reasonably accurate, and has created a system of compensation that turns on screen credit. It is not an exaggeration to say that a union determines the authorship of film and TV. The fact that the Writers Guild controls authorship has important consequences for those who work in the industry and for the way we consume their work.

Nor is it an exaggeration to say that the absence of a union in advertising is one reason why, as said by Don Draper, the creative director of the fictional ad agency at the center of the TV show *Mad Men* (2007-2015), there are no credits in commercials. I did not find evidence of a serious push among advertising agency staff writers for unionization, except one effort in the late 1940s that fizzled rather quickly. There wasn't even a serious effort to change the norms of credit, except for the 1955 policy at JWT that briefly gave screen credit for agency-produced TV shows just as the agency was getting out of the business of producing TV. It is nonetheless clear that unionization of freelance radio and television writers forced ad agencies to give air credit when they were the producers of radio and TV shows in the late 1940s and early 1950s. The demise of commercial radio storytelling with the advent of TV and the rise of the magazine format for TV resulted in the nonattribution norms of advertising agencies governing the ads and the attribution rules of the WGA governing the programs. Had the labor relations in advertising been different, or had the divorce of ad agencies from television production never occurred, it is not impossible to imagine a different kind of advertising, different norms of attribution, and a different approach to interpreting advertisements as cultural artifacts.

But there is an even more important conclusion to be drawn from the history of the Writers Guild's approach to credit and compensation in contrast to the nonunion and anonymous culture in advertising. That difference illuminates the possibilities for collective representation of white-collar or creative workers in so-called "new economy" jobs. In the United States today, a mere 7 percent of the private sector workforce is unionized, and many people seem unable even to imagine what joining a union would do for a white-collar worker, much less whether a unionized work force would benefit the companies for which they work.[2]

Guild representation and the credit and compensation systems that it administers have lasted, even amid a collapse in union representation in the rest of the private sector. Given how difficult it is to break into film and TV writing and the number of people who would like to work as writers, why don't aspiring writers cooperate with studios and networks to create nonunion productions? And when streaming services like Netflix, Hulu, and Amazon started producing original content, why did they adopt the union model and sign onto the Minimum Basic Agreement (MBA), complete with the requirement to give screen credit, pay residuals, and so on? The usual answer is a combination of path-dependence and Hollywood exceptionalism: Hollywood talent unionized in the 1930s, and they've just gone along the same way ever since; there's enough money around that it's not necessary to break the union; lowering labor costs is simply not a priority; and the most high-quality writers want to be in the WGA because of its health and retirement benefits. All of that is true, but there is more to the story than that.

Writers as Authors Today

Path dependence does not alone explain why new businesses entering the industry would follow the old path. Nor does it explain the process by which new writers are recruited to be such dedicated unionists that they would strike for 100 days in 2007–2008 at considerable personal cost. The absence of corporate hostility to unions is also an inadequate explanation. However profligate studios and networks can be in compensating directors, actors, executives, and writers, most studios are owned by publicly traded corporate conglomerates and are not immune to the Wall Street imperative to increase share price by lowering labor costs. And, as the work of many scholars and journalists has shown, they have done so with a vengeance by outsourcing special effects work to low-wage international suppliers, filming in locations where they can use nonunion and low-wage below-the-line labor, and on and on.

The labor and attribution practices of the mid-twentieth century are a major legacy for the labor and attribution practices today. To understand labor in Hollywood, and in allied industries—including advertising, online gaming, and web-based entertainment like YouTube—we can learn from what writers today say about how the Writers Guild manages the dramatic difference of interests between highly paid showrunners and struggling staff writers, why new entrants into the industry hired unionized writers, why writers struck in 2007–2008 and what they think they gained from the strike, and why some writers believe that belonging to a union is an acceptable trade-off for the agreement each one enters at the time of hiring that their creative products are works made for hire and they are therefore not the copyright owner.

In 2013 and 2014, with a colleague, I interviewed thirty-two writers and two executives working in television. Fourteen are (or were) showrunners. Most have worked in the industry for ten years or more, but five were relatively junior staff writers at the time, and one is a novelist who was under contract to write a pilot for a cable network. All of the writers are members of the WGA except one who is a member of the Animation Guild.[3] Twenty-four are men, ten are women. The thirty-four interview subjects are, without exception, highly educated. Most are graduates of elite colleges and universities. Several are lawyers; others worked as journalists or as playwrights before working in Hollywood. One is a doctor. They are extremely articulate, which matters because writing for TV is collaborative and social. Successful writers get hired by pitching themselves and their ideas in meetings with studio executives, and they succeed in the writers' room by being able to talk. As one said, "To succeed in the business you have to be able to sell, to pitch—whether it's pitching my thumbnail to the room, or pitching a show, or pitching yourself in a hiring meeting, or pitching to the network that the idea they want to throw out is really worth taking a second look at."[4] The writers were almost certainly pitching themselves as they spoke to me—though they professed to being candid and occasionally invoked my offer that they could decide that anything they said was off the record.

There was a surprising degree of unanimity among the writers about what screen credit means to them, why writing for TV remains a union job, and why even showrunners—who hire and fire writers and manage the production of TV shows—are union members and conceive of themselves as labor. Almost everyone identified fair credit determinations, residuals, minimum compensation, and the generous health insurance and pension plans as important. As Terence Winter (creator, writer, and executive producer of HBO's *Boardwalk Empire*, 2010–2014) said, "I think they should put up a statue of the man who invented or the woman who invented the residual. The fact that I get checks in the mail for stuff I did five years ago is pretty mind blowing. I think that's pretty great. So assuming that would all go away if we didn't have a union—I think that's a good reason to have a union."[5] Many characterized the Minimum Basic Agreement (MBA) as the absolute minimum of fairness to writers who, after all, sell the intellectual property rights in their work as a condition of hire. They were unanimous in noting the importance of Guild determination of screen credit, even though many noted that, occasionally, arbitrations make a mistake and that credit arbitrations are relatively rare in TV. And, asked to explain why new media companies like Netflix and Amazon agreed to the MBA, all told the same story: talented writers insist on working under the jurisdiction of the WGA, and studios and production companies want, and want to be known for having, talented writers.

A number of writers connected unionization to the work-for-hire doctrine of copyright law; unionization is a necessary trade-off for the loss of intellectual property rights. As Glen Mazzara (showrunner and executive producer of Seasons 2 and 3 of AMC's *The Walking Dead*, 2011–2013) explained: "[Y]ou're giving up your intellectual property. . . . I sign a contract to work for a studio. I also sign a certificate of authorship—I'm signing that my work is owned by the studio. . . . So I think with the Guilds, you know the reason that the Writers Guild still exists is, it puts forward a writers agenda." He said a union is necessary because he takes direction as an employee, his contract says he works for a studio, and he has no hope of owning the rights in his work. And, because writers are willing to tolerate this state of affairs, and are willing to work in a world in which "these companies just make gazillions of dollars," unionization is "a matter of just making sure that the writers don't get pushed back to zero."[6]

This point of view is not just sour grapes by a showrunner whose contract was not renewed, even though he led the most highly rated show on TV. Every writer I interviewed offered the same defense of unionization for Hollywood writers. Matthew Weiner (creator of AMC's *Mad Men*), who could not possibly be fired because he has attained the status of auteur that is rarely attained by any TV writer, echoed Mazzara's sentiment. Weiner observed that the 2007–2008 strike, which halted production on his show, resulted in him losing a great deal of money. Yet he honored the strike to protect the contractual protections that writers fought for in the past: "I'm involved with the Guild because I'm obsessed with fairness. . . . [W]hen I saw the power of that collaboration, of collectivization, it was amazing." Although the strike caused him to lose money, Weiner said, "Just the idea that writers were valuable in some way, and this was going to be an embarrassment, that they were going to picket at the Academy Awards, which is the Super Bowl of entertainment, it is the single biggest viewing audience celebration of, promotion of that business. That's what ended it [the strike]. . . . And that feels like justice. So that's why I'm involved with the Guild." Howard A. Rodman, Jr., a film writer who became president of the Writers Guild in 2015, described the challenge and the obligation of writers as being to preserve the system that the Guild fought for in the 1930s: "[T]here are people who are in the Writers Guild now who grew up as independent filmmakers in a very DIY kind of way. And for them unions are those things, among those things you have to work around in order to get your vision up on the screen. You know, "Fuck the Teamsters," Fuck SAG, Fuck the Writers Guild, I'm making my movie." . . . I don't think they understand either the larger context of labor struggle or the smaller history of the Guild within that and the sacrifice made by the generations that came before them, to get that stuff that they now take for granted." But Rodman said that he is "the beneficiary" of the "signature advances of the Guild: the right to determine credits, so that studios couldn't just arbitrarily assign credit to anybody they wanted—the Son-in-Law Also Rises, that kind of thing—; the ability to set minimums for our work; the ability to have residuals so that when people make money off the re-use of our work we get some share of that; the ability to have health insurance so that if we get sick, you know, we don't have to throw ourselves on the mercy of . . . the health-care system; the ability to have a pension because, if you really want to be accurate about it, the working lives of screenwriters are about as long as the working lives of professional athletes. . . . I want to make sure of something that seems increasingly difficult: That it remains possible to make one's living as a writer. And if one does make a lot of money for the people who are employers, he gets something approaching a fair share."[7]

Writers connect the somewhat surprising fact that they went on strike in 2007–2008 to the importance of protecting the health of the industry. Show-runner Matt Nix (*Burn Notice*, 2007–2013) prefaced his analysis of his status as labor with an anecdote: "I got a call during the strike from a lawyer friend of mine who was like, "What the fuck are you guys doing? You're management! Who pulled you into behaving like labor?" Then he said that he and other showrunners "behaved like labor" because everybody's contractual protections are vulnerable to studio and network cost-cutting, and it is essential to protect the right to compensation in new media to attract and keep talent in the industry. If TV writing were moderate- or low-wage salaried employment like software, web, and video game design, he said, the industry would burn through young people but not keep enough experienced people in the business to produce really good shows. Plus, he said, "there is a perception that, and it's the truth, that if you're up one day, you're likely to be down the next."[8]

Almost all the writers said the point of collective bargaining, and striking, in today's entertainment industry is not really to increase compensation to current writers working in the industry as it is currently constituted, but rather to ensure that writers will be fairly compensated in the industry of the future—in which content is streamed over the internet as much as or more than broadcast by advertising-supported networks or aired by basic (advertising supported) or premium-subscription supported cable. As Rodman said, "very soon it will all be what's now called new media" and unless writers "fought for the future in 2008 it is quite possible by 2015 there wasn't going to be any future anymore."[9]

A major issue that sparked the 2007–2008 strike was the question of payment for use of work in new media. While writers had wanted some form of royalty or profit-sharing system since the 1930s, the need for it became acute when TV offered studios the chance to profit from the reuse of television programs and movies. Writers struck in 1952 to secure a provision in the MBA requiring payment of residuals to the credited writers any time a television show was reused on TV after its initial run. Writers who worked on successful network television programs can make a considerable amount of money (tens or hundreds or thousands of dollars) in residual payments on top of the weekly salary and script fees they are paid during the season in which they wrote on a show. When cable TV developed, and later when videocassettes, DVDs, and the internet provided ways to reuse content, the studios originally refused to pay residuals, and the Guild struck repeatedly (in 1973, 1981, 1985, 1988, and 2007–2008) to secure residual payments for use of work in these new media. And writers are also acutely aware of the residuals that they do not get paid, as for pre-1948 movies, and take the lesson from history that giving into the studios today will never be repaid by higher salaries or residuals in the future.

When I asked writers what they thought of residuals, they almost uniformly looked at me as if the question were idiotic—of course they love residuals. When I pointed out that residuals are unknown in any industry other than above-the-line talent in film and TV production, they said things like, "residuals are nice. They're gravy. It's unexpected though. The fact that a network re-airs a show that you write is just a nice bonus. And the fact that you get paid for it is awesome." Many acknowledged that getting paid for reuse of work is unusual generally, and also that it's not fair that writers (and actors and directors) get residuals when other contributors to film and TV do not. As Rick Murriagui (executive story editor, *Suits*, 2011–2013) said, "Why doesn't the cinematographer get residuals? Why doesn't one of the grips? We are creating something, but other people—It takes 200 people to make an episode of television. So it's amazing that we get them, but it's manna from heaven." Yet he, too, acknowledged the importance of the history of writers and residuals: "Someone a lot smarter than me, several years ago, felt that writers deserved residuals. Someone who had thought this through. . . . This was put in place for writers, and who knows if compensation was adjusted because of residuals that like, 'Maybe we won't pay writers as much, because they're gonna get residuals later.' " And when the networks and studios decide to reduce residuals or not pay them for new media, to him that felt like "they're trying to undercut writers and they—To me, just on principle—From a moral point of view, that's wrong. . . . It's like the big guys trying to bully the little guys, on some level. And the writers have a lot of power. The writers are the ones who are creating the content that keeps these networks up and running."[10]

A consistent story told by the writers is a decline in residuals. Marti Noxon, one of the longtime writers on *Buffy the Vampire Slayer*, talked about her good fortune to work on a show that lasted so long (seven seasons, 1997–2003) in its first run and then had become a show that many people discovered later or watched on Netflix. But about residuals for the show, she said, "No, I mean they're dead now. I mean if something plays that much your residuals are like a penny now. They go down with each successive, you know—. So, literally, I get residual checks that are like 13 cents." And then she laughed. Yet she, too, is a dedicated supporter of the WGA.[11]

While recognizing that there is a certain unfairness in great shows not being the kind of show that works well in reruns and therefore those writers not getting much in the way of residuals while some shows are rerun all the time, writers nevertheless describe residuals in terms of basic fairness. Ashley Gable (a writer on *Buffy* and *The Mentalist*, 2008–2015) explained: "Residuals reward success. If a show tanks and never airs anywhere else, the company doesn't have to pay residuals. But in success, the company has to share with the creator some portion of that success, a tiny portion of that success. . . . And that was the whole mantra of the strike, 'When the company makes money, writers make money.' That's all we want. So, in new media, if the company is making money, they can't just—If they're making money, they can't turn around and say, 'Oh, we don't know the business model.' Well, you know what? You got some money in your pocket. That's your business model."[12]

Part of the reason writers in Hollywood have fought so hard to defend and extend the rights to screen credit and residuals to new media is that the changing nature of the industry has forced them to be far more entrepreneurial about their careers than studio-era writers were or than advertising agency copywriters were. Copywriters, and even some writers employed by studios, could emphasize professionalism while making light of themselves as "pencils for hire" because they had steady jobs, very good paychecks, and very little control over what they did. With a steady job, whose name went on the completed project mattered less than it does when a freelance writer constantly must pitch herself to new employers, and notions of professionalism and commitment to excellence in the craft compensated for absence of creative autonomy. As Miranda Banks explained, quoting a 1978 interview with Maurice Tombragel, a writer on *Walt Disney's Wonderful World of Color* (1961–1969), the decline of steady employment forced writers not only to create their material but also "to raise the money for it," to direct, to produce, and to sell their work. Writers in the old days, he said, "just couldn't do that nor were we interested in doing it. . . . To sit down and write something, fine. To try to sell it? Just leave me alone. I don't even want to go on a set. I don't want to be involved in the studio."[13] Writers occasionally echoed this today; Vanessa Taylor, in explaining why she left the writing staff of *Game of Thrones* after Season 3 (2013) to return to writing for film, said, "television is a group process" and "as you get higher up in TV you get your producer credit and hopeful you actually know how to produce, so that means you're involved in casting and wardrobe and post production and everything else on set. And these are simply things I don't care about. . . . I honestly feel like once I push the script across the desk, now it's yours, you do what you want. I really love writing alone." All the creative control a writer can have, in one sense, as a writer-producer in TV (which Taylor described as being "like you're the queen. Everybody cares what you want") doesn't compensate for the group nature of the project, where "you're a writer for hire." Unless you're the show's creator, the show "will always be theirs" and "[a]t the very, very best, I can contribute and not mess anybody up but it's never going to be mine, it doesn't belong to me."[14]

When studios adopted a different business model, laid off writers in droves in the late 1940s, and started reusing scripts, rerunning TV programs, and selling their film libraries to TV, writers recognized that they had to be entrepreneurial. Writers had to be sure that the world knew who had written the films and TV shows so that they could get another job and share some of the profits of the reuse of their work. The struggle over how writers should be paid and credited that began in the 1940s and continued through the 2007–2008 strike was hugely contentious among writers, and the dividing lines were complicated. The 1946–1947 controversy over the American Authors Authority and the licensing rather than sale of copyrights divided writers not along the lines of ideology, or occupation, or success, but rather, according to their views of their work and their profession. Supporters of the elimination of the outright sale of copyrights included communists, moderates, and conservatives, and writers of film, print, radio, and stage. Opponents included people from all those groups. The dividing line was between those who thought of writing as paid employment without any prospect of true creative autonomy in which a system was needed to prevent exploitation, and those who thought of writing as an independent profession and wanted to preserve writers' autonomy.[15] A similarly dichotomous view of the nature of writing illuminates the longstanding differences of approach to attribution between advertising writers and film and TV writers.

The industrialization of writing in the studio system, including the requirement that writers work on the lot and keep regular hours, had the unintended consequence in the 1930s of fostering esprit de corps that facilitated the organization of writers, and organization proved crucial to writers' ability to negotiate collectively. The studio model is long gone, and even in TV, the writers' room is a group of four, or eight, not the huge studio workforce of the 1930s. Yet, writers today understand the value of their collective action and its rarity among workers in almost every other field. The contrast between the more industrialized forms of employment in films during the studio era and even in TV, and the more autonomous forms of employment experienced by dramatists, novelists, short story writers, and playwrights, complicated the efforts to form a national union of writers, especially in the 1950–1955 period when the Screen Writers Guild debated at length with the Authors League over organization of television.

The basic difference was over a conception of writers who sold finished works (the eastern model) and those who sold the labor of writing (the Hollywood model). An exasperated member of the SWG summed it up in a 1952 executive board meeting, reporting on two days of meetings with Authors League Chairman Rex Stout, who was a successful mystery novelist based in New York. The main stumbling block to resolving the dispute over who should represent television writers was the need "to educate some of the less labor minded representatives in New York about labor union practices in general. This blind spot is due primarily to the Authors Guild, which is made up entirely of independent contractors." A few years later, after the jurisdictional dispute had been formally resolved by the creation of the Writers Guild of America West and East, still the cultural differences persisted. Representatives of WGA East spent two days in Los Angeles discussing how to combine the credit rules for the two branches of the Guild, how to have greater influence over revisions of copyright law, and what the Guild should do to prevent self-interested dealings by agents who were taking double commissions by packaging the deal and representing the talent. The Eastern representatives, according to the Guild's longtime Executive Secretary Francis Inglis, "said that they had no idea that such unity could exist. They . . . pointed out that in the East the writers were isolated from each other and did not have this feeling of unity."[16]

This feeling of unity is a rare thing indeed in the contemporary workplace. JWT tried to create it by adhering to norms of anonymity, professional decorum, and agency authorship. I haven't interviewed three dozen writers working in advertising today, but I suspect that the feeling of unity is no more prevalent there than it is in law firms or any other nonunion workplace today. It was hard for Hollywood writers to develop, and it may be hard to maintain. But solidarity, and its absence, has been the key to the attribution and compensation regimes described here. As more and more people work as freelancers, whether they are driving an Uber car, cleaning houses, designing web pages, or writing for hire, their hopes for good compensation and respect may turn on whether they can find that feeling of unity and force their employers to bargain collectively over pay and recognition in the decades to come.

NOTES

ARCHIVAL SOURCES

ACKNOWLEDGMENTS

INDEX

Notes

Introduction

The epigraph is from C. Wright Mills, *White Collar: The American Middle Classes* (New York: Oxford University Press, 1951, 2002), 151.

1. This account of the 1973 credit arbitration is based on WGA files. I am grateful for the WGA's permission to read dozens of WGA credit arbitration files. Because revealing the names of the films and the writers might upset the participants and damage the credit arbitration process, and is unnecessary to understanding the credit arbitration process, I promised not to reveal the names of people or projects.

2. 17 U.S.C. § 201.

3. Andrew Sarris is generally credited with introducing French auteur film theory to America with a series of articles in journals and then his book, *The American Cinema: Directors and Directions, 1929–1968* (New York: Dutton, 1968).

4. Charles Brackett, "Address for the Samuel Goldwyn Award for Creative Writing," Apr. 22, 1957, folder 20.f-48, Charles Brackett Papers, Herrick Library; David Kipen, *The Schreiber Theory: A Radical Rewrite of American Film History* (Hoboken, NJ: Melville House Publishing, 2006). I am grateful to Ronny Regev's superb dissertation for introducing me to the cited document in the Charles Brackett papers at the Herrick. Ronny Regev, " 'It's a Creative Business': The Ideas, Practices, and Interaction that Made the Hollywood Film Industry" (PhD diss., Princeton Univ., 2013).

5. Mark Rose, *Authors and Owners: The Invention of Copyright* (Cambridge: Harvard University Press, 1993).

6. WGA, Alliance of Motion Picture and Television Producers Theatrical and Television Basic Agreement, 29 (2011) [hereinafter 2011 MBA], available at http://

www.wga.org. The current MBA, in effect from 2014, is largely the same as the 2011 version, but at the time of this writing is in the form of a Memorandum of Understanding, listing revisions to the 2011 MBA. Theatrical Schedule A to the Basic Agreement has provided without substantial change for several decades that the "decision of the Guild Arbitration Committee, and any Policy Review Board established by the Guild in connection therewith, with respect to writing credits, insofar as it is rendered within the limitations of this Schedule A, shall be final, and the Company will accept and follow the designation of screen credits contained in such decision and all writers shall be bound thereby." Schedule A, 2011 MBA, at 270; WGA, *Screen Credits Manual* (2010); Statement of the Credits Review Committee to all WGA Members (June 2008); Screen Credits Review Committee File (2009); Constitution and By-Laws of WGAW, Art. VII, § 6 (revised June 17, 2009), *available at* http://www.wga.org/uploadedFiles/who_we_are/leadership/constitution09.pdf.

7. See Stone v. Writers Guild of Am. W., Inc., 101 F.3d 1312, 1314 (9th Cir. 1996) (holding state law claims for fraud and intentional infliction of emotional distress are preempted by federal labor law); Marino v. Writers Guild of Am. E., Inc., 992 F.2d 1480, 1481 (9th Cir. 1993); Eddy v. Radar Pictures, Inc., 215 Fed. App'x. 575 (9th Cir. 2006) (rejecting claims that WGA's participating writer determination was arbitrary, discriminatory, or in bad faith; finding other claims against union and production companies preempted).

8. The separated rights provision allows the credited writer of an original story to retain some rights to write a derivative work based on the story elements of a script other than through the film or TV show (such as the right to publish a novel or play based on the story) and also allows a writer to reacquire a script that is not produced within a stated term. 2011 MBA, art. 16. To be eligible for separated rights, the writer must receive "story by," "written by," or "screen story by" credit on a motion picture; or "story by," "written by," or, in certain circumstances, "television story by" credit on a television movie; or "created by" credit on an episodic television series. Ibid.

9. Melville Nimmer & David Nimmer, *Nimmer on Copyright,* vol. 1, ch. 5 (2011) (form contracts for hiring for writing services or sale of screenplay).

10. David Weil, *The Fissured Workplace: Why Work Became So Bad for So Many and What Can Be Done to Improve It* (Cambridge: Harvard University Press, 2014).

11. The quote is from a 2009 memo in the files of the WGAW Screen Credits Review Committee. The WGAW Executive Director made the same point about the importance of credit determinations in a news interview. Charles Schreger, "Screen Credits: Who Gets What—and How," *L.A. Times,* Apr. 16, 1979, F1.

12. Actually, since 1954 the WGA has been two unions: the Writers Guild of America—East (which represents writers in the eastern part of the United States)

and the Writers Guild of America—West (which represents writers in the west). I refer to them collectively as the WGA or Guild or Writers Guild except where the differences between them matter. The WGAE and WGAW were formed by an amalgamation of the Screen Writers Guild (which represented film writers from 1933 onward), the Radio Writers Guild, and various groups that formed to represent television writers in the 1940s and 1950s. Abbreviated histories of the formation of these guilds are in Chapters 2, 4, and 5.

13. Alan Hyde, *Working in Silicon Valley: Economic and Legal Analysis of a High-Velocity Labor Market* (Armonk, N.Y.: M. E. Sharpe, Inc., 2003).

14. Catherine L. Fisk, "The Modern Author at Work on Madison Avenue," in Paul K. Saint-Amour, ed., *Modernism and Copyright* (New York: Oxford University Press, 2011).

15. Staff Meeting Minutes, October 26, 1932, Box 5. In describing the history of the Jergens Lotion campaign, Ruth Waldo noted, "Mr. Steichen, by the way, has taken the photographs almost from the beginning of the [Jergens] Lotion advertising." Patricia Johnston, *Real Fantasies: Edward Steichen's Advertising Photography* (Berkeley: University of California Press, 1997), 55–65; Fisk, "The Modern Author at Work," 181.

16. Michele H. Bogart, *Artists, Advertising, and the Borders of Art* (Chicago: University of Chicago Press, 1995).

17. Thomas Frank, *The Conquest of Cool: Business Culture, Counterculture, and the Rise of Hip Consumerism* (Chicago: University of Chicago Press, 1997), 71.

18. On attribution in scientific authorship, see Mario Biagioli & Peter Galison, eds., *Scientific Authorship: Credit and Intellectual Property in Science* (New York: Routledge, 2003).

19. Catherine L. Fisk, "Credit Where It's Due: The Law and Norms of Attribution," *Georgetown Law Journal* 95 (2006), 49, 88–92.

20. Erik Barnouw, *Media Marathon: A Twentieth Century Memoir* (Durham: Duke University Press, 1996), 121; Miranda Banks, *The Writers: A History of American Screenwriters and Their Guild* (New Brunswick: Rutgers University Press, 2015), 12, quoting Erik Barnouw, interview by the Writers Guild Oral History Project (Los Angeles: Writers Guild Foundation, 1978), 11.

21. Erik Barnouw, *The Television Writer* (New York: Hill & Wang, 1962), 18.

22. In 2009, the Guild polled its members about a variety of issues ranging from their views on the status of writers to their experience with status-based discrimination to their views on whether there should be more or fewer types of credits or whether credit bonuses should be prohibited; 54 percent of respondents said that there should be more credit for all writers. Credits Poll, in WGA File. WGA Screen Credits Review Comm. (2009).

23. 17 U.S.C. § 201; see Catherine L. Fisk, "The Origin of the Work for Hire Doctrine,"

Yale Journal of Law & Humanities 15 (2003), 1; Catherine L. Fisk, *Working Knowledge: Employee Innovation and the Rise of Corporate Intellectual Property, 1800–1930* (Chapel Hill: University of North Carolina Press, 2009); Banks, *The Writers;* John Thornton Caldwell, *Production Culture: Industrial Reflexivity and Critical Practice in Film and Television* (Durham: Duke University Press, 2008); Vicki Mayer, Miranda J. Banks & John Thornton Caldwell, eds., *Production Studies: Cultural Studies of Media Industries* (New York: Routledge, 2009); F. Jay Dougherty, "Not a Spike Lee Joint? Issues in the Authorship of Motion Pictures under U.S. Copyright Law," *UCLA L. Rev.* 49 (2001), 225.

24. John Gertner, *The Idea Factory: Bell Labs and the Great Age of American Innovation* (New York: Penguin, 2012). For example, the Wikipedia entry on the Apple Macintosh "1984" commercial that aired during the 1984 Superbowl (http://en .wikipedia.org/wiki/1984) attributes it to Ridley Scott as director and to the ad agency Chiat/Day generally, with "written by" credits to Steve Hayden (copywriter), Lee Clow (creative director), and Brent Thomas (art director). On the attribution of inventions in the iPod and iPhone, see Walter Isaacson, *Steve Jobs* (New York: Simon & Schuster, 2011).

25. Greg Lastowka, "The Trademark Function of Authorship," *Boston University Law Review* 85 (2005), 1171; Greg Lastowka, "Digital Attribution: Copyright and the Right to Credit," *Boston University Law Review* 87 (2007), 41. See also Laura A. Heymann, "The Trademark/Copyright Divide," *Southern Methodist University Law Review* 60 (2007), 55.

26. Countries that protect moral rights have had to grapple with figuring out who is the "author" entitled to attribution with respect to collaborative works such as most films and TV shows.

27. Peter Decherney, *Hollywood's Copyright Wars: From Edison to the Internet* (New York: Columbia University Press, 2012), 116.

28. The Supreme Court rejected trademark law as a source of rules requiring accurate screen credit to authors or creators in Dastar Corp. v. Twentieth Century Fox Film Corp., 539 U.S. 23 (2003). Prior to *Dastar,* some misattribution claims by writers did succeed under the Lanham Act. One famous one was brought by the writer/actors known as Monty Python, who objected to ABC showing edited versions of the programs they had made for the BBC on the ground that the editing amounted to mutilation of their work. The court enjoined broadcast of the edited shows pending determination of whether the edits amounted to mutilation. Gilliam v. American Broadcasting Companies, Inc., 538 F.2d 14 (2d Cir. 1976). Twentieth Century Fox had contracted for rights to distribute videos of a television series about World War II, the copyright to which had expired. When Dastar, a competitor, released videos using the original version of the TV series (which was in the public domain), Fox sued for a violation of section 43(a) of the

Lanham Act and state unfair competition law, asserting that the release of the videos without screen credit to Fox (which had owned the rights to the original TV series) constituted "reverse passing off." (Reverse passing off is the misrepresentation of someone else's goods as one's own.) The Lanham Act prohibits the "false designation of origin, false or misleading description of fact" that is "likely to cause confusion . . . as to the origin . . . of goods." 15 U.S.C. § 1125(a)(1). The Court held that the failure to grant credit was not a false designation of origin because the "origin" of the goods, for purposes of the statute, was Dastar (the seller). The Court noted that the law of copyright is the sole source of protection for authors of motion pictures, and that it contains no requirement of designating the actual author.

29. A handful of student law review notes and articles by practitioners address screen credit. See Rick Mortensen, "D.I.Y. after *Dastar:* Protecting Creators' Moral Rights through Creative Lawyering, Individual Contracts and Collectively Bargained Agreements," *Vanderbilt Journal of Entertainment & Technology Law* 8 (2006), 335, 356–62; Dana N. Glasser, Note, "Stranding Dorothy in Oz and Keeping the Wizard behind the Curtain?: Writer's Guild Determination of Screenwriting Credits through Arbitration," *Pepperdine Dispute Resolution Law Journal* 3 (2002–2003), 271; Shawn K. Judge, Note & Comment, "Giving Credit Where Credit Is Due? The Unusual Use of Arbitration in Determining Screenwriting Credits," *Ohio State Journal on Dispute Resolution* 13 (1997), 221; Karen L. Gulick, Note, "Creative Control, Attribution, and the Need for Disclosure: A Study of Incentives in the Motion Picture Industry," *Connecticut Law Review* 25 (1994–1995), 53; Bayard F. Berman & Sol Rosenthal, "Screen Credit and the Law," *UCLA Law Review* 9 (1962), 156.

30. Catherine L. Fisk & Robert W. Gordon, "Foreword: 'Law As . . .' Theory and Method in Legal History," *University of California Irvine Law Review* 1 (2011), 519; Christopher Tomlins & John Comaroff, "Law As . . . Theory and Practice in Legal History," *University of California Irvine Law Review* 1 (2011), 1039.

31. Howard Becker, *Art Worlds* (Berkeley: University of California Press, 1982).

32. Pierre Bourdieu, "The Field of Cultural Production, or: The Economic World Reversed," *Poetics* 12 (Nov. 1983), 316; Pierre Bourdieu, *The Rules of Art: Genesis and Structure of the Literary Field* (Stanford: Stanford University Press, 1996).

33. Fisk, *Working Knowledge*, 125, 209–210.

34. See Jeff Gerth, "Military's Information War Is Vast and Often Secretive," *New York Times*, Dec. 11, 2015, A1 (reporting on US government efforts to place US-government-produced reports on the occupation of Iraq in Iraqi and US news media as if the reports were written by Iraqi or US news media employees); Decherney, *Hollywood's Copyright Wars*, 128–129 (on the Alan Smithee credit).

35. David Thomson, *The Whole Equation: A History of Hollywood* (New York: Vintage, 2004), 9.

36. Jane M. Gaines, *Contested Culture: The Image, the Voice, and the Law* (Chapel Hill: University of North Carolina Press, 1991); Robert Spoo, *Without Copyrights: Piracy, Publishing, and the Public Domain* (New York: Oxford University Press, 2013); Brenda R. Silver, *Virginia Woolf Icon* (Chicago: University of Chicago Press, 1999); Fisk, "Credit Where It's Due," 49.

37. See Cal. Civ. Code 3344; Midler v. Ford Motor Co., 849 F.2d 460, 463 (9th Cir. 1988); Wendt v. Host International, Inc., 125 F.3d 806 (9th Cir. 1997). In *Wendt*, the court held that two actors who portrayed characters in the TV show *Cheers* could bring statutory and common law right of publicity and trademark infringement claims against the owner of airport bars that installed animatronic figures of their *Cheers* characters in bars decorated to resemble the *Cheers* set. The court explained that, although Paramount owned the copyright in the show and thus could license the copyrighted work (the TV program), the actors nevertheless had a right to prevent the use of their likeness in ways other than use of the copyrighted television programs. 125 F.3d at 810–14.

38. Lugosi v. Universal Pictures, 25 Cal. 3d 813, 824–28 (1979) (Mosk, J., concurring).

39. And of course the claim to absolute originality is an overstatement. Rosalind E. Krauss, *The Originality of the Avant-Garde and Other Modernist Myths* (Cambridge: MIT Press, 1985).

40. Clement Greenberg, "Modernist Painting," in *Modern Art and Modernism: A Critical Anthology* (London: Harper and Row, Ltd., 1982; Francis Frascina & Charles Harrison, eds., 1982), 5, 6; Amy Adler, Note, "Post-Modern Art and the Death of Obscenity Law," *Yale Law Journal* 99 (1990), 1359, 1363–1364.

41. Kevin J.H. Dettmar & Stephen Watt, eds., *Marketing Modernisms: Self-Promotion, Canonization, and Rereading* (Ann Arbor: University of Michigan Press, 1996); Andreas Huyssen, *After the Great Divide: Modernism, Mass Culture, Postmodernism* (Bloomington: Indiana University Press, 1986). As Robert Spoo has pointed out, when James Joyce sought to prevent an American publisher, Samuel Roth, from selling an unauthorized and expurgated edition of *Ulysses,* he could not invoke copyright law because *Ulysses* was not protected by American copyright. Instead, he invoked a state law of unfair competition that prevented the passing off of a product as being something that it was not or as being produced by a person or entity that it was not. Joyce's American lawyer succeeded in getting a New York court to enjoin Roth and his company "from using the name of the plaintiff [Joyce] for advertising purposes or for purposes of trade." If Joyce could not exercise control over the text itself, at least he could prevent the use of his name in connection with it. Robert Spoo, Note, "Copyright Protection and Its Discontents: The Case of James Joyce's *Ulysses* in America," *Yale Law Journal* 108 (1998), 633, 640, quoting Joyce v. Roth (N.Y. Sup. Ct. Dec. 27, 1928), in *Letters of James Joyce,* vol. 3, 185.

42. Clement Greenberg, "Avant-Garde and Kitsch," *Partisan Review* (1939), 1, 5; Paul K. Saint-Amour, "Introduction: Modernism and the Lives of Copyright," in Paul K.

Saint-Amour, ed., *Modernism and Copyright* (New York: Oxford University Press, 2009), 5; Huyssen, *After the Great Divide*, vii, ix.

43. Michael Szalay, "HBO's Flexible Gold," *Representations* 126 (2014), 112–124; Michael Szalay, "Pimps and Pied Pipers: Quality Television in the Age of Its Direct Delivery," *Journal of American Studies* (Oct. 2015), 1–32.

44. Amy Adler recounts this incident in "Against Moral Rights," *California Law Review* 97 (2009), 263, 296: "Boasting his lack of connection with his own objects, addressing a group of admiring interviewers, Warhol said: 'Why don't you ask my assistant Gerry Malanga some questions? He did a lot of my paintings.'" (quoting Caroline A. Jones, *Machine in the Studio: Constructing the Postwar American Artist* (Chicago: University of Chicago Press, 1996), 422 n.35).

45. Pierre-Michel Menger, "Artistic Labor Markets and Careers," *Annual Review of Sociology* 24 (1999), 541.

46. Ibid., 557–558 (citation omitted).

47. James Boyle, *The Public Domain: Enclosing the Commons of the Mind* (New Haven: Yale University Press, 2008); Joanna Demers, *Steal This Music: How Intellectual Property Law Affects Musical Creativity* (Athens: University of Georgia Press, 2006).

48. The process of record collecting and sampling emphasizing the labor, knowledge, skill, and creativity in hip-hop composition (also known as production) is described in a detailed ethnomusicology of the hip-hop artists of Seattle, Washington by Joseph G. Schloss, *Making Beats: The Art of Sample-Based Hip-Hop* (Middletown: Wesleyan University Press, 2004).

49. See, e.g., Samantha Brand, Note, "Four Thousand Words on *Finnegans Wake:* The Misuse of Copyright Doctrine and the Controversy Surrounding the Estate of James Joyce," *Cardozo Arts & Entertainment L.J.* 25 (2008), 1229. The *Shloss v. Joyce Estate* litigation, which involves Joyce's heir's effort to prevent a scholar from including certain materials in a book, is chronicled at http://cyberlaw.stanford.edu/case/shloss-v -estate-of-joyce. The controversy is described in D.T. Max, "The Injustice Collector: Is James Joyce's Grandson Suppressing Scholarship?" *The New Yorker* (June 19, 2006).

50. Roland Barthes, *The Death of the Author* (1968) was a satirical essay that became known, perhaps wrongly, for advocating this. See J. C. Carlier & C. T. Watts, "Roland Barthes's Resurrection of the Author and Redemption of Biography" *The Cambridge Quarterly* 29 (2000), 386–393.

51. On the literature debating whether writers or producers should be deemed the authors of TV, see Muriel Cantor, *The Hollywood TV Producer: His Work and His Audience* (New York: Basic Books, 1971); Bridget Conor, *Screenwriting: Creative Labor and Professional Practice* (New York: Routledge, 2014); Horace Newcomb and Robert S. Alley, *The Producer's Medium: Conversations with Creators of American TV* (New York: Oxford University Press, 1983); Alisa Perren & Thomas Schatz, "Theorizing Television's Writer-Producer: Reviewing *The Producer's Medium*," *Television and New Media* (October 2014), pp. 1–8.

There are also very good reasons to treat others—both talent and craft workers—as authors of TV, and I do not mean by focusing on writers to privilege the work of writers over that of the many so-called "below-the-line" contributors. Among the scholars who have analyzed the significant creative contributions of people other than writers, producers, and directors, see John T. Caldwell, "Authorship Below-the-Line," in Jonathan Gray and Derek Johnson, eds., *A Companion to Media Authorship* (Malden, MA: John Wiley & Sons, 2013); Vicki Mayer, *Below the Line: Producers and Production Studies in the New Television Economy* (Durham: Duke University Press, 2011); Matt Stahl, "Nonproprietary Authorship and Uses of Autonomy: Artistic Labor in American Film Animation, 1900–2004," *Labor: Studies in Working-Class History of the Americas* 2005 2(4): 87–105.

1. The Cloak of Anonymity and the Literary Gunman

1. The Mother Goose book was reprinted in 1998 by the Museum of York County, South Carolina, which has a number of Grant's works, as he lived in Rock Hill, South Carolina from 1947 until his death in 1990. Vernon Grant, *Mother Goose* (New York: Harry N. Abrams, Inc., 1998).
2. Grant v. Kellogg, 58 F. Supp. 48 (S.D.N.Y. 1944).
3. Ibid., 54.
4. Courts prior to the enactment of the 1909 Copyright Act had begun to distinguish between employees working on salary and those specially commissioned to produce work, awarding copyrights to the former by default and awarding copyrights to the latter only if the parties specifically agreed. A draft of the 1909 Act provided that an author would be entitled to copyright if it was produced "by an employee during the hours for which salary is paid." Catherine L. Fisk, *Working Knowledge: Employee Innovation and the Rise of Corporate Intellectual Property, 1800–1930* (Chapel Hill: University of North Carolina Press, 2009), 226.
5. Ibid., 52–53.
6. Cases ruling against the artist include: Dielman v. White, 102 F. 892 (D. Mass. 1900) (involving photographs of a mosaic in the Library of Congress); Yardley v. Houghton Mifflin Co., 108 F.2d 28 (2d Cir. 1939) (photographs of a mural in a public school building); Lumiere v. Robertson-Cole Distrib. Corp., 280 F. 550 (2d Cir. 1922) (involving a photographer creating stills eventually used in a motion picture). But courts still sometimes adhered to the older law ruling in favor of the artist, at least when doing so would not materially harm the interest of the corporation. See, e.g., Uproar Co. v. National Broadcasting Co., 81 F.2d 373 (1st Cir. 1936).
7. Michele H. Bogart, *Artists, Advertising, and the Borders of Art* (Chicago: University of Chicago Press, 1995).

8. Ibid., p. 56.

9. Advertisement of J. Walter Thompson, Jan. 23, 1919, Colin Dawkins Papers Box 12, File JWT Company 1917–1921 (House Ads).

10. Roland Marchand, *Advertising the American Dream: Making Way for Modernity* (Berkeley: University of California Press, 1986), 6–10; Colin Dawkins Interview with Kennett Hinks, Sept. 10, 1979, Colin Dawkins Papers Box 17; Howard Henderson to Stanley Resor, Nov. 2, 1959, quoting *The Lever Standard* (October 1950), Henderson Papers; "Some Basic Roots of the J. Walter Thompson Company" Bertram Metter Files Box 2; Stephen R. Fox, *The Mirror Makers: A History of American Advertising and Its Creators* (New York: Morrow, 1984), 80–82.

11. Robert Haws Interview, Nov. 18, 1964, pp. 1–2, Bernstein Company History Files, Box 1; Biographical File on Paul T. Cherington, Bernstein Company History Files, Box 4. On advertising being for men with business experience rather than a college education, see Fox, *The Mirror Makers,* 53.

12. "Report of the National Committee on Agency Service," (April 1918) in "Some Basic Roots of the J. Walter Thompson Company," Bertram Metter Files Box 2; Fox, *The Mirror Makers,* 90. On the similar goals and methods of lawyers in this era, see Robert B. Stevens, *Law School: Legal Education in America from the 1850s to the 1980s* (Chapel Hill: University of North Carolina Press, 1983); Robert W. Gordon, "The American Legal Profession, 1870–2000," in Michael Grossberg & Christopher Tomlins, eds., *The Cambridge History of Law in America* vol. III (New York: Cambridge University Press, 2008).

13. JWT "Forum," Jan. 7, 1936. On agencies paying elite salaries, see Fox, *The Mirror Makers,* 61 (Lord & Thomas in the early twentieth century "hired writers . . . at salaries of unprecedented generosity").

14. Marchand, *Advertising the American Dream,* 26, 18–20.

15. John Hall Woods, "Glorifying the American Copy Writer," *Printers' Ink* (Feb. 13, 1930), p. 121; Mac Artzt, "Should Copy Writers Sign Their Copy?" *Printers' Ink* (Jan. 30, 1930), p. 61; Fox, *The Mirror Makers,* 56; Marchand, *Advertising the American Dream,* 41.

16. Jim Wood, "Copy Writers Need Their Cloak of Anonymity" *Printers' Ink* (Feb. 20, 1930), p. 44.

17. *J. Walter Thompson News Bulletin,* June 1926. Newsletters 1910–25. Box MN5, File 1926.

18. Marchand, *Advertising the American Dream,* 26–28.

19. "Scientific Advertising" by Claude Hopkins – Comments by Alfred Politz, with a handwritten note across the top: "Mr. Meek – This is terrific stuff. AAP," Samuel Meek Papers Box 6; Marchand, *Advertising the American Dream,* 42–43.

20. The copyright entry reads: "'A skin you love to touch,' © Alonzo Kimball 1915." Catalogue of Copyright Entries, Part 4, p. 45, Library of Congress, 1916. https://

books.google.com/books?id=IEEhAQAAIAAJ&pg=PA64&lpg=PA64&dq=alonzo
+kimball+a+skin+you+love+to+touch&source=bl&ots=Q_F35NZ3Zz&sig
=80S4WKtTz4pjXldsLpsYiMel8tw&hl=en&sa=X&ved=0CCsQ6AEwBWoVCh
MIhbDOkpyLxgIVhT2SCh2zxQB6#v=onepage&q=alonzo%20kimball%20a
%20skin%20you%20love%20to%20touch&f=false.

21. "Helen Landsdowne Resor—1886–1964," *J. Walter Thompson Company News* (Jan. 10,
    1964) (obituary including images of some of her famous ads, including the Wood-
    bury ad); Howard Henderson Papers, Box 1, File: Helen Landsdowne Resor; Staff
    Meeting Minutes, October 16, 1932; Presentation of Edward Steichen, Minutes
    of the Representatives Meetings, Jan. 31, 1928; Patricia Johnson, *Real Fantasies:
    Edward Steichen's Advertising Photography* (Berkeley: University of California Press,
    1997), 35–37; Carl Sandburg, *Steichen the Photographer* (New York: Harcourt Brace,
    1929), 51–52; Marchand, *Advertising the American Dream*, 26.

22. "Through the Years with Howard Kohl," p. 13, Howard Kohl File, Colin Dawkins
    Papers, Box 2.

23. Account Histories: U.S. Gutta Percha Paint Company, February 5, 1926, JWT
    Account Files, Box 18.

24. Henry Flower Interview, Helen and Stanley Resor File, Colin Dawkins Papers,
    Box 3, pp. 6–7; Walter Lord Interview Transcript, Colin Dawkins Files, Box 17.

25. Interview with Sam Meek, JWT Bernstein Company History, Box 1.

26. Colin Dawkins, in his notes for *Ain't It Hell on a Windy Day,* says Day said this in
    a Jan. 19, 1932 staff meeting. pp. 281–282. The manuscript is found in the Colin
    Dawkins Papers, Box 22. On William Day, see Michele H. Bogart, *Artists, Advertising,
    and the Borders of Art* (Chicago: University of Chicago Press, 1997), and Charles F.
    McGovern, *Sold American: Consumption and Citizenship, 1890–1945* (Chapel Hill:
    University of North Carolina Press, 2009).

27. "Creative Organization Staff Meeting," May 5, 1932, JWT Staff Meeting Minutes,
    Box 5.

28. Robert Haws Interview, Nov. 18, 1964, pp. 5–7, Bernstein Company History Files,
    Box 1.

29. William Howard to John Devine, June 16, 1949, John F. Devine Files.

30. Edward G. Wilson Files, Box 48, Box 51.

31. Edward G. Wilson Files, Box 48, Box 65,

32. James W. Young Interview Transcript, Nov. 1963, p. 6; Client File on Chesebrough-
    Ponds, Bernstein Company History Files, Box 5 (the Pond's slogan); Biographical
    File on Ruth Waldo, Bernstein Company History Files, Box 5 (the gender segre-
    gation of departments); Colin Dawkins Papers, Box 1, Offers and Staff file on
    Carroll Carroll (attributing "a skin you love to touch" slogan for Woodbury Soap
    to Landsdowne in 1911); Kennett Hinks Interview with Colin Dawkins, Sept. 10,
    1979, Dawkins Papers, Box 17.

33. "Notes on JWT Compensation Policies, Written 1949 by EGW-LL," JWT
    Bernstein Company History Box 7 (emphasis in original).
34. Many examples are found in the JWT Newsletter Files. See *JWT News*, Nov. 21,
    1962 (Pan Am ad campaign won awards; firm credited as a whole), *JWT Michigan
    Avenues*, May 1, 1970 (Uncola campaign credited to a group headed by named
    individuals); Interview with Robert Haws, JWT Bernstein Company History,
    Box 1.
35. Memo from Robert Castle to Peggy King, June 25, 1956, John F. Devine Papers,
    Box 37 (Personnel): "The favorable reaction to our 1–1/2 min. Skol commercial
    has exceeded the usual response. The client has repeatedly spoken of its high
    quality. . . . In addition to this, I have heard from several people in the industry
    already. . . . One of these was a long distance call from Mr. Walter H. Annenberg,
    owner and Managing Editor of *TV Guide*, who wanted me to know it was the
    finest commercial he had ever seen on television."
36. Eileen Boris, *Art and Labor: Ruskin, Morris and the Craftsman Ideal in America* (Phil-
    adelphia: Temple University Press, 1986).
37. The story of race relations in authorship is extremely difficult to tell because
    whites excluded blacks (and, it appears, anybody else who seemed to them to be
    of color) from advertising, film, and television production for the period covered
    here. According to Writers Guild Executive Board minutes, the first black writer
    was not hired at MGM until 1952. Elizabeth Vroman was hired as a technical
    advisor on a screenplay based on her story and would also do some writing. So
    the Guild's Board voted to make her a member, even though she had not yet sat-
    isfied the credits requirements for membership: "As she is the first negro writer
    employed at MGM, some of the writers there wanted to present her with mem-
    bership in the Guild." Executive Board, April 21, 1952. At J. Walter Thompson, the
    General Counsel insisted in memoranda to the executives in the 1950s that the
    company did not discriminate on the basis of race. The absence of even a single
    black creative employee, he said, was simply that they had never had a qualified
    black person apply. Edward Wilson Files. He did not interrogate what he meant
    by "qualified" or what had happened to whatever applications the agency had
    received from blacks who aspired to work or had worked in advertising.
38. Jeffrey Kastiner, "Out of Tiffany's Shadow, a Woman of Light," *New York Times*,
    Feb. 25, 2007, AR33; Martin Eidelberg & Nina Gray, *A New Light on Tiffany: Clara
    Driscoll and the Tiffany Girls* (New York: New York Historical Society, 2007).
39. Eidelberg & Gray, *A New Light on Tiffany*, 34, 49, 119–121.
40. Tiffany was widely known as the head of a business more than an artist himself,
    although he did maintain "an artistic control over production that other art man-
    ufacturers rarely achieved." Eileen Boris, *Art and Labor* at 144. See also Robert
    Koch, *Louis Tiffany: Rebel in Glass* (New York: Crown, 1964); Robert Koch, *Louis*

Tiffany's Glass-Bronzes-Lamps (New York: Crown, 1971); Ellen Mazur Thomson, "Alms for Oblivion: The History of Women in Early American Graphic Design," *Design Issues* 10 (1994), 27, 29–30 (noting some Currier & Ives lithographs were done by Frances Flora Bond Palmer).

41. Howard Henderson to Howard Kohl, Ruth Waldo, Eleanor Taylor, and Henry Flower, June 14, 1939, Henderson Papers, Box 7, File: Special Projects – Personnel, Recruitment, and Training, 1939, 1954–60; *Printers' Ink*, Aug. 1926, pp. 82, 86, *Printers' Ink*, Oct. 7, 1926, p. 112; Marchand, *Advertising the American Dream*, 33–35.

42. *JWT News*, Oct. 15, 1956; Ruth Waldo Bio, JWT Bernstein Company History, Box 5 (emphasis in original); Interview with Margaret King Eddy, JWT Bernstein Company History, Box 1; Margaret King Interview with Colin Dawkins, Oct. 19, 1979, Dawkins Papers, Box 17; Fox, *The Mirror Makers*, 289; David Ogilvy, "Ogilvy on Advertising: Six Giants Who Invented Modern Advertising," *Adweek*, Aug. 8, 1983 (excerpt from *Ogilvy on Advertising* (New York: Crown Publishers, 1983).

43. "J. Walter Thompson Company," *Fortune*, Nov. 1947, pp. 95, 205; Colin Dawkins Papers, Box 3, File: Resor, Helen and Stanley; Fox, *The Mirror Makers*, 289, 292; "Copy Seminar Study: Summary of What We Learned," Henderson Papers, Box 7, File: Copy Seminar Study Findings 1958; Howard Henderson to Howard Kohl, Ruth Waldo, Eleanor Taylor, and Henry Flower, June 14, 1939, Henderson Papers, Box 7, File Special Projects – Personnel, Recruitment and Training, 1939, 1954–60; Wallace W. Elton to O'Neill Ryan, Feb. 18, 1957, Wallace Elton Papers, Box 1, File: JWT Company Policies.

44. Staff Meeting Minutes, October 26, 1932, Box 5.

2. The New Story System

1. Matthew Weiner, interview with the author, Los Angeles, October 11, 2013.

2. Leo C. Rosten, *Hollywood: The Movie Colony, the Movie Makers* (New York: Arno Press & The New York Times, 1970), 314–315. Rosten's account of the specialization among writers in the late silent and early talk era is echoed by Thomas Schatz, *The Genius of the System: Hollywood Filmmaking in the Studio Era* (Minneapolis: University of Minnesota Press, 2010) (originally published 1989), 51–52.

3. Douglas Gomery, *The Hollywood Studio System: A History* (London: British Film Institute, 2005); Miranda Banks, *The Writers: A History of American Screenwriters and Their Guild* (Rutgers University Press, 2014); Ian Hamilton, *Writers in Hollywood, 1915–1951* (1991); Marc Norman, *What Happens Next: A History of American Screenwriting* (2007); Nancy Lynn Schwartz, *The Hollywood Writers' Wars* (1982); Lizzie Francke, *Script Girls: Women Screenwriters in Hollywood* (1994); Todd Gitlin, *Inside Prime Time* (1983); William T. Bielby & Denise D. Bielby, "Organizational Mediation of Project-Based Labor Markets: Talent Agencies and the Careers of

Screenwriters," *American Sociology Review* 64 (1999), 64, 65; Richard E. Caves, *Creative Industries: Contracts between Art and Commerce* (Cambridge: Harvard University Press, 2000), ch. 5; Michael Storper & Susan Christopherson, "Flexible Specialization and Regional Industrial Agglomerations: The Case of the U.S. Motion Picture Industry," *Annals of Ass'n of American Geographers* 77 (1987), 104; Susan Christopherson & Michael Storper, "The Effects of Flexible Specialization on Industrial Politics and the Labor market: The Motion Picture Industry," *Industrial & Labor Relations Review* 42 (1989), 331; Murray Ross, *Stars and Strikes: Unionization of Hollywood* (New York: Columbia University Press, 1941); Louis Perry & Richard Perry, *A History of the Los Angeles Labor Movement, 1911–1941* (1963), 337–344.

4. "Fox to Try New Story System," *Hollywood Reporter,* Sept. 9, 1930, 4: "Christie Short Subject Department Disbanded," *Hollywood Reporter,* Oct. 10, 1930, 1; "Paramount Using Book Title for Farce," *Hollywood Reporter,* Sept. 22, 1930, 2; "Old Copyrights Sought for Titles," *Hollywood Reporter,* Sept. 23, 1930, 2; "More Than $17,630,000 Tied Up in Story Material by Producers: Some Will Never Reach Screen," *Hollywood Reporter,* Oct. 1, 1930, 1; Clifford Howard, "Writers and Pictures," *Close Up* (September 1928), 38. On the drive for organization and efficiency in studio film production in the teens and twenties, and the related development of the system of writing by committee, see Eileen Bowser, *The Transformation of Cinema, 1907–1915* (Berkeley: University of California Press, 1994); Thomas Schatz, *The Genius of the System: Hollywood Filmmaking in the Studio Era* (Minneapolis: University of Minnesota Press, 1988), 51–54; David Bordwell, Kristin Thompson & Janet Staiger, *The Classical Hollywood Cinema: Film Style and Mode of Production to 1960* (New York: Columbia University Press, 1985), 146.

5. Schatz, *The Genius of the System,* 106. On Thalberg's relations with writers and recruitment of outstanding novelists, dramatists, and short story writers from New York to Hollywood, see Mark A. Viera, *Irving Thalberg: Boy Wonder to Producer Prince* (Berkeley: University of California Press, 2010).

6. Gerald Horne, *Class Struggle in Hollywood, 1930–1950: Moguls, Mobsters, Stars, Reds, & Trade Unionists* (Austin: University of Texas Press, 2001) (quoting Joseph North, "The New Hollywood," 32 *The New Masses* 14, July 11, 1939), 45; "Talbot and Flynn Off to Write 'Yankee,'" *Hollywood Reporter,* Sept. 18, 1930, 2; "MGM Writers Are Now in Seclusion," *Hollywood Reporter,* Oct. 16, 1930, 2. An excellent study of the development of the American film industry as a modern system of labor is Ronny Regev's dissertation, "'It's a Creative Business': The Ideas, Practices, and Interaction That Made the Hollywood Film Industry" (PhD diss., Princeton University, 2013).

7. "The Screen Writers Guild and the N.R.A.," *The Screen Guilds' Magazine,* vol. 2, no. 2 (Apr. 1935), pp. 3–5 (summarizing early history of Guild); Catherine L. Fisk, "Authors at Work: The Origins of the Work-for-Hire Doctrine," *Yale Journal of*

Law & the Humanities 15 (2003), 1, 64; Christopher Dudley Wheaton, "A History of the Screen Writers Guild (1920–1042): The Writers' Quest for a Freely Negotiated Basic Agreement" (Ph.D diss. University of Southern California, 1974), 3; Author's League Bulletin, vol. 22, no. 10 (1938), 6.

8. "Guild Contract Cut—Producers Eliminate the Clause Giving Publicity to Writers," *The Script,* vol. 2, no. 5, Feb. 3, 1923, p. 1.; "Annual Guild Meeting, April 6," *The Script,* vol. 1, no. 18, Mar. 25, 1922, p. 1; "Club's Prosperity Shown in Figures by Manager Platt—Growth in Membership and Attendance Parallels Increase in Service and Facilities," *The Script,* vol. 2, no. 6, Feb. 10, 1923. These issues of *The Script* are in the Herrick Library.

9. Some apparently feared copyright infringement suits from the owners of the copyrights in the component parts (script, music, and so on), and so they sought to minimize the risk of litigation by acquiring the copyright in all the elements, rather than simply licensing them for use in the film.

10. "Actors Equity Unable to Join Art Federation—Reason That Federation of Labor Must Be Considered," *The Script,* vol. 1, no. 24, May 6, 1922, p. 1; "Will Hays Told about What the Guild Stands For," *The Script,* vol. 1, no. 28, June 3, 1922, p. 3. Herrick Library.

11. John Bright, "The Painful Vainful," *The Screen Guilds' Magazine,* vol. 1, no. 4 (August 1934), p. 9; C. Gerald Fraser, "John Bright, 81, a Screen Writer," *New York Times,* Sept. 16, 1989 (obituary).

12. Gerald Horne, *The Final Victim of the Blacklist: John Howard Lawson, Dean of the Hollywood Ten* (Berkeley: University of California Press, 2006), 91–92; Norman, *What Happens Next,* 141; Hamilton, *Writers in Hollywood,* 91–92.

13. Norman, *What Happens Next,* 142. The same quote appears in Hamilton, *Writers in Hollywood,* 91. Horne, *The Final Victim of the Blacklist,* 91.

14. Executive Board, Aug. 26, 1935, Oct. 7, 1935, Nov. 12, 1935; "Valuation Placed on Screen Credit," *The Screen Guilds' Magazine,* vol. 3, no. 1 (Mar. 1936), p. 27.

15. "Here's an Idea with Some Sense—Suggestion of Page Adv't in Trade Journals for Writers," *The Script,* vol. 1, no. 27, May 27, 1922, p. 1.

16. "Boylan Will Do Yankee Dialog," *Hollywood Reporter,* Sept. 29, 1930, 3; "Counselman Hired for "Yankee" Treatment," *Hollywood Reporter,* Oct. 16, 1930, at 2; Francke, *Script Girls,* 41 (quoting DeWitt Bodeen, *Frances Marion: Part II, Films in Review,* Mar. 1969, at 129, 139); Hamilton, *Writers in Hollywood,* 184; Letter from Al Cohn, Chairman, Writers Branch, to Bud Schulberg, Chairman, Producers Branch (July 10, 1931), WGA File Blacklist AMPAS & Screen Writers Guild Correspondence.

17. *History & Organization of the Academy,* Academy of Motion Picture Arts & Sciences, http://www.oscars.org/academy/history-organization/index.html; Academy of Motion Picture Arts & Sci., Revised Admin. Procedure and Reprint of Text of Writer-Producer Code of Practice, Writers Branch Bulletin (July 14, 1934) WGA

File Blacklist AMPAS & Screen Writers Guild Correspondence; Hugh Lovell & Tasile Carter, *Collective Bargaining in the Motion Picture Industry: A Struggle for Stability*, Berkeley: Institute of Industrial Relations, 1955, 35–36.

18. Horne, *The Final Victim of the Blacklist*, 93; Schwartz, *Hollywood Writers' Wars*, 9–12; Banks, *The Writers*, 28–32; Viera, *Irving Thalberg*.

19. Schwartz, *Hollywood Writers' Wars*, 18–29; Horne, *The Final Victim of the Blacklist*, 93–96. The formation of the Guild and the politics of the candidates for office were covered in *Variety* (Mar. 14, Mar. 28, Apr. 11, 1933).

20. "Warning!" *The Screen Guilds' Magazine*, vol. 2, no. 10 (Dec. 1935), p. 14; "Comparison of Guild Demands and the Academy's Proposed Revised Writer-Producer Agreement," *The Screen Guilds' Magazine*, vol. 2, no. 8 (Oct. 1935), p. 4; Schwartz, *The Hollywood Writers' Wars*, 49; Lovell & Carter, *Collective Bargaining in the Motion Picture Industry*, 37. The critiques of the codes of fair competition for talent were discussed at some length in *The Screen Guilds' Magazine* in 1934.

21. Minutes of the Annual Meeting of the SWG, Apr. 4, 1935; Executive Board, Apr. 22, 1935.

22. Dudley Nichols, "Cooking a Goose," *The Screen Guilds' Magazine* (May 1936), p. 7.

23. "Commission on Conciliation, Arbitration, and Ethics Report," *The Screen Guilds' Magazine*, vol. 2, no. 4 (June 1935), p. 4; "Report of the Conciliation Committee," *The Screen Guilds' Magazine*, vol. 2, no. 6 (Aug. 1935), p. 10; Lovell & Carter, *Collective Bargaining in the Motion Picture Industry*, 37.

24. Horne, *The Final Victim of the Blacklist*, 94; Schwartz, *The Hollywood Writers' War*, 21.

25. Horne, *The Final Victim of the Blacklist*, 97.

26. See, e.g., W. R. Wilkerson, "Tradeviews," *Hollywood Reporter*, Sept. 18, 1930, p. 1 (discussing a contract between producer Samuel Goldwyn and writer Frederick Lonsdale that provided for profit sharing but left unresolved various issues in the calculation of the writer's share).

27. Horne, *The Final Victim of the Blacklist*; Schwartz, *Hollywood Writers' Wars*; Francke, *Script Girls*; Danae Clark, *Negotiating Hollywood: The Cultural Politics of Actors' Labor* (Minneapolis: University of Minnesota Press, 1995); Tom Sito, *Drawing the Line: The Untold Story of Animation Unions from Bosko to Bart Simpson* (Lexington: University Press of Kentucky, 2006); Notice from "The Executive Board of the Screen Writers Guild" to "All Members of the Screen Writers Guild" in anticipation of a May 1936 meeting, WGA File Blacklist AMPAS & Screen Writers Guild Correspondence.

28. "8 New Members Elected by Board," *The Screen Guilds' Magazine*, vol. 3, no. 1 (Mar. 1936), p. 12.

29. Executive Board, Mar. 9, 1936; "An Award Worth Winning," *The Screen Guilds' Magazine*, vol. 3, no. 1 (Mar. 1936), p. 1; Schwartz, *Hollywood Writers' Wars*, 51–54.

30. *Variety,* Feb. 26, 1936, pp. 1, 31.

31. Schwartz, *Hollywood Writers' Wars,* 135; *Variety* (May 25, 1938) (reporting credit dispute over *Lord Jeff* in which SP member received screenplay credit and Guild members received lesser credits for story and research); Executive Board, May 27, 1936, July 20, 1936.

32. General Membership Meeting, July 28, 1937; National Labor Relations Board v. Jones & Laughlin Steel Corp., 301 U.S. 1 (1937). The Guild easily satisfied the law's threshold requirement that labor relations in film production affect interstate commerce and could therefore be subject to federal regulation. In those days, about 70 percent of all motion pictures shown throughout the world were produced in the United States, and more than 90 percent of those films were made in Los Angeles County. The working conditions of writers clearly mattered to the national and international film industry. Moreover, labor relations in the movie business affected many people: the United States Bureau of the Census reported that in 1935, 27,417 people were engaged in the production of motion pictures and that 85 percent of them were employed in Los Angeles County, earning a collective $95.7 million, which constituted over half of the total cost of production. Metro-Goldwyn-Mayer Studios, 7 NLRB 662, 669 (1938).

33. Metro-Goldwyn-Mayer Studios, 7 NLRB 662, 687–89 (1938).

34. Schwartz, *Hollywood Writers Wars,* 139–140.

35. Executive Board, Nov. 28, 1938.

36. Executive Board, Nov. 28, 1938, Dec. 5, 1938.

37. Tim Palmer, "Side of the Angels: Dalton Trumbo, the Hollywood Trade Press, and the Blacklist," *Cinema Journal* 44 (2005), 57, 63.

38. Executive Board, Aug. 15, 1938. It was: Charles Brackett (*Ninotchka* (1940), *The Lost Weekend* (1945)), Sheridan Gibney (*The Story of Louis Pasteur* (1936), *Once Upon a Honeymoon* (1942)), Lillian Hellman (*The Children's Hour* (1934), *The Little Foxes* (1941)), Donald Ogden Stewart (*Holiday* (1938), *Philadelphia Story* (1940)), and Anthony Veiller (*Stage Door* (1937), *The Stranger* (1946)).

39. Rosten, *Hollywood,* 324 (estimating weekly salary of writers in 1938 based on studio payroll information; nearly 41 percent earned less than $250 a week); Ceplair & Englund, *The Inquisition in Hollywood,* 4 (citing *Variety,* estimates the median weekly wage of screen writers in 1939 at $120); *Variety,* Feb. 29, 1940, pp. 1, 5; Budd Schulberg, *What Makes Sammy Run?* (New York: Vintage, 1990, 1941), 142, 171, 190.

40. Executive Board, Jan. 31, 1938.

41. Schwartz, *Hollywood Writers' Wars,* 188.

42. Christopher Dudley Wheaton, "A History of the Screen Writers' Guild (1920–1942): The Writers' Quest for a Freely Negotiated Basic Agreement" (PhD diss. University of Southern California, 1974).

43. Executive Board, January 31, 1938; Special Meeting of SWG Membership, Aug. 22, 1938.

44. Executive Board, Nov. 28, 1938.

45. Annual Membership Meeting, November 8, 1939.

46. Executive Board, July 10, 1939, July 17, 1939, July 24, 1939.

47. Seth Freeman, "Some Relevant History on Credits," *Credits Forum* (Credits Review Committee) (June 2002); Executive Board, June 17, 1942, June 29, 1942, Mar. 31, 1947.

48. Executive Board, Mar. 31, 1947.

49. Executive Board, Oct. 26, 1942, July 27, 1942, Aug. 5, 1942, Dec. 6, 1948.

50. Executive Board, Oct. 7, 1942. The Board also discussed plagiarism and idea theft allegations on many other occasions, especially before the Guild developed arbitration as a mechanism to deal with such disputes between writers. Executive Board, Dec. 22, 1937, Nov. 28, 1938; Annual Membership Meeting, Nov. 8, 1939.

51. Executive Board, June 29, 1942, April 2, 1945, May 28, 1945, Mar. 31, 1947; Maurice Rapf, "Credit Arbitration Isn't Simple," *The Screen Writer*, vol. 1, no. 2 (July 1945), p. 31.

52. Executive Board, Oct. 25, 1943, Jan. 31, 1944.

53. Executive Board, Aug. 17, 1942.

54. Executive Board, Apr. 2, 1945, Nov. 11, 1946, Jan. 6, 1947.

55. Among the many accounts of who wrote which parts of *Gone with the Wind* is one that the legendarily talented screenwriter Ben Hecht rewrote the first nine reels of the movie in seven days but that David O. Selznick, the producer, wanted Sidney Howard's name alone on the screenplay. Richard Corliss, *Talking Pictures: Screenwriters in the American Cinema, 1927–1973* (Woodstock, NY: Overlook Press, 1974), p. xxiii.

56. Norman, *What Happens Next*, 200, 210; Rosten, *Hollywood*, 311.

57. Royce Mathew Pirates of the Caribbean file, WGA Files.

58. "Revised Administrative Procedure and Reprint of Text of Writer-Producer Code of Practice," *Writers Branch Bulletin* (Acad. of Motion Picture Arts & Scis.) (July 14, 1934); Blacklist AMPAS & Screen Writers Guild Correspondence (includes the 1932 Code and the 1934 proposal for revision of the administrative procedure on credits).

59. Ibid.

60. "Historical Highlights of the Credits Manuals," WGA Screen Credits History Files.

61. Executive Board, Apr. 1, 1946 (voting to submit to membership the following recommendations of Credits Committee: percentage required for screenplay credit shall be 33 percent for one writer, 40 percent for team). Membership approved the proposal. General Membership Meeting, Apr. 29, 1946.

62. Special Meeting of SWG Membership, Aug. 22, 1938; Executive Board, Aug. 29, 1938.

63. Annual Meeting, Feb. 19, 1947; Executive Board, Mar. 31, 1947.

64. Screen Credits Manual.

65. *Credits Survival Guide,* WGA, *available at* http://www.wga.org/subpage_writers resources.aspx?id=153#9 (last visited Oct. 12, 2011).

66. This account of the evolution of the rules from 1948 to 1996 is from two WGAW files: "Historical Highlights of the Credits Manuals," from a file: Screen Credits: History of the Screen Credit Manual, and Memorandum from Mary Devlin to Ann Widdifield & Cathy Reed (June 16, 1995).

67. Executive Board, Apr. 4, 1949.

68. Occasionally, a question will arise whether a writer is entitled to invoke the credit determination arbitration process. Under the MBA, "a writer who has participated in the writing of a screenplay, or a writer who has been employed by the Company on the story" is a participating writer. 2008 MBA, at 267; *Screen Credits Manual,* at 4; WGA, *Television Credits Manual* 4 (2010). http://www.wga.org/ uploadedFiles/writers_resources/credits/tvcredits_manual10.pdf. Disputes over whether a writer meets this definition sometimes arise, and when they do, they are resolved through arbitration. *See* Eddy v. Radar Pictures, Inc., 215 Fed. App'x. 575 (9th Cir. 2006)

69. Executive Board, Aug. 26, 1935.

70. Executive Board, Mar. 6, 1945, Mar. 19, 1945.

71. TWB Executive Board, April 18, 1955.

72. The history of the Guild's struggles with production executive hyphenates after the period I cover is told with insight and detail by Miranda Banks in chapter 4 of *The Writers.*

73. Executive Board, September 24, 1951. *Streetcar* was released September 19, and *Force of Arms* on August 13, 1951,

74. David Bordwell & Kristin Thompson, *Film Art: An Introduction* (McGraw Hill, 9th ed. 2010) 33, 475; Peter Wollen, *Signs and Meanings in the Cinema* (Bloomington: Indiana University Press, 1972), chapter 2, "The Auteur Theory"; Andrew Sarris, "Notes on the Auteur Theory in 1962," *Film Culture* 27 (1962), 1. No less a respected film critic than Pauline Kael questioned auteur theory, and Sarris's particular exposition of it, at the start. Pauline Kael, "Circles and Squares," *Film Quarterly* (1963), 12–26.

75. Jesse Hiestand, "Whose Movie Is It Anyway?" *Hollywood Reporter,* Mar. 31, 2005; David Robb, "A Dispute by WGA and DGA over Film Credit," *Daily Variety,* Aug. 2, 1999 at 1; Notice from WGA to WGA Members (June 4, 2001) (explaining negotiations for and provisions of 2001 MBA, including efforts to get AMPTP to limit use of possessory credit). The history of the WGA's struggles with the possessory credit, including in the period after the era covered in this book, is told well by Miranda Banks in *The Writers,* 159–165.

76. Executive Board, November 18, 1940.
77. Notice from WGA to WGA Members (June 4, 2001).
78. WGA Files: 1998, 2005, 2007 Possessory Credits. Vanity Credits 1994–1997, 1999.
79. Executive Board, October 17, 1938.
80. TWB Executive Board, May 16, 1955.
81. Executive Board, December 11, 1939.
82. Executive Board, November 14, 1938, November 21, 1938.

3. Agency-Built Storytelling

1. Michele Hilmes, *Hollywood and Broadcasting: From Radio to Cable* (Urbana: University of Illinois Press, 1990), 53–55.
2. Erik Barnouw, *The Sponsor: Notes on a Modern Potentate* (New York: Oxford University Press, 1978), 22–25; Martin J. Maloney, "The Collision of Radio, Unions, and Free Enterprise," in *Broadcasting and Bargaining: Labor Relations in Radio and Television,* Allen E. Koenig, ed. (Madison: University of Wisconsin Press, 1970), 12–15.
3. Hilmes, *Hollywood and Broadcasting,* 80; Erik Barnouw, *Tube of Plenty: The Evolution of American Television* (New York: Oxford University Press, 2d ed. 1990), 57.
4. Michele Hilmes, ed., *NBC: America's Network* (Berkeley: University of California Press, 2007), 150.
5. Hilmes, *NBC,* 17–19.
6. *JWT News* (June 3, 1946), File JWT Newsletters.
7. Hilmes, *Hollywood and Broadcasting,* 82; Richard Fine, *James M. Cain and the American Authors' Authority* (Austin: University of Texas Press, 1992), 75, 92.
8. Hilmes, *Hollywood and Broadcasting,* 84–85.
9. Hilmes, *Hollywood and Broadcasting,* 92; Executive Board, June 17, 1942.
10. Executive Board, June 17, 1942, Dec. 21, 1942, Jan. 4, 1943.
11. Erik Barnouw, *Media Marathon: A Twentieth-Century Memoir* (Durham: Duke University Press, 1996), 70.
12. Relations with Radio Writers Guild: History of Developments, June 1948, Edward G. Wilson Files; Fine, *James M. Cain and the American Authors' Authority,* 76 (quoting a RWG pamphlet in the RWG archive at the New York Public Library).
13. John U. Reber to W.F. Lochridge, August 5, 1948, Edward G. Wilson Papers Radio Writers Guild Correspondence June–August 1948.
14. Legal: Major Time-Consuming Matters, 1949, January 23, 1950, Edward Wilson Papers, Box 43, File Annual Reports 1948–49 (listing the items for which JWT registered a copyright on behalf of clients and the clients in whose behalf the copyright was registered).

15. William Howard to John Devine, June 16, 1949, John Devine Papers.

16. Mike Mashon, "NBC, J. Walter Thompson, and the Struggle for Control of Television Programming, 1946–1958," in Hilmes, ed., *NBC*, 139–140.

17. Barnouw, *The Sponsor*, 32.

18. Barnouw, *Media Marathon*, 112; Michele Hilmes, "Never Ending Story: Authorship, Seriality, and the Radio Writers Guild," in Jonathan Gray & Derek Johnson, eds., *A Companion to Media Authorship* (Wiley-Blackwell, 2013), 181–199.

19. Writers Guild Sets Contract for Freelancers, *Variety*, Dec. 11, 1946 (clipping in Edward G. Wilson Radio Writers Guild Files).

20. Memorandum for Legal Files, November 11, 1946, Edward G. Wilson Radio Writers Guild Files.

21. Barnouw, *Media Marathon*, 113.

22. Erik Barnouw to Joel S. Mitchell, May 28, 1948, Edward G. Wilson Papers, Radio Writers Guild. Correspondence 1948 Feb.–May.

23. An internal memo of JWT's in-house counsel listed the RWG demands: arbitration of disputes; all rights in the script to belong to the writer and writers would lease them for one-time use only; air credits to writers; writers would be paid on delivery (not broadcast); writers hired not with a specific commission but simply to generate material would be paid a monthly salary; no two writers would be hired to work on the same script; writers could be hired to write "trial scripts" (on spec) only by a written agreement, and would be paid half the broadcast fee if the script was not used, in which case the script would be returned in fifteen days so the writer could sell it to someone else, and would be paid the full fee if the script was used. Comedy writers were to be guaranteed three weeks of employment. Rewriting would be done only by the first writer, or by an alternate chosen by the writer, and the writer would be forced to rewrite "only if he thinks it should be." Memorandum to Miss Pedersen from A.K. Spencer, November 13, 1945 (enclosing a draft RWG release with Spencer's notes on the back), Edward G. Wilson Files.

24. "Radio Writers Guild," memorandum by Edward G. Wilson, October 16, 1947, Edward G. Wilson Files; "Memorandum of Meeting between Radio Writers Guild and Agency Representatives," January 6, 1948, Edward G. Wilson Files.

25. Annual Report, Dec. 31, 1948, Edward Wilson Papers, Box 43.

26. "Radio Writers' Guild," Edward G. Wilson memo to file, February 4, 1948, Edward G. Wilson Papers.

27. Ibid.

28. "Summary of Proposed Radio Writers' Guild Agreement," JWT Legal Dept., January 9, 1948, Edward G. Wilson Files.

29. Memo: Radio Writers' Guild, American Association of Advertising Agencies, May 29, 1940, Edward G. Wilson Papers.

30. Edward G. Wilson to Daniel Danker, Jr., May 23, 1940, Edward G. Wilson Files.

31. Memo for Legal Files by Edward G. Wilson, August 29, 1947, Edward G. Wilson Files (expressing surprise to learn that Lever brothers had licensed to another the rights in a script written by a freelance radio writer).

32. Memorandum for Files re: Lux Radio Theatre Theme Song, December 18, 1947, Edward Wilson Files, Box 48; File Labor Union Matters, 1946–1961.

33. Barnouw, *Tube of Plenty*, 41.

34. Hilmes, *NBC*, 67.

35. Barnouw, *The Sponsor*, p. 34.

36. "Functions of BBDO in Servicing the Du Pont 'Cavalcade of America' Program on Television," July 23, 1954, DuPont Advertising Department Cavalcade of America Files, BBD&O Organization, 1954–1957.

37. Catherine L. Fisk, *Working Knowledge: Employee Innovation and the Rise of Corporate Intellectual Property, 1800-1930* (Chapel Hill: University of North Carolina Press, 2009), 196–206.

38. Teletype to E. Wilson from Fidler, June 24, 1948, Edward G. Wilson Files; Radio Writers' Guild, August 15, 1947, Edward G. Wilson Files; JWT Free Lance Writers, August 29, 1947, Edward G. Wilson Files.

39. Harold L. Blackburn to F. Lyman Dewey, September 8, 1949, DuPont Advertising Department Files, Cavalcade of America—Biographies, A-M, 1948–1952.

40. "Summary of Proposed Radio Writers' Guild Agreement," JWT Legal Dept., January 9, 1948, Edward G. Wilson Files.

41. Barnouw, *Media Marathon*, 114.

42. *Ain't It Hell on a Windy Day*, pp. 335–336, Colin Dawkins Papers, Box 22 (some internal punctuation omitted).

43. "Radio Writers' Guild," Edward G. Wilson memo to file, February 4, 1948, Edward G. Wilson Files.

44. Teletype from Devine to Rorke, July 1, 1948, Edward G. Wilson Files.

45. Edward G. Wilson to Art Farlow, January 14, 1948, Edward G. Wilson Files.

46. John U. Reber to W.F. Lochridge, JWT Chicago Office, August 5, 1948, Edward G. Wilson Files.

47. Edward G. Wilson to W.F. Lochridge, JWT Chicago Office, January 22, 1948, Edward G. Wilson Files.

48. "Radio Writers' Guild" Edward G. Wilson memo to file, January 27, 1948, Edward G. Wilson Files; Leonard T. Bush to Erik Barnouw, February 2, 1948, Edward G. Wilson Files.

49. "Radio Writers' Guild," Edward G. Wilson memo to file, February 4, 1948, Edward G. Wilson Files.

50. "A Report from the President," Erik Barnouw to membership of RWG, May 15 & June 1, 1948, Edward G. Wilson Files; "A Report from the President: Where We

Stand with the Advertising Agencies," *The Scriptwriter*, June 1948, Edward G. Wilson Papers.

51. Radio Writers Guild: JWT Radio Shows—Effect of Complying with Proposed RWG Agreement (Aside from Anti-Trust Point), July 28, 1948, Edward G. Wilson Files; "Radio Writers Guild," July 23, 1948, Edward G. Wilson Files.

52. Radio Writers Guild: JWT Radio Shows—Effect of Complying with Proposed RWG Agreement (Aside from Anti-Trust Point), July 28, 1948, Edward G. Wilson Papers.

53. Erik Barnouw to Leonard T. Bush, October 5, 1948, Edward G. Wilson Papers.

54. Executive Board, Feb. 17, 1947, Mar. 31, 1947, November 1, 1948.

55. Form letter from Austin Fisher to members of the Association of National Advertisers seeking adherence to collective bargaining agreement, June 24, 1949, Edward G. Wilson Files, File RWG 1949 Correspondence; Barnouw, *Media Marathon*, 120.

56. Barnouw, *Media Marathon*, 121–122.

57. John F. Devine Memorandum to Mr. Mygatt, August 28, 1953, commenting on proposed Writers' Contract for Commercial Radio for Canada, Edward Wilson Files, Box 48, Labor Matters 1950–1953.

58. Annual Report, December 31, 1948, Edward Wilson Files, Box 43: File Annual Reports 1948–1949.

59. Barnouw, *Media Marathon*, 121–122.

60. Digest of Talk by William A. Hart, Advertising Department Clinic, May 28, 1953, DuPont Advertising Department Files.

4. The Revolution Will Be Televised

1. Executive Board, Sept. 17, 1951.

2. Erik Barnouw, *Tube of Plenty: The Evolution of American Television* (New York: Oxford University Press, 2d ed. 1990), 101; Eric Hoyt, *Hollywood Vault: Film Libraries before Home Video* (Berkeley: University of California Press, 2014), chapters 4 and 5; Christopher Anderson, *Hollywood TV: The Studio System in the Fifties* (Austin: University of Texas Press, 1994); William Boddy, *Fifties Television: The Industry and Its Critics* (Urbana: University of Illinois Press, 1992); Michele Hilmes, *Hollywood and Broadcasting: From Radio to Cable* (Urbana: University of Illinois Press, 1990).

3. Barnouw, *Tube of Plenty*, 113–114.

4. United States v. Paramount Pictures, Inc., 334 U.S. 131 (1948); Barnouw, *Tube of Plenty*, 116; Hoyt, *Hollywood Vault*.

5. "Writers, Actors, Meggers Cut in Economy Drive," *Daily Variety*, May 13, 1948, p. 1 (as a result of the box office dip, studios switched to hiring actors, writers, and

directors by the picture rather than on long-term contracts); "Par Drops Contract Scribes," *Daily Variety*, March 22, 1948, p. 51 (with the exception of a few on longer-term contracts, Paramount writers all work on week-to-week basis as part of retrenchment scheme); Hugh Lovell & Tasile Carter, *Collective Bargaining in the Motion Picture Industry: A Struggle for Stability* (1955), 39–41; "Screen Composers Assn Gets Authors League TV Protection," *Daily Variety*, July 3, 1950 (Screen Composers League joined with SWG, Radio Writers Guild, Dramatists Guild, Authors Guild and Television Writers Group to present a united writers' front in negotiation with TV producers, networks, and ad agencies); Anderson, *Hollywood TV*, 156, 159, 249; Erik Barnouw, *The Television Writer* (New York: Hill and Wang, 1962), 16; Tino Balio, ed., *Hollywood in the Age of Television* (London: Unwin Hyman, 1990).

6. The Screen Writers Guild's early anxieties about television, with particularly rich accounts drawn from a wealth of oral histories of early participants in TV, is recounted by Miranda Banks in her book, *The Writers: A History of American Screenwriters and Their Guild* (New Brunswick: Rutgers University Press, 2015), 123–137.

7. "J. Walter Thompson Company Television Firsts," Copy September 29, 1952, January 20, 1950 revised, John Devine Files, Box 1.

8. Partial Agreement Reached between Television Authority (TvA) and Broadcasters. American Association of Advertising Agencies Bulletin 1834C, November 21, 1950, Edward Wilson Papers, Box 65, File TvA Negotiations 1950.

9. Executive Board, May 4, 1953.

10. Executive Board, February 12, 1952.

11. Barnouw, *Tube of Plenty*, 134.

12. Edward Wilson, "Report on Activities from January 1, 1942 to March 15, 1943," Edward G. Wilson Papers, Box 43.

13. Barnouw, *Tube of Plenty*, 125–126, 129.

14. "Television, Radio and Motion Pictures," Henderson Papers, Box 9. File: Special Projects, Television Advertising 1957–1959.

15. Ruth Franklin's resume, for example, was a one page document titled "Introducing . . . The Little Boy's Voice on the Levy's Cinnamon Raisin Bread current radio spot now in its second 13-week cycle on 5 N.Y. radio stations and going strong. 'I want Wevy's Cimminum Waisin Bwead . . .'" The resume then lists "Some previous and current accounts" and a number of advertising agencies and Empire Broadcasting. Dan Seymour Papers, Box 2, Talent. John Devine Papers, Box 37, Personnel, 1956 (folder 1 of 2). A resume for Evelyn Barnes Peirce in 1956 was a long list of agencies or other employers and credits: "Co-Casting Director, J. Walter Thompson. Star Tonight. Brillo. May, 1955 to Present. "Producer and Casting Director. Fuller & Smith & Ross. Program: "Home" Network: NBC.

Sponsor: WearEver Foil. Program: 'Freedom Rings' Network: CBS. Sponsor: Westinghouse." December 1952 to May 1955." In the Samuel Meek papers, Box 4, Policy Letters 1961–1962, a form memo dated June 12, 1962, "re: Unsolicited Ideas," describes the company's refusal to consider unsolicited ideas.

16. Erik Barnouw, *The Sponsor: Notes on Modern Potentates* (New York: Oxford University Press, 1978), 27.

17. Barnouw, *The Sponsor*, 28; Barnouw, *Tube of Plenty*, 194–195.

18. Executive Board, Nov. 14, 1938; Executive Board, Nov. 21, 1938.

19. Executive Board, Nov. 21, 1938; Executive Board, Dec. 11, 1939.

20. Executive Board, May 14, 1945.

21. Executive Board, May 28, 1945, June 18, 1951.

22. Executive Board, June 11, 1945, December 3, 1951, December 17, 1951.

23. Executive Board, November 29, 1948, April 18, 1949.

24. Executive Board, July 25, 1949, September 11, 1950; Mary McCall, Jr., "Good News: TV Contract Shapes Up," *Bulletin of the Screen Writers Guild*, June–July 1950, p. 1, Herrick Library; Karl Tunberg, "Report to the Board of the SWG on the National Television Conference," July 25, 1951; Morgan Cox to Executive Board, Screen Writers Guild, July 25, 1951; Executive Board, August 13, 1951. On the formation of the TWA, see Banks, *The Writers*, 118.

25. Executive Board, April 17, 1950; Valentine Davies, "From the President," *Bulletin of the Screen Writers Guild*, September–October 1950, p. 1; Banks, *The Writers*, p. 118 (quoting Nate Monaster, a writer on *The George Burns and Gracie Allen Show*).

26. Executive Board, May 4, 1953, June 8, 1953. Miranda Banks has an excellent account of the processes by which the jurisdictional dispute was resolved. Banks, *The Writers*, 127–138.

27. Executive Board, July 9, 1951, October 13, 1952.

28. Executive Board, July 9, 1951 (Temporary Code of Working Rules), Mar. 3, 1952, August 27, 1951.

29. Deane F. Johnson to John F. Devine, June 30, 1952, enclosing a copy of the Screen Writers Guild proposed contract. Edward Wilson Papers, Box 65, File: Television Writers of America Film Negotiations 1952–1953.

30. Executive Board, Sept. 17, 1951, Apr. 30, 1951, June 4, 1951, May 15, 1951.

31. Executive Board, February 4, 1952.

32. Ibid.; Marvin Borowsky, "Are You Considering TV Writing in NY???" *Bulletin of the Screen Writers Guild*, March 1951, p. 4 (offering advice to film writers based in Los Angeles about the good prospects for writing for TV in New York).

33. Executive Board, June 18, 1953; TWB Executive Board, January 27, 1955. Jordan Segall, *A Guild Don't Go Its Own Way, It's Nothing: The Reorganization of the Authors League, 1951–1954* (unpublished manuscript in the WGA Files). As on all of this

material, Banks has a particularly good account of the ultimate merger of the different writer organizations into the WGA. Banks, *The Writers*, 134.

34. "Indies Face Split on TV," *Daily Variety*, April. 3, 1951, at 1 (summarizing proposals for the MBA covering independent producers); "SWG Seeks Pact with Indies," *Daily Variety*, Mar. 6, 1951, at 1 (with MBA for major studios in effect, Guild negotiating similar agreements with two different associations of independent producers); "$500 to $750 Tilt Offered Screen Writers by Prods," *Daily Variety*, Jan. 25, 1950 (separated rights provision in new MBA with film producers "still needs clarifying and will be subject to further negotiation"); "Guild Taps Screen Scribes for Coin to Build Kitty," *Daily Variety*, Apr. 10, 1950 (SWG members asked to increase dues to build emergency fund in event negotiators fail to come to terms over SWG's demand for separated rights covering TV rights); "SWG Seeks Per-Usage TV Pact," *Daily Variety*, Aug. 25, 1950 (describing writers' bargaining demands entering TV negotiations as including that writers would sell original material for only one use or performance on TV and would retain all rights to material and be paid a percentage of the total sale of the package to a sponsor).

35. "For Advertising People Only!" Edward Wilson Papers, Box 48, Labor–Union Matters, 1946–1951.

36. Executive Board, Feb. 3, 1947, Feb. 17, 1947.

37. Memorandum to Robert Ballin from Edward Wilson, January 3, 1952, Edward Wilson Papers, Box 65, File: Television Writers of America Correspondence 1951–1954.

38. "Television Talent—Employees—Agency or Sponsor" October 19, 1950, Edward Wilson Papers, Box 48, File: Labor Matters 1950–1953.

39. John F. Devine to Richard Scheidker, March 27, 1952, Edward Wilson Papers, Box 65, TVA Negotiations.

40. Howard Kohl to Edward Wilson, March 10, 1952, requesting and receiving information about ownership and compensation practices on three shows: *Fairmeadows, U.S.A., Kraft Television Theatre*, and *Lux Video Theatre*.

41. W.F. Howard to John F. Devine, May 25, 1949; John F. Devine to W.F. Howard, June 13, 1949. Edward Wilson Papers, Box 48.

42. Samuel Meek Papers, Box 6: "Scientific Advertising" by Claude Hopkins— Comments by Alfred Politz, with a handwritten note across the top: "Mr. Meek— This is terrific stuff. AAP" (n.d., probably 1950s).

43. John Devine, "Re: Air Credits for J. Walter Thompson Company Employees," Aug. 15, 1955, September 27, 1955, John Devine Papers, Box 1, File Miscellaneous, 1955–1958. Quotes are substantially identical in both versions of the memo.

44. Howard Kohl to Mr. Wilson, et al., "Re: Air Credits for Company Employees," October 5, 1955, John Devine Papers, Box 1, Miscellaneous 1955–1958.

45. Dorothy Copeland to John F. Devine and Committee on Television and Radio Administration, November 7, 1960, John Devine Papers, Box 20.

46. Report from Marvin Borowsky, Chairman, on the Credits Committee.

47. Executive Board, August 3, 1950.

48. TWB Executive Board, February 21, 1955.

49. Stephen Fox, *The Mirror Makers: A History of American Advertising and Its Creators* (Urbana: University of Illinois Press, 1997), 213–214; Barnouw, *The Sponsor*, 47–58.

50. "Points Concluded with Companies," January 23, 1951, Edward Wilson Papers, Box 65, File TVA Negotiations 1951.

51. Executive Board, Feb. 4, 1952, April 21, 1952.

52. Horace Newcomb and Robert S. Alley, *The Producer's Medium: Conversations with Creators of American TV* (New York: Oxford University Press, 1983); Alisa Perren and Thomas Schatz, "Theorizing Television's Writer-Producer: Reviewing *The Producer's Medium*," *Television and New Media* (October 2014): pp. 1–8; Muriel G. Cantor, *The Hollywood TV Producer: His Work and His Audience* (New York: Basic Books, 1971).

53. Executive Board, July 13, 1953.

54. Executive Board, July 13, 1953, August 10, 1953; Rule 16, Working Rules; TWB Board January 26, 1955, May 16, 1955.

55. Executive Board, Jan. 21, 1952, March 24, 1952; Banks, *The Writers*, 140.

56. The Guild's struggles to fit the role of TV writer-producer into its framework and the controversy over Jess Oppenheimer's role on *I Love Lucy* and his relations with Madelyn Pugh and Bob Carroll, Jr., are discussed in Banks, *The Writers*, 119–122.

57. Executive Board, August 10, 1953.

58. Executive Board, Jan. 21, 1952, March 24, 1952; Banks, *The Writers*, 140.

59. TWB Executive Board, January 17, 1955.

5. The Writer's Share

1. Jonathan Handel, *Hollywood On Strike! An Industry at War in the Internet Age* (Los Angeles: Hollywood Analytics, 2011), 473. Handel's proposed reform to the calculation of residuals, Ibid., 473–476, is thus largely what the Guild first proposed in the 1940s.

2. Ring Lardner, Jr., "First Steps in Arithmetic," in "One Percent of the Gross: An Economic Primer of Screen Writing," *The Screen Writer*, vol. 3, no. 3 (Aug. 1947), p. 16.

3. Residuals are explained in the WGA's *Residuals Survival Guide* and under the Writer's Resources tab of the WGA website www.wga.org, where the *Residuals Survival Guide* may also be found and downloaded.

4. 2011 MBA Art. 16.A. The MBA in effect May 2014 to May 2017 is, at the time of this

writing, in the form of a Memorandum of Understanding and various side letter agreements modifying the 2011 MBA; these amendments will eventually be integrated into the 2011 MBA, but they don't materially change the basics of the residual and separated rights provisions, and therefore it's easiest to understand the provisions by reading the 2011 MBA. The description in the text is an oversimplification of the film separated rights provisions, which constitute thirty pages of the 2011 MBA, and only grew longer and a bit more complex in 2014 with the effort to apply the residuals and separated rights principles to streaming video on demand and other new media.

5. 2011 MBA Art. 16.B. Made for Internet Sideletter.

6. In film, a writer who receives "written by," "story by," "screen story by," screenplay by," "adaptation by" or "narration written by" credit is entitled to residuals. In TV, a writer who receives "written by," "story by," "television story by," "teleplay by," "adaptation by," "narration written by," or "created by" credit is entitled to residuals. Article 15, which contains the residuals provisions of the 2011 MBA, is over fifty pages long. A description of how residuals worked in the 1950s is in Robert W. Gilbert, "'Residual Rights' Established by Collective Bargaining in Television and Radio," *Law & Contemporary Problems* 23 (1958), 102, 103; Blacklist Credits Comm. Memos and Letters 1950s (Mar. 11, 1959); Carl DiOrio, "MGM Lets UA Off on Cruise Control," *Hollywood Reporter*, Jan. 8, 2008; Carl DiOrio, "Script Goes as Planned: WGA Signs Off on New Deal," *Hollywood Reporter*, Feb. 27, 2008. Art. 15.A.3.e. (reuse of films), Art. 15.B.2 (television reruns) 2011 MBA. *Residuals Survival Guide* 5 (Dec. 2013), available at http://www.wga.org/uploadedFiles/writers_resources/residuals/residualssurvival2013.pdf.

7. Anthony A.P. Dawson, "Hollywood's Labor Troubles," *Industrial & Labor Relations Review* 1 (1948), 638, 640 (1948) (lamenting the difficulties caused by the fact that "[t]he movie labor market is casual in the fullest sense of the word" and quoting screenwriter Ring Lardner, Jr. as saying that "while the situation is bad enough if you think of approximately 1500 writers competing for some 421 jobs (as of July 1, 1947), consider how it looks if you estimate that at least 200 of our members are almost constantly employed. Then we have the far grimmer picture of about 1300 writers competing for little over 200 jobs.")

8. The credit bonus term in a 2001 contract by which a studio hired a writer (by "leasing" the writer's services from the corporation owned and managed by the writer) provides: "If the Picture is produced as a feature-length theatrical motion picture and Artist receives sole 'screenplay by' or sole 'written by' credit therefore . . . , then Lender shall be entitled to receive a bonus in the amount of $500,000. . . . If . . . Artist receives shared 'screenplay by' or 'written by' credit . . . , then in lieu of the foregoing, Lender shall be entitled to receive a bonus in the amount of $75,000." The same agreement also provided that if the

writer received sole "screenplay by" or "written by" credit, the writer's company ("Lender") would receive contingent compensation in the amount of 5 percent of 100 percent of the "Defined Contingent Proceeds." The contract provided that the writer would be paid $225,000 for writing in addition to the bonuses. WGA File of correspondence between a writer and the WGA concerning litigation filed by the writer challenging the credit determination on a major motion picture of the 2000s; *WGA Credits Forum,* Aug. 2002, at 1.

9. Homer Croy, "A Chapter on Radio," *The Screen Guilds' Magazine,* vol. 3, no. 2 (May 1936), p. 13.

10. Executive Board, July 1947; Eric Hoyt, *Hollywood Vault: Film Libraries before Home Video* (Berkeley: University of California Press, 2014).

11. Mary McCall, Jr., "Facts, Figures on your % Deal," *The Screen Writer* (June 1945), pp. 32–35; Executive Board, Nov. 18, 1946. The Guild also considered whether or how to urge other Guilds to take action on the problem of reissues at a meeting on June 9, 1947, but referred the matter to committee for further study. Lester Cole, in *The Screen Writer,* vol. 3 (Aug. 1947), p. 42, made the argument that appears in the epigraph to this chapter.

12. Executive Board, Mar. 4, 1946.

13. Richard Fine, *James M. Cain and the American Authors' Authority* (Austin: University of Texas Press, 1992), 92.

14. ASCAP and BMI are slightly different than the AAA would have been. They do not get the copyright in the song, but rather a nonexclusive license. The ASCAP/BMI licenses are only for the public performance rights, and only for nondramatic public performances, and ASCAP/BMI must grant a license to anyone who requests one and can pay for it.

15. "American Authors Authority Looms, a la ASCAP, to Embrace All Scribes," *Variety,* July 31, 1946; James M. Cain, "An American Authors' Authority," *The Screen Writer* (July 1946), p. 13; Fine, *James M. Cain and the American Authors' Authority,* 96, chapters 2 and 4 (the quote is drawn from a letter Cain wrote to H. L. Mencken on July 16, 1947 that Fine found in the Cain papers in the Library of Congress, Washington, D.C.).

16. Fine, *James M. Cain and the American Authors' Authority,* 50–51.

17. Ibid. George E. Sokolsky, "Proposed: Thought Monopoly." *New York Sun,* Aug. 29, 1946 (clipping in Edward Wilson Radio Writers Guild Files).

18. "American Authors Authority Looms, a la ASCAP, to Embrace All Scribes," *Variety,* July 31, 1946.

19. Fine, *James M. Cain and the American Authors' Authority,* 220 (quoting a letter from Cain to H. L. Mencken, July 16, 1947, in the Cain Papers in the Library of Congress, Washington, D.C.).

20. Executive Board, Mar. 16, 1946.

21. Executive Board, Apr. 22, 1946. At the Executive Board meeting of June 10, 1946 the Board approved Ring Lardner's suggestion that the Committee should draft specific proposals for putting the licensing resolution into effect to be submitted to the Authors League and its member Guilds, thus implementing what the membership approved at the April 29 meeting. Executive Board Mar. 31, 1947.

22. *The Screen Writer,* vol. 3 (August–September, 1947), p. 42.

23. Emmet Lavery, "A Time for Action," *The Screen Writer,* vol. 1, no. 12 (May 1946), p. 1.

24. Editorial Committee, "What of the Market for Originals?" *The Screen Writer,* vol 3, no. 3 (1947), p. 29. Executive Board, Jan. 22, 1945. Executive Board, May 26, 1947.

25. Ring Lardner, Jr., "First Steps in Arithmetic," *The Screen Writer,* vol. 3, no. 3 (Aug. 1947), p. 16. Martin Field, "Twice-Sold Tales," *The Screen Writer,* vol. 2, no. 12 (May 1947), p. 1. Martin Field, "No Applause for These Encores," *The Screen Writer,* vol. 3, no. 3 (Aug. 1947), p. 24.

26. "The Writers' Share: Some Comments on the Contribution of Writers to the Screen Industry and Vice Versa," *The Screen Writer,* vol. 3, no. 4 (Sept. 1947), pp. 29–33 (with responses by Samuel Goldwyn, James Hilton, Stephen Longstreet, Irving Pichel, Howard Lindsay, David O. Selznick, and Millen Brand).

27. General Membership Meeting, September 8, 1947.

28. Executive Board, October 25, 1948, Dec 20, 1948. Richard Fine's book has a detailed argument about the relationship between the HUAC hearings and the failure to establish the American Authors Authority. Fine, *James M. Cain and the American Authors' League,* chapter 8.

29. Executive Board, December 20, 1948.

30. Executive Board, April 18, 1949, June 20, 1949.

31. Executive Board, April 24, 1950, May 8, 1950, September 24, 1951.

32. Executive Board, Feb. 6, 1951, Feb. 26, 1951, Nov. 20, 1950, Jan 29, 1951; Proposed Code of Working Rules, Jan. 17, 1951, April 30, 1951.

33. Executive Board, March 3, 1952, March 24, 1952. John Klorer, "Writing for Percentage," *The Screen Writer,* vol. 1, no. 9 (Feb. 1946), p. 7.

34. Executive Board, July 14, 1952. "Crisis Looms in TV Contract Fight," *SWG Bulletin,* July 1952, p. 1. Herrick Library.

35. Executive Board, July 14, 1952.

36. Ibid.

37. By late July, it was clear that the SWG considered but rejected trading off ownership and payment of a royalty for sale of the script with payment for reuse (the residual system it ultimately adopted). In early August, the SWG called a strike against independent television production companies making mainly filmed TV programs in the west. The National Television Committee (the entity created by the Authors League to negotiate over live television in the east), the SWG, and the

RWG asserted overlapping claims to represent writers working in various forms of TV in the east and the west, and the logistics of having multiple different guilds responsible servicing the various contracts began to seem complicated. Executive Board, July 14, 1952, Aug. 4, 1952,

38. In September of 1952, the SWG studied carefully the contract that the National Television Committee had concluded with the networks and noted that if the writer is paid above the minimum, the overage could be applied to residuals. While, as a practical matter, the SWG had jurisdiction over live TV west of the Rockies, it recommended to the NTC that the network contract in the west be administered by the NTC and that dues be put in escrow or used to pay off expenses of negotiating the network contract. Executive Board, September 29, 1952, October 13, 1952.

39. Executive Board, Sept. 3, 1952 (Stulberg quote). As Everett Freeman, an Executive Board member, explained about a TV deal he had been offered in 1952, the producer "was very receptive to residuals and [payment for] reuse, but could not figure out—in terms of a sponsored show—what is considered a percentage of the gross in such case." Executive Board, Aug. 27, 1952 (Freeman statement).

40. Erik Barnouw, *Tube of Plenty: The Evolution of American Television* (New York: Oxford University Press, 2d ed. 1990), 197. Hoyt, *Hollywood Vault: Film Libraries*.

41. Executive Board, Feb. 23, 1953; Special Membership Meeting, April 22, 1953.

42. Executive Board, March 2, 1953. The question whether writers could accept a percentage in lieu of minimum compensation recurred frequently in the early days of television. Michael Wilson had agreed to such a deal for *Salt of the Earth*, but his deal guaranteed him the MBA minimum in the event that was more than the 15 percent of the producer's share that was the sum for which Wilson leased the script.

43. Television Writers Branch Executive Board, Apr. 18, 1955, May 16, 1955, Sept. 19, 1955.

44. Executive Board, March 3, 1952 (for quote); Television Writers Branch Executive Board, Sept. 19, 1955 (on policing reruns).

45. Memorandum of August 14, 1946, Edward G. Wilson Radio Writers Guild Files.

46. Comments of AAA Radio Committee Members on RWG Proposal for Standard Lease Contract on Single-Shot Scripts. Edward Wilson Radio Writers Guild Files. Writers' ownership of characters emerged as an issue before the Executive Board in the fall of 1939 when Fannie Hurst sued Warner Bros. over use of characters in *Four Daughters* (1938), who were reused in *Daughters Courageous* (1939), *Four Wives* (1940), and *Four Mothers* (1941). It came up again in 1952, when Dashiell Hammett won a case about ownership of his character Sam Spade. Warner Bros. had purchased one of Hammett's novels featuring Spade to make into a movie, but Hammett had sold another story involving the same character to CBS for a radio

show. In the case holding that Hammett owned the character notwithstanding the sale of a novel to be made into a movie, the Guild saw an important principle of writer ownership. It was important in principle, and important if the original sale of a script did not allocate rights, but careful drafting could deal with it. Afterward, studios simply had to be more careful to purchase the rights to characters as well as the rights to the literary property. Writers did not generally wind up owning the characters in the stories they wrote, and Hammett's situation became the exception rather than the rule. Executive Board, Jan. 7, 1952.

47. Executive Board, Sept. 17, 1951.

48. TWB Executive Board, April 11, 1955.

49. When the Guild planned to negotiate with the networks in the fall of 1955 for a renewal of the 1952–1955 MBA, one of the major points was whether the writers' demands for residuals were too high in comparison to what actors settled for after a two-week strike in the summer of 1955 and also whether writers should insist on residuals for foreign TV release (on which actors did not demand residuals). The writers decided to stick with the principle of payment on the first rerun, but did moderate their percentages because actors had not gotten what the writers proposed to demand. TWB Executive Board August 15, 1955.

50. TWB Executive Board, August 15, 1955.

51. TWB Executive Board, April 18, 1955. Negotiations went on simultaneously with the majors and the networks, and by the end of 1955, the Television Writers Branch Board was informed that progress had been made in both sets of negotiation in the crucial areas of "money, terms, and rights." With the majors, the most contentious issues were that the majors wanted to give the writers nothing more than they gave the actors with respect to return payments. On foreign rights, the majors absolutely refused to talk, and the writers feared they would have to strike, but the networks were more flexible. On remakes, the majors and the networks both insisted they would give writers nothing because they saw a danger to the theatrical motion picture contract, but the writers insisted that the right to remake could "wipe out entirely the effect of separation of rights and reversion of rights." In negotiations with the networks the big issues were that the networks wanted a separate contract for staff writers. TWB Executive Board, Dec. 20, 1955.

52. Commissioner v. Wodehouse, 337 U.S. 369 (1949); Melville Nimmer and David Nimmer, *Nimmer on Copyright*, vol. 1 (2011), ch. 5; Hugh Lovell and Tasile Carter, *Collective Bargaining in the Motion Picture Industry: A Struggle for Stability* (1955), 42–43.

53. Warner Bros. Pictures v. Columbia Broad. Sys., 216 F.2d 945 (9th Cir. 1954). In Gaiman v. McFarlane, 360 F.3d 644, 660 (7th Cir. 2004), the court suggested that

the Sam Spade case is no longer good law. Another example of cases struggling to discern when one use of a character infringes the copyright in a work featuring that character was Metro-Goldwyn-Mayer, Inc. v. Am. Honda Motor Co., 900 F. Supp. 1287 (C.D. Cal. 1995), which held an advertisement featuring a handsome, debonair man and an attractive female companion in a speeding sports car escaping from a grotesque villain through use of intelligence, dry wit, and clever gadgets infringed the copyright in the James Bond movies.

6. The Blacklist

1. Richard Fine, *James M. Cain and the American Authors' Authority* (Austin: University of Texas Press, 1992), 236. On the attacks on craft labor, see Mike Nielsen & Gene Mailes, *Hollywood's Other Blacklist: Union Struggles in the Studio System* (London: British Film Institute, 1995); Gerald Horne, *Class Struggle in Hollywood, 1930–1950* (Austin: University of Texas Press, 2001).

2. Among the excellent accounts of the blacklist are Larry Ceplair & Steven Englund, *The Inquisition in Hollywood: Politics in the Film Community, 1930–60* (Urbana: University of Illinois Press, 1979); Nancy Schwartz, *The Hollywood Writers' Wars* (New York: Knopf, 1982); Victor S. Navasky, *Naming Names* (New York: Hill & Wang, 2003, 1980). Most recently, Miranda Banks's excellent history of the Writers Guild has a short and highly readable account of the Guild during the blacklist era. *The Writers,* chapter 2. The biographies and memoirs of famous blacklisted writers on which I have drawn include Bruce Cook, *Trumbo* (New York: Scribner's, 1977); Larry Ceplair, *The Marxist and the Movies* (Lexington: University Press of Kentucky, 2007); Larry Ceplair & Christopher Trumbo, *Dalton Trumbo* (Lexington: University Press of Kentucky, 2015); Gerald Horne, *The Final Victim of the Blacklist: John Howard Lawson, Dean of the Hollywood Ten* (Berkeley: University of California Press, 2006). My personal favorite account of the blacklist is the one by Jean Rouverol, *Refugees from Hollywood: A Journal of the Blacklist Years* (Albuquerque: University of New Mexico Press, 2000). Rouverol, an actor turned writer, was married to Hugo Butler and describes what happened after US Marshals turned up at their house at dinner time in late winter of 1951 to serve a HUAC subpoena on Butler. The book recounts how the Rouverol-Butler family, joined by the Trumbo family because Dalton had just finished serving his sentence for refusing to testify, fled to Mexico where they lived, raised their many children, and wrote under fronts or pseudonyms and sold their work on the black market.

3. Executive Board, Sept. 15, 1947.

4. Cook, *Trumbo*, 180–185.

5. Lawson v. United States, 176 F.2d 49 (D.C. Cir. 1949); Erik Barnouw, *Tube of Plenty:*

The Evolution of American Television (New York: Oxford University Press, 2d ed., 1990), 109; Ceplair & Englund, *Inquisition*, 254–298, 325–360, 455.

6. Cook, *Trumbo*, 193.

7. Executive Board, December 8, 1947, Aug. 3, 1950. Ceplair & Englund, *Inquisition*, 250–251, 292–297.

8. "Writers Will Sue Prods," *Daily Variety*, May 28, 1948, p. 1; "SWG Sues 7 Majors on Blacklist," *Daily Variety*, June 2, 1948, p. 1; Chronology on Blacklist Suit, WGA; Executive Board, January 19, 1948.

9. Executive Board, May 2, 1949 (placing about 100 members in bad standing, including Dwight Taylor, Edwin Justus Mayer, Louise Rousseau, Fred Rinaldo, Jay Dratler, and Ring Lardner, Jr.); Executive Board, May 19, 1949 (Dwight Taylor resigning from negotiating committee because he had been placed in bad standing at prior meeting of Executive Board); Executive Board, October 25, 1948 (placing 120 members on bad standing list, including Dalton Trumbo, Donald Ogden Stewart, Frances Marion); Executive Board, October 24, 1949 (placing Herman Mankiewicz, Hugo Butler, Paul Gangelin, Budd Schulberg, Salka Viertel, and Orson Welles on the bad standing list, along with 70 other people).

10. Executive Board, May 8, 1950, May 31, 1950, Aug. 3, 1950, Aug. 21, 1950. Frank Nugent, "Attorney for SWG Resigns," *Bulletin of the Screen Writers Guild*, June–July 1950, p. 1. Herrick Library.

11. Cook, *Trumbo*, 196.

12. Bayard F. Berman & Sol Rosenthal, "Screen Credit and the Law," *UCLA Law Review* 9 (1962), 156, 188 (law review article by two Hollywood entertainment lawyers providing sample language of morals clause in talent contracts). RKO Radio Pictures, Inc. Agreement with Paul Jarrico, (Jan. 17, 1951) (WGA file); Seton I. Miller Contract, no. 12631B, Mar. 24, 1936, Warner Bros. Archive, USC; James R. Webb Contract, no. 12591A, Feb. 4, 1946, Charles Hoffman Contract, no. 12836A, May 4, 1942, Warner Bros. Archive, USC; Scott v. RKO Radio Pictures, Inc., 240 F.2d 87 (9th Cir. 1957); Twentieth-Century Fox Film Corp. v. Lardner, 216 F.2d 844 (9th Cir. 1954); Loew's, Inc. v. Cole, 185 F.2d 641 (9th Cir. 1950); RKO Radio Pictures, Inc. v. Jarrico, 274 P.2d 928 (1954).

13. J.I. Case Co. v. NLRB, 321 U.S. 332 (1944); National Licorice Co. v. NLRB, 309 U.S. 350 (1940); James Webb Contract, paragraph 18.

14. Am. Arb. Ass'n, Adm'r Voluntary Labor Arb. Tribunal, In the Matter of the Arb. between Radio Writers Guild and Columbia Broad. Sys., L-7847, NY-1–211–51 (Arbitrators Lewis Gannett, Albert Gilbert & Harold Taylor); Letter from Gordon Stulberg, Counsel for the Writers Guild, to Ross Hastings, of RKO (Jan. 10, 1952).

15. *Lardner*, 216 F.2d 844, 851 (holding writer Ring Lardner, Jr. was properly fired for breach of morals clause based on contempt of Congress citation for refusal to answer questions before HUAC).

16. "Writers Tussle on Arnold Fee," *Daily Variety*, Mar. 22, 1948, p. 51; Executive Board meetings (Jan.–Mar. 1948); Ceplair & Englund, 249–253, 361–397.

17. Executive Board, September 10, 1951, November 19, 1951.

18. Executive Board, January 19, 1948, May 21, 1951.

19. Executive Board, July 2, 1951.

20. SWG Memorandum from Frances Inglis (Dec. 28, 1951); Executive Board, Dec 6, 1948, April 18, 1949; Morris Cohn to Thurman Arnold, Dec. 2, 1948, in Executive Board Meeting Minutes File for 1948.

21. RKO Radio Pictures, Inc. Agreement with Paul Jarrico (Jan. 17, 1951) (WGA File); WGA File Blacklist RKO Lawsuit 1951–1953; Ceplair, *Marxist and the Movies*, 118–127; Cook, *Trumbo*, 214–215. I owe a debt to Miranda Banks for introducing me to the Jarrico quote that is the epigraph to this chapter. Dick Vosburgh, "Paul Jarrico: Obituary," *The Independent*, November, 5 1997, quoted in Banks, *The Writers*, 109.

22. Executive Board, March 28, 1952, March 24, 1952; Memorandum from Frances Inglis, Exec. Sec'y (Feb. 12, 1952) (describing conversation with SWG lawyer Gordon Stulberg in which he requested Executive Board to give him authority to go to court for temporary injunctive relief against RKO for breach of the MBA; a handwritten note on the memo dated Feb. 13 says: "Gordon says cannot find law to support this"); Letter from Howard Hughes to Screen Writers Guild (Mar. 27, 1952).

23. Minutes of a Special Meeting of the Exec. Bd. (Mar. 28, 1952); Press Release for Monday, Mar. 31, 1952.

24. Executive Board, April 28, 1952.

25. Executive Board, March 28, 1952.

26. RKO Radio Pictures, Inc. v. Jarrico, 274 P. 2d 928, 930 (Cal. Ct. App. 1954); J.I. Case Co. v. NLRB, 321 U.S. 332 (1944).

27. "Dear Guild Member" letter signed by Lester Cole, Edward Huebsch, John Howard Lawson, and others (May 10, 1952) (WGA File).

28. Advertisement "To members of the Screen Writers Guild" appearing in *Variety* and *The Hollywood Reporter* (May 21, 1952).

29. Chronology on Blacklist Suit, WGA Blacklist Files.

30. Edward Wilson, JWT's General Counsel, put a clipping of December 7, 1952 *New York Times* article about the Paul Jarrico case in his labor matters file. Edward Wilson Papers, Box 48, Labor Matters 1950–1953.

31. Telephone Conversation with Judge Thurman Arnold (June 2, 1952), WGA File Blacklist Credits Comm. Memos & Letters 1950s; Executive Board, July 28, 1952; Executive Board Misc. Correspondence 1952; Letter from Mary McCall to Loew's Inc. ("This will confirm that Robert Pirosh's name does not appear on the petition to nominate Lester Cole and Ring Lardner to the slate for election to the

1948–1949 Executive Board") (June 23, 1952); Letter from Frances Inglis to Art Cohn ("I have searched our records and can find no support by you at any time of the Hugo Butler Resolution passed at the membership meeting of November 17, 1948") (Apr. 14, 1952); WGA File Committee Blacklist & Anti, 1948–1959; Letter from Curtis Kenyon to Louis Pollock (Dec. 31, 1959); Letter from Fred Schiller to Bob Chandler, *Daily Variety* ("your article about Louis Pollock having been black-listed for the past five years through a case of mistaken identity has shocked and distressed me immensely") (Dec. 20, 1959), WGA File Committee Blacklist & Anti, 1948–59.

32. Executive Board, November 6, 1952.

33. Lizzie Francke, *Script Girls: Women Screenwriters in Hollywood* (London: British Film Institute, 1994), 41–42.

34. Executive Board, Nov. 19, 1952, Dec. 29, 1952.

35. Executive Board, Jan. 26, 1953, March 23, 1953.

36. Telegram from Frances Inglis to Thurman Arnold announcing that the member-ship voted to settle (Feb. 5, 1953); Article 6 of the MBA was approved by the Guild at a contentious meeting on April 22, 1953; "SWG OK's Removal of Commies' Credit," *Hollywood Reporter*, Apr. 23, 1953, p. 1; Berman & Rosenthal, *Screen Credit and the Law*, 188–89; Navasky, *Naming Names*, 184; Cathy R. Reed to Brian Walton, November 11, 1997 (WGA File).

37. Ceplair, *Marxist at the Movies*, 129.

38. Executive Board, Jan. 17, 1951, Nov. 26, 1951, Jan. 7, 1952.

39. Larry Ceplair, "Who Wrote That??? A Tale of a Blacklisted Screenwriter and His Front," *Cineaste* 18 (1991), 18.

40. Executive Board, Mar. 24, 1952, April 6, 1953, June 29, 1953, Aug. 15, 1955, Dec. 20, 1955.

41. Michael Wilson & Deborah Rosenfelt, *Salt of the Earth* (New York: The Feminist Press, 1978).

42. Executive Board, Feb 23, 1953.

43. Executive Board, July 13, 1953, Aug. 31, 1953, Sept. 14, 1953, Sept. 21, 1953.

44. Executive Board, September 21, 1953.

45. Executive Board, March 31, 1952.

46. Executive Board, Nov. 26, 1951, Jan. 21, 1952,

47. Melville Nimmer to Albert Maltz, Apr. 1, 1957, WGA File Committee Blacklist & Anti 1948–59; Letter from Mary Dorfman to Columbia Pictures (Aug. 16, 1957); Memorandum from Gordon Stulberg, Counsel for the Writers' Guild (Mar. 30, 1953); Blacklist RKO Lawsuit Clippings, in WGA File; Dalton Trumbo, *The Time of the Toad: A Study of Inquisition in America, by One of the Hollywood Ten* (Hollywood 1949), 30.

48. TWB Executive Board, Feb 21, 1955.

49. TWB Executive Board, Jan 23, 1956.

50. Letter from Mary Dorfman, Credits Adm'r, WGA, to Allied Artists, in WGA File Blacklist RKO Lawsuit—Clippings, etc. (Mar. 22, 1956).

51. Navasky, *Naming Names,* 185: Letter from Allied Artists Legal Dep't to Mary Dorfman, Credits Adm'r, WGA (Mar. 26, 1956).

52. Ceplair & Trumbo, *Dalton Trumbo,* 339–342.

53. Meeting of the Screen Branch Negotiating Comm. (Mar. 11, 1959); Cathy R. Reed to Brian Walton, November 11, 1997; Ceplair & Trumbo, *Dalton Trumbo,* 356–357.

54. Ceplair & Englund, *Inquisition,* 418–419.

55. Berman & Rosenthal, *Screen Credit and the Law,* 162; Ceplair & England, *Inquisition,* 418–419; Ceplair & Trumbo, *Dalton Trumbo,* 359.

56. *Corrected Blacklist Credits,* WGAW (July 17, 2000); Cathy R. Reed to Brian Walton, November 11, 1997. At one point, writer Del Reisman, blacklisted writer Paul Jarrico, and former WGA president George Kirgo were working on WGA's Blacklist Credit Committee. "WGA Announces Six Credit Corrections for Films Written by Blacklisted Writers," *WGA News,* Mar. 12, 2005. In weighing the interests of accuracy versus access to evidence, the Committee favored accuracy. "The research was rigorous and conservative, and for all the credits it amended, the Guild reluctantly denied many that could not be substantiated," Stephen Bowie, *Another Good Reason to Hate the Internet Movie Database, Classic TV History Blog* (Jan. 28, 2008), http://classictvhistory.wordpress.com/2008/01/28/another-good-reason-to-hate-the-internet-movie-database; "Getting Credit Where It's Due," *Daily Variety,* Sept. 11, 1996.

57. Lesley Macky McCambridge to WGAW Board of Directors, July 15, 2011; Ceplair & Englund, *Inquisition,* 371.

58. Cathy R. Reed to Brian Walton, September 1996; Cathy R. Reed to Brian Walton, November 11, 1997.

7. Pencils for Hire and Mad Men in Gray Flannel Suits

1. Nancy Lynn Schwartz, *The Hollywood Writers' Wars* (New York: Knopf, 1982), 110.

2. Jean-Christian Vinel, *The Employee: A Political History* (Philadelphia: University of Pennsylvania Press, 2013); Ed Bernero interview with author, Los Angeles, Nov. 8, 2013.

3. Grant v. Kellogg, 58 F. Supp. 48 (S.D.N.Y. 1944); Herbert S. Gardner, Jr., *The Advertising Agency Business: The Complete Manual for Management and Operation* (Lincolnwood, IL: NTC Business Books, 1988), 102.

4. C. Wright Mills, *White Collar: The American Middle Classes* (New York: Oxford University Press, 1951, 2002), 150–151.

5. Among the novels in this genre are, in rough chronological order, Frederic Wakeman, *The Hucksters* (New York: Rinehart & Co., 1946); Arkady Leokum,

Please send me, absolutely free . . . (New York: Harper & Bros., 1946); Robert Alan Aurthur, *The Glorification of Al Toolum* (New York: Rinehart & Co., 1953); Eric Hodgins, *Blandings' Way* (New York: Simon and Schuster, 1950); John G. Schneider, *The Golden Kazoo* (New York: Rinehart & Co., 1956); George Panetta, *Viva Madison Avenue!* (New York: Harcourt Brace, 1957); Harold Livingston, *The Detroiters* (Boston: Houghton Mifflin, 1958); James Kelly, *The Insider* (New York: Henry Holt, 1958); Shepherd Mead, *The Admen* (New York: Simon and Schuster, 1958); and Edward Stephens, *A Twist of Lemon* (Garden City, NY: Doubleday & Co., Inc., 1958). Another novel about an ad agency writer is Eric Hodgins, *Mr. Blandings Builds His Dream House* (New York: Simon and Schuster, 1946), which was more about home renovation and life in suburbia than about advertising; the sequel, *Blandings Way,* was about advertising. Herman Wouk's first novel, *Aurora Dawn* (New York: Simon and Schuster, 1947), was also about advertising. Wouk did not work as a staff copywriter for an advertising agency directly, but he did freelancer writing for radio between 1935 and 1941. The only advertising novel to feature a woman as the protagonist (but not the narrator, who was a man, an art director who is in love with the woman) was Matthew Peters (pseudonym for Walter McQuade & Harry Middleton), *The Joys She Chose* (New York: Dell, 1954) (it was based on a story that McQuade & Middleton published in *Cosmopolitan,* vol. 129, no. 3, Sept. 1950).

6. Matthew Weiner, "The Art of Screenwriting No. 4," *The Paris Review* 56 (Spring 2014), 107, 113; Matthew Weiner Interview with author, Los Angeles, October 11, 2013.

7. Sean Wilentz, *Chants Democratic* (New York: Oxford University Press, 1984); David Montgomery, *Fall of the House of Labor* (New York: Cambridge University Press, 1983); Paul E. Johnson, *Sam Patch, The Famous Jumper* (New York: Hill and Wang, 2003).

8. Eric Hodgins, *Blandings' Way* (New York: Simon and Schuster, 1950), 36; John Kenneth Galbraith, "Onward and Upward with the Admen," *The Reporter* (May 2, 1957), 48. The best of them, Galbraith said, was *Blandings' Way,* because "the author had studied his subject at close range; he wasn't using the novel to assuage any sense of personal guilt at the reader's expense. His people exist, or could. They talk informatively about the business, and there is about the right amount of satire."

9. "J. Walter Thompson Company," *Fortune,* Nov. 1947, pp. 95–233; Colin Dawkins Papers, Box 3, File: Resor, Helen and Stanley.

10. Howard A. Rodman, Jr., Interview with author, Los Angeles, Nov. 8, 2013; Leo Rosten, *Hollywood: The Movie Colony, the Movie Makers* (New York: Arno Press & The New York Times, 1970), 310.

11. Miranda J. Banks, *The Writers: A History of American Screenwriters and Their Guild* (New Brunswick: Rutgers University Press, 2015), 8 (quoting Barbash); Neal Baer Interview with the author, Los Angeles, Jan. 21, 2014. On the 1998 strike, Aljean

Harmetz, "Tentative Accord Reached in Strike of Screen Writers," *New York Times,* July 12, 1981.

12. Seton I. Miller Contract, March 24, 1936, item number 12631B, Warner Bros. Archive, USC; Ian Hamilton, *Writers in Hollywood, 1915-1951* (New York: Carroll & Graf, 1991), 35, 49, 74–75; Marc Norman, *What Happens Next: A History of American Screenwriting* (New York: Three Rivers Press, 2007), 95.

13. Seton I. Miller Contract, March 24, 1936, item number 12631B, Warner Bros. Archive, USC. John Twist, who had a career writing westerns and other B-movie action pictures from the 1930s to the early 1960s, signed a similar year-long contract with Warners with an option for a one-year renewal, in 1953. John Twist Contract, October 28, 1953, item number 12840A, Warner Bros. Archive, USC. Rosten, *Hollywood,* 324 (reporting data on 1938 salaries of writers at Warner Bros., Twentieth Century Fox, and Columbia; 13 percent received $1,000 or more a week, and 6 percent received $1,500 or more a week); *Metro-Goldwyn-Mayer Studios,* 7 NLRB 662, 689 (1938) (describing terms of standard writers' contracts submitted in case seeking union representation of writers); Christopher Anderson, *Hollywood TV: The Studio System in the Fifties* (Austin: University of Texas Press, 1994), 237, 252.

14. Hortense Powdermaker, *Hollywood, the Dream Factory: An Anthropologist Looks at the Movie-Makers* (Boston: Little, Brown, 1950), 85.

15. Rosten, *Hollywood,* 306–307 (emphasis added).

16. Powdermaker, *Hollywood.* Jill B.R. Cherneff, "Dreams Are Made Like This: Hortense Powdermaker and the Hollywood Film Industry," *Journal of Anthropological Research* 47 (1991), 229

17. Pierce Bourdieu, *The Field of Cultural Production* (New York: Columbia University Press, 1994), 101. This argument is elaborated in Catherine L. Fisk & Michael Szalay, "Story Work: Nonproprietary Autonomy and Contemporary Television Writing," *Television and New Media* (forthcoming 2016). See also Michael Szalay, *New Deal Modernism: American Literature and the Invention of the Welfare State* (Durham: Duke University Press, 2000).

18. Hamilton, *Writers in Hollywood,* 184.

19. *Metro-Goldwyn-Mayer,* 7 NLRB 662, 669, 686–687 (1938).

20. The NLRB's findings about the industrialized process of script development was drawn from testimony of both writers and studio executives, including Benjamin Cahane, Vice President of Columbia Pictures, who described in detail the way that the producer chose a literary property and hired a writer to adapt it for the screen and then assigned other writers to write dialogue and to add jokes. *Metro-Goldwyn-Mayer,* 7 NLRB 662, 669, 686–687 (1938). My account draws on the NLRB decision and on Ronny Regev's dissertation, for which she read the full record of the case in the NLRB archive in the National Archive, College Park, Maryland, Case No. XXI-R-149, Boxes 515, 516, 517, 518.

21. On this in 1959, see Banks, *The Writers*, 142.

22. *Metro-Goldwyn-Mayer*, 7 NLRB at 688.

23. Ibid., 687–689; Robert A. Gorman & Matthew W. Finkin, *Basic Text on Labor Law* (Minneapolis: West Publishing Co., 2d ed. 2004), 37–38.

24. "Radio Writers' Guild," August 15, 1947. Edward G. Wilson Papers.

25. A Report from the President, Erik Barnouw to membership of RWG. May 15, 1948. Edward G. Wilson Papers.

26. At the beginning, the RWG wanted to get some kind of agreement signed before the August 22, 1947 effective date of the Taft-Hartley Act because the new law would require an employee vote and NLRB certification to be conducted specifically on the issue of whether writers would be required to join or pay dues to the union. It would also require every union official to sign a noncommunist affidavit, which some Guild leaders resisted on principle, and the Guild also wanted to avoid the red-baiting that was sure to surround the affidavit issue. But that deadline came and went with no contract. The ad agencies thought that requiring the Guild to seek certification from the NLRB would eliminate possible antitrust problems, and they hoped the Board would impose a narrower definition of employees on whose behalf the Guild could negotiate than the Guild was seeking. Those agencies (principally JWT and Young and Rubicam) that were not so implacably opposed to unionization of freelancers recognized that what mattered was whether writers were in fact employees, and whether the Board thought they were would not decide the issue for antitrust law. Confidential Memo: Agency Committee Recommendation—Radio Writers Guild, August 26, 1948. Edward G. Wilson Papers RWG Correspondence, June–August 1948.

27. *Loewe v. Lawlor*, 208 U.S. 274 (1908); Daniel Ernst, *Lawyers against Labor: From Individual Rights to Corporate Liberalism* (Champaign: University of Illinois Press, 1995).

28. *Ring v. Spina*, 148 F.2d 647, 652 (2d Cir. 1945).

29. Jessica Litman, "The Invention of Common Law Play Right," *Berkeley Technology Law Journal* 25 (2010), 1381, 1420, 1422

30. American Association of Advertising Agencies Bulletin no. 1439A, "Radio Writers' Guild Seeks Minimum Basic Agreement with Agencies," June 22, 1945, American Association of Advertising Agencies Bulletin no. 1441A, "AAAA Radio Committee Counter Proposal to Radio Writers Guild," July 17, 1945. Edward G. Wilson memo to John Reber, April 1, 1947. All in Edward G. Wilson Radio Writers Guild Files.

31. Memorandum to Miss Pederson & Mr. Colwell from A. K. Spencer, June 21, 1945. Edward G. Wilson Papers; Erik Barnouw, *Media Marathon: A Twentieth-Century Memoir* (Durham: Duke University Press, 1996), 112.

32. Edward G. Wilson, Memo for Legal Files, JWT Free Lance Writers, Aug. 29, 1947. Edward G. Wilson Files.

33. Radio Writers Guild, August 15, 1947. Edward G. Wilson Files.

34. "Radio Writers' Guild," January 12, 1948; "Radio Writers' Guild" Edward G. Wilson notes to file, January 19, 1948. Edward G. Wilson Files.

35. Nancy Lynn Schwartz, *The Hollywood Writers' Wars* (1982), 46.

36. Ibid.

37. John Crosby, "Radio in Review: Revision, Modification or Changes," newspaper clipping from unidentified source, September 17, 1948, in Edward G. Wilson Papers; Leonard T. Bush to Erik Barnouw, September 13, 1948 and attached "Definition of Employee," September 13, 1948. Edward G. Wilson Papers.

38. Erik Barnouw to Leonard Bush, September 22, 1948. Edward G. Wilson Papers.

39. Executive Board, Sept 3, 1952.

40. David Miller to Mr. Brockway, January 20, 1949. Edward G. Wilson Files. RWG 1949 Correspondence.

41. WGA, 2001 Theatrical and Television Basic Agreement, Art. 1.B (theatrical), Art. 1.C (television); Barnouw, *Media Marathon*, 122.

42. Hamilton, *Writers in Hollywood*, pp. 50–52, quoting Frances Donaldson, *P.G. Wodehouse: The Authorized Biography* (London: Weidenfeld & Nicolson, 1982), 139, and Jay Martin, *Nathaniel West: The Art of His Life* (London: Secker & Warburg, 1970), 205; Executive Board, Oct. 25, 1948.

43. Executive Board, Jan. 6, 1947, Oct. 24, 1948, Nov. 1, 1948, June 4, 1951; TWB Executive Board, Jan. 26, 1955, May 16, 1955; Hamilton, *Writers in Hollywood*, 78

44. Rosten, *Hollywood*, 81, quoting Mary C. McCall, Jr., "Hollywood Close Up," *Review of Books*, May 1937, p. 44.

45. Glen Mazzara interview with author, September 24, 2013, Culver City, CA.

46. Stephen R. Fox, *The Mirror Makers: A History of American Advertising and Its Makers* (Urbana: University of Illinois Press, 1997), 179–180, 213–214. In the DuPont advertising department files from the 1950s, employees of DuPont's advertising department and its agency, BBD&O, marked up scripts for episodes of *Bat Masterson*, for example, offering tepid suggestions about plot and character.

47. "J. Walter Thompson Company: A Program for Its Growth and Development," Wallace Elton Papers, Box 1; Norman H. Strouse, "The Seven Areas of Opportunity," Mar. 13, 1957, Colin Dawkins Papers, Box 12, File: Handbook for Personnel; Fox, *The Mirror Makers*, 173, 253, 255. The memo was from Howard Kohl, longtime senior executive of JWT, to Winfield Taylor, a senior executive at the New York Office. Colin Dawkins Papers, Box 2, Howard Kohl File. On the role of JWT in introducing professionalism and "science" into advertising, see Robert Haws Interview, Nov. 18, 1964 at pp. 1–2, Bernstein Company History Files, Box 1; Biographical File on Paul T. Cherington, Bernstein Company History Files, Box 4; *JWT News*, Feb. 1984, Sept. 3, 1956 (*JWT News* was the company's internal newsletter); Bertram Metter Papers, Box 2.

48. *Breaking the Rules at JWT*, p. iii. Bertram Metter Papers, Box 2.

49. Memorandum from Howard Kohl to Winfield Taylor, Mar. 8, 1957, Colin Dawkins Papers, Box 2; Howard Kohl, "Creative Procedures at J. Walter Thompson Company," November 1960, Colin Dawkins Papers, Box 12, File: Handbook for Personnel.

50. Memo from Elton to Strouse and other executives, 1957, and "Program for Growth and Development," JWT Company Policies File, Wallace W. Elton Papers, Box 1. Colin Dawkins, *Ain't It Hell on a Windy Day*, 281–82. The manuscript is found in the Colin Dawkins Papers, Box 22. "Program for Growth and Development," JWT Company Policies File, Wallace W. Elton Papers, Box 1. Robert Haws Interview, Nov. 1964, pp. 5–7, Bernstein Company History Files, Box 1. Wallace W. Elton Papers—Personal. Thomas F. Naegle to Dan Seymour, "Year End Report—TV Art Group," December 1956, Dan Seymour Papers, Box 2. "Springboarding Background," Henderson Papers, Box 9, File Special Projects Personnel Department Seminars, 1957–1960.

51. Fox, *The Mirror Makers*, 177, 209, 253–255, 262; Matthew Peters, *The Joys She Chose* (New York: Dell, 1954).

52. Memo from Bill Gibbs to Jack Devine and cc to Dan Seymour re "Personnel Evaluation—Television Commercial Production JWT New York," May 28, 1963; Report on Activities from Jan. 1, 1942 to Mar. 15, 1943. Edward G. Wilson Papers, Box 43.

53. John Monsarrat, "Professionalism in Advertising Agency Practice (1964), Dan Seymour Papers, Box 23.

54. Wallace Elton to Academy of Television Arts and Sciences, April 5, 1956; Memorandum from John McQuigg to Messrs. Strouse, Flower, Ryan and Elton, May 3, 1956. Wallace Elton Papers, Box 14, File Ford Advertising Awards.

55. Letter from J. C. Roberts, JWT Detroit Office, to Winfield Taylor, NY Office, January 28, 1953, Winfield Taylor, Box 1, Ford Correspondence & Memoranda.

56. "Too Many Awards? Amen" *Advertising Age* (January 20, 1969), clipping in the Edward Wilson Files, Box 77; Steve Riordan, ed., *Clio Awards: A Tribute to 30 Years of Advertising Excellence, 1960–1989* (New York: Clio Enterprises/Rizzoli Int'l Publications, Inc. 1989), Foreword (not paginated); John Devine to John Sherman, Feb. 23, 1971, John Devine Papers, Box 30.

57. Fox, *The Mirror Makers*, 292.

58. "J. Walter Thompson Company," *Fortune*, Nov. 1947, pp. 95, 205. Colin Dawkins Papers, Box 3, File: Resor, Helen and Stanley.

59. Fox, *The Mirror Makers*, 293.

60. "Dean of Them All," *Advertising Age*, Jan. 13, 1964.

61. Fox, *The Mirror Makers*, 294–295.

62. Lucene Fergus memo to Mr. Foote, Jan. 9, 1958. Henderson Papers, Box 7, File Copy Seminar Study Memoranda 1957–1958.

63. "John M. Willem—4th Appearance," Henderson Papers, Box 9, File: Special Projects – Presentation to Sunkist Growers 1960; "Mini Over Midi by a Landslide," *Michigan Avenews* (May 18, 1970); "And Then There Was One: A Look at Advertising Services," *Michigan Avenews* (Sept. 8, 1970) (*Michigan Avenews* was the company newsletter of JWT's Chicago office).

64. David Weil, *The Fissured Workplace: Why Work Became So Bad for So Many and What Can Be Done to Improve It* (Cambridge: Harvard University Press, 2014); Noam Scheiber, "Growth in the 'Gig Economy' Fuels Work Force Anxieties, *New York Times,* July 13, 2015, A1.

65. "Mary C. McCall, Jr., "The Unlick'd Bear Whelp," *The Screen Writer,* vol. 2, no. 3 (Aug. 1946), 27; Martin Field, "Independents' Day," *The Screen Writer,* vol. 2, no. 4 (Sept. 1946), 12; TWB Executive Board Jan 26, 1955. The 1955 working rules for writers prohibited freelancers from engaging in certain types of uncompensated work that, in the Guild's view, were proper only if either specifically paid for or if the writer was hired on staff under an exclusivity arrangement. These included requiring the writer "to confer, with the producer or with other writers, on another writer's work unless the specific object of such conference is employment to revise said other writer's work for a fee" and "[r]equiring the writer to view stock film for more than one calendar day per assignment."

Conclusion

The epigraph to this chapter is from Dorothy Parker, "To Richard with Love," *Screen Guilds Magazine* (May 1936). I found it in Nancy Lynn Schwartz, *The Hollywood Writers Wars* (New York: Knopf, 1981), 69–70.

1. Miranda J. Banks, *The Writers: A History of American Screenwriters and Their Guild* (New Brunswick: Rutgers University Press, 2014), 145–146; Christopher Anderson, *Hollywood TV: The Studio System in the Fifties* (Austin: University of Texas Press, 1994), 271.

2. Of course, white-collar unionization is stronger in the public sector.

3. Both the percentage of women and the percentage of showrunners make the group not representative. And of course the fact that the sample consists of working writers makes it unrepresentative of all WGA members, the majority of whom are unemployed at any given moment. The sample is about evenly divided between those who write or have written primarily for network broadcast TV and those who write primarily for cable. Two members of the sample write for low-budget TV and for even lower-budget webisodes. And at least six (and perhaps more) said they have served as an officer or as a member of a WGA committee, so the group may be unrepresentative in reflecting writers' views about the benefits of involvement with the Guild.

4. Speed Weed, interview with the author, Los Angeles, Aug. 14, 2013.

5. Terence Winter, interview with the author, Los Angeles, Dec. 23, 2013.

6. Glen Mazzara, interview with the author, Los Angeles, Sept. 24, 2013.

7. Matthew Weiner, interview with the author, Los Angeles, Oct. 11, 2013; Howard A. Rodman, Jr., interview with the author, Los Angeles, Nov. 8, 2013.

8. Matt Nix, interview with the author, Los Angeles, Aug. 30, 2013.

9. Rodman, interview with the author in Hollywood, Nov. 8, 2013.

10. Rick Muirriagi, interview with the author, Santa Monica, Aug. 30, 2013.

11. Marti Noxon, interview with the author, Los Angeles, Jan. 16, 2014.

12. Ashley Gable, interview with the author, Los Angeles, Feb. 4, 2014.

13. Banks, *The Writers,* p. 16.

14. Vanessa Taylor, interview with the author, Los Angeles, Dec. 11, 2013.

15. Richard Fine, *James M. Cain and the American Authors' Authority* (Austin: University of Texas Press, 1992), 242.

16. Executive Board, July 14, 1952, April 18, 1955.

Archival Sources

The major advertising agency archive on which I rely is the J. Walter Thompson collection at the Hartman Center for the Study of Advertising of the Perkins Library at Duke University in Durham, North Carolina. I also consulted the DuPont company's advertising department archive at the Hagley Museum and Library in Wilmington, Delaware, which contains documents from its ad agency during this era, Batten, Barton, Durstine & Osborn, Inc. I gratefully acknowledge the assistance of archivists and permission to consult and quote from these archives.

The major source on film and television production on which I rely is the files of the Writers Guild of America, West, in Los Angeles, California. The WGAW files were not open to the public when I conducted my research, but the Guild gave me access and permission to quote from them. Since then, some have been archived at the Library of the Writers Guild Foundation, thanks to the urging of the WGA leaders and counsel. I am grateful to Anthony Segall, the WGAW's General Counsel, for permission to read and quote from them, and to the talented Guild staff, especially Lesley Mackey McCambridge and Sally Burmester, who allowed me to see the files and answered my questions. I reviewed not only the Writers Guild's extensive files on the history and administration of the screen-credit system since 1940, but also the verbatim minutes of its Executive Board meetings from the founding of the union in 1935 to 1960. These are voluminous but reveal quite a bit about the goals and conflicts of writers. As Frances Inglis, the Guild's longtime executive secretary, complained at a September 1952 Executive Board meeting, "the taking and transcribing of verbatim minutes was a laborious and time consuming process." Reading them was, too, but scholars are indebted to the Guild for making and keeping this valuable record. I also rely on the archives of film and television studios, primarily Warner Bros. and Paramount, at the University of Southern California Library in Los Angeles and the Margaret Herrick Library of the Academy of Motion Pictures Arts and Sciences in Beverly Hills. The Conclusion and a few chapters draw on interviews I conducted with thirty writers working in contemporary television in Los Angeles in late 2013 and early 2014. I am grateful to the writers who spent time talking with me and to my colleague, Michael Szalay.

Acknowledgments

Many colleagues and friends read parts or all of the manuscript at various stages. Erwin Chemerinsky was the first to read it and, as he always does, offered incredibly perceptive comments. Then Dirk Hartog, Carrie Hempel, Tony Reese, and Tony Segall read and commented on the entire manuscript. I cannot thank them enough for their generosity and insight. I am also grateful to many others for reading papers that became parts of chapters. Paul Saint-Amour and Chris Tomlins made especially valuable suggestions. Other wonderful readers and interlocutors include Jane Anderson, Funmi Arewa, Anne Barron, Miranda Banks, Lionel Bentley, Susannah Blumenthal, Eileen Boris, Jamie Boyle, Dan Ernst, Paul Frymer, Nan Goodman, Ariela Gross, Jonathan Handel, Eric Hoyt, David Lange, Dick Langston, Nelson Lichtenstein, Mona Lynch, Bill Novak, Andy Russell, Hilary Schor, Ellen Seiter, Carrol Seron, Clyde Spillenger, Bob Spoo, Matt Stahl, Susan Sterrett, Nomi Stolzenberg, Michael Szalay, David Vaver, and Barbara Welke. I presented parts of this research at so many different conferences and workshops over the years that I can't list them all, but I particularly benefitted from faculty and students at UC Irvine and its Center in Law, Society, and Culture; UC Berkeley; Cambridge University; the University of Colorado; Duke University; Georgetown University; the Hagley Museum; the London School of Economics; the University of Michigan; the University of Minnesota; the University of New Mexico; New York University; Northwestern University; Oxford University; Princeton University; UC Santa Barbara; the University of Tulsa; the University of Western Ontario; and Yale University. I am grateful to fellow panelists and attendees at meetings of the Law & Society Association, the American Society for Legal History, and the Society for Cinema and Media Studies.

The UC Irvine Law Library is an incredible resource; I am especially grateful to librarians Dianna Sahhar and Christina Tsou for their research assistance. My students have been another extraordinary resource. I'm indebted to the many who helped, including Richard Allen, John Bridge, Rachel Diggs, Laura Durity, Anya Engel, Alisa Hartz, Tilman Heyer, Sowmya Krishnamoorthy, Amy Lieberman, Josh Mayer, Donna Nixon, Margaux Poueymirou, Katherine Scott, Xenia Tashlitsky, Kathrin Weston, Andrew Woods, and Christina Zabat-Fran. Nicola McCoy has been indispensable in preparing the manuscript.

I develop themes initially presented in my earlier works, and I am grateful to the editors of the following publications for sharpening my ideas: "Credit Where It's Due: The Law and Norms of Attribution," 95 *Georgetown Law Journal* 49 (2006), "The Modern Author at Work on Madison Avenue," in *Modernism and Copyright* (Paul Saint-Amour, ed., Oxford University Press, 2010), and "The Role of Private Intellectual Property Rights in Markets for Labor and Ideas: Screen Credit and the Writers Guild of America, 1938–2000," 32 *Berkeley Journal of Employment and Labor Law* 215 (2011).

As with the authors about whom I have written, I have huge debts to my friends and family. Jim and Doriane Coleman made my archival trips to Durham a joy. Alex's vast knowledge and love of movies inspires me, as does Mara's belief that words are magical and that we are the authors of our own life stories. The eleven years I spent researching and writing this book were when my children grew up, and I am ever so grateful to Adam, Alex, Andrew, Jeff, Kim, and Mara Chemerinsky for their love and support. The very best chapters of my life story are those I've spent with them and Erwin. The dedication hardly begins to cover it.

Index

CPSIA information can be obtained
at www.ICGtesting.com
Printed in the USA
BVHW030303190121
597835BV00012B/139/J